Fashion Nation

fashion nation

PICTURING THE UNITED STATES IN THE LONG NINETEENTH CENTURY

Sandra Tomc

University of Michigan Press
Ann Arbor

Copyright © 2021 by Sandra Tomc
All rights reserved

For questions or permissions, please contact um.press.perms@umich.edu

Published in the United States of America by the
University of Michigan Press
Manufactured in the United States of America
Printed on acid-free paper
First published September 2021

A CIP catalog record for this book is available from the British Library.

Library of Congress Cataloging-in-Publication Data

Names: Tomc, Sandra, author. | Michigan Publishing (University of Michigan), publisher.
Title: Fashion nation : picturing the United States in the long nineteenth century / Sandra Tomc.
Description: Ann Arbor : University of Michigan Press, 2021. | Includes bibliographical references (pages 261–282) and index. |
Identifiers: LCCN 2021012972 (print) | LCCN 2021012973 (ebook) | ISBN 9780472074891 (hardcover) | ISBN 9780472054893 (paperback) | ISBN 9780472129010 (ebook)
Subjects: LCSH: Fashion—United States—History—19th century. | Clothing and dress—United States—History—19th century. | United States—Civilization—19th century.
Classification: LCC GT610 .T66 2021 (print) | LCC GT610 (ebook) | DDC 391.0097309/034—dc23
LC record available at https://lccn.loc.gov/2021012972
LC ebook record available at https://lccn.loc.gov/2021012973

Cover (*left to right*): Alexandre Lacauchie, *Costumes Portugais*; Joseph Reinhard, *Costumes du Canton de Zoug*; Alexandre Lacauchie, *Costumes Écossais*; Edward Harding, *A Female Mestscheraik*; William Alexander, *A Standard Bearer*; James Brown, *F.S. Chanfrau in the Character of Mose*. Image design by Sandra Tomc.

CONTENTS

Digital materials related to this title can be found on
the Fulcrum platform via the following citable URL:
https://doi.org/10.3998/mpub.11719661

ACKNOWLEDGMENTS

In 1968, my parents, sister, and I traveled to what was then communist Yugoslavia to meet for the first time my grandmother, aunts, uncles, and cousins. Among the many memorable events of that fantastic trip was the discovery that my Aunt Reska, my father's sister, made little souvenir national dolls that were sold at tourist sites. Their heads, made out of some kind of smooth papier-mâché, arrived in a plastic bag. They all had blushing cheeks, tiny little lips, and different colors of hair. We watched Reska sew their bodies out of white cloth and helped her stuff the skins with sawdust, after which the heads were sewn on. Then we sewed on a little satin shawl, a brightly colored skirt, and a black apron. To top it all off there was a funny puffy white hat with a gold and black band. The dolls were about seven inches tall when they were done. She made two kinds. The one I just described was for western Slovenia, with Alpine clothes (dirndl, apron, shawl); the other one she made was for eastern Slovenia, with its Croatian influence. It consisted of all-white skirts, all-white blouses, and a white turban-like headdress, finished off with a crimson belt and crimson beads. There were male dolls too with outfits to match their female partners. It was all thrilling. My sister and I were so taken with these dolls and their clothes that Reska sewed us our own Croatian-style Bela Kranja outfits to wear ourselves. Made out of homemade flax, they had stiff white petticoats and blousy layers and a crimson belt, topped by the turban thing on our heads. Of course, we outgrew these outfits in short order. The next summer they would not fit.

When I started doing research for *Fashion Nation*, I went back to question my parents about what they remembered about their clothes. I learned that my mother's family, who lived in Croatia but only two miles from the Slovenian border where my father grew up, still wore the puffy white skirts and blouses as a child in the 1920s and 1930s. Certain women in their village were assigned to sew the richly pleated skirts from locally woven flax. Their clothes were not pure white, though. They had colorful aprons, the fabric of which was purchased in the city. My parents both came from impoverished families, but my father who lived in Slovenia across the river from my mother, dressed in Western dress. He remembers how his village looked down on the girls in the Croatian villages, with their old-fashioned voluminous skirts and aprons. Before my father was born, his father, my grandfather, Janes Tomc, left Slovenia and went to the United States, to Pittsburgh, to work in the steel mills to earn money to repair his farmhouse. He left in 1912 and stayed for eight years. As a child many years later, my father was fascinated by the American things his father had brought back from the United States. These included beautiful silk shirts, a heavy gold watch for Sunday, and a silver watch for work days. In 1939, my mother and grandmother left Croatia to travel to Canada. They traveled by train to England and sailed for Nova Scotia on the last ship leaving London before the outbreak of war. They started on their travels dressed in their usual finery. They quickly realized that their white skirts and blouses were unsuitable for travel and changed. My mother, who was twelve at that time, does not remember wearing those clothes again. My father fought in World War II with the Partisans, then escaped from Yugoslavia in 1952, finally landing in Canada a year later.

Some of the things I saw and learned from my family went into this book, but only a little. Really, this book is about the dolls. How did ordinary farm clothes in Croatia—or anywhere else for that matter—get turned into the stuff of souvenirs to be sold in shops in tourist spots? This book traces the curious, circuitous path that folk clothes followed in one national story—the story of "America"—in the nineteenth century.

The initial research for this project was done over many years at a small handful of libraries and research institutions: the British Library, the Houghton at Harvard, and the Osborne Collection at the Toronto Metropolitan Library. Just at the moment I needed to sit down and finally order up all the marvelous images I had discovered, it was March 2020 and the world went into lockdown and my major libraries closed. I had more than fifty images slated for my book but could get none of them scanned for publication. I then set about trying to piece together all my images from smaller libraries and rare book shops in regions less affected by COVID-19. It has taken me five months and not an insignificant amount of work. Some of the images I didn't end up finding elsewhere and have had to put in substitutes.

So my first thank-you's go to the wonderful librarians and staff at the many libraries I turned to who helped in sometimes heroic and surprising ways. I especially want to thank Gayle O'Hara at the Butler Theatre Archive at Washington State University, who went above and beyond in securing images that matched the ones I had seen at the Houghton. I also want to thank Mack Frost, who took twenty-four hours to send an image that I had waited two months for from another library, and Andrea Immel at the Cotsen Children's Library, Princeton University Library, who rushed through an image for me with limited staff. But let me say also that I am immensely grateful to all the many librarians who offered guidance and help with my research both after and before the lockdown, especially the librarians at Houghton and Osborne who were kind and generous with their time and knowledge.

I owe a huge debt to the friends who read various chapters of this study and who encouraged my work, especially Dina Al-Kassim and John Culbert, who were such willing sounding boards and who championed the project and invited me into the Critical Nationalisms and Counterpublics Conference in 2019. I am also grateful to Deanna Kreisel and Ronda Arab, who read early drafts of chapter 1, and to Coll Thrush, who offered invaluable advice for chapter 3.

Many graduate students were part of the research for this book. Karl Manis, Emilia Halton-Hernandez, and Lionel Widmer did painstaking research at libraries. Most of all, I want to thank Craig Stensrud, who did a great deal of work on this project, from indexing and organizing illustrations to offering advice around arguments. The project would not have been the same without his intellectual input. I am also truly grateful to the readers and staff at the University of Michigan Press, especially Sara Cohen, who exhibited unflagging faith in my work even at points where it did not go smoothly. The anonymous readers who commented on my manuscript wrote some of the most helpful responses to my work I've ever encountered anywhere and I remain indebted to their insights.

The research for this project was generously funded by a Social Sciences and Humanities Research Council of Canada Insight Grant, as well as a UBC Aid to Scholarly Publishing Grant. A significantly earlier version of chapter 2 was published as "Restyling an Old World: Nathaniel Parker Willis and Metropolitan Fashion in the Antebellum United States," in *Representations* 85 (2004): 98–124. An earlier version of chapter 3 was published as "'Clothes Upon Sticks': James Fenimore Cooper and the Flat Frontier," in *Texas Studies in Literature and Language* 51 (2009): 142–78.

I save my most heartfelt thanks for my family: my parents, Barbara Tomc and Joseph Tomc, my late aunt Reska Cimmerman, my sister Kristina, who shares my love of the clothes and dolls and went with me to libraries, my daughter, Scarlett, who listened to a lot of clothes talk, and my husband Roger Larry, whose father was a clothing designer and who brought his heart and mind, as well as his eye for visual detail, to every draft of this manuscript.

ILLUSTRATIONS

INTRODUCTION

Traveling in the United States in 1906 and suffering from a depressive malaise he termed "boredom," the Russian novelist Maxim Gorky was taken by his friends to Coney Island. There, as Gorky later recounted, he saw the epitome of everything he loathed about the United States. It was a place full of aggressive and meaningless visual surfaces. "From the very first moment of arrival at this city of fire, the eye is blinded. It is assailed by thousands of cold, white sparks, and for a long time can distinguish nothing in the scintillating dust round about. Everything whirls and dazzles and blends into a tempestuous ferment of fiery foam." These bewildering assaults on the "eye" have a deadening, stupefying effect on the subject. "[T]he visitor is stunned; his consciousness is withered by the intense gleam." Millions of electric lights "prick the eye with the sharp needles of their dead, indifferent sparkle." Gorky observes how "people wander about in the flashing, blinding fire intoxicated and devoid of will."[1]

Gorky's description of Coney Island—and by analogy the whole of the United States—as a glittering, surreal visual extravaganza with no spiritual or political content was neither unusual at the time nor destined to fade. Late nineteenth- and early twentieth-century chroniclers of what was called U.S. "civilization" agreed that "America" was distinguished by empty sparkle, flashiness, and vistas of highly colored façades, lights, and signs. E. L. Godkin called U.S. society "chromo-civilization."[2] Describing various American "broadways" and boardwalks in 1922, Lewis Mumford noted, "The dazzle of white lights, the colour of electric signs, the alabaster architecture of the moving-picture palaces, the aesthetic appeals of the shop windows." He concluded, "Broadway . . . is the façade of the American city: a false front."[3] This idea of the United States remained prominent in political and philosophical thinking until the late twentieth century, achieving a kind of climax in the writing of Jean Baudrillard, for whom "America" is to be found in all its technologized, hyperactively visual soullessness, "in the speed of the screenplay, in the indifferent reflex of television, in the film of days and nights projected across an empty space, in the marvellously affectless succession of signs, images, faces."[4]

The idea that the United States might be linked with extravagant visual display is, of course, familiar to students of U.S. culture, especially students of late nineteenth-century culture. In twentieth-century critical traditions, such descriptions were typically thought to chronicle the devious materializations of capital. For William Leach in *Land of Desire* (1993), America's "facades of colour, glass, and light" are the apparatus of consumer modernity; the superficial, tricky quality of these visual displays mimics the trickiness of the commodity itself, an object that seems magnificent and magical but is in reality trivial.[5] Recent scholars reject the political terms of traditional consumer theory. Instead of trying to define the political aims of late nineteenth-century visual extravaganzas, recent material culture scholars, including Robert Rydell and Rob Kroes in *Buffalo Bill in Bologna* (2005) and Lauren Rabinovitz in *Electric Dreamland* (2012), see them as part of the interactive relationships between subjects and modern embodied entertainment experience. Rydell argues that as it was exported around the world, U.S. mass entertainment, though understood as "American" and "capitalist," performed a variety of functions that cannot reliably be mapped onto racial, national, imperial, or economic ideologies.[6] According to Rabinovitz, the amusement park's assault on the senses helped Americans weave new industrial and manufacturing technologies into both their sensible lives and into "a sense of national belonging." "Uniquely *modern mechanized* responses" to a changing nation, amusement parks "taught Americans to revel in a modern sensibility that was about adapting to new technologies, to hyperstimulation analogous to the nervous energies of industrial cities, to mechanical rhythms and uniformity, and to this perceptual condition as itself American."[7]

It is not insignificant, however, that while Rydell and Rabinovitz renounce the idea of coherent political meaning in the experiences of material culture, they continue to understand the forms of the new entertainments as "American" and "national."[8] The question I want to ask is why visual overload of the kind described by Gorky would be understood as American in the first place. Can a display of light—the glare of sunlight, the glow of electric bulbs—be "American" without first being part of a regime of meaning that articulates connections between certain visual effects and the imputed characteristics of a nationality or ethnicity?

In fact, a closer look at the origin of the kind of scenery that strikes Gorky and others as typically "American" reveals the extent to which these scenes were in the first place generated not around consumer pleasure or technology or urban entertainment, as scholars suggest, but around performances of national and ethnic characteristics. Touring Coney Island in 1906, Gorky was viewing a set of architectural and scenographic elements that had first been developed for competitive national displays at the World's Columbian Exposition in Chicago in 1893. The three Coney Island amusement parks, Steeplechase, Luna Park, and Dreamland, were all constructed between 1897 and 1904 in frank imitation of the Midway Plaisance and White City that had been the most distinctive and profitable features of the Columbian Exposition. What is revealed in descriptions of these features at the Columbian Exposition is the extent to which both the language used to describe them and the material and visual components of the features themselves drew on an existing repertoire of national and ethnic stereotypes, in which "America" already appeared as a site of emptiness and visual overload. In other words, what Gorky encountered at Coney Island was neither the emptiness of commodity capitalism nor precisely some actual embodied experience produced by electric bulbs and giant machines but a conventional way of imagining the material instantiation of "America" in the international community of the late nineteenth and early twentieth century.

These conventional ways of imagining "America" had a long history. In late eighteenth-century racial and national theory, the landscape of a given place and the appearance of its population were thought to be continuous. Thus one of the first things we notice if we look at the history of American appearance is that the features imputed to landscapes at the end of the century—the visual overload, the technologized surfaces, the glittery colors—first appear on American bodies in the early nineteenth century. Americans feature in the descriptions of both domestic and international travelers as a people whose surfaces are noisy and confusing. Americans are given to visual bravado, to florid colors, glittery jewels, varnished boots, and gaudy patterns. Touring New York City in 1842, Charles Dickens remarked, "Heaven save the ladies, how they dress! We have seen more colors in these ten minutes, than we should have seen elsewhere, in as many days. What various parasols! what rainbow silks and satins!"[9] In *New York by Gas-Light*, published in 1850, George Foster describes Broadway at night, with its whirling Drummond light and its beautiful ladies: "their complexions are pure white and red, and their dresses are of the most expensive material, and an ultra fashionable make. Diamonds and bracelets flash from their bosoms and bare arms, and heavily-wrought India shawls, of that gorgeous scarlet whose beamy hue intoxicates the eye, hang carelessly from the superb shoulders, almost trailing on the walk."[10]

On the one hand, this imagery of excess summons up stereotypes of class and racial degeneracy that were common in this period. Like other peripheral populations, U.S. settler colonial groups were typified in transatlantic ethnographic discourse as a quaint, underdeveloped people attracted to showiness and inferior consumer objects. Thus, in the above descriptions, we learn from Dickens that the colorful dresses of the ladies of New York are a mark of backwardness and inferiority. Dickens shortly reveals that Americans are a violent, childish group who live in a nation that still enslaves human beings. We learn from Foster that the flashy clothes of the women of Broadway are not signs of sophistication; they are linked to "large feet" and low morals.[11]

These stereotypes of "Americans," which proliferated in the transatlantic art and intellectual scene from the early 1820s to the 1840s, were produced by diverse groups. They were produced by British and European travelers trained to see all provincial populations, whether white or people of color, as primitive and non-modern; they were produced by U.S. performers and intellectuals who identified with the metropole and looked upon local populations with disdain or disaffection; and they were produced by local writers looking to invest the United States with regional particularity through the elucidation of a peculiar "folk." Drawing on ethnic nationalist and racialist visual itineraries that were being developed in Britain and Europe around clothes and that were relayed in transatlantic print and theater networks, the gaudy clothes and habitats of U.S. populations signaled for contemporaries a debased national or regional character. And this was a completely conventional construction; it was taken for granted by everyone in the transatlantic intellectual world that Americans, who lived in the provinces of empire, were a peripheral, unsophisticated, and even morally questionable population with an undeveloped taste that led to a love of cheap and shiny mass-produced consumer goods.

But beginning in the 1830s, I argue, significant branches of U.S. cultural nationalism responded to these stereotypes by producing a new set of stereotypes that focused not on the gaudy inner character revealed in American clothes but on the gaudy surface itself as a central symbol of U.S. nationality. Imagined as purely technological and formal, a site where the look of the spectator was short-circuited and reflected back to itself, the dazzling, refractive surface did not convey ethnicity, nationality, or race in any conventional sense. On the contrary, it functioned as a site where the transmission of these properties was broken and short-circuited in an incoherent wash of visual information. It was this meaningless surface, often associated with glitter, lights, and reflections, that had achieved hegemony as a kind of mythical, transcendent sign of U.S. nationality by the end of the nineteenth century. When Gorky saw Luna Park on the horizon of Coney Island, he was seeing the materialization of an ethnic national personality whose chief feature was its confusion of the conceptual terms of race and ethnicity, terms that were exploded through the overloading of perception.

In *Fashion Nation*, then, I trace the history of this idea of America as a flashy, meaningless surface from its early proliferation in the 1830s, when it was associated primarily with loud, colorful clothes, masks, and cosmetics, to its fruition in late nineteenth-century mass entertainment, when it shifted from clothes to elaborate lights and scenics. I argue that discussions of the United States as a contentless visual extravaganza, rather than having anything to do with technology or modernity, were rooted in the early nineteenth-century emergence of ethnic and racial nationalism in Britain, Europe, and the United States. In the wake of pressure in the first half of the nineteenth century to embrace ethnically and racially saturated national types, significant branches of U.S. nationalist culture developed national types distinguished by their refusal to divulge ethnic and racial affiliation. Elaborate visual surfaces purported to short-circuit precisely those visual signals that were thought to transmit ethnic and racial information.

The Ethnic Nation

What exactly is ethnic nationalism and how might we include it in existing histories of U.S. nationalism and consumer modernity?

Writing about his travels in England in the late 1820s and early 1830s, James Fenimore Cooper recapitulated beliefs about nationhood that were typical for metropolitan intellectuals of this period. The English, Cooper said, seemed to be held together by powerful bonds of history, tradition, heritage, and kinship. Americans, by contrast, had few such affiliations. Citizens of a recently founded nation-state, often émigres from the far corners of the earth, Americans, Cooper felt, merely held in common "a consciousness of living under a system that protects their rights and interests." "An Englishman, or a Frenchman," says Cooper, "goes into distant countries, with a consciousness that he leaves behind him, a concentrated and powerful sentiment of nationality, that will throw its protection around him, even to the remotest verges of civilization, but the case is altogether different with the American"[12]

Cooper's distinction between U.S. nationalism and the nationalism of the European nations nicely marks out what in the early nineteenth century was a growing distinction between different forms of nationhood. The United States was conceived and structured as what historians today call a "civic nation." Writing on the nation in his now classic *Imagined Communities*, Benedict Anderson argues that the chief goal of the modern nation-state was to impose itself as an imaginative structure or fiction on a diverse population. Replacing older, dynastic, imperial, and religious obligations, the modern nation-state worked as an entity by offering subjects new objects of communal affiliation; populations who had once paid obeisance to a monarch, a pope, or an emperor were now encouraged to give their devotion to "France" or "Italy." The modern nation utilized a variety of cultural and pedagogical technologies, including print, maps, museums, education, administrative bureaucracy, and linguistic uniformity, to encourage its populace to imagine themselves as part of a larger definable collective. According to Anderson, capitalism itself, with its requisite lawyers, mapmakers, accountants, and officials, aided in the establishment of administrative structures that were readily transformed in the late eighteenth century into apparatuses of national unity.[13]

Traditional histories of U.S. nationalism see the United States as one of the earliest examples of the civic nation materializing itself through bureaucratic, pedagogical, marketplace, and print apparatuses in the late eighteenth century. In the words of Lloyd Kramer, the United States rapidly "narrated" itself into positive existence after 1775, imposing unity on a "diverse, scattered population" through a combination of "political institutions, schools, religious rituals, public celebrations, family memories, literature, and history books."[14] Anderson himself identifies the United States as one of several creole entities in the Americas whose national apparatus merely harnessed an existing colonial administrative structure.[15]

Nevertheless, as Cooper's comments suggest, in the early years of the nineteenth century, a new and different idea of nationhood surged to the fore in Europe, what historians sometimes call "romantic nationalism" or "ethnic nationalism." Unlike civic nationalism, which took its shape from a bureaucratic or economic apparatus, ethnic nationalism was built on the perception that a given group of people belonged together because they shared powerful cultural and kinship attributes. They spoke the same language, adhered to a specific religion, claimed a common ancestry, and shared the same national personality or character. In this formulation, certain population groups existed as a coherent people *prior to* the existence of the apparatus of the nation-state itself. Indeed, the nation-state was often seen as a fulfillment of the destined oneness of "a people." Whereas the civic nation was conceived as a voluntary organization, one that citizens could join or leave at will, ethnic nationality was conceived as something deeply ingrained in the body and spirit of a given people. When German or Italian people traveled outside of their home region, they did not merge into a formless cosmopolitanism or take on the identity of the populations among whom they traveled. They remained immutably "German" or "Italian." This is what Cooper means when he senses that the "English" take with them a "sentiment of nationality" wherever they go. There is a quality of Englishness, in Cooper's mind, that exceeds the nation-state. Indeed, the language of nations in the nineteenth century developed a whole vocabulary that emphasized the modern nation's comparability to a family or kinship system: "mother tongue," "homeland," "fatherland," "mother country." These words signified powerful national affiliations that went well beyond merely legal, economic, and governmental apparatuses. Cooper's very impulse to compare the "American" to the "Englishman" participates in the production of a national character that exceeds the mere "protection of rights and interests" that the civic nation purports to guarantee. Describing ethnicity in *Race, Nation, Class*, Étienne Balibar and Immanuel Wallerstein call it a nation's alleged "personality."[16] Thus France is not simply a collection of bureaucratic and educational structures; it is occupied by "the *French*." The "French" have a shared personality. To be "French" means something other than to live in France and be educated in a national culture.[17] In Immanuel Wallerstein's words, ethnicity denotes a culture and a heritage. It describes "a people."[18]

It is useful to pause for a moment to define my terminology. The word "ethnic" was not used in the early nineteenth century to indicate nation or natal origin. The words used to indicate one's "people" at that time were words like "tribe" or "race." "Ethnic," in the eighteenth century, meant "neither Christian nor Jewish," "pagan" (OED). In the mid-nineteenth century, "ethnic" came to denote exotic, provincial, or nonmetropolitan populations and places. Thus, Thomas Moore could, in 1804, refer to "All the charm that ethnic fancy gave / To blessed arbours o'er the western wave." Writing in 1846, Henry Wadsworth Longfellow imagined "These . . . ancient ethnic revels / Of a faith long since forsaken" (OED). It was in the twentieth century that "ethnicity" acquired its modern meaning, indicating a person's natal relationship to a country or a people. The OED definition of "ethnic" as it is used now is: "Of or relating to peoples with regard to their (actual or perceived) common descent"; and "Of or relating to national or cultural origin or tradition." Accordingly, the term "ethnic nationalism" stems from twentieth-century meanings of the word "ethnic." Although the term "ethnic nationalism" was not used in the early nineteenth century, it is used by scholars today to describe the nationalisms of this period that take ancestry, language, and birthplace as their defining feature. I also want to say at the outset that I am siding with scholars who see ethnic culture as a social construction rather than as an innate or essential property of persons with common genetic ancestry, territory, or language. I regard ethnic nationalism as a governing symbolic system and biopolitical discourse, a way of grouping and classifying human populations that fell in line with other biopolitical discourses developed during the late eighteenth and early nineteenth centuries. Ethnic nationalism could serve a just purpose, helping local groups and communities resist larger imperial and monarchical forces. But it also produced a pernicious set of doctrines and ideologies, the most extreme of which evolved into modern white nationalism and Germanic supremacy theory.[19]

Ethnic nationalism—the belief in the purity or oneness of a people or nation—swept over British and European intellectual culture in the 1790s and early 1800s. Its most famous British proponents included Edmund Burke and Walter Scott. Its German proponents included Johann Gottfried Herder, Johann Gottlieb Fichte, and the Brothers Grimm. Offering itself as an alternative to republican anonymity and empire and often catering to conservative political opinion, ethnic nationalism celebrated regional affiliation and vernacular cultures, delighting in insularity, quaint tradition, and ancestral histories that escaped enlightenment modernity. Unlike the civic nation, which was represented by abstract symbols like the flag, ethnicity was postulated as an embodied, intimate phenomenon. Whereas the "nation" referenced legal, pedagogical, and bureaucratic unity, an ethnic group indicated ancestral formations closely linked to regional location, to ancient languages and religions, and to the land of one's birth. In addition, the ethnic nation was thought to be powered by destiny. From the 1790s to the 1880s, as Europe's so called "stateless nationalities"—the Greeks, the Germans, the Italians, the Hungarians, the Slavs—struggled against Hapsburg and Ottoman control, they were animated by a powerful belief in the destiny and right of a given "people" to unify themselves into a state based on perceived ethnic allegiances.

Ethnic nationalism had a profound effect on nationalist cultures in the United States. At the simplest level, U.S. intellectuals from about 1820 onward became entranced by the idea that there might be one "American" people linked through common taste, language, and culture. Ethnic nationalism's influence on U.S. culture manifested itself in numerous ways. It manifested itself in passionate interest among Americans themselves in the creation of a distinctive national character. Traveling in Europe in the 1820s and 1830s, Cooper and the generation of cultural nationalists who followed closely on his heels were responsible for contriving an "American" national personality and appearance that could at every turn be contrasted with the British and Europeans they met. The French, said Cooper, were "short."[20] The English, according to Ralph Waldo Emerson, were "ruddy," violent, and obsessed with the eradication of nature.[21] Ethnic nationalism also manifested itself in the determination of U.S. writers and entertainers to create a set of what were called national "types," fictional characters who seemed to embody a quintessential "American" personality, one that was not generically metropolitan but colloquial or vernacular in nature. Figures like Ichabod Crane, Natty Bumppo, Davy Crockett, and Brother Jonathan became stock characters in transatlantic theater and political cartoons. They joined a host of newly nationalistic British and European caricatures who now collectively peopled transatlantic fiction, theater, and political cartoons.

In addition, ethnic nationalism provided a new lens through which to understand relationships among regional and immigrant populations inside the United States. In the eighteenth century, it had been common in the United States to imagine the country's population as a composite of the ethnicities of its various settler groups. J. Hector St. John de Crèvecoeur's famous question in 1782, "What is an American?" imagines Americans as a diverse, informal collective of European immigrants, each with its own "national genius": Americans are "English, Scotch, Irish, French, Dutch, Germans, and Swedes."[22] By the 1840s, the strands of ethnic nationalism prominent in the United States were insisting on the separateness of these nationalities and developing a hierarchy among them in accord with emerging Anglo-Saxon and Germanic supremacy theory, which flourished in early nineteenth-century England, France, and Germany. Writing his poem "Our Country" in 1841, Henry David Thoreau lists the "nationalities" populating the United States in much the same way Crèvecoeur does. The difference is that he uses the term "Saxon" as a way of distinguishing Anglo-Protestants from other groups. According to Thoreau, various immigrant groups are creating in the United States a "congress of the world"; they are led by a superior Germanic people, the "Anglo-Saxons."

> Look nearer,—know the lineaments of each face,—
> Learn the far-travelled race, and find here met
> The so long gathering congress of the world!
> The Afric race brought here to curse its fate,
> Erin to bless,—the patient German too,
> Th' industrious Swiss, the fickle, sanguine Gaul,
> And manly Saxon, leading all the rest.[23]

Dividing various U.S. populations not just by familiar racialist categories ("Afric race") but also by ethnicity (the Irish, or people of Erin, the Germans, the Swiss, the "Gauls" or French), Thoreau uses the terminology of a powerful branch of ethnic nationalist thought, Germanic supremacy theory, to indicate that the "manly Saxon" is the natural leader of these other peoples.

But in addition to U.S. cultural nationalists manufacturing their own American "types," myths, and symbols, U.S. people were also the objects of similar efforts on the part of the British and Europeans. Along with hundreds of other localities around the world, the United States was typified in metropolitan intellectual culture from about 1800 onward not just as a nation-state or settler empire but as its own peculiar region with its own distinctive people, its own "folk" and customs. The United States was now understood to be home to a national "personality": the

American. Some of this "American" identity, as I have said, was generated by U.S. writers and performers, but much of it was not. Between 1815 and 1850, the United States featured prominently in British and European-authored theater, journalism, travel literature, and political cartoons. On a practical level, the United States was a special object of interest to transatlantic readerships because so many Britons and Europeans contemplated emigrating there. The early nineteenth century witnessed an explosion of documentary and travel writing on the United States. Historians calculate that between 1790 and 1860, more than 330 separate book titles on North American travel appeared.[24] But more than that, the United States offered itself as a site for the production of political, national, and ethnic difference. With its diverse populations, its republican political systems, its settler colonial imperatives, and especially its continued tolerance of enslaved labor, the United States emerged in the early nineteenth century as a kind of counter to Britain and Europe, a place against which metropolitan audiences could take the measure of their own nations. As Rob Kroes puts it, "America" was not just a foreign nation; it was "a constituent element in the history of European ideas."[25]

It was in this climate of nationalistic typification that the notion of an "American" look or a peculiar American style became important. One of the central features of ethnic nationalism was that it codified and mandated certain regimes of appearance and style for human groups. Ethnic nationalism believed that each nation had its own style and look. Racial scientific discourse, which developed in this same period, from roughly 1780 to 1860, took the skin or cranial structure as its primary signifier. Ethnic nationalism hypothesized a set of differences that were not reliably present in the morphological features of the unadorned biological body. Instead, one of the key instruments of distinction in ethnic nationalism was clothing; and, if the description of certain human groups or a certain subject had to go beyond the features of the visible body, habitat. In the early nineteenth century, clothing did the work of distinguishing the ancestral or "tribal" spirit of populations in scenes of nationalist awakening and self-assertion. Indeed, clothing acted as a kind of extension of the body, a place where, for good or ill, the "genius" of a people was coalesced and brought into vivid materialization. This was the logic behind the new concept of "national dress," also called "folk dress," which was thought to embody the ancient spirits and energies of a given national "people."

To be sure, we would not immediately think that this discourse of clothing as a medium of ethnic national personality would have much application to the study of dress in the nineteenth-century United States. Virtually all histories of U.S. fashion and material culture treat nineteenth-century fashion, consumer objects, and mass entertainments as indicative of modernity and thus symbolically severed from archaic tradition. That is, items of modern fashion and décor are typically treated as phenomena whose major feature was that they floated free of allegedly arcane or primitive caste, race, and ethnic structures, especially structures that might have been invested with notions of ancestry and destiny. Indeed, for most historians, the very definition of "mass culture" and "consumer culture" is that these were homogenizing forces that actualized liberal and democratic alternatives to traditional modes of social organization, even if they often provided new sites for the diffuse operations of gender and political power.

We can see examples of this thinking in major studies not just of early twentieth-century U.S. mass culture and entertainment but also of early nineteenth-century fashion and spectacle. In these studies, colorful fashions are understood to be part of an expanding and democratizing mass culture industry. Michael Zakim, for example, begins his study of modern clothing manufacture by pointing out that the early nineteenth-century United States was the scene of the world's first cheap, ready-to-wear men's clothing industry. Flush with cloths woven by the newly mechanized looms of northern England, tailors in New York in the late 1810s and early 1820s began to manufacture men's coats, shirts, and pantaloons that were sold off the rack at cut rate prices. Zakim argues that these new, ready-made clothes were more than just a modern convenience; they became powerful symbols of the transformative powers of the capitalist marketplace. Decimating traditional sartorial cultures of rank and station, they promised an equal opportunity society, a "democracy of broadcloth," in which everyone had access to a polished genteel appearance.[26]

In its emphasis on the liberal, egalitarian sensibility of consumer culture, Zakim's work follows in the footsteps of an older tradition of material culture scholarship that links together an expanding marketplace for consumer goods and a middle-class ideology that promised U.S. populations the instruments of social mobility and prosperity. Karen Haltunnen's *Confidence Men and Painted Women* (1982), John Kasson's *Rudeness and Civility* (1990), and Richard Bushman's *The Refinement of America* (1993) all discuss antebellum fashions and bodily adornments in the context of an expanding consumer marketplace and the ideology of individualist self-fashioning and class aspiration that went with it.[27] More recently, Monica Miller suggests that in the expanding marketplace of material goods, opportunities for self-fashioning were open not just to middle-class whites but to poor whites and people of color who could take advantage of the possibilities for transformation that clothes offered.[28] To be sure, some studies of U.S. material culture, including Lori Merish's *Sentimental Materialism* (2000), argue that middle-class people in the nineteenth century urban United States were instantiated as docile subjects through their commitment to what Merish calls a "cult of fashion."[29] Nevertheless, while she disagrees with the political possibilities often attributed to the "ornamental" American body, Merish still sees it as a site that was supposed to offer, if it never really actualized, endless novelty and the possibilities of transformation.

However, this exclusive focus on the egalitarian and marketplace dimensions of clothing, I argue, overlooks clothing's powerful capture in early nineteenth-century's developing systems of nationality, ethnicity, and race. Indeed, as numerous scholars emphasize, modern clothing and consumer items, even as they potentially promised a liberal social order, tended to work along with rather than superseding caste and race systems. Anne Anlin Cheng's studies of clothing, skin, and race, *Second Skin* (2013) and *Ornamentalism* (2019), trace the complex ways in which adornment worked together with the surfaces of the body in late nineteenth- and early twentieth-century U.S. modernity to capture subjects in extended racializing systems that went beyond the merely biovisual realm. Modern scholars are almost unanimous in emphasizing the extent to which modern fashion and consumer culture freed subjects from traditional identities. In *Fashion Nation* I look at the ways in which arguments around U.S. nationalism and often violent obsessions with "tribal" affinities and ethnic differences played themselves out in the realm of material culture, inhabiting the world of sartorial signs and habitat design where the nation was supposed to materialize itself as an embodied entity. Instead of assuming that modern fashion and consumer culture represented a homogenizing, anodyne force, I look at how modern fashion and consumer culture encoded and aided fierce struggles around ethnic and racial supremacy, struggles that would reach a violent fruition in the extremist forms of ethnic nationalism that flourished at the end of the nineteenth century.

From the late eighteenth century to the end of the nineteenth, U.S. nationalists adopted and did their part to contribute to the major conceptual frameworks of British and European ethnic and racial thought. Indeed, in the case of authors like Thomas Jefferson, Washington Irving, and James Fenimore Cooper, U.S. intellectuals very much helped in the building of transatlantic ethnic nationalist mythologies, especially around German origins theory. But it is also the case that in the late 1820s, U.S. intellectuals were faced with new challenges. Like other biopolitical and racially animated discourses of this period, ethnic nationalism worked as a double-edged sword, encouraging the coexistence in nationalistic discourse of congratulatory adulation of one's own nation and the derogation and abjection of other nations. Even as U.S. cultural nationalists celebrated the United States as a Germanic nation powered by white racial destiny, the United States itself came under the scrutiny of British and European ethnic nationalists, many of them also fired up by Germanic supremacy theories, who challenged U.S. claims.

In the late 1820s, as ethnic nationalism in general grew more bullish and chauvinistic, and as the international political status of the United States altered substantially over the morality of Indigenous dispossession and slavery, the United States became the target not just of political and touristic description but of often vicious satire and caricature. In particular, travel literature, novels, political cartoons, and transatlantic comic theater would provide voluble and widely viewed forums for a new generation of what historians sometimes call "anti-American" journalists, illustrators, and performers.[30] The U.S. nation in this discourse was not identified as one of the triumphant modern nations. Instead, nationalists in Britain and Europe targeted the United States as a violent, backward country destined to fall well short of the civilizational summit where truly superior nations, it was thought, would soon hold court. The United States appeared in this literature as a land filled not with noble adventurers but with mediocrities and moral degenerates. This strand of anti-Americanism was not minor or invisible. It appeared in the works of such famous authors as Frances Trollope and Charles Dickens. It was published in the form of popular novels and countless essays. It appeared in the most widely read British reviews and it flooded theaters and magazines in the United States in the late 1820s and 1830s.

My book argues that U.S. nationalists invented novel ways of deflecting these ascriptions. As I show in chapter 1, in ethnic nationalist doctrines, as these developed in transatlantic visual and theater culture in the first half of the nineteenth century, colorful and ornate clothes acted as a shorthand for degeneracy. Critical accounts of Americans were thus filled with accounts of their gaudy dress. And precisely because clothing in the ethnic nationalist regime was so closely linked to national character, clothing itself emerged as a site of significant political struggle among Anglo-European and U.S. nationalist factions in the decades between 1820 and 1860. Scholars have long understood that antebellum cultural nationalist groups, in addition to coming under the negative scrutiny of the British and Europeans, experienced a series of profound crises between the 1830s and the late 1850s, crises provoked by the growing abolition movement and politicization of slavery, by intensifying settler colonial violence and war with Mexico, by new revelations of class inequality and the plight of the poor. Such studies as Jared Gardner's *Master Plots* (1998), Elisa Tamarkin's *Anglophilia* (2008), Lara Langer Cohen's *The Fabrication of American Literature* (2011), J. Gerald Kennedy's *Strange Nation* (2016), and Jason Richards' *Imitation Nation* (2017) chronicle the fraught relationship between U.S. cultural nationalists and their own shifting and often violently negative image of the United States during this period.[31] In Kennedy's words, U.S. nationalism often served "to cover an abyss of insecurity produced by the peculiar circumstances of the country's origins."[32]

It was in this transatlantic climate, I suggest, fueled with nationalistic vitriol and one-upmanship, that U.S. nationalist culture produced unconventional tropes for the visual signage of embodied "Americanness." These tropes initially represented a revolt against and challenge to British and European ethnic nationalist frameworks. The central tenet of the nineteenth-century ethnic nationalist visual regime was faith in the transparency of the signal sent out by the surface of the body to the eye of the beholder. In this sense, as I show in chapter 1, although the ethnic body relied upon the signifiers produced by clothes, it operated almost exactly like the skin and bones of the racialized body, in the sense that here too the surface of the body purported to offer a transparent window into the moral and intellectual abilities of the embodied subject. Indeed, in ethnic nationalist discourse, particularly white supremacist discourse, the racial and ethnic body were virtually the same, often functioning as interchangeable constructs. Once viewed by a knowing observer, according to this powerful mythology, the ethnic/racial body unconsciously revealed the complex totality of the subject's moral and intellectual character to its beholder. In this formulation, the surface of the body, whether clothes or bare skin, was not a "covering." It was a sensual materialization of the moral and spiritual impulsions, the deep ancestral character, of the ethnic or racial group to which the subject belonged. Thus portraits of Americans as a gaudily dressed people were not a minor insult. They hit at the powerful white supremacist belief systems that justified U.S. settler colonial and enslaver violence. They suggested that "Americans," instead of being members of a triumphant Germanic people destined to rule over inferior ethnic and racial groups, were themselves impure and inferior. But precisely because this structure depended on the clarity of a visual signal—the signal sent from the surface of the body to the eye of the beholder—this signal could also be deflected or blocked.

Beginning in the late 1830s, I argue, significant branches of U.S. cultural nationalism responded to popular transatlantic stereotypes of gaudy Americans by producing a new set of stereotypes that focused not on the gaudy inner character supposedly revealed in American clothes but on the gaudy surface itself as a central symbol of U.S. nationality. Already associated with the curious, ornate clothes of provincial populations, the American subject was reimagined in the entertainment culture of the early nineteenth-century northern United States as a subject whose visual signals contained a glitch, a place where the touristic eye met the surface of the body only to encounter an unexpected blockage or flare of light that stopped information about ethnic or racial character from being transmitted. Imagined as purely technological and formal, a site where the look of the spectator was short-circuited and reflected back to itself, the dazzling, refractive surface of this revised

American body did not convey ethnicity, nationality, or raciality in any conventional sense. On the contrary, it functioned as a site where the transmission of these properties was broken. The popular picture of Americans and their habitats as visually noisy, covered in shining color, glitter, and light, was the manifestation of this fantasy of short-circuiting, in which the eye of Europe, looking for positive signals of ethnicity and race, met a flashy, reflective surface and was blinded, distracted, or turned back on itself in a wash of visual noise. The American body, in this formulation, refused to divulge racial or ethnic information. It was thus understood as something empty, a kind of visually audacious but dead technological shell.

In the 1830s, this fantasy of Americans as a mass of overbright surfaces that refused to divulge positive information circulated both in urban entertainment in the United States and in the exploding field of transatlantic journalism, where U.S. and British intellectuals taunted each other with vicious nationalist jokes and insults. Toward the end of the century, it also increasingly described American interiors, scenes, and landscapes. But it is also the case that by the end of the century, the glittery, empty American subject produced in antebellum fantasy as a repudiation of the ethnic body had been naturalized as itself a kind of ethnic figure, a sign of "Americanness." At the world's fairs and amusement parks that flourished in the 1890s and early 1900s, Americanness materialized itself as a nationalist entity in reflective surfaces and blinding lights, in the flickers of cinema projectors and the flashes of cameras, in machines that claimed to be devoid of positive embodiment. When Gorky saw Luna Park on the horizon of Coney Island, he was seeing the materialization of this revisionist ethnic personality, a personality whose chief feature was its confusion of the conceptual terms of race and ethnicity, terms that were exploded through the overloading and short-circuiting of perception. By the end of the century certain visual arrangements that could be read as excessive (and sometimes this excess had an objective existence, sometimes it was the fantasy of viewers) signified as "American." Offering to vaporize racial and ethnic content in the blur of a utopian capitalist modernity, in what Baudrillard would call a dizzyingly "spectral form of civilization,"[33] these images of "America" still retained at their heart an ethnic and racialist logic, fitting themselves with the imperial projects that preoccupied the United States at the close of the nineteenth century.

In the chapters that follow, I not only offer a detailed study of the arguments and invective that flowed back and forth across the Atlantic between U.S. intellectuals and their counterparts in Britain and Europe, but I also look closely at the central and largely unexamined role played by clothing and other bodily and cultural surfaces in these arguments. To a degree that has not been remarked on by scholars, U.S. cultural nationalists in the antebellum period were obsessed with clothes. There are the various veils and badges in Nathaniel Hawthorne's tales "The Minister's Black Veil" (1832), *The Scarlet Letter* (1850), and *The Blithedale Romance* (1852). There is Anna Cora Mowatt's costume-centered satire of American manners, *Fashion* (1845), and Nathaniel Parker Willis's obsessive focus on fashion and dandyism. There is James Fenimore Cooper's final Leatherstocking novel, *The Deerslayer* (1841), with its mirrored lake and elaborately deceptive clothes. There are the extended passages on clothing in Henry David Thoreau's *Walden* (1854) and Ralph Waldo Emerson's *English Traits* (1856) as well the preoccupation with clothes in Herman Melville's novels and stories, from *White Jacket* (1850) and "Benito Cereno" (1855) to the *Confidence Man* (1857). Lydia Maria Child, Caroline Lee Hentz, and Horace Bushnell were a few of the many writers who wrote about clothes. Clothes mattered to these writers not because they were concerned with literal garments but because by the 1830s, clothes had acquired international currency as the language and signature of nations. How U.S. cultural nationalists responded to these mandates and how "Americanness" was remade as a defensive, compensatory structure in the light of ethnic nationalist sartorial imperatives are the topics of this book.

What Were People Wearing?

It is worth stressing that this book does not deal with material culture in any conventional sense. It is not a history of fashion or consumer culture in the United States, and with few exceptions it does not look at what people actually wore or purchased. Instead, the book is a history of a certain visual regime, one in which the surfaces of bodies and their habitats were understood in Anglo-European intellectual culture as densely *meaningful*, their signals pinging ardently on the eye of the knowing viewer. In some cases, as in its discussion of *The Scarlet Letter* and *The Deerslayer*, this book looks at fictional accounts of dress. In other cases, for example, in its reading of costume albums, political cartoons, children's books, and theatrical comedies, it looks at illustrations and performances that purport to document what actual individuals and cultures wore. And in still other cases, as in the case of Nathaniel Parker Willis, William Cody, and Óta Kté (Luther Standing Bear), this book does in fact look at the actual clothes worn by actual people, but it does so in order to specify that clothes as material objects in these instances are impossible to separate from their heavily symbolic, almost fictitious air as ethnic nationalist dress.

In contrast to material culture histories, which either look at the economic and political dimensions of consumer culture or seek to recover the subject's intimate experience of clothing, consumer items, or artifacts, *Fashion Nation* is a study of the mediation of cultural objects and landscapes within nineteenth-century visual regimes. It emphasizes the inability of populations to grasp objects in their unique simplicity. In this sense, my study has less in common with conventional material culture histories than with recent discussions of outsized sartorial items: the "veil," the "turban," the "hoodie," the war bonnet, the MAGA hat, items whose meanings have ballooned in chaotic fashion beyond the control of their wearers and beyond their origination in a particular cultural group or political moment.[34] In this study, I look at how some clothes existed as symbols, aesthetic constructs, fictions, theatrical devices, fantasies, and projections. Their purpose was to produce and police symbolic systems and to teach people how to see and decode signs, in this case the signs of nationality.

In looking at clothing as an ethnic nationalist trope, I am not only drawing attention to a prominent and overlooked feature of U.S. nationalist discourse, but I am also hopefully adding to our knowledge of the many ways in which the nineteenth-century Western ideological regimes of colonization and nationalistic competition multiplied themselves in unexpected nooks and crannies of U.S. life, extending themselves well beyond arenas that we typically associate with the reproduction of biopolitical, racial, and settler colonial norms. In *Skin Acts*, Michelle Ann Stephens looks at how racialized difference has historically been produced in the United States and other Western nations at the level of skin. The racialized subject is theorized as part of a visual regime in which the skin of any given unadorned body is fetishized as an object of peculiar ontological importance. In Stephens' words, skin is not just an extension of bodily flesh. It is "a cutaneous medium and bodily contact zone through which modern subjects negotiate and enact a profound desire to see difference."[35] The racialist gaze fixates on skin as the place where racial difference is produced. Indeed, the racial gaze consists of the "denaturalizing of the givenness of human difference," so that accidental features of the body become indicators of character and personality. In racializing discourse, "The skin . . . becomes the primary signifier of the *meaningfulness* of difference, producing racialized difference *as* significant, as signifying."[36]

At the same time, precisely because its importance as a site of difference was part of an extended semiotics of legibility, skin has not been alone in its ability to arbitrate difference. In her study of Black U.S. music star Josephine Baker, Anne Anlin Cheng draws attention to the easy convertibility of naked skin and the synthetic surfaces seemingly produced in early twentieth-century transatlantic art and entertainment. Her study "revisits the visceral possibility of raced skin, not in order to recuperate notions of corporeal authenticity, but to attend to the curious interface between that skin and inorganic surfaces emerging out of the first quarter of the twentieth century." Cheng attempts to understand "raced skin as itself a *modern material fascination*, one that speaks not just to a history of objectification but paradoxically also to an emerging concept of matter as mutability, thereby redefining raced skin as 'dumb flesh.'"[37] But more recently Cheng herself has spoken of the limitations of skin as an analytic when it comes to understanding the history of race in the United States. In *Ornamentalism*, which theorizes the category of the "woman of color," Cheng wonders whether the "'epidermal racial schema' hardened for us into a thing of untroubled legibility? To what extent have the 'hieroglyphics of the flesh' prevented us from seeing an alternative materialism of the body?"[38] Cheng goes on to consider the extent to which structures that seem to be superfluous to the biological body, such as clothes, fabrics, décor, and aesthetic devices, have a racializing function. I explore the extent to which this signifying practice, which seems to Cheng to belong to nineteenth-century aesthetic and orientalist culture, permeated metropolitan ethnic nationalist and racialist thinking across a multiplicity of populations and genders.

By characterizing clothes and other cultural devices as sites of ontological significance, nineteenth-century ethnic nationalism and the ethnographic disciplines that often went with it multiplied opportunities for scopic differentiation and proliferated sites of potential hierarchization beyond the corporeal body to cultural and aesthetic practices. In this sense, ethnic nationalism worked in tandem with more familiar racializing techniques and strategies, offering to hierarchize and taxonomize a broader range of populations across the globe. In this discourse, the visible signs of the adorned body became fail-safe proofs of the subject's genetic inheritance and intellectual abilities, ciphering the imperatives of what was now elaborated as racial and national destiny. At the same time, by studying clothing and habitats as opposed to the biological attributes of the body, *Fashion Nation* draws attention to the odd, often uncanny way that plainly nonbiological objects—shiny cloth, gold watches, veneers, ornate shoes, even a flash of light—can nevertheless function as signs of ethnic embodiment as surely as religion, ancestry, or literal flesh and bones.

Fashion Nation contains four chapters, each of which focuses on an episode in the history of U.S. visual extravagance that cohered around U.S. status in the community of Western nations. The chapters begin in the opening years of the 1800s as the first ethnic nationalist figures appeared in transatlantic visual and theater culture. It was at this point that the United States was swept into ethnic nationalist visual systems as a site of degeneracy, a degeneracy announced by its inhabitants' loud clothes. The book then moves on to consider the 1830s and 1840s, when alternatives to the visual techniques of conventional ethnic ascription proliferated in antebellum literature and entertainment and when the American subject, instead of being imagined as a gauche, noisily dressed creole cousin of Europe, appeared in the scene of nations as a figure of mystery whose clothes refused to divulge information about its ethnic and racial provenance. The final two chapters trace the migration of these embodied ethnic characteristics into a topographical imaginary that purported to extend the features of the ethnic body to the features of a people's habitat. In these chapters, I not only illustrate the development of scenic visual repertoires that matched the flashy, confusing body of the American developed earlier in the century, but I also look at the extent to which these image regimes were normalized within U.S. nationalist discourse by the end of the century. In the bold patchwork of militaristic nations formed around British and European imperial might at the end of the century, the United States appeared, not as a positive embodied presence, but as a flash of light or glittery façade, something the eye could not properly assess.

Chapter 1, "American Looks," serves as a broad introduction to the pictorial and discursive fields that frame the book as a whole. The chapter begins by tracking the emergence of a regime of national "looks"—the idea that a nation's people are identifiable in the appearance and style of the adorned body—that came into vogue in the late eighteenth and early nineteenth century, partly in concert with a new emphasis on the visible body as an indicator of moral and intellectual character, here expanded to include national and regional character as well. In this chapter, I not only give a more detailed description of ethnic nationalism and its sartorial regimes but I also emphasize the influence of ethnic nationalist concepts and imagery in the United States. In fact, sartorial symbols played a crucial political role in the American Revolution, which was distinguished by its rejection of "Old World" finery and embrace of plain, unornamented "homespun" as the proper dress of patriots. Ethnic nationalism, which gained ascendancy after 1800, drastically inverted these symbols in redesignating plainness as a symbol of aristocratic elegance.

With this in mind, I trace the changes in the way "Americans" were depicted and thought to appear to the eye in both transatlantic and domestic description in the early years of the nineteenth century. When tourists like Frances Trollope, Charles Dickens, Thomas Chandler Haliburton, and Hugo Playfair remarked on the American love of rainbow colors, they were not identifying the United States as a site of consumer modernity. They were identifying what were understood to be the peculiarities of white U.S. populations, who were now defined as a separate ethnic group, one whose status as an ethnic population was announced and guaranteed by their love of gaudy finery and their inability to control or understand the language of their own bodies. Americans' love of gaudy clothes typified them as part of a degenerate, debased group, something affirmed in the eyes of Europeans by Americans' ongoing embrace of slavery. Overall, this chapter surveys not just the characterization of "Americans" by British, European, and Canadian travelers, but also the lush visual world of early nineteenth-century costume albums and ethnic clothing prints that flourished in transatlantic print culture. Chapter 1 concludes with an account of the visual and sartorial itineraries of early nineteenth-century U.S. nativism and white nationalism, both of which, I argue, relied heavily on the tropes of ethnic nationalism in their development of a rhetoric of the body for white supremacy.

Chapter 2, "Restyling an Old World," examines the development in the United States of visual arrays designed to defy ethnic nationalist itineraries. A vicious competitive nationalism—self-aggrandizement, ethnic slurs, demeaning jokes—flourished in British and U.S. travelogues and magazines in the 1820s and 1830s. British writers took special delight in ridiculing Americans. In this chapter, I look at a figure—the poet and travel writer Nathaniel Parker Willis—whose celebrity crystallized a larger set of fantasies aimed at escaping and transcending the debased nationalized body at the heart of these critiques. Famous for his social climbing, his outlandish clothes, and his imitation of English "men of fashion," Willis developed a peculiar brand of metropolitan polish whose signature feature, I argue, was its highlighting of the surface of the body as a site of visual blockage and trickery. Willis's clothes were so overdone and so confusing that they could not be relied upon to convey accurate information about the ethnic attributes of their wearer. Instead, Willis was a figure of mystery and amorphous embodiment. He achieved transatlantic fame in the 1830s by writing a kind of revenge travelogue, in which, armed with his "European mask" and dandyish clothes, he snuck into the homes of English elites and reported back to U.S. audiences on their secrets. In this chapter I rely not just on Willis but also on a variety of other antebellum entertainment and literary forms that featured clothing and visual sleight of hand, including Nathaniel Hawthorne's clothing tales, "The Minister's Black Veil," *The Scarlet Letter*, and *The Blithedale Romance*, Herman Melville's *The Confidence Man*, and the many popular Barnumesque entertainments of this period that relied on fakery, visual trickery, and hoaxes. Reliant on motifs of visual confusion and distraction, these texts modeled the construction of a counterethnic national body for the American subject, one that rejected and remade ethnic nationalism's central visual tropes. It reimagined the American body not as a site of transparent transmission but as a confusing and noisy surface where the racializing look of Europe was distracted and lost in a wash of bold color and glitter that refused to divulge coherent information.

The third chapter, "Clothes Upon Sticks," looks at how this initially marginal representation of Americanness, powered by a desire to challenge and subvert ethnic hierarchies, became part of mainstream nationalist symbol systems in the second half of the nineteenth century. I use James Fenimore Cooper as a hinge figure whose novels and reputation help us understand how these earlier defensive nationalist strategies, which seemed to occlude and even vaporize the biological body, could nevertheless be translated later in the century into global imperial scenes that relied on racist biopolitical ideologies. An expansionist and believer in white racial destiny who borrowed heavily from Anglo-European ethnic nationalist and race theory, Cooper had been the central architect of nationalist frontier mythology in the early 1820s, a mythology that celebrated the epiphanic fusing of white settlers and a "virgin" land waiting for their arrival. In the late 1830s, however, Cooper returned to the United States after twelve years in Europe to find a novel situation. In the time that Cooper had been away, locals had, in effect, "settled" his family's parkland at Three Mile Point on Otsego Lake. Suddenly on the other side of a property debate he had always controlled, Cooper published a series of vitriolic anti-American diatribes. He then turned to a revision of his own frontier mythology in his last Leatherstocking novel, *The Deerslayer* (1841), which takes place on the very land that his fellow Cooperstown inhabitants claimed was theirs.

What is remarkable about this novel is that it mirrors the fantasies set out in Willis's celebrity. Cooper rewrites settler mythology so as to obliterate white racial destiny from its scope, something he achieves by turning to the tropes of shallow glitter and emptiness developed in urban entertainment of this period. I argue that Cooper's strategies in this novel predict a later nineteenth-century trend in U.S. settler nationalism. As the specter of Indigenous war and genocide on the one hand and the threat of a revived Confederacy and its white supremacist ideology on the other came to haunt narratives of Western and noncontiguous settlement in the years after the Civil War, various nationalist constituencies reimagined settler colonial "frontiers" not as natural spaces but as stagy artificial vistas populated by stick figures from which scenes of both racial violence and racial destiny have been expunged. Initially a challenge to ethnic nationalist ideology, these shiny, artificial figures came, by the end of the century, to represent a kind of essential folk "America." This chapter concludes with a consideration of the contrast between the experience of Indigenous people on the frontiers of settler war, looking in particular at the writings of Luther Standing Bear and the representation of the "West" in Buffalo Bill Cody's Wild West shows, which relied heavily on tropes of ethnic nationalism. I argue that the Wild West climaxes a larger project to deflect from and obliterate evidence of settler violence through strategies of visual audacity and sleight of hand, a project that by the 1890s had been normalized within conventional representations of "America."

In chapter 4, "Some Inscrutable Flattery of the Atmosphere," I look at the extent to which languages of visual extravagance and hyperbole, which were central to defining the figure of a stereotypical "American" person in the late nineteenth century, readily transferred themselves to what were now seen to be typical American scenes, in the process helping to normalize the gaudy surface as a kind of ethnic nationalist attribute of the United States. In fact, landscape and scenery had all along featured as potent signifiers in the articulation of regional character, playing dynamically with ethnic clothing in the production of national and ethnic personalities. But new imperatives around landscape's importance to Eurocentric nationalist thinking manifested themselves in the late nineteenth century at the site of world's fairs. What ethnic costume had done for ethnic nationalism in the early nineteenth century, world's fairs and amusement park sites did again now, materializing an alleged eternal character not just in the ethnic body and its adornments but in a people's habitats. Flourishing between 1885 and 1910, site-specific and immersive entertainments offered visitors a chance to visit the various regions of the globe in virtual form, through painstakingly recreated villages, castles, streets, and bazaars. As in the case of ethnic costumes, which seemed to corporealize the timeless characteristics of a "people," turn-of-the-century world's fairs invited nations and ethnicities to perform their quintessential selves in elaborate visual and immersive scenes.

It was in this environment, I argue, that "America" materialized itself as a series of bewildering façades and fiery assaults on the eye. Instead of associating this hyperbolic visuality with unthinking consumerism and technological modernity, as scholars traditionally do, I argue that this notion of America as an array of colorful lights and "boardwalk" façades represented a transposition of the distracting American body with its colorful, garbled, and illegible surfaces into an equally colorful, garbled, and illegible ethnic landscape, one that here again short-circuited the sign systems of conventional racial and ethnic typification, seeming to deflect the eye from detecting positive content. In this chapter, accordingly, I offer an extended reading of the many national and ethnic sites of the 1893 World's Columbian Exposition in Chicago, focusing in particular on how "America" was symbolized in the fair's famous architectural and design elements, most prominently in its "White City," with its glaring electric lights and weirdly Venetian façades. I argue that with its parodic deployment of European architectural themes and its emphasis on the showiness of surfaces, the exposition theorized the façade itself as a privileged site of American expression and dominance. The chapter closes by considering the replication of these same white structures in amusement parks worldwide, parks that seemed "American" not because they sported new lighting technologies or embodied consumer modernity but because they incorporated the vocabulary of nineteenth-century nation and ethnicity, which had already decided what America looked like.

Overall, then, *Fashion Nation* traces the history of a crucial but undertheorized theme in U.S. nationalist discourse, one that threads its way through descriptions of U.S. populations from the 1820s to the 1970s and beyond. It looks at how in discussions of "America" seemingly inorganic, technological visual elements—the glint of a shining surface, the glimmer of gold thread—which are traditionally understood by scholars as artifacts of market capitalist and consumer modernity, were in fact developed in the early nineteenth century as part of an intensely nationalistic, often biologized discourse of "American" appearance. The very objects that seem most ethereal and most quintessentially the products of modern consumerism and entertainment, whether mass-produced fabric or the haze of Coney Island, were, I am suggesting, caught up in nineteenth-century symbolic circuits of the ethnic body and its habitats, hence their ability to seem "American" in the first place. I look at the history of this trope of the shining surface from its initial appearance in anti-American discourse, when it signified ethnic degeneracy, through its defiant reappropriation by U.S. writers and entertainers, when it came to signal a challenge to ethnic nationalism, to its transformation back into an ethnic nationalist sign, one seemingly absolved this time of biovisual embodiment while nevertheless still freighted with ethnic nationalist meaning. The shining surface, the glare of light, the flash of a sequin, acquired a strange, lasting importance at the end of the nineteenth century as signs of U.S. nation and empire. I would like to think, moreover, that *Fashion Nation* speaks to a global resurgence of ethnic nationalism happening in 2020 as I write. The presidency of Donald Trump in the United States with its signature encapsulation in a peculiar sartorial sign—the red baseball cap with "Make America Great Again" embroidered in white across the front—makes a study of ethnic nationalist sartorial symbol systems in the United States particularly important and urgent. It is not a coincidence that Trump's white nationalism has a red hat as its symbol. As I show in the following chapters, these odd items of clothing have been central features of ethnic and white nationalism since its beginnings. It is to these beginnings that I now turn.

ONE

AMERICAN LOOKS

Touring New York City in 1842, Charles Dickens was struck by the extravagant look of its inhabitants:

> Heaven save the ladies, how they dress! We have seen more colors in these ten minutes, than we should have seen elsewhere, in as many days. What various parasols! what rainbow silks and satins! what pinking of thin stockings, and pinching of thin shoes, and fluttering of ribbons and silk tassels, and display of rich cloaks with gaudy hoods and linings! The young gentlemen are fond, you see, of turning down their shirt-collars and cultivating their whiskers, especially under the chin; but they cannot approach the ladies in their dress or bearing, being, to say the truth, humanity of quite another sort.[1]

Descriptions of Americans as lovers of extravagant clothes and other forms of "gaudy display" lard the commentary of early nineteenth-century observers. In some cases, these observers were, like Dickens, travelers from Europe. In other cases, it was U.S. writers themselves remarking on the showiness of American dress. Describing the working-class "b'hoy" on the streets of New York, Cornelius Mathews told audiences, "He rolls down the Bowery a perfect Meteor" in "stark staring blue for coat, brick-red for waistcoat, breeches with a portentous green stripe, hat brushed to the highest gloss, shiny as a new kettle."[2]

Almost without exception, scholars suggest that these accounts of extravagantly dressed Americans had their basis in a combination of objective facts and cultural perception. The U.S. economic system proliferated consumer goods, which a liberal ideology prompted the population to buy. In *Ready-Made Democracy*, Michael Zakim demonstrates that the United States was the site of history's first ready-to-wear men's clothing industry. "[U]nprecedented quantities and the low cost of cloths being dumped by British firms in the United States" after the War of 1812 inspired a few enterprising U.S. tailors to abandon traditional made-to-measure men's garments in favor of a new concept: "genteel . . . ready mades." The first ready-made menswear shops opened in New York in 1816. "Promising . . . the standard rich assortment of cloths," these shops offered customers "complete suits available 'at a moment's notice.'" Within a few years, these shops, in addition to selling finely sewn coats, pantaloons, shirts, and waistcoats at relatively low prices, were also selling "a wide assortment of cravats, handkerchiefs, hosiery, suspenders, collars, undervests, and drawers."[3]

Moreover, historians agree that this proliferation of material culture goods took place within a liberal social milieu that argued for the primacy of choice and self-expression when it came to dressing. These beliefs dated to the years before the American Revolution. To advertise their renunciation of British rule, American patriots had made a show of rejecting clothes made of fine British cloth. Instead, they appeared in clothes made of the rough, domestically woven cloth called "homespun." As Zakim and others note, this powerful conceptual link between clothing and political self-fashioning remained a critical orienting point for later U.S. consumers of clothing. People in the United States continued to believe that clothing was a means by which individuals fashioned themselves and their political order. In this formulation, the multitudinous fashion choices U.S. populations appear to have enjoyed—whether manifested as the choice to be plainly dressed or to appear in rainbow silks—is linked with popular ideals of egalitarianism and social mobility. Many historians of material culture, accordingly, contend that accounts of extravagant dress in the antebellum United States reflect the growth of a consumer middle class in the urban northeast that could afford to purchase items of dress usually vouchsafed for the wealthy.[4] In Zakim's view, the antebellum United States was the scene of a modern "broadcloth democracy" in which all men, regardless of birth, were offered access to bright, new, fashionable clothes. Monica Miller suggests that in the growing market for material goods, opportunities for self-fashioning were open not just to middle-class whites but to poor whites and people of color who could take advantage of the possibilities for transformation that clothes offered.[5]

Nevertheless, it remains unclear what exactly observers like Dickens were actually seeing. If nineteenth-century tourists were observing the proliferation of clothing options for U.S. populations, why would the vocabulary used to describe American clothing so frequently extend itself into passages devoted to the description of American streets or towns? In *American Notes*, for example, Dickens describes the architecture and landscape of Boston in much the same way that he describes the dresses of the ladies of New York. In both cases, the American scenes are "gaudy," over bright:

> When I got into the streets upon this Sunday morning, the air was so clear, the houses were so bright and gay; the signboards were painted in such gaudy colors; the gilded

> letters were so very golden; the bricks were so very red, the stone was so very white, the blinds and area railings were so very green, the knobs and plates upon the street doors so marvellously bright and twinkling; and all so slight and unsubstantial in appearance—that every thoroughfare in the city looked exactly like a scene in a pantomime.[6]

In addition to the seeming continuity between descriptions of clothes and descriptions of landscape, there is almost invariably a moral and cultural dimension to the descriptions of Americans and their clothes and surroundings. The clothes are prompted by a desire for "display"; they are "curious," "pinching," and made up of too many colors. The streets are "bright and insubstantial" and look "like a scene in a pantomime." It isn't just that Americans' clothes are new, but also that their clothes seem to hint of childishness, of undeveloped powers of discernment. Written by travelers and chroniclers of local culture, these accounts do not represent a neutral documentation of liberal or consumer society; on the contrary, they seem to reflect on the United States as a nation and on Americans as a distinct population group that is unaware of how their clothes appear to others.

In this chapter, I want to propose that the narrative of fashion as an instrument of liberal ideology, which dominates current studies of U.S. sartorial culture, fails to take account of a crucial development in the Western sartorial scene in the early nineteenth century. Most historians, as we have seen, assume that "homespun ideology" or "broadcloth democracy" remained active in the transatlantic cultural imaginary throughout the nineteenth century, ensuring that debates around clothes remained tied to notions of equality, wealth, and consumer choice. This assumption, however, overlooks a powerful new sartorial symbol system that emerged in the first years of the nineteenth century, one that exempted clothes from the realms of political agency or consumer desire: the symbol system linked to ethnic dress and ethnic nationalism. Fashion and culture historians agree that the evolution of the modern Western fashion system turned clothes into a complex system of signs that purported to reveal and materialize the agency of individual wearers. Ethnic clothing, by contrast, hypothesized a set of sign and symbol systems that were explicitly not controlled by individual subjects. On the contrary, they were rigidly determined by ancestry and geographical place. Often associated with bright colors, pattern variation, and intricate embroidery, ethnic clothes grew out of the systems of thought responsible for essentialist theories of ethnic and racial difference, which emerged in this same period. Indeed, these three signifying complexes—ethnicity, race, and nation—were all closely related.

In the following pages, I retell the history of clothing in the United States by taking into account the critical missing puzzle piece of ethnic dress. The first part of the chapter looks at homespun activism during the American Revolution. In this section, I not only look at early U.S. iconographies of dress but I also look at how clothes generally are thought to function within any given era or social group. I then turn to consider the peculiar sartorial sign and symbol systems introduced by European ethnic nationalism in the early years of the nineteenth century. Developed as a stopper on liberal political ideology and its promises of transformation and mobility, the ethnic clothing system represented a radical revision of the fashion system that emerged in the late eighteenth-century revolutionary era, insisting not on clothing's powers of transformation but on its materialization of the stubborn changelessness of ancestral and inherited character. In this section I show that the gaudily dressed American figures who populated transatlantic scenes in the early nineteenth century were not figures of democracy and consumer choice. Rather, they track almost exactly with the figures being produced in transatlantic pictorial and discursive amplifications of ethnicity and race, something made clear if we look at the history of the Uncle Sam costume. Typified by bright colors, lush fabrics, and intricate patterns, ethnic dress, I will suggest, was essentially the equivalent of the biovisual body of early nineteenth-century ethnic and racialist ideology, allowing the extension of ethno-racialization across a wide range of cultural practices that included adornment.[7]

Finally, I turn to the travelogues penned by writers like Dickens as well as to other nineteenth-century texts written by Americans but purporting to view a white U.S. population with a touristic eye. In this section, I emphasize that, here again, brightly colored fabrics, twinkling buttons, and luxurious waistcoats were not offered in these texts as the signs of wealth and consumer choice, nor even of the as-yet undeveloped tastes of American *nouveaux riches*. When tourists like Dickens remarked on the American love of rainbow colors, they were identifying the peculiarities of Americans as a separate nationality or "ethnic" group, one whose status as a peripheral population was announced and guaranteed by their love of colorful finery and their inability to control or understand the language of their own bodies.

I should note that apart from a few material culture studies (Haltunnen, Bushman, Zakim), there has been little scholarly research on clothing as a sign system in the nineteenth-century United States. I therefore rely not just on material culture histories of clothing and bodies but also on a large corpus of scholarship on Western fashion and costume that does not address the United States in particular but nevertheless offers important accounts of fashion that are relevant to all of the modern West. As I will show, the United States, like other provincial and settler colonial precincts, was stitched into a Western clothing imaginary that determined its simultaneous continuity with metropolitan fashion regimes and its status as an outlier and repository of sartorial curiosities. My account of ethnic dress relies on a substantial visual archive of illustrated costume books, popular journals, prints, and gift books produced in London and the United States in the first half of the nineteenth century, an archive that has not, to my knowledge, been examined by scholars. Vividly conceived, beautifully executed, and often enlivened with color, this visual archive brings to life the intricate, kaleidoscopic yet carefully taxonomized world that the ethnic dress imaginary ended up producing. In addition, because this chapter deals partly with ethnic and national caricature and stereotype, I rely not just on books of costume but also on political cartoons and theater archives. Often overtly engaged in the generation of crude stereotypes, cartoons and theater prints furnish important information about how "nationality" was visually and performatively conceived in the transatlantic milieu where notions of what nations might look like were first consolidated. Subsequent chapters of this book examine the attempts of U.S. cultural nationalists to rebel against the ethnic clothing apparatus and to renounce the implications of ethnoracial embodiment that ethnic clothing brought in its wake. In this chapter, however, my aim is simply to trace ethnic clothing's sway over national iconography and conceptions of identity from the turn of the nineteenth century to the 1850s, a story that begins earlier, in the discourse of the American Revolution.

The Styles of Revolution

Clothing, as scholars have long understood, played a critical symbolic and material role in the rise of revolutionary sentiment in British North America. The American patriots' famed renunciation of British political control over the colonies initially took its shape not from political discourse, precisely, but from inside the lively consumer culture that defined the mid-eighteenth-century British Atlantic economy. Throughout the early eighteenth century, the thirteen colonies were significant consumers of English manufactured goods and other products of imperial trade, including china, tea, spices, silverware, rifles, books, and, most important for our purposes, textiles.[8] But precisely because the colonial economy hinged so heavily on imported goods, these goods were weaponized in the conflict with Britain. Having in common a set of consumer habits, the otherwise diverse and geographically distinct settler populations of the thirteen colonies were able to coalesce political feeling around a common cause; they could all register disaffection and rebellion by participating in the boycott of British imports.

As the Seven Years' War ended in 1763 and Britain raised taxes on the imported luxuries that so many colonists took for granted, colonists fought back by refusing to purchase British merchandise. The chief target of their dissent was the centerpiece of the import market: cloth. Advertisements and descriptions of consumer goods for sale in British North America brim with lists of cloth and related sartorial commodities. In North Carolina in 1765, merchants advertised: "Cyprus and figur'd gauzes," "Cambricks and lawns, Calimancoes and durants, Shalloons and tammies."[9] Even as conflict with Britain threatened in 1774, Boston consumers were offered "Calicoes, Chintz," "Satins," "Black and white blond lace," "India taffetas" and "Crimson damask."[10] A staple of the colonial economy and a powerful symbol of wealth, high status, and personal choice, cloth and clothes emerged as primary objects of anti-British sentiment. "Fashion," in the words of Timothy Breen, "became a measure of ideological commitment."[11] United States patriots in the years before the revolution enjoined fellow anti-British sympathizers to boycott British cloth, to cast off their British finery, to renounce "laces, Ribbons, [and] gaudy Flowers."[12] Patriots were exhorted to wear instead the rough, undyed, locally manufactured cloth called "homespun."

Celebrations of homespun as the proper garb of a free American people were henceforth part of the rhetoric of the revolution. According to one journalist writing in 1770, "America, from one end to the other, can now boast of Gentlemen and Ladies, used to all the delicacies of life, encouraging industry, and submitting to eat and drink and wear, what every peasant may procure."[13] Patriots announced, "[T]hat man is the most respected who appears clad in Homespun."[14] One Boston writer told readers, "I laugh at a man who talks of facing cannon and red coats." Yet this same man "cannot conquer his foppish empty notions of grandeur." Is he "a true lover of his country . . . who would soon be seen strutting about the streets, clad in foreign fripperies, than to be nobly independent in russet gray[?]"[15]

In one sense, this association between plain clothes and revolution was not new. Radical Protestant sects in Europe and Britain had long associated ornate dress with a decadent Catholicism, with aristocracy, and with moral corruption. One of the signal features of the Parliamentarian side of the English Civil Wars in the 1640s and 1650s was the Puritans' renunciation of lavish courtly dress. But the widespread rearrangement of the meaning of fashion in British North America in the eighteenth century represented something new. It was linked to a permanent transformation in modern political life. In the final decades of the eighteenth century, the picture of revolutionaries divested of ornate clothes flourished as a central trope of modern Republicanism in both the United States and Europe. Late seventeenth- and early eighteenth-century intellectuals had taken for granted that dress was evidence of "the achievements of civilization."[16] People all over the world had always associated lavish clothes and jewels with status, wealth, power, and even virtue. In the late eighteenth century, however, as the state of "nature" was conceived as a condition prior to "government," simple, unembellished clothes were suddenly linked not to poverty but to egalitarian social movements seeking to free themselves of traditional governmental controls. Associated with wealth and hierarchy and denigrated in transatlantic political writing, ornate dress emerged as a metaphor for the power of oppressive regimes. In the opening paragraphs of *Common Sense*, Tom Paine warned, "Government, like dress, is the badge of lost innocence; the palaces of kings are built on the ruins of the bowers of paradise."[17] Plain dress, by contrast, functioned as both the instrument and symbol of rebellion. The radical, lower-class factions of the French Revolution were called "sans-culottes"; instead of wearing the fashionable silk knee breeches of the wealthy, called "culottes," they wore long baggy pantaloons or trousers and were hence "sans culottes." Plain clothes were the badge of the revolutionary subject.

Now, it is important to stress that these developments, in which clothes were swept into emancipatory and civic nationalist projects, took for granted the viewer's cognizance of certain semantic conventions where clothes were concerned. The nature of these conventions is worth discussing, given their importance to the arguments that follow. Historians and anthropologists have long debated how exactly clothes work. For late nineteenth-century sociologists like Thorstein Veblen, clothing functioned mainly as an indicator of power and social position.[18] The more opulent and contrived the clothing, the more socially exalted or wealthy the wearer. For twentieth-century semioticians, including Umberto Eco and Roland Barthes, clothing functions as a complex sign system, transmitting information from the wearer to the observer in much the same way as a language does. In this analysis, clothing is a kind of speech.[19]

Many scholars emphasize, however, that clothing does not map exactly onto the model of linguistic code. In Fred Davis's words, clothing cannot be "generally equated with the language rules that govern speech and writing." Davis argues that clothing can perhaps best be viewed as "an incipient or quasi-code, which, although it must necessarily draw on the conventional visual and tactile symbols of a culture, does so allusively, ambiguously, and inchoately, so that the meanings evoked by the combinations and permutations of the code's key terms (fabric, texture, color, pattern, volume, silhouette, and occasion) are forever shifting or in process." Davis goes on to suggest that clothes in fact work rather like an aesthetic structure. They aim "to communicate notions, subtleties, [and] complexities which have not yet been formulated" or precisely perceived as code.[20]

More recent anthropologists and material culture scholars question whether the rules governing the system of "fashion" that dominates the modern West can even offer themselves for generalization about the function of clothes as a whole. In their discussion of clothes in early modern England, Ann Rosalind Jones and Peter Stallybrass draw attention to an older way of understanding clothes not as "fashion" but as "fashioning." Instead of acting as a transmitter of information from the wearer to the observer, clothing in premodern Western societies functioned as a form of capture, enveloping the wearer within a pregiven net of social relations. "Clothing is a worn world: a world of social relations put upon the wearer's body."[21] The modern Western view of clothing as constantly changing fashion, as a surface put on the body and changed according to whim, obscures the extent to which clothing was traditionally "investiture": the robe of the king, the habit of holy orders, the livery of the servant. According to Jones and Stallybrass, modern fashion's "opposing of clothes and person was always in tension with the social practices through which the body politic was composed. . . . It was investiture, the putting on of clothes, that quite literally constituted a person as a monarch or a freeman of a guild or a household servant. Investiture was, in other words, the means by which a person was given a form, a shape, a social function, a depth."[22]

It is important to add that whether clothing is viewed as a set of signs to be decoded, as an aesthetic structure, or as a form of investiture, its meanings and uses at any given time or in any given social milieu are governed by what Webb Keane calls a "semiotic ideology." As Keane says, "By semiotic ideology I mean people's background assumptions about what signs are and how they function in the world.[23] Indeed, we can look at the various eras discussed by scholars, from Veblen and Barthes, who look at the modern Western fashion system, to Jones and Stallybrass, who look at premodern liveries and other habits, as each governed by its own semiotic ideology. Rooted in a specific human group's shared assumptions, "semiotic ideology" generates the system of meanings through which the bodily coverings of that particular collective are understood.

In the case of the revolutionary-era United States, for example, we can assume that homespun's association with independence was founded on a number of shared standards. Colonists clearly took for granted that homespun was part of a hierarchy of fabrics; it was less desirable than lawn or cambric. For that very reason it appears to have suggested itself as a site of self-abnegation; already bound up with inferiority, it could also be harnessed as a symbol of virtuous self-discipline and self-control. It could thus function as a marker of independence. Made in the colonies, moreover, it could be seen to promote the expansion of domestic manufacture and thus economic independence from Britain. And associated with the poor, with "peasants," it could reorganize the members of the thirteen colonies, transforming elites into the seeming equals of the middling classes and poor, uniting all in the struggle against Britain.

At the same time, most contemporary accounts suggest that homespun clothing, when it was worn by elites as a political statement, did not trespass entirely on the standards of genteel luxury associated with imported cloth. On the contrary, part of the political power of homespun clothes seems to have resided in the fact that a rough cloth was being used in the making of genteel clothes. According to the *Virginia Gazette*, a "Ball at the Capitol" in 1769 featured precisely this contrast:

> [I]t is with the greatest pleasure we inform our readers that the same patriotic spirit which gave rise to the association of the Gentlemen on a late event, was most agreeably manifest in the dress of the Ladies on this occasion, who, to the number of near one hundred, appeared in homespun gowns; a lively and striking instance of their acquiescence and concurrence in whatever may be the true and essential interest of their country. It were to be [wished] that all assemblies of American Ladies would exhibit a like example of public virtue and private economy, so amiably united."[24]

The fabric of ball gowns, homespun could in these circumstances transmit a combination of virtuous independence and genteel fashionability, insofar as refinement could still be implied in the overall form of the garment.

The other assumption that appears to have animated early U.S. associations between plain, rough cloth and virtuous patriotism, democratic equality, and independence was the notion that clothing was a message system that offered an unproblematic insight into the character and intentions of its wearer. Here again, it is important to underline when considering this proposition the existence of a shared set of ideas about how clothing operates. How would you know, looking at the colonial ladies at the Washington ball, that they were not merely too poor to afford fine fabrics? Similarly, how would you know that homespun represented a rejection of another cloth rather than a preference in and of itself? For that matter, how are preference or deliberation or personality broadcast in the case of clothes? You would not assume that the clothes at a masquerade party or the clothes worn by actors on a stage transmitted the true, real character of their wearers. The masquerade party and stage are governed by a different set of conventions than those that govern day-to-day life. Nor would the assumption of transparency be a concept readily generated in a system in which clothes operated as instruments of investiture. Under the aegis of investiture, on the contrary, you would expect the disappearance of unique character and personal choice in favor of the memorial or institutional identity bestowed upon the wearer by the clothing: the livery, the habit, the judicial robes, the wig, the crown, and so on. In these systems, as Daniel Defert argues, "The garment is a rule of conduct and the memory of this rule for the wearer as well as for others."[25] The garment here subsumes the individual within a tradition.

The principles respecting homespun, however, are different, as evidenced in the language used in the passage cited above: The homespun ball gowns do not make their wearers. They rather express a "patriotic spirit." In choosing homespun, the ladies self-consciously display "public virtue and private economy." In this formulation, clothing is part of a political decision on the part of the subject and indicates the subject's control over their own appearance. One chooses one's clothes as one chooses to be part of the party of independence. These clothes belong to the realm of signs identified by Eco and Barthes; they are deliberately arranged representations of abstract spiritual, political, and affective affiliations. In the words of Webb Keane, these clothes are treated not as objects in and of themselves but "as illustrations of something else, as . . . communicating meanings or identities"; they are figured as "the garb of meaning."[26] Moreover, these meanings are assumed to be generated by the wearers of the clothes who voluntarily "acquiesce and concur" in their submission to an abstract ideal of "country."

It is important to stress that this modern semiotic ideology not only described new ways of wearing clothes but also new models of personhood and identity and their relationship to new political entities. Generated in the mid-eighteenth century, the tropes of homespun and plain dress contributed to what Susan Manning calls a new "poetics of character," "a rhetoric of the body" through which the new entity of the republican nation was performed and personated.[27] In the eighteenth century and throughout the early part of the nineteenth, minimalist dress offered to figure the structures of civic nationalism that glued together the subjects of the modern nation-state. In civic nationalism, the citizens of a nation were bound together not by allegiance to monarchies or social elites but by voluntary submission to abstract principles: liberty, democracy, equality. The central trope of U.S. democracy, according to Joan Copjec, is "divestment." "Democracy," says Copjec, "is the universal quantifier by which America—the 'melting pot,' the 'nation of immigrants'—constitutes itself as a nation. If *all* our citizens can be said to be Americans, this is not because we share any positive characteristics but rather because we have all been given the right to *shed* these characteristics, to present ourselves as disembodied before the law. I divest myself of positive identity, therefore I am a citizen."[28]

We can speculate that the figurative power of plain clothes came from their seeming to perform this divestment; they summoned up a prior condition of sartorial complexity in order to perform the act of simplification, to divest the subject and its visual representation of what were now declared to be its decorative or ornamental features (see fig. 1). With homespun garments, this denuding seems to have been conveyed not in the fact that patriots were wearing quantifiably *fewer* clothes than their British counterparts but rather in the lack of visual patterns or variegated color on the fabric, as well as in a lack of trim and fancy buttons. Again, the outlines and construction of the garments remain the same but the tactile and visual variations are erased. What homespun garments offer, in other words, is a kind of bleached or colorless version of clothes normally made with high-quality, often figured imported British fabric. The cut of the garments might be the same, but the surfaces lack pigment, variation, and intricacy. They can thus suggest a kind of blank slate, a freedom from insignia. They seem to cast off or divest themselves of a prior inscription.

In the years following the American and French Revolutions, the emancipatory connotations of plain clothes permanently altered Western fashion, changing men's garments forever. The long pants of the sans-culottes became the norm in men's fashions after about 1800, when modern trousers were born. Rich fabrics and vivid colors, which had typified upper class men's dress in virtually all cultures since the medieval era and had spoken of wealth, power, and station, now permanently disappeared from Western men's dress. Instead, Western men's dress acquired the spare outlines of the uniform that still dominates them today in the form of the men's suit: long trousers, dark coat, vest, white shirt, neck tie, all very stark, dominated by monotones, flat planes and angles, containing minimal variation in pattern. Implying rebellion, equality, self-transformation, and individual choice, plain clothes were called upon to define scenes of liberal governance and, increasingly, the scenes of finance and marketplace society where individual choice and personal transformation continued to play key roles. This was precisely the role played by plain and unornamented clothes in conventional U.S. nationalist iconography of the late eighteenth and early nineteenth century. Pictorial images of "Americans" as a national people—that is, as citizens of what was called a "republic" or "democracy"—produced at the turn of the nineteenth century represent them as denuded and plain compared to their European counterparts, the implication being that they are liberated, freed from the oppressive burdens of custom and class specificity.

John Trumbull's *The Death of General Warren at the Battle of Bunker's Hill, 17 June, 1775*, painted between 1815 and 1831, identifies the American figures by depicting them in glowing white dress, mostly hatless and coatless, either in bright white

Fig. 1. Eighteenth-century homespun coat. *Coat*, Isle of Wight County, Virginia. Ca. 1780. Cotton and wool with wooden buttons covered with fabric. Accession #1964–174, A, image #TC2001–577. *The Colonial Williamsburg Foundation. Museum Purchase.*

shirts or flimsy white coats that could be shirts. The British, by contrast, appear with their signature brilliant scarlet coats and black tricorn hats, their breeches a gold pigment that suggests heft and richness (see fig. 2). According to the iconographic and visual conventions of the late eighteenth century, the American figures imply carelessness, daring, freedom from tradition and formality; the British are freighted with their regimented class and monarchical formations.

A prominent personification of the United States, Columbia, possessed similar qualities. The links between Columbia, Americanness, and white clothes that indicate a scene of divestment are on display in John Gast's 1872 painting *American Progress* (see fig. 3). Here Columbia, armed with electrical wire, travels across the North American continent in a state of dishabille, her purity and virtue transmitted in a luminous white dress that seems ready to blow away from her body entirely. She is bringing freedom, light, and modernity to the West; and her blowing clothes, seemingly on the verge of leaving her divested of coverings, promise a state of freedom.

The Ethnic Dress Imaginary

In the first years of the nineteenth century, the citizens of metropolitan modernity were figured, via their dress, in a sort of permanent state of revolution and change; they were the subjects of futurity, teleological time, and progress. In this sartorial fantasy, modern Western male subjects, dressed in their newly plain suits, were full of possibility, without inscription, waiting to be written upon. But it was precisely the now-primitive state of inscription, represented by color, patterning, and variation, that the ethnic clothing regime sought to return to. The development of an elaborate visual itinerary for clothes related to ethnicity was part of a larger, violent shift in nationalist feeling in Europe and the Americas in the wake of the French and Haitian Revolutions. Plain clothes were the signs of what historians call "civic nationalism," signifying the subject's self-conscious submission to abstract principles: justice, liberty, equality. Ethnic clothes, by contrast, developed out of postrevolutionary "ethnic" nationalism, sometimes called "romantic" or "folk" nationalism, which represented a powerful repudiation of republican and revolutionary values. Sweeping across Europe in the years of the Napoleonic Wars, ethnic nationalism insisted on the cohesive powers not of monarchy or nation-state but of ancestry and tribe, highlighting geographical region, common language, religion, and kinship as the indelible forgers of subjectivity. Whereas civic nationalism celebrated the possibility of divestment before an exteriorized abstract ideal, ethnic nationalism believed that identity was immutable; it could no more be shed than one's

Fig. 2. John Trumbull, *The Death of General Warren at the Battle of Bunker's Hill, June 17, 1775*. After 1815, before 1831. Oil on canvas. Museum of Fine Arts, Boston; Gift of Howland S. Warren, 1977.853 Photograph © 2020 Museum of Fine Arts, Boston.

Fig. 3. George A. Crofutt, *American Progress*. 1872. Chromolithograph. After the painting *American Progress* by John Gast. Library of Congress Prints and Photographs Division LC-DIG-ppmsca-09855.

skin or bodily organs. In this formulation, the removal of clothes or other signs of positive identity did not signal one's affinity with abstract principles but merely brought into greater clarity the true and essential particularity of the ethnic group to which the subject belonged. In Anthony Smith's words, in ethnic nationalism, "Whether you stayed in your community or emigrated to another, you remained ineluctably, organically a member of the community of your birth and were for ever stamped by it."[29]

Reviving the strains of regionally based nationalism that had flourished in pockets of Britain and Europe since the Reformation, early nineteenth-century ethnic nationalism invested these older forms of nationalism with fiery romantic beliefs in national and racial destiny. Like revolutionary republicanism, ethnic nationalism promoted resistance to "government," but in this case it was resistance not just to disintegrating empires like the Hapsburg and Ottoman Empires but to revolutionary modernity itself, now represented by Napoleon and the French Empire. Ethnic nationalism flared up among European intellectuals as a fierce, defiant refusal to be swallowed up by the winds of revolutionary change. As French armies rolled over Prussia in 1806 and took the city of Berlin, Johann Gottlieb Fichte thundered praise for the idea of an insurmountable organic "Germanness," a property that could not be erased by advancing armies, that lived deep in the spirit of the "volk," in a common language, an ancient past, and seemingly shared tribal roots; he predicted future German greatness in spite of this local defeat. "[Y]ou will see the German name exalted . . . to the most illustrious among all the peoples, you will see in this nation the regenerator and restorer of the world."[30]

On the one hand, ethnic nationalism was part of a political strategy. It stood at the center of mid-nineteenth-century nationalist unification movements in Germany, Italy, Poland, Hungary, and the Balkans. Under the leadership of people like Giuseppe Mazzini, who founded and inspired the "Young Italy," "Young Germany," "Young Poland," and "Young Switzerland" movements in the 1830s and 1840s, ethnic nationalists agitated for the right of a "people" to form a nation-state based on shared linguistic, cultural, religious, natal, and alleged ancestral ties. Instead of celebrating the anonymous figures associated with the civic nation (the flag, the classical allegory), ethnic nationalism celebrated regional uniqueness and peculiarity, privileging what they called the "tribe," the "clan," the "volk," as superior units of human community. The German philosopher Johann Gottfried von Herder believed that modern conquest, empire, and the bureaucratic nation-state were all unnatural social formations imposed on what were originally ancient, homogeneous familial groups. "Nature produces families; the most natural state therefore is one people [Volk] with a natural character. . . . Nothing seems more obviously opposed to the purposes of government than the unnatural enlargement of states, the wild mixing together of different human species and nations under one sceptre."[31] Edmund Burke praised the existence among the British of "pedigree and illustrating ancestors."[32] Instead of seeking to unite disparate groups under the umbrella of the modern bureaucratic and legal state, ethnic nationalists believed in the slumbering power of primal, premodern communities that were, they believed, destined to be revivified and to rise up in ethnic unity against modern oppressors.

Yet ethnic nationalism was more than just a political strategy. It was a theory of hierarchy and difference that meshed with this period's extended biopolitical projects, most obviously with attempts to catalogue and hierarchize human populations through what would become known as "race science." Herder's belief in the familial oneness of a people does not directly reference racial differences and hierarchies, but such hierarchies were implicit in early German nationalism and were in fact intrinsic to this era's ethnic nationalist belief. In Fichte's view, the "Teutonic" peoples in Europe, who include the Slavs, the Germans, and the Scandinavians, were all descendants of one "German" tribe described by Tacitus in *Germania*. "In the peoples of Germany," wrote Tacitus, "there has been given to the world a race untainted by intermarriage with other races, a peculiar people and pure, like no one but themselves."[33] Early nineteenth-century British and European intellectuals debated each other over which of the surviving "German races" was most pure and thus superior to the others. According to Fichte, the Germans in Germany were a superior distillation of the original Teutonic seed, for unlike the Slavs and Scandinavians who had moved away from their geographic roots, the Germans had remained in central Europe, living "in the original dwelling-places of the ancestral stock," and thus presumably marinating in a kind of originary Teutonic spirit that was unmixed with other peoples and languages.[34] Similar arguments around purity were being made for the so-called "Anglo-Saxon" people in Britain, now conceived as one of the original "pure" tribes described by Roman observers. Not surprisingly, this emphasis on the supremacy of Germanic and Anglo-Saxon people supported various imperialist and colonizing projects, both inside and outside Britain and Europe. In a work on political economy published in 1841, German nationalist Friedrich List divided Europe into three races based on linguistic groups, the Slavic, the Germanic, and the Latin. He believed that "providence has by preference dedicated the Germanic races by means of their nature and character, to the solution of the great task of leading world-affairs, civilizing wild and barbaric countries and populating those that are still uninhabited."[35]

Motivated by the belief that future success was encrypted in the documents of the past, ethnic nationalist intellectuals in England, Scotland, Germany, France, and Italy passionately engaged in the recovery (and sometimes the fabrication) of vernacular and nonmetropolitan cultural forms: ancient songs, forgotten folk stories, ballads, legends, and fairy tales. Ethnic nationalism's favorite scenery consisted of landscapes hidden from enlightenment modernity, protected from what were deemed to be modernity's sterile, homogenizing effects: dark haunted forests, misty shores, quaint villages, and decaying castles. The landmark works of early nineteenth-century ethnic nationalist literary culture were the Brothers Grimm's *Kinder-und Haus-Märchen* (*Children and Household Tales*), a collection of European folk tales that appeared in 1812 and 1815, and Walter Scott's blockbuster historical adventure novels, *Waverley* (1814), which details the 1745 Scottish Rebellion against England, and *Ivanhoe* (1819), which recovers the myths of medieval England to tell the story of the Anglo-Saxon Wilfred Ivanhoe and Robin Hood in their struggle against the Norman ruler Prince John. The conceit of these works is that a nation's people, whether they reside in the formal political unity of the modern state or not, are animated by mysterious, sometimes violent ancestral spirits from a deep past, spirits that can wake in the modern world to either crush or fulfill the nation's rightful destiny.

Transferred to the United States in the late eighteenth century, ethnic nationalism would have a powerful influence on U.S. nationalism, most obviously through Anglo-Saxon supremacy theory. The most famous U.S. proponent of Anglo-Saxon language and history was Thomas Jefferson, who from his early days as a law student devoted himself to the promotion and study of the Anglo-Saxon language. As a law student, Jefferson was exposed to a myth prevalent in seventeenth- and eighteenth-century English legal thought: the idea that the English Parliament and common law, including the elective monarchy, the folkmoot, and trial by jury, were legacies of the Anglo-Saxons. Jefferson imagined the founding of the United States as both a continuation and revival of this Anglo-Saxon heritage and even proposed engraving on the great seal of the United States the figures of Hengist and Horsa, "the Saxon chiefs from whom we claim the honor of being descended, and whose political principles and form of government we have assumed." The "descent" Jefferson imagined here was not just cultural, the mere continuation of legal and social practices. He believed that the people of the United States had a mystical, intimately familial relationship with England's ancient peoples, one that would come to life if Americans learned Old English, for they "will imbibe with the language their free principles of government."[36]

Jefferson was not destined to remain alone in his thinking. By the mid-1840s, the idea of Anglo-Saxon uniqueness, supremacy, and brotherhood across white Atlantic populations had suffused both intellectual and popular culture in the

United States. At the simplest level, the term "Anglo-Saxon" became a common way of distinguishing various white populations inside the United States, especially in the wake of mass migration from Ireland in the early 1840s, as well as waves of immigration from the regions of Austria-Hungary, including people from modern Germany, Switzerland, and Poland. "Anglo-Saxon" also became a common way of referring to imagined continuities between the British and Americans. When Emerson traveled to England in the late 1840s, he was well armed with the ethnic distinctions of transatlantic intellectual culture. Instead of identifying all of the English as Anglo-Saxons, however, he followed other racial theorists of the day in seeing two races in England, one "Norman" or French and one (the superior one and the one most closely related to Americans) "Anglo-Saxon." "I found plenty of well-marked English types, the ruddy complexion, fair and plump, the robust men, with faces cut like a die . . . a Norman type, with the complacency that belongs to that constitution." But Emerson also finds "Others, who might be Americans, for anything that appeared in their complexion or form," whose "speech was much less marked, and their thought much less bound. We will call them Saxons."[37]

In addition to imagining a patchwork United States and forming new entanglements with British heritage, the language of Anglo-Saxonism animated the U.S. discourse of Manifest Destiny. One of the chief tenets of Anglo-Saxonism and other Germanic supremacist theories developing in England and Europe in the eighteenth and early nineteenth centuries was the idea that "pure," northern races, whether called the "Germans," the "Caucasians," or "Aryans," had originated somewhere north of India and were compelled by their superior vitality and ambition to move west into Europe. In the United States, this alleged westward momentum of Germanic peoples was readily equated with the founding of the United States itself and with continued continental expansion of settler populations. Magazine editor John O'Sullivan, who coined the term "Manifest Destiny" in 1845, argued for the righteousness of U.S. claims to western lands, including California, by summoning the language of racial self-actualization that came to dominate U.S. nationalism: "The Anglo-Saxon foot is already on its [California's] borders. Already the advance guard of the irresistible army of Anglo-Saxon emigration has begun to pour down upon it"[38] The rhetoric of Anglo-Saxonism would, of course, continue to power U.S. imperial and colonial propaganda until the end of the century.

Clothing played a unique role in ethnic nationalism, one that both complemented and opposed its role in civic nationalism. The clothes that came to be representative of ethnicity as a cultural ideal were linked not to systems of state, imperial, or class organization but to what were now conceived as regional and ancestral allegiances that predated modernity. With their stark, simple lines and monotones, modern Western men's clothes emerged as the equivalent of revolutionary clothes; they signified blankness, lack of inscription. Ethnic clothes were the opposite of modern metropolitan dress. Instead of being sleek and plain, they were saturated with color, filled with patterns, cut into odd shapes, and bursting with curious details. It was this period, from about 1798 to 1820, that gave birth to the whole idea of "national" or "folk dress." Whereas the plain metropolitan male suit of clothes was meant to be unscripted, signaling only potentiality, ethnic clothes offered themselves as dense agglomerations of signs that spoke of ancient habits, languages, and beliefs. Seeming to be written upon, inscribed with the peculiarities that modern metropolitan dress expelled, ethnic dress indicated a people's primordial origins and isolation from metropolitan modernity.

It is important to stress in discussing these clothes that a distinction must be made between modes of dress particular to the various regions, populations, and unique cultures of the globe and the idea of "ethnic dress" as it was consolidated in the early nineteenth-century West. Of course, different parts of the globe had different customs and fashions when it came to adornment. Moreover, as historians of dress emphasize, these differences had long been a source of fascination, not just in Europe but across medieval and early modern North Africa and Asia. Cosmopolitan travelers, especially merchant and aristocratic classes in medieval and early modern Japan, China, Persia, Venice, the Iberian Peninsula, and the Ottoman and Holy Roman Empires, took great delight in observing and sharing different ideas about clothes, fashions, and textiles. The first formal illustrated guides to the costumes of the world, often called "costume albums" and "costume geographies," appeared in the late medieval period and continued to be produced throughout the early modern period.[39]

But scholars of dress underline that the early nineteenth-century Western ethnographic imagination now engulfed the different customs of the globe within a single totalizing system.[40] Within the ethnic nationalist imaginary, all the populations of the globe, whether in Africa and the Middle East, in Western Europe, the British Isles, Asia, or South America, were reimagined as a patchwork of discrete tribes, each dressed in its own peculiar clothing. Even while the regions under consideration all had customs of dress already in place at this period, the early nineteenth-century Western ethnographic imagination now endowed these customs with certain properties that rendered them "ethnic" according to metropolitan definitions of these ideals. In other words, ethnic clothes, no matter what their provenance, were all endowed with certain features that relayed their ethnic quality. These features of ethnic dress, which illuminate the ethnic wardrobe's relationship to Western fashion, are worth enumerating.

First, ethnic clothing was thought to be changeless, even across multiple generations and vast expanses of time. In this fantasy, modern metropolitan men and women occupied sped-up teleological time, always developing, moving forward into the future. This constant progress and inveterate updating was something reflected not just in the unadorned blankness of the male sartorial uniform, but also in the ever-changing fashions of metropolitan women. Ethnic clothing, by contrast, belonged to ancient, unchanging custom.[41] Ethnic clothing was thus linked to the larger traditions of European romantic historicism and veneration of place. In *Reflections on the Revolution in France* (1790), Edmund Burke wrote that unlike the French, who championed natural rights, the English were happy "to derive all we possess *as an inheritance from our forefathers*." Whereas the French were addicted to upheaval and revision, the English were typified by "a sullen resistance to innovation" and "cold sluggishness." Burke intoned, "We are not the converts of Rousseau; we are not the disciples of Voltaire." "We are generally men of untaught feelings, . . . and instead of casting away all our old prejudices, we cherish them to a very considerable degree, . . . [a]nd the longer they have lasted and the more generally they have prevailed, the more we cherish them."[42] Ethnic clothing was thus clothing that remained tethered to a people's past, unchanged across potentially dozens of generations. In some cases, the clothing of the past prefigured the future. In *Ivanhoe*, for example, England's Anglo-Saxon tribes, though they suffer defeat against the Normans in the medieval era, signal their incipient role as the heralds of global modernity by preferring the garb of the republican spirit: plain dress. Indeed, the Anglo-Saxon leader Cedric consents to be reconciled with his son Wilfred Ivanhoe only on condition that Ivanhoe vow to dress according to simple Anglo-Saxon traditions. Cedric commands, "[L]et me see thee use the dress and costume of thy English ancestry—no short cloaks, no gay bonnets, no fantastic plumage in my decent household. He that would be the son of Cedric, must show himself to be of English ancestry."[43] In this case, a taste for plainness is understood to be a changeless feature of the Anglo-Saxons as an ancient people.

But more than being associated with those who defied Western patterns of change, ethnic clothes were frequently associated with people who were deemed by Western intellectuals to be incapable of change. They belonged to those who would not be moving forward into modernity. Discussing how clothing and other material objects changed meaning across the spaciotemporal regions of Western modernity, Jones and Stallybrass draw attention to the instantiation of a contrast between the European metropolis, imagined throughout modernity as a site of change, development, and achievement, and a "periphery" imagined as timeless. "The Other is imagined as eternally itself (Turkish, or Navaho, or Ashanti), subject to the mobile and restless observation of the European observer: the Other is changeless, outside of fashion; the European is the marker and bearer of fashion and of historicity itself."[44] Representing a changeless past, ethnic clothes were part of what historians call "stadial" or conjectural historiography, the belief that all human societies pass through similar evolutionary changes on their inevitable way to modernity and perfection, with some societies succeeding but many failing and doomed to vanish from history. Ethnic clothes thus purported to allow the Western viewer a glimpse into earlier stages of human development, often stages that would, for the populations in question, never be transcended or left behind.

Second, ethnic clothes were thought to express in unmediated form the specific "genius" or spirit of a people. In civic nationalism, the features of clothes (patterns, colors, shapes) were presented as optional; one dressed in certain ways to represent such things as refinement or station, but one could also signal style or choice or political affiliation through the addition or subtraction of complexity or color. In the system developed for ethnic clothing, by contrast, clothing was conceived as the unintended symptom of a people's indelible character. While clothing conveyed information to observers, it did so without the wearer's intention or cognizance. In this sense, the signifying regimes of ethnic clothes were closely linked to the consolidation of ethnographic and pseudoscientific racial theory in this same period. The prevailing late eighteenth century theory of the world's "races," monogenesis, held that a population group's temperament and the morphological features of their bodies were determined by environment: certain human groups were pale or dark or short or tall purely because of climate, with harsher climates producing extremities of color and height.[45] In the early nineteenth century, this privileging of environment as the deciding factor of ethnic and racial appearance was superseded by the privileging of heredity and even Biblical predetermination: differences among human groups, it was increasingly believed, were determined by God. But in both systems of thought, the visible features of the body had importance as *evidence* of the abilities of the mind. In Denise Ferreira da Silva's words, racial theory "rewr[o]te the human body, which had been safely disavowed (displaced and negated) in the founding statements of modern thought, as a signifier of the mind." In early nineteenth century racialist formulations, "man's organic parts and movements become the extended determinants of his mind's unique attributes." And because the physical body and mind were now understood as interrelated, the body's "exteriority" came to be considered "ontologically relevant."[46]

In ethnic nationalism, this exteriority of the person was extended to clothes. Like phenotypical bodily features (height of forehead, hair, shade of skin, etc.), which were understood as clues to a subject's inherited moral and intellectual capacities, ethnic clothing purported to disclose the true, immutable character of an imagined regional or ethnic group. In some ways, because they are cultural artifacts, ethnic clothes seem to belong to older theories of race as situationally determined and thus potentially malleable. Unlike skin or height, which are inherited, morphological properties, clothing can be changed or removed. But it is also the case that because clothing in this system only ever provided the evidence of an alleged existing, inherited interiority (a German was immutably German and this Germanness would always reveal itself in choice of bodily adornment) it overlapped with and expanded theories of racial difference and supremacy that focused on the phenotypical body alone. Thus, we might think of ethnic clothes as forming part of an extended ethno-racializing assemblage, a system of signs, ontologies, material artifacts, and institutions assuring the primacy of visual appearance in the arbitration of human hierarchy and difference. Popular ethnographies and geographies whose focus was costume were frequently patterned after eighteenth-century physiognomies, such as Johann Lavater's 1750 *Essays on Physiognomy*, which purported to decipher and hierarchize Europe's prevailing "races" and "tribes" through study of inherited facial and cranial features.[47] Ethnic dress books often began by noting the continuity between biovisual features and dress on their first pages. In *Costume of the Russian Empire*, first published in 1803, the author begins, "Dress is a no less striking distinction of nations than customs, language, and bodily configuration."[48] Interchangeable with "bodily configuration," ethnic clothes expanded the possibilities and intricacies of Western biopolitical and pseudoscientific systemization across all global populations, bringing far-flung populations into the same analytical framework.[49]

Finally, as their temporal and representational features suggest, ethnic clothes relied entirely on a Western system of signs in which clothing and other bodily surfaces acted as symbols or signifiers. Metropolitan clothes from the early modern period onward were understood as, in Keane's words, the "garb of meaning";[50] they offered to divulge clues about the wearer's heritage, station, and personality. Ethnic clothes similarly offered themselves as a kind of code or hieroglyph to be read by Western tourists and intellectuals. They thus had their own visual itinerary; they were typified by curious detail, profusion, and intensity of color. As art historians underline, color itself had a lively history in the nineteenth century as a property of racialized and ethnic persons and landscapes. In the words of David Batchelor, color was "made out to be the property of some 'foreign' body—usually the feminine, the oriental, the primitive, the infantile, the vulgar, the queer, or the pathological."[51] According to nineteenth-century French art critic Charles Blanc, "Colour . . . is the peculiar characteristic of the lower forms of nature."[52] At the turn of the nineteenth century, Western fashion revered anonymous neoclassical design and clothes for metropolitan men and women. Accordingly, vivid colors emerged in the early years of the nineteenth century as a kind of default sign of peripherality and foreignness. Indeed, the development in this period of a monotone, largely unadorned suit of clothes for metropolitan men contributed to the reclassification of colorful men's clothes as by definition nonmetropolitan.

Relationally defined, ethnic and plain clothes were part of the same sign system; both treated the body as a system of codes and messages, but the wearer's relationship to these messages was different in each case. Plain clothes hypothesized the wearer's control over the appearance of the body and thus over its messages. Ethnic clothes were unselfconscious, innocent of intent. In an important sense, ethnic clothes, as they appear in ethnographies and geographies, were part of a Western fantasy of semiotic visibility, in which Western observers became the only ones trained to read or manipulate ethnic and racial signification in clothes and bodies.

These properties of ethnic clothes—their association with a frozen past, their connection to modern racializing regimes, and their peculiar visual itinerary—had a profound effect on the visual and fantasy life of early nineteenth-century transatlantic culture. The emergence of ethnic nationalism in the early nineteenth century was coincident with new technologies of printing for illustrations and with a general shift of political commentary from the printed word to the visual media of cartoon and stage.[53] The result was that the early nineteenth century witnessed a booming scholarly and hobbyist interest in costume and its history. Scott himself was a famed scholar of historical dress and the inventor of Scottish folk dress in its modern form: For George IV's visit to Scotland in 1822, Scott and his associates designed the famous Highland folk costume that still prevails as Scotland's national costume today: short English jacket, brilliant red tartan kilt, tartan socks, and sporran.

Scott was part of a generation of scholars, connoisseurs, collectors, and readers fixated on dress. Their interest included not just the dress of bygone periods in history but also the contemporary dress of peripheral and rural populations living in the present world, which were here again thought to channel curious, ancient energies. By the 1810s it was fashionable among British and European elites to be fascinated by the dress of Europe's rural, non-metropolitan groups. In Benjamin Disraeli's bestselling novel *Vivian Grey* (1826 and 1827), which details the life of the English aristocracy, the protagonist stays in a luxury hotel in the Duchy of Nassau, Germany, which features a shopping arcade on its first floor: For sale here, among the "varieties of national bijouterie," are not just expensive china, jewelry, pipes, and "crosses of Mont Blanc crystal" but also "costumes of Swiss peasantry."[54]

Nor was this interest limited to Britain and Europe. In the United States, *Godey's Lady's Book* regularly ran serial features on "Costumes of All Nations," in which it detailed the dress of the ladies of the world, from Portugal and Turkey to Soleure and Unterwalden.[55]

This interest in clothing, moreover, flourished across genres, markets, and media. Indeed, clothing came spectacularly to life in the visual and performance media that were major vectors of transatlantic ethnic nationalist transmission, including engravings, illustrated books, political cartoons, and theater. Travelogues in the early nineteenth century began to feature minute descriptions of the local dress of inhabitants of various lands, often accompanied by elaborate illustrations. Children were taught geography through illustrations of the costumes of the world. Racial and national caricatures familiar to us today came into vogue in political cartoons as the pictorial field itself emerged as a new realm of consolidation for political, national, and regional identity. And illustration was not alone in its influence on repertoires of national and ethnic appearance. After the War of 1812, the booming transatlantic theater business had a powerful influence on the promotion and solidification of what was now understood as ethnic appearance, giving life to a variety of national, ethnic, and racial caricatures and personifications that would have a lasting impact on nationalistic doctrine.[56]

The Picture of Ethnicity

Perhaps nowhere are the dominant tropes and principles of ethnic dress better represented than in popular "costume geographies" or "costume albums" that were produced in Britain and Europe in the early nineteenth century. Launched at the turn of the nineteenth century and promoted by renowned artists and engravers, nineteenth-century costume albums came in a striking variety of forms, everything from ornate and costly giftbooks filled with a cornucopia of color to cheap books for children illustrated with woodcuts. Albums compiled of illustrations of costumes, sometimes printed, sometimes hand-painted, had circulated in European, Middle Eastern, and Asian courts since the early modern period. What was new in the early nineteenth century was the deployment of the traditional visual tropes of these albums not to affirm global cosmopolitan life but to elaborate new versions of human difference and hierarchy. Often built around the conceit of a tour of the world, ethnic costume books offered discursive and pictorial illustrations of seemingly strange and distant populations dressed in their everyday clothing. In some cases, these albums involved actual sketches from life. In other cases, the illustrations were inspired by earlier costume albums or by purely imaginary and fanciful ideas of the dress of a given people, ideas taken from images in Cook's *Voyages* or from the stage or romantic literature. Nevertheless, in all their forms, these books drew on and elaborated the principles of ethnic dress I outlined above: the peoples depicted were associated with timelessness and lack of change, they were depicted according to modern racializing regimes with their peculiar visual itineraries, and their clothes belonged to Western semiotic schemas.

In one popular costume geography, *Cosmorama*, written for children and published in London in 1826, readers are introduced to cultures that are frozen in time. Icelanders possess "language, dress, and mode of life" that "have been invariably the same for the last nine centuries"; "they exhibit a faithful picture of their Scandinavian progenitors." The "dress of the Japanese is the same, except in quality, from the emperor to the peasant, fashions never changing among them."[57] As visual media, these illustrations exploited unusual color, lush surfaces, and multitudinous ornament as signifiers of archaism, exoticism, and distance from metropolitan temporality. Color and ornament were thus the equivalent of a kind of genetic script. The more colorful and ornate the costumes of a given people, the more lost in primitive or ancestral times these people seemed.

In *Costume of the Russian Empire, Illustrated By Upwards of Seventy Richly Coloured Engravings*, published in London in 1803, readers are invited into a world of unfamiliar vibrancy and bewildering ornamental detail. In this book, readers tour the panoply of European, Asian, and Indigenous peoples inhabiting the vast terrain of the Russian Empire, from the Baltics and Finland to northern Mongolia and Siberia. Each "chapter" describes a different population group and provides a detailed illustration of their dress, combining breathtaking engraved and hand-colored plates with a seeming taxonomic rigor. We hear of how Sámi Indigenous women manufacture a glinting "tin thread" with a mechanism made of "reindeer antlers" and employ "silver and a kind of mock or false gold" to ornament and embroider different parts of their dress.[58] They "wear . . . trowsers, shoes, doublets, and close coats. . . . Sometimes they wear caps plaited like turbans, and sometimes they are made to fit close to the head: they are always ornamented with brass wire, or strips of cloth of different colours" (see fig. 4).[59]

But it is the illustrations themselves, filled with color and rich graphic detail, that do the heavy lifting when it comes to the vivification of exotic cultures. In these illustrations, both unexpected swaths of color and graphic patterns suggest densely ornamented and embroidered clothes. The brilliant vermilion of the Sámi costume finds its conceptual equivalent in the ornamental detail of the clothes of the Mordvin and "Mestscheraik" women (see figs. 5 and 6). Accompanying textual descrip-

Fig. 4. John Dadley, "A Female Inhabitant of Lapland," *Costume of the Russian Empire, Illustrated By Upwards of Seventy Richly Coloured Engravings.* London: William Miller, 1804. Plate 2. Hand-painted stipple engraving. Special Collections, Harold B. Lee Library, Brigham Young University.

Fig. 5. Edward Harding, "A Mordvin Woman of the Mokchanien Tribe," *Costume of the Russian Empire: Illustrated by Upwards of Seventy Richly Coloured Engravings*. London: T. Bensley for J. Stockdale, 1811. Plate 12. Hand-painted stipple engraving. Author's collection.

tions replicate the emphasis on color and detail purveyed in the illustrations. Of the Mordvin woman's costume we read, "Glass beads of various colours serve them for necklaces: the apron is formed of four fillets or bands, which are united by small clasps, trimmed with tassels, and loaded with coral."[60] Indeed, wordy and minute descriptions of dress are typical of the nineteenth-century costume album genre generally. Describing the garb of the "Woman of Finland," the author spec-

Fig. 6. Edward Harding, "A Female Mestscheraik," *Costume of the Russian Empire: Illustrated by Upwards of Seventy Richly Coloured Engravings*. London: T. Bensley for J. Stockdale, 1811. Plate 28. Hand-painted stipple engraving. Author's collection.

ifies, "The jacket is of silk, longer than ordinary, and trimmed with a border like a furbelow, of a different colour to the jacket. In the front it is ornamented, from the knee to the furbelow, with elegant embroidery and glass pearls. The apron, though narrow, is striped with various colours, embroidered, and richly ornamented with medals and glass pearls."[61]

Costume of the Russian Empire was part of a series of luxury ethnic costume books produced by London engravers and publishers between 1800 and 1820: *The Costume of China* (1800, 1805), *The Costume of Turkey* (1802), *The Costume of the Russian Empire* (1803, 1811), *The Costume of Hindostan* (1804), *The Costume of the Hereditary States of the House of Austria* (1804). Published in both French and English, these volumes set the tone and style of travel and national dress illustrations for years to come.

Costume taxonomies and geographies of this period included the regions of central and northern Europe and Britain. Traditionally provinces of large imperial and monarchical domains, the regions of Europe were now divided into discreet ethnic and regional groups, each with its own peculiar character and ancient sartorial customs. As in the case of the *Costume of the Russian Empire*, many of the costume books and prints that flourished in this period were upscale and included sophisticated artwork and cutting-edge experiments in color printing. Costume albums attracted such artists and engravers as William Alexander, who served as the "draughtsman" for the Macartney Expedition to China in 1792; the famed Swiss engraver Joseph Reinhard, who chronicled the dress of the Swiss peasantry; Norwegian painter Johan Frederik Eckersberg, who painted the rural people of Norway; and the Paris-based Alexandre Lacauchie, who, in addition to his fine engravings of characters from theater, offered especially lush renditions of all the standard ethnic costumes of the world. These upscale productions were complemented by a large variety of more affordable productions. Costume albums, prints, and geographies flourished in all markets, becoming especially popular as children's books and geographies. What all these costume books and prints had in common, regardless of their cost or geographic focus, was an emphasis on color, complex patterns, and unconventional cuts of clothes to indicate a people's peculiar spirit and isolation from metropolitan modernity.

In *Costume of China*, William Alexander represents the people he sees during his travels in washes of rich, surprising color, floral patterns, and intricate graphic detail (see figs. 7 and 8).[62] In the productions of Reinhard, Eckersberg, and Lacauchie quirky short jackets, dense embroidery, and unusual floral and checkered cloth distinguish the clothes of nonmetropolitan populations. We are invited to contemplate the embroidered bodices and flower-topped hats of the Swiss and Norwegian

Fig. 7. William Alexander, "A Standard Bearer," *The Costume of China. Illustrated in Forty-Eight Engravings*. London: William Miller, 1805. Aquatint. Getty Research Institute via Internet Archive.

Fig. 8. William Alexander, "A Soldier of Chu-San," *The Costume of China. Illustrated in Forty-Eight Engravings*. London: William Miller, 1805. Aquatint. Getty Research Institute via Internet Archive.

peasants;[63] we view the wild plaid skirts of the Highlanders, the lavishly trimmed boots of the Portuguese man, and the shimmering yellow and green dress of the Turkish woman (see figs. 9, 10, 11, 12, and 13). In more affordable books and prints by such artists as George Scharf and Jacques Grasset de Saint-Saveur, provincial people are more rudimentarily rendered. They are, however, likewise identified by the bright stripes, lively colors, and floral patterns in their clothes: the quaint rural people of "Unterwalden" wear oversized flower-daubed straw hats and red-striped vests; the woman of Bordeaux wears a striped shawl, turquoise bows, and a floral petticoat (see figs. 14 and 15).[64]

These same visual idioms prevailed throughout the market. At the turn of the nineteenth century, upmarket costume geographies were replicated in illustrated juvenile reading materials that offered to teach children the geographical regions of the world by associating each region with a different costume. These books

Fig. 9. Joseph Reinhard, "Costumes du Canton de Zoug," *Collection de Costumes Suisses en 44 feuilles*. J. Whatman, 1808. Outline etching and aquatint. Gugelmann Collection, Prints and Drawings Department, Swiss National Library.

Fig. 10. Johan Fredrik Eckersberg, *Udvalgte Norske Nationaldragter* (*A Selection of Norwegian National Costumes*) Christiania: Chr. Tønsberg, 1861. Plate 2. Hand-colored engraving. National Library of Norway.

Fig. 11. Alexandre Lacauchie, "Costumes Écossais," *Les Nations. Album des Costumes de Tous les Pays* (publisher unknown). c. 1850. Hand-colored lithograph. Paris. Author's collection.

Fig. 12. Alexandre Lacauchie, "Costumes Portugais," *Les Nations. Album des Costumes de Tous les Pays* (publisher unknown). c. 1850. Hand-colored lithograph. Paris. Author's collection.

Fig. 13. Alexandre Lacauchie, "Costumes Turc," *Les Nations. Album des Costumes de Tous les Pays* (publisher unknown). c. 1850. Hand-colored lithograph. Paris. Author's collection.

Fig. 14. George Scharf, "Unterwalden," *Swiss Costume*. London: Rodwell and Martin, 1824. Hand-colored engraving. Courtesy of Swiss National Library (NL), Bern.

Fig. 15. Jacques Grasset de Saint-Saveur, *Artisanne de Bordeaux*, c. 1797. Hand-colored engraving. Author's collection.

were more rudimentary in their engraving and painting techniques. But precisely because children's book authors and artists worked with a drastically reduced palette of signs, they tended to distill those signs into their most simplistic forms. In *Cosmorama*, the "Highlanders" and the "Dutch" appear, once again, in splashes of color and quirky shapes (see fig. 16). Indeed, this particular illustration, which features not only "Highlanders," "Dutch," and "English Peasants," but also an elegantly dressed metropolitan couple, "Londoners," emphasizes the extent to which peripheral groups were identified with bright colors while fashionable metropolites arrayed themselves in sober black, white, and dark blue. Similarly, in *The Costume, Manners and Peculiarities of Different Inhabitants of the Globe*, the most colorfully dressed people are the most alien to the metropole and its norms. In the entry for "Spaniards," readers are warned: "Stand clear, my little friends, stand clear, / The haughty Spanish Don comes here, / With waving plumes and ample cloak." The "Spaniard's" ornate dress indicates a violent character: "[H]ot and testy, oft he draws / His rapier for the slightest cause." In the entry for "Persians" we not only see colorful non-western dress, but we also hear of beheadings, battles with knives, and fierce jealousy when it comes to wives (see fig. 17).

Because the codes of ethnic dress drew on the codes being established for racial difference, clothes and biovisual properties tend to function in these illustrations as mutually reinforcing and even interchangeable elements. In some cases, unusual and colorful clothes are displayed in conjunction with racialized bodies, as in the case of a print of the Wolof people of western Africa ("Jalofs"), in which the bright clothes and jewels indicate the tropical isolation of the population (see fig. 18).[65] At the same time, what is being identified in this print is an ethnicity, "Jalofs," rather than a racial group, and like other ethnicities they are associated with vivid clothes that indicate arcane and unfamiliar customs. In other cases, particularly in the cheaper books, these illustrations worked within a symbol system in which clothing alone, irrespective of bodily features, was responsible for delineating ethnic and racial character. In two different children's publications illustrating the people of Tahiti, *The Costume, Manners and Peculiarities of Different Inhabitants of the Globe* and *The Little Traveller*, the particularities of complexion color are clearly haphazard, a choice of the individual colorists who hand-tinted the illustrations. In the *Little Traveller*, the faces of the family members under the entry "Chinese" are painted different colors. In these illustrations, it is the costume alone that performs all the work of ethnic and racial differentiation (see figs. 19, 20, and 21).[66]

This convertibility of clothes and the features of the racialized body is made especially clear in monochrome illustrations. We can see the racializing work done by costume in the illustrations produced for a luxury gift book on costumes of the

Fig. 16. "Londoners, English Peasants, Scottish Highlanders, Hollanders or Dutch," *Cosmorama: The Manners, Customs, and Costumes, of all the Nations of the World Described* by J. Aspin. New Edition. London: John Harris, 1834. Plate 5. Hand-colored engraving. Special Collections and University Archives, Iowa State University Library.

PERSIANS. 7

A CUSHION supporting her back,
Her legs bent most awkwardly under,
A beauty of Persia, good lack !
Appears to a Briton a wonder.
Yet tell me, young friend, would not some of the fruit
To which she is pointing, your palate just suit?
But hold, there's a man by her side
With a knife, I suppose, and a sword ;
Should she happen to be this man's bride,
And he prove her master and lord,
The only sure way to shun losing one's head,
Will be to run home, and get quickly to bed.

Fig. 17. "Persians," *The Costume, Manners, and Peculiarities of Different Inhabitants of the Globe, Calculated to Instruct and Amuse the Little Folks of All Countries.* London: John Harris, 1831. Page 7. Hand-colored wood engraving. Courtesy of Princeton University Library.

world, *Finden's Tableaux*, published in London in 1838.[67] In the plate illustrating "England," the central figure conveys her Englishness by being dressed in clothing that is entrenched in the English past—in this case, a fantasized medieval past. In the background is a castle with the rudimentary features of the Tower of London, suggesting that we are in the eleventh century (see fig. 22).[68] In this illustration, ethnic dress is both part of the present (it represents the dress of essential Englishness in the here and now) and yet fixed in the distant past, in a timeless yet archaic moment in which the spirit of Englishness appears to have been born. At the same time, almost all these illustrations contain figures who are implicitly attached to an

Fig. 18. Jacques Kuyper, *Jalofs*, [1836?]. Hand-colored engraving. Author's collection.

12 OTAHEITANS.

THIS man is a comical blade,
He 's cloth'd in a very odd way:
And what to the good-looking maid
Who stands by his side shall I say?

The lady 's a dancer, I guess,
But why in the world has she got
Such things sticking out from her dress?
Are they wings pray, or fans, Sir, or what?
Indeed, Miss, the question propos'd is a task,
So step to Taheite*, and there you may ask.

* The name given by the natives to Otaheite.

Fig. 19. "Otaheitans" [Tahitians]. *The Costume, Manners, and Peculiarities of Different Inhabitants of the Globe, Calculated to Instruct and Amuse the Little Folks of All Countries.* London: John Harris, 1831. Page 12. Hand-colored wood engraving. Courtesy of Princeton University Library.

even deeper past. "Venice," "Scotland," and "India" all feature central female figures in lavish costumes that, like "England," gesture at a vague romantic "past" (see figs. 23, 24, and 25). But in all cases these central figures are surrounded by background figures whose clothes and faces are more shadowed. In many cases, as with the harlequin-like page in "Venice" or the highland characters in "Scotland," their clothes are more ornate, more specific than those of the central, brightly lit woman figure. These shadowy figures freighted with ornamental detail give the impression of being simultaneously recessed from the foreground (further back in distance) and more deeply ensconced in their ethnic and racial specificity, members of an even more distant temporality. By contrast, with their pale, less ornamented

THE LITTLE TRAVELLER. 31

OTAHEITEANS.

The inhabitants of Otaheite are a fine, stout, active people; in their dispositions they are mild, good-natured, and friendly. Their complexion is of a pale brown; their hair and eyes, black, with small noses, and rather large mouths, and beautiful white teeth. The men of consequence wear their finger-nails long, which is thought a very grand mark of distinction, but the nail of the middle finger on the right hand is always kept short. The men generally wear their beards.

Fig. 20. J. Steerwell, "Otaheiteans," *The Little Traveller; or, A Sketch of the Various Nations of the World*. London: A. K. Newman, 1825. Page 31. Courtesy of Princeton University Library.

clothes, the central female figures, even as they inhabit frozen ethnic and racial historicity, intimate a potential jump into the modern West. In "India," the central figure, bathed in a white glow, sets a lamp afloat on a river, signaling her alignment with light and with the forward flow of time.[69] In these engravings, shadow, pattern density, and ornament play dynamically with biovisual markers of race, offering to extend ethnic and racial character across a range of surfaces and temporalities beyond the plane of fleshly corporeality.[70]

THE LITTLE TRAVELLER. 21

CHINESE.

China is remarkable for the great antiquity of its government, which can be traced back to about four thousand years. The Chinese are the most numerous of any known nation in the world, the population being estimated at no less than three hundred millions. In their persons, they are of a good stature, with round broad faces, little black eyes, and small sunk noses, they shave their heads, except only a small portion of hair on the top, which they wear plaited and very long. The people of high rank suffer their finger nails to grow long. Their com-

Fig. 21. J. Steerwell, "Chinese," *The Little Traveller; or, A Sketch of the Various Nations of the World.* London: A. K. Newman, 1825. Page 21. Courtesy of Princeton University Library.

Fig. 22. [Edward] Finden, "England," *Finden's Tableaux. A Series of Picturesque Scenes of National Character, Beauty, and Costume* [ed. Mary Russell Mitford]. London: Charles Tilt, 1838. Engraving. Author's collection.

Fig. 23. W. Hall, "Venice," *Finden's Tableaux. A Series of Picturesque Scenes of National Character, Beauty, and Costume* [ed. Mary Russell Mitford]. London: Charles Tilt, 1838. Engraving.

Fig. 24. E. Scriven, "Scotland," *Finden's Tableaux. A Series of Picturesque Scenes of National Character, Beauty, and Costume* [ed. Mary Russell Mitford]. London: Charles Tilt, 1838. Engraving.

Fig. 25. H. Egleton, "India," *Finden's Tableaux. A Series of Picturesque Scenes of National Character, Beauty, and Costume* [ed. Mary Russell Mitford]. London: Charles Tilt, 1838. Engraving.

American Ethnic Dress

In the early nineteenth century, as the vogue for regional and ethnic personalities gained ascendency in Britain and Europe, U.S. writers joined in a general transatlantic rush to introduce worldly readerships to their own quaint, local personages who claimed ethnic and folk status. In the 1810s, U.S. writers were galvanized by the idea that "America" might have its own storied "national" literature and joined in a general clamor among artists of various countries to produce a literature expressive of their own national personality. "America" in this literature was conceived not merely as the anonymous civic state of patriot fantasy but as a patchwork of distinctive cultures and ethnicities, each with its own ancient past, locales, and forms of dress. The masters of this genre were Washington Irving and James Fenimore Cooper. Living in England and Europe between 1815 and 1832 and close friends with Walter Scott, Irving followed Scott's advice and concocted seemingly ancient folk tales for New York and New England inspired by the work of the Brothers Grimm. His most famous short stories, "Rip Van Winkle" and "The Legend of Sleepy Hollow" appear in the *Sketchbook of Geoffrey Crayon, Esq.*, which was published serially in 1819 and 1820 to great transatlantic acclaim. Cooper's talent lay in transposing Walter Scott's dramas of antique Britain wholesale into the history of British settler colonialism in North America. Cooper's famous Leatherstocking novels, the first of which, *The Pioneers*, was published in London and New York in 1823, took their plots and characters directly from *Waverley* and *Ivanhoe*. Set between the 1740s and 1804 and fixated on ethnic groups in colonial North America—the English, the French, the Haudenosaunee, the Spanish, the Dutch, the Wendat—the Leatherstocking novels chronicle what Cooper saw as the nation's turbulent but preordained emergence.

But it is also the case that as ethnic nationalist culture ballooned in popularity in the late 1810s and early 1820s, the United States as a whole was reconceived as an ethnic precinct. Irving and Cooper follow Scott in imagining the clash of ethnicities and their "folk" cultures as part of an arcane historical past that modernity overcomes. "Rip Van Winkle," for example, is about a man in eighteenth-century New York who one day, when he is lost in the mountains, meets the ghosts of the Dutch colony's founders, with their fuzzy beards and "antique Dutch" dress. Under their spell, he falls asleep for twenty years and wakes up after the Revolution. The tale opens with an epigraph from a seventeenth-century poem hailing, "Woden, God of Saxons." Irving's tale thus retells the story of the United States's self-actualization not just through reference to the rupture from British monarchy but also through reference to an ancient ethnic past (the past of a Germanic people, the Dutch) that is ferried into modern consciousness, much like the Anglo-Saxon spirit in *Ivanhoe* is assumed to be ferried into modern England. Cooper's Leatherstocking novels tell a similar tale of regional ethnicities and factions overcome by a unifying revolutionary modernity.

But "America" in this period was not always conceived by writers and performers as the modern entity of the civic nation-state. Rather, within broader transatlantic literature and performance culture between about 1815 and 1840, the whole of the United States came to be understood as itself a provincial "folk" region, like the Swiss cantons or the hidden recesses of the Russian Empire, a region whose people, *Americans*, had their own peculiar character and personality. For Irving and Cooper, who spent substantial portions of their careers living in Britain and Europe, genteel Anglo-Protestant Americans were indistinguishable from genteel metropolitan people in London or Edinburgh. They were all generic gentlemen indebted to British intellectual and social traditions. Their chronicling of local types in their tales and novels was a kind of imaginative, ethnographic exercise, a peek behind the scenes at a forgotten yokel culture unconnected to their own status. But by the mid-1820s, as the United States was plunged into internal turmoil around slavery and settler expansion, and as British and European ethnic nationalist culture grew more belligerent and chauvinistic, the United States as a whole began increasingly to feature in British and European discourse as its own peripheral region, a vast rural backwater uniformly peopled by oddities who were now in their aggregate conceived to be an ethnicity. They were "*American*."

Nowhere are these new ethnic nationalist "American" figures more clearly displayed than in the history of the "Yankee," an eighteenth-century stereotype of regional New Englanders that eventually morphed into a personification of the United States. The earliest Yankee figures were called "Brother Jonathan"; in the 1850s, they would evolve into the figure of Uncle Sam. These new "American" figures were not the generic genteel types who strolled the spaces of older public sphere culture. They were quirky, brightly dressed rural figures, personifications of an "*American folk*." As in the case of other objects of Western ethnographic interest, "Americans" in this branch of commentary were possessed of specific features: they were part of a regressive and even violent past, locked into ancestral customs and modes of dress; their external appearance was an unintended symptom and uncomplicated sign of their character as a people; and they wore dress that invoked the codes of ethnic costume. As contemporary descriptions of "Americans" by travelers suggest, the codes of ethnic dress infiltrated not just stage and cartoon culture but also tourist literature, flâneur journalism, and even local nativist doctrine, all of which now associated Americans with ornate, colorful clothes.

The Yankee proper would enter the lists of transnationally recognized ethnic caricatures in the 1820s. To a large extent, he was a figure from the stage. Throughout the eighteenth century, British theater companies toured British North America and the Caribbean. While subsiding during the Revolutionary War and the War of 1812, this theater traffic continued to thrive unabated throughout the nineteenth century. With its vivid costumes and increasingly elaborate sets, theater offered a unique venue for the mobilization and transmission of ethnic nationalist visual and symbolic palettes. Theater historian S. E. Wilmer speculates that the major images and themes of U.S. nationalism were delivered to U.S. populations not through print but through popular theatrical representations on stage. A vogue for "ethnic types" and crude national and racial caricatures exploded on the transatlantic stage in the years after the War of 1812, which was thronged with comedy routines representing the Irish, Jews, Muslims, Spanish, and English.[71] The U.S. side of the Atlantic provided fodder for these shows, introducing new caricatures to the repertoires of performers, including Black and Indigenous characters, as well as the "Yankee," who emerged as a stock low comedy figure on the transatlantic theater circuit.

Rural New Englanders, called "Yankees" and personified by a figure named "Brother Jonathan," had appeared as country bumpkin figures in U.S. letters in the late eighteenth century. But the Yankee in his modern incarnation was not concocted by U.S. writers and performers. He was the brainchild of a British actor, the famous dialect comedian Charles Mathews. In 1822 and 1823, Mathews was touring parts of the United States with his one-man show, a vaudeville-style slate of ethnic impersonations. In the words of theater historian Francis Hodge, Mathews "lightly ridiculed through songs, skits, and monologues the Scots, Welsh, Irish, many of the English county types, and the French, German, and Dutch. His shows were realistically conceived galleries of national types."[72] When Mathews was back in England in 1824, he premiered a farce called *Trip to America* in which a raft of new ethnic impersonations was featured, all of them "American." An 1824 print advertising "The Mathew-Orama" shows him performing in the guise of fourteen different U.S. regional types, from "Colonel Hiram Peglar, A Kentucky Shoemaker" and "Mr. O'Sullivan, an Irish Improver of His Fortune," to "Mon. Capot, French Immigrant Taylor" and "Agamemnon," an escaped slave.[73]

But the enduring hit of Mathews' show was Jonathan W. Doubikin, the "*Real Yankee*" who came equipped with his own peculiar expressions: "I *guess*," "I *reckon*," "I *calculate*."[74] *Trip to America* was shortly followed by another Mathews concoction, *Jonathan in England*. In these pieces, the Brother Jonathan Yankee took what would become his time-honored form as a personation distinguished by his vanity, his shrewd dealings with money, his dialect, his indiscriminate violence, and his love of telling rambling tall tales that never reach a climax. Touring London in 1827, the U.S. actor James Henry Hackett seems to have seen Mathews' caricatures of American types and then performed his own rendition of a Yankee character,

Fig. 26. Amos Doolittle, *Brother Jonathan Administering a Salutary Cordial to John Bull.* 1813. Hand-painted engraved print. New Haven, CT: Yankee-Doodle Scratched. American Antiquarian Society Polit. Cart. B872.

first in front of London audiences and then in front of U.S. audiences. By the early 1830s, the Yankee was a stock figure in a transatlantic comedy circuit fixated with the production of crude national, racial, and ethnic personalities.

In the late eighteenth century, the Jonathan Yankee was outfitted in the clothes of a rural farmer. Appearing in Royall Tyler's 1787 comedy *The Contrast*, Jonathan was dressed in what theater historian Francis Hodge calls "plain linen," his costume making a sharp "contrast with the fancy linen of the city characters"[75] A famous political cartoon produced in Connecticut in 1813 features Brother Jonathan in a plain suit apparently made of homespun, the garb of revolutionary feeling. John Bull, the personification of England, is dressed in the uniform of eighteenth-century wealth and power, represented by the red of his coat and white wig (see fig. 26).[76] As late as 1827, James Kirke Paulding's comic political allegory *The Diverting History of John Bull and Brother Jonathan* specifies that Jonathan likes "to dress in homespun."[77] But by the late 1820s, Brother Jonathan's typical rural costume had transformed itself into the colorful, vividly decorated dress that signified ethnic peoples. Both textual descriptions of Yankee figures and illustrations of actors in costume suggest the transformation of the Yankee costume into what contemporaries would have recognized as ethnic garb.

Fig. 27. George Hill [in a whittling pose]. Theatrical Portrait Prints. TCS 44 (Hill, George). Hand-painted print. Houghton Library, Harvard University.

Appearing on the Covent Garden stage in 1827, the U.S. actor James Hackett was, in the words of Hodge, "clothed in what was taken for the genuine Yankee dress: a black hat, blue coat, flowered waistcoat, and blue-striped trousers. His hair was set in a pigtail and tied with a green eelskin."[78] This colorful dress became a standard in the Yankee repertoire. The actor's edition of the well-known Yankee comedy *Jonathan in England* gives a description of the clothes of the Yankee character Soloman Swap: "Yankee coat; striped trowsers and vest; shoes; red wig."[79] Engravings of famed Yankee actor George Hill depict him in the densely patterned waistcoat and striped trousers that were the stage Yankee's signature wardrobe elements (see fig. 27). "Yankee Hill," as George Hill was called, also frequently appeared in the red, white, and blue dress that would later be made famous in the figure of Uncle Sam (see fig. 28). As in the case of the Swiss and Portuguese provincials, whose peripheral status is conveyed in the love of bright colors, stripes, and effusive patterns, the Yankee's striped pantaloons, brightly colored neckerchief, and loud vest typify him as the member of an ethnic hinterland. Other Yankee characters played by Hill similarly sported audacious colors. The hand-colored engraving of Hill as "Major Enoch Wheeler," "a bustling, inquisitive Yankee, ready for anything," shows him in a rich purple coat, checkered trousers, red stockings, and red neckerchief (see fig. 29).[80]

Nonstage representations of Yankees followed these same principles. As the Yankee and Brother Jonathan became popular national personifications of the United States in the 1830s, illustrations of them confirmed what was now understood to be their ethnic character. In a series of satirical papers called *The Playfair Papers, or, Brother Jonathan, The Smartest Nation in All Creation*, published in three volumes in 1841, the British writers Hugo Playfair and Robert Cruikshank offer a portrait of Americans from the point of view of British travelers (see fig. 30). The volumes are notable for containing color illustrations, engraved by Cruikshank, of American persons and scenes. In the illustration, "Scene on Battery Point, New York," the clothes of Brother Jonathan stand out for their bold colors and patterns: the green coat, the short, red striped pantaloons that would in later years be made famous in the figure of Uncle Sam. Brother Jonathan's companion is another curiosity in this scene; like the figures in the depiction of Swiss country people, this figure wears a large straw hat. He is supposed to represent an Andrew Jackson–like character who in the narrative turns up at a dinner party with "huge gray woollen stockings drawn over his boots and over his trousers, up to the middle of his thighs. He was a Down-Easter, and a genuine Yankee Politician."[81] In this illustration, the vivid clothes and curious accessories of the Yankee figures indicate their difference from the metropolitan gentlemen who stand on the right side of the engraving.

In the 1780s, the plain, homespun garments of American patriots had mod-

Fig. 28. George Hill [in stripes]. Theatrical Portrait Prints. TCS 44 (Hill, George). Hand-painted print. Houghton Library, Harvard University.

Fig. 29. George Edward Madley, *Mr. Hill as Major Wheeler in the Farce of New Notions.* Hand-painted print. Robert Cushman Butler Collection of Theatrical Illustrations; Manuscripts, Archives, and Special Collections; Washington State University Libraries. Color corrected to match Houghton copy of this print.

Fig. 30. Robert Cruickshank, "Scene on Battery Point, New York," in Hugo Playfair and Robert Cruikshank, *The Playfair Papers, or, Brother Jonathan, the Smartest Nation in All Creation*, vol. 1 of 3 (London: Saunders and Otley, 1841). Special Collections, Harold B. Lee Library, Brigham Young University.

eled a new kind of citizenry based on the divestment of idiosyncratic features of identity and dress. As we have seen, plain clothes remained the standard-bearers of metropolitan subjectivity and continued to be associated with scenes of modernity, egalitarianism, and free market choice, as these were imagined in early nineteenth-century transatlantic culture. By the 1830s, however, it was no longer characteristic for Americans to be associated with such clothes. In 1841, when *Playfair Papers* was published, Brother Jonathan and the Yankee, with their bright colors and curious outfits, were routinely standing in for a more general projection of a fabled Yankee ethnicity onto all white U.S. populations. Not only in *Playfair Papers* but in Dickens' *Martin Chuzzlewit*, in travelogues by Emmeline Stuart Wortley and Michel Chevalier, and in essay series by Canadian writer Thomas Chandler Haliburton, the features of the Yankee encompass all "Americans," who are now classed as a separate people with their own tastes, customs, intellectual abilities, and bodily features.

Now, as Zakim suggests, U.S. working- and middle-class consumers appear to have had access to an exceptionally wide assortment of cloths and clothes. It was this access to clothes itself, I would suggest, that was influential in defining

"Americanness" as an ethnic property. Americans were understood, both in tourist discourse and in critical ethnographic observation at home, as a race of people attracted to shiny new clothes. In this writing, the peculiar "folk" features given to the Yankee—his seeming to exist outside of metropolitan temporality, his possession of a biovisual embodiment, and his commitment to visually audacious clothing—are extended to the U.S. population and to the country generally. Americans become typified as a people who, at first glance, wear metropolitan dress, but this dress is marked by an overly modern, hyperconsumerist flashiness (often a literal shininess or glitter) that reveals a peculiar American ethnicity to viewers.

In an essay series called *The Clockmaker, or the Sayings and Doings of Samuel Slick of Slicksville*, published in Nova Scotia beginning in 1835, the Canadian writer Thomas Chandler Haliburton describes his travels with a Yankee character named Sam Slick. The word "slick" itself entered U.S. dialect in the early 1800s as a New England colloquialism, meaning "shiny" and "superficially attractive; glibly clever." (OED). When he first meets Sam Slick on the road, the narrator is uncertain of his identity. Then he notices his fine clothes and excess ornaments and knows he's a Yankee. "His clothes were well made, and of good materials. . . . A large brooch, and some superfluous seals and gold keys, which ornamented his outward man, looked 'New England' like." Sam Slick's taste for shiny ornament is echoed in the clock he sells: "a gawdy [*sic*], highly varnished, trumpery looking affair."[82] Traveling in Illinois in the early 1840s, British author William Oliver noted that "In the west, the Yankee is not very generally nor highly esteemed, as he is considered 'too quirky.' If anyone has been cheated, he is said to have been 'yankeed'; and any worthless thing, which is tinselled and varnished, is said to have been 'yankeed over.'"[83]

The tropes of slickness, shininess, and excess feature in many travelogues. Visiting the United States in 1849, the British poet Emmeline Stuart Wortley marveled at the dress of American men, with their "lemon-coloured kid gloves, or Parisian boots." Some of what Whortley sees is exotic. "Yankee speculators" wear "curious boots turned up at the points, something like Turkish cimeters." But most of these peculiarities are related to consumerist excess. According to Wortley, even the poorest class of men appear "in black silk waistcoats . . . and well-brushed hats."[84] According to French traveler Michel Chevalier, "the American mechanic . . . dresses like a member of Congress" and "every woman ha[s] her cloak and bonnet of the latest Paris fashion."[85]

American "folk" and vernacular personages were, as we have seen, frequently promoted by prominent U.S. writers and performers, most famously Washington Irving and James Fenimore Cooper. But ethnic nationalist figures, by their very nature, contained potentially powerful energies of derogation. Caught up in the semiotic universe of conjectural historiography and race pseudoscience, ethnic clothes opened a conceptual door into a racialist worldview; their mere presence purported to lead the viewing (Western) subject into a mysterious realm of archaic, nonmetropolitan beliefs and behaviors, of dubious morality, limited intellectual powers, and violent social practices. In the popular ethnographic language that permeated touristic commentary of this period, the mention of bright color and intricate detail were a shorthand. They allowed readers to peg various populations within stadial and racialist models of human history and development. In Aspin's *Cosmorama* the reader is taken on a virtual tour of every inhabited region of the globe known to Europeans. Each region's population and clothing are described, as well as each nation's habits and abilities. The narrator of the book is the "transparent I" of Silva's analysis, the subject who stands at the perceived pinnacle of civilization and looks back over the dim, descending stairs of human history and development. For Aspin, color, ornamentation, and patterns in clothing are not just the signs of ethnic and racial peculiarity; they also feature as signs of the inferior developmental stage of their wearers. Simplicity and lack of color are things that only the most enlightened civilizations can achieve. "The higher classes of the English," Aspin says, "observe great simplicity in their dress, except on public occasions, when they display much of elegance and somewhat of magnificence. The same characteristic neatness usually pervades their houses and equipages, which are rarely distinguished for useless pomp or parade."[86]

For Aspin, all the people of the world are subsequently placed on a spectrum between this stark simplicity and various explosions of color and pattern that correlate with their place on the scale of human development. The French, who seem to exist just beneath the English, have different bodies, different tastes, and different clothes. "In their persons, the French are slender, well-proportioned, and rather shorter than the English. Their eyes are black, and their complexions brown, or sallow." The French are also more prone to sartorial display. "Paris sets the fashions of all Europe; and an immense trade in articles of dress and new patterns is carried on by tailors, dress makers, and milliners." France also has its less developed folk who linger in the shadows of an evolutionary past, and their clothes are correspondingly more rustic and peculiar, untouched by modernity. "The peasants . . . remain faithful to the ancient costume of an enormously large hat, loose breeches, and wooden shoes, for the men; and the jerkin and short petticoat, with a high cap, for the women."[87]

As a general rule, the more allegedly primitive, exotic, and backward a population, the more ornamented and colorful are their clothes. In this formulation, sartorial, phenotypical, and moral and intellectual attributes are all interchangeably indicative of each other. Aspin reports, "The Georgians are in general tall, well proportioned, and elegant in shape; and their language is soft, harmonious, and expressive; but their minds, unrestrained by education and virtuous habits, are depraved and vicious." In harmony with their depravity, the Georgians have extravagant taste in clothes and cosmetics. "They usually dye their hair, beard, and nails, of a red colour; and the women do the same to the palms of their hands. The latter have on their heads a cap, or fillet, under which, in front, their black hair falls upon the fore head, and behind, it is braided into tresses. They paint their eyebrows black, so as to give them the appearance of one entire line; their faces are coated with red and white; and their air and manner are voluptuous in the extreme." Those human groups who are most "fierce, warlike," and "inhumanly savage" tend to be most attracted to color. The Tatars love the color red. "Red is the color highest in esteem with the Tatars: their chiefs, though otherwise meanly attired, seldom fail to have a scarlet robe for state occasions; and a woman of quality would not think herself well dressed, were she without a garment of this hue."[88]

It was precisely in these terms that Americans were figured. Their modern flashy clothes, in this literature, indicated their lack of correspondence with true modernity, opening a window instead into violent and degenerate social practices. To be sure, these attacks on the United States were fundamentally political in nature. Travelers from England and Europe were preoccupied with what today are considered the ugliest and most exploitive features of the antebellum United States, including its legalized enslavement of Black and people of color populations, its genocidal settler colonial projects, and its peculiarly brutal forms of capitalism. Indeed, in the 1830s and 1840s, as sectional debates over slavery and expansion reached a crescendo, negative accounts of Americans in travelogues grew more intense.[89] Nor were these accounts all penned by foreign tourists. As J. Gerald Kennedy shows, the 1830s and 1840s witnessed violent repudiations of their nation and its policies by U.S. intellectuals and reformers.[90] But the thing to note about these critical accounts is their reliance on what was now understood as a peculiar American appearance that was thought to be symptomatic of moral depravity. As in the case of the populations described in *Cosmorama*, the extravagant, modern surfaces of Americans, often signified by twinkling surfaces and shiny fabric, are a metonym for a combination of violent social practices and embodied pollution and degeneracy.

In many travelogues by British writers, readers are introduced to the United States through descriptions of Americans' lavish, colorful dress and extravagant display. In Charles Dickens' *Martin Chuzzlewit*, Martin's trip to Boston includes meeting young women "very gorgeously attired in very beautiful colours," who are "great proficients in the French fashions"[91] In Hugo Playfair's the *Playfair Papers*, a thinly fictionalized travelogue detailing U.S. life, the English narrator, Playfair, is invited to the home of wealthy New Yorkers, the Palavers. The Palavers hold court in a drawing room of "full flowery brilliancy," with a "crimson and gold damask-covered and gilded canapé," "a rich crimson-and-gold coloured Beauvais tapestry," "full, flowing window-curtains, of the same materials," "magnificent French mirrors," "tables profusely covered with green, scarlet, and gold" (86–87). Mrs. Palaver's friend, Mrs. Philog, carries "a glittering Parisian reticule" (93).

To be sure, the properties of excess attributed to Americans by British travelers were also class properties, frequently projected onto a generic transatlantic bourgeoisie and *nouveaux riches*. Indeed, in its opening pages *Martin Chuzzlewit* includes descriptions of an English family whose excesses seem to be mirrored, albeit more shabbily, by families across the Atlantic. But the idea that there might be a transatlantic category of poorly dressed white people and that Americans were, as a nationality, descended from this substandard group was itself an ethnic nationalist construct. It suggested that class and taste were linked not, as they traditionally had been, to wealth and station or to easily traversed social hierarchies based on money, but to genetic, biological properties. Class was like a high forehead or elegant feet: you were born with it. In these accounts, Americans appear as descendants of a degenerate "stock," a degraded, unevolved, and disreputable branch of Anglo-European populations.

As is the case in *Cosmorama*, where fiery colors indicate the presence of violence and cruelty, the colorful, shiny appointments and costumes of the American people indicate a violent nature, one that for Playfair and other observers of the day was crystallized in the institution of slavery and in the capitalistic behaviors with which it was closely linked. In most travelogues and fictionalized accounts of the day, references to slavery are overt. The narrator of *Playfair Papers* calls the United States the "Land of Bondage and Boasting" (235) where all the inhabitants boast of living in "freedom" while slavery is legal and respectable gentlemen engage in "a sneaking slave trade with Africa." (79). In many accounts, both fiction and nonfiction, including *Cosmorama*, *Playfair Papers*, and Dickens' *Martin Chuzzlewit*, visitors to the United States travel to the South to see the enslaved laborers and plantations for themselves. In *Cosmorama*, slavery is virtually the only thing mentioned about the United States. Aspin informs readers, "Slavery is permitted among men who vaunt of their own freedom. In the southern states, religion is almost totally disregarded, and slavery prevails with all its concomitant demoralizing effects."[92] In *Martin Chuzzlewit*, the good-hearted Martin, desperate for money, journeys into the Deep South to a fever-ridden swamp where he's told he will make a killing working for land and cotton speculators. Plain garments in liberal revolutionary sign systems had represented self-consciousness and choice; they pegged the United States as the site of modern liberty where ancient prejudice and custom had been cast off.

The glittery American clothes that feature in mid-nineteenth-century commentary mark the site where, thanks to slavery, modern liberty is shut down.

The Jonathan Yankee, for example, with his quaint, colorful dress and gold accessories, was often identified as a slave trader; in this sense, American folk clothes were continuous with a violent, allegedly racial inclination to traffic in human beings. Indeed, the Jonathan Yankee was from the first connected to slavery. The British actor Charles Mathews, who invented the stage Yankee, imagined him as a slave owner. Mathews' *Jonathan in England*, the first full-length Yankee comedy, featured Jonathan Doubikin, the Yankee character who had earlier appeared in *Trip to America*, but this time traveling in England with his enslaved black servant Agamemnon. Instead of playing the good-natured clown in this play, Jonathan is the crude, avaricious villain of the piece who mistreats Agamemnon and tries to sell him at a cheap price.[93] These antislavery parts of *Jonathan in England* were excised by James Hackett, who brought the play back to the United States, but subsequent characterizations of stereotypical Americans by Britons and Europeans suggest that slavery remained an orienting trope in the conceptualization of American character and appearance. The first scenes of *Uncle Tom's Cabin* feature Haley the Yankee slave trader dressed in flamboyant, peculiar clothes with many patterns and fixtures of gold. "He was much overdressed, in a gaudy vest of many colors, a blue neckerchief, bedropped gayly with yellow spots, and arranged with a flaunting tie." "His hands, large and coarse, were plentifully bedecked with rings; and he wore a heavy gold watch-chain, with a bundle of seals of portentous size, and a great variety of colors, attached to it, which, in the ardor of conversation, he was in the habit of flourishing and jingling with evident satisfaction."[94] In these accounts, the appearance of Americans—their taste for finery and shiny gold objects—transmits a debased moral and intellectual interiority. As Martin Chuzzlewit says at one point to the flashy silk of the American flag, "you're a gay flag in the distance. But let a man near enough to get the light upon the other side and see through you; and you are but sorry fustian!" (273).

In *Cosmorama*, the clothes and bodies of the "Georgians" and "Tatars" are assumed to be interchangeable; the red, ornamented clothes intimate and elaborate the existence of a racialized phenotypical body, helping to ferry the biological body into the realm of visible evidence as a signifier of character. By the same token, ancestral or tribal character in the ethno-racial imaginary expresses itself in glaring clarity in the combined arrangements of the phenotypical body and its clothes. In this circular scheme, clothes, flesh, and character are mutually generative and convertible. The same is true for American clothes in accounts by travelers. The violent character of Americans not only reveals itself in shining jackets and gold seals but also in the phenotypical American body, which is depicted in these travelogues in stereotypical ethnoracialist terms.

In the *Playfair Papers*, Hugo Playfair's initial impression is that the United States as a whole is "heathenish" (36) and filled with "uncivilized monsters" (47). The citizens Playfair meets are revolting to look upon; a wealthy woman of Boston has a complexion the color of "meager whey" "like that of one wretchedly sea-sick" (198). Her lips are "especially repulsive, from their only half overlaying the black jagged remains of what were formerly teeth" (206). At one point, Playfair, just because he is British, is challenged to a duel by the white Kentucky frontiersman General Boon. Boon is "large-boned, sinewy, and tough-looking, with hickory-coloured skin—a keen eye, hooked nose, short lips, and long under-jaw" (18). Boon's body bears the marks of a national personality defined by violence. The men of Kentucky, Playfair tells readers, take great pleasure in gouging out eyes and biting off ears. "Every second man in Kentucky had an eye gouged out and every third a nose or ear gander-plucked—that is, bitten off" (n. 37). Instead of dueling with swords or pistols, General Boon opts for "pitchforks or hatchets" (51), neither of which "are used by civilized nations" and "could only be tolerated during the ages of barbarism" (52). One character, witnessing the duel, cries, "This is atrocious, it is barbarous, savage beyond precedent" (55).

The "savagery" and "barbarism" of Americans are conveyed not just in these racialized dueling technologies but also in scenes of gorging and gluttony. These appear not just in the *Playfair Papers* but also in *Martin Chuzzlewit* and feature a violent rending of flesh in the name of omnivorous, insatiable appetites. The theme of avarice in these scenes is heightened by references to the American Revolution and its cause of universal liberty. Taken to the ironically named "Liberty Hall Hotel," Playfair has dinner in the dining room with upward of a hundred people of "the most heterogeneous casts of origin" (10), who talk without pause of the proceeds of textile capitalism: "cottons, molasses, Yorkshire cloths, Manchester calicoes, Michigan lands, rum, railroads, packet-shares, bills, and papers dollars" (25). The only thing that stops them is the arrival of the meal. They all fall upon the food "with that extraordinary celerity with which all moves forward in this nation of *progressers*." Playfair witnesses a terrifying scene, the sudden "demolition of soups, fish, geese, fowls, turkeys, beef, mutton, pork, rumpsteaks, meat pies, sausages, and hams, with puddings, pastry, omelets, fruit," "the annihilation of roast and boiled, of huge joints and unfeathered birds, great and small."

In these scenes, the description of grotesque consuming bodies mingles with ethnographic spectatorship of the dining habits of an exotic culture. "Here a tall broker stretched over the table, and pulled towards him a turkey; there a lathy, long-nosed, short-lipped Yankee hoisted over . . . a dish from two yards' distance. . . . [Y]onder a Kentuckian who despised the art of carving, tore with his bony claws a capon into atoms" (15–16). A similar scene of feeding and gorging takes place in *Martin Chuzzlewit*. As he sits down to his first meal in New York, also at a hotel, Martin is dumbfounded. "It was a solemn and an awful thing to see. Dyspeptic individuals bolted their food in wedges; feeding, not themselves, but broods of nightmares, who were continually standing at livery within them. Spare men, with lank and rigid cheeks, came out unsatisfied from the destruction of heavy dishes, and glared with watchful eyes upon the pastry" (205). Later in the novel, Dickens identifies American diners as "dirty feeders" (402).

The insatiable hunger of Americans in these scenes corresponds, the writers suggest, to other violent appetites and to a general subordination of fleshly creatures to American greed. At several points, Dickens draws connections between American ravenousness for animal flesh and slavery. Americans think it "incalculably more criminal and dangerous to teach a negro to read and write than to roast him alive in a public city" (273). At one point, Martin and his companion Mark meet an enslaved Black man. Mark tells Martin his history: "[H]e was shot in the leg; gashed in the arm; scored in his live limbs, like pork; beaten out of shape; had his neck galled with an iron collar, and wore iron rings upon his wrists and ankles. The marks are on him to this day." Treated like "pork," the slave is an item the American republic consumes and with which it energizes itself. Unlike the New York diners, Mark can't stomach these scenes. "When I was having my dinner just now, he stripped off his coat, and took away my appetite" (213). Not surprisingly, for Dickens this collective American body gorging itself on human and animal misery is "so maimed and lame, so full of sores and ulcers, foul to the eye and almost hopeless to the sense, that her best friends turn from the loathsome creature with disgust" (279).

This loathsomeness was perhaps nowhere more clearly condensed than in notorious accounts of American chewing tobacco use, which required spitting. In these accounts, the American body is a site of pollution. Americans might look like Europeans, according to Aspin, but they are at odds with them in one critical respect: "the cleanliness both of person and habit." "The use of tobacco pervades the whole frame of society, from the President of the United States to the meanest pauper; neither the chair of state, the senate, the pulpit, the bar, nor the drawing-room, is exempt from this annoyance and its loathsome consequences, the marks of which are witnessed upon the floors and walls even of the best apartments."[95] Of course, tobacco was another product of the South and the slave states. Like the "dirty feeding," the American fondness for tobacco mars Americans' pretensions to European sophistication, staining the very luxuries that the American rich are so eager to buy. In many travelogues, scenes of spitting appear in proximity to gorgeous fabrics, carpets, and upholstery. In Frances Trollope's famous *Domestic Manners of the Americans*, which appeared in 1832, the narrator finds herself in a cabin "handsomely fitted up . . . and well-carpeted; but oh! That carpet! I will not, I may not describe its condition; indeed it requires the pen of a Swift to do it justice." Rather than sitting with Americans in this room, Trollope would "infinitely prefer sharing the apartment of a party of well conditioned pigs." She goes on, "I hardly know any annoyance so deeply repugnant to English feelings as the incessant, remorseless spitting of Americans."[96] I will have more to say about Trollope in a moment but for now it is important to note that it is essentially two products of the slave economy, cloth and tobacco, that end up functioning in these accounts as signs of American embodiment, the one, colorful and ornamented cloth, marking the outside of the body, the surfaces whose meanings Americans are unable to control, the other, tobacco, the inside, whose various orifices and porosity are always already determined by the extended assemblage of cloth and clothes. What Americans wear and what they are on the "inside" are here coproduced.

The Garb of White Nationalism

In sum, then, colorful, tinseled clothes acted in travelers' accounts as elements in the racializing and ethnographic discourses that helped to cohere white Americans into their own ethnic group, separate from metropolitan populations and, along with other ethnic and racial groups, hindered by heredity when it came to the teleological journey into the future. But these links between lavish, colorful clothes, racialized bodies, and regressive, violent character were not just promoted by the British and Europeans. They were also embraced and celebrated by significant populations inside the United States. In the late 1830s and 1840s arguments over slavery, formal imperialism, and settler expansion contributed to the growing ferocity of racist belief in the United States. Germanic supremacy doctrines and imagery, with their belief in highly specialized white races, became central to antebellum white supremacy, feeding burgeoning white nationalist and nativist movements in the United States. Combining labor unrest with anti-British, anti-Irish, and anti-Black agitation, these movements were distinguished by the new idea of a peculiar "American ethnicity," what Amy S. Greenberg calls an "imaginary race of American 'Anglo-Saxons' [that] was destined to dominate lesser races."[97] By the mid-1840s, certain U.S. writers, performers, and political actors had developed the idea that the United States was not just the home of a subsection of Anglo-Saxons but a repository of the purest Anglo-Saxons, *American* Anglo-Saxons, who were superior to their English counterparts. The staple personalities of ethnic theater and political caricature, with their raucous colors, their belligerence, their boisterous lack of respect for Britain and Europe, featured in these movements with a vengeance, appealing to a disaffected white working class that loathed "aristocracy" and professed to fear competition from immigrants and free people of color. Centering these movements was, again, a codification of ethnic bodies and persons through symbol systems that relied heavily on clothes.

Precisely because they were ethnic nationalist figures, the personifications Brother Jonathan and the Yankee were co-opted in the late 1830s not as a critique of the United States but as defiant symbols of white working-class pride. They became symbols of a white ethnic American "folk." In these years, Brother Jonathan became the figurehead of various nativist associations and publications, including, most famously, the weekly New York penny paper, *Brother Jonathan* (1839–1862). Two of the most popular character types on the New York stage in the 1840s were the "b'hoys" and "g'hals" of the Bowery, symbols of urban working-class nativist defiance. Most famous were working-class firefighter Mose and his girlfriend Lize.[98] New York was also home to a new generation of flâneur journalists who brought ethnographic discourse to their reporting on familiar urban scenes. One of the most well-known of these urban ethnographers was George G. Foster, who loved to describe the audaciousness of "genuine" Americans, "the most original and interesting phase of human nature yet developed by American society and civilization."[99] In these accounts, colorful clothes function once again as signifiers of ethnicity and race, but in this case, they elaborate a defiant people who embrace what are confessed to be their violent, chauvinistic ancestral traits with pride. In turn, these ethnic people come to stand, as they do in travelogues by the British and Europeans, for Americans in general as a national type.

In Foster's accounts, working-class "g'hals" are distinguished by their "independence," "defiance," and "free talk." They love riotous profusion and color; their layered skirts and stomachers, says Foster, sport "a light pink contrasting with a deep blue, a bright yellow with a brighter red, and a green with a dashing purple or maroon," all topped with a hat "trimmed with a perfect exuberance of flowers and feathers, and gigantic bows and long streamers of tri-colored ribbons."[100] Engravings of fireman Mose depict him in a striking costume that once again looks like ethnic dress: a brilliant red shirt, tall black hat, baggy pantaloons, and slick curls of black hair (see fig. 31). Other nativist figures are depicted in gaudily patterned coats. A piece of sheet music from the period features a depiction of a nativist "Uncle Sam" (a spin-off of the Jonathan Yankee), in a "patch-work" coat whose patterns evoke folk dress (see fig. 32). Contemporary descriptions of Bowery characters confirm this ethnic framework; they contain the ethnographic rhetoric used to describe ethnic groups in travel books. One observer of the day describes the Bowery boy in a "black silk hat, smoothly brushed . . . hair well oiled, and lying closely to the skin . . . vest of fancy silk, large flowers." This traveler adds, "He has a peculiar swing, not exactly a swagger, to his walk, but a swing, which nobody but a Bowery boy can imitate."[101]

According to Foster "the b'hoy of the Bowery, the rowdy of Philadelphia, the Hoosier of the Mississippi" are all "alike." All typified by their costumes and regional peculiarities, these figures are also part of a now ethnicized white working class. "The secret and key of the entire class of characters represented by Mose . . . and Davy Crockett . . . is just this—*free development to Anglo-Saxon nature*" (emphasis in original). Foster quickly adjusts his claim and calls this group not *Anglo-Saxon* precisely (and thus of British and European origin) but "Anglo-American," aligning his commentary with the notion that there existed an American race closely linked to the Anglo-Saxon but entirely different, something enabled by the transatlantic taxonomizing and hierarchizing of populations as ethnic groups. According to Foster, "There can be no doubt that, thus far, the Anglo-American is the highest and most perfect specimen of the human being."[102] In the work of Foster and other writers, ethnic nationalism energized nativist sentiment, helping to consolidate and vividly personify local white supremacist beliefs.

The Return of Plain Clothes

In this chapter, I have surveyed the installation of a sartorially materialized ethnic and racial personhood in early nineteenth-century transatlantic nationalist regimes, focusing in particular on "Americanness" as it came to be represented in theater, illustrations, and travel literature. Instead of arguing that descriptions of Americans as a gaudily dressed people were linked to U.S. consumer culture and the expansion of the marketplace, I argue that visual tropes of sartorial audacity were part of a broad transatlantic obsession with discovering a peculiar appearance for each of the "nationalities," "races," and "ethnicities" of the world. "Americans" in this discourse were treated not as a nation on the cutting edge of consumer modernity, as modern scholars assume, but as a "folk" people whose colorful clothes indicated their unworldliness and degeneracy. In the next chapter, I will look at how U.S. writers and entertainers from about 1830 to 1855 responded to these insults to

Fig. 31. James Brown, *F.S. Chanfrau in the Character of Mose*, 1848. Chromolithograph. New York: E & J Brown. In Joseph Norton Ireland, *Records of the New York Stage from 1750 to 1860*. TS 939.5.3 vol. II, part XII, Houghton Library, Harvard University.

Fig. 32. Howard Paul, *Uncle Sam, An American Song*. 1854. Lithograph (illustrated song sheet). Philadelphia: Lee & Walker. Library of Congress Music Division LC-USZ62–91849.

U.S. character. Before moving on to that discussion, however, I want to emphasize how profoundly typifications of Americans as a violent, debased people reverberated through the world of the U.S. intelligentsia.

When Frances Trollope's *Domestic Manners of the Americans* was first published in 1832, it created a convulsion in U.S. genteel and intellectual society. Trollope was unsparing in her condemnation of the United States. An abolitionist and friend of Frances Wright, Trollope was, of course, a fierce enemy of slavery, and some of her disgust with the United States stemmed from that source. Americans, she believed, had managed "to extract all that was most noxious both in democracy and in slavery, and had poured the strange mixture through every vein of the moral organization of their country."[103] "[I]t is impossible for any mind of common honesty not to be revolted by the contradictions in their principles and practice." "[Y]ou will see them with one hand hoisting the cap of liberty, and with the other flogging their slaves." Trollope did not limit herself to criticism of slavery. She also condemned the United States for its crimes against Indigenous people. "[L]ecturing their mob on the indefeasible rights of man" one moment, Americans were in the next "driving from their homes the children of the soil, whom they have bound themselves to protect by the most solemn treaties" (180).

But Trollope also dwelled on American appearance and personal habits. Americans, she declared, suffer from a "total and universal want of manners, both in males and females" (56). They are "dull" and "silly" and "coarse" (56). Their homes are "dirty" (188). Almost everything Trollope sees in the country "jars the feeling and shocks the taste" (56). Most offensive for Trollope, as we have seen, is the American love of chewing tobacco and "obsessive, remorseless spitting" that goes along with it. American walls and carpets in the "best apartments" everywhere are stained with yellowy spit. As yet "'unrazored lips'" are "polluted with the grim tinge of the hateful tobacco" (271). Even dashing young men in "the most elaborate toilet" can be seen pulling lumps of tobacco from the pockets of "silk waistcoats." Drawing on late eighteenth-century theories of race, Trollope finds in spitting an explanation for the peculiar facial and bodily features of Americans:

> I am inclined to think this most vile and universal habit of chewing tobacco is the cause of a remarkable peculiarity in the male physiognomy of Americans: their lips are almost uniformly thin and compressed. At first I accounted for this upon Lavater's theory, and attributed it to the arid temperament of the people; but it is too universal to be so explained; where the habit above mentioned, which pervades all classes (except the literary) well accounts for it, as the act of expressing the juices of this loathsome herb, enforces exactly that position of the lips which gives this remarkable peculiarity to the American countenance. (189)

Reading these words in 1832, the U.S. intelligentsia and its bourgeois audiences were horrified, filled with shame and outrage. Local papers all over the United States teemed with reviews and articles attacking Trollope and defending Americans. Many years later, Mark Twain remembered how "Mrs Trollope was . . . cursed and reviled by this nation." "MRS TROLLOPE has abused us," fumed the *Traveller and Spirit of the Times* before lambasting the English for their inveterate gambling and horrific sports involving the suffering of animals.[104] Other papers accused Trollope of "downright stupid lying" and "misrepresentation."[105] Not surprisingly, the antebellum period saw numerous struggles among U.S. cultural arbiters to wrest control of the American image away from the British and Europeans. At a time when virtually all U.S. writers aspired to transatlantic readerships and publishers, assaults on the "American" character were not a neutral or distant phenomenon that the U.S. intelligentsia could ignore. The devaluation of American character potentially impacted the lives of authors, actors, publishers, intellectuals, and entertainers.

At one point in *Domestic Manners*, Trollope announces, with reference to ethnic nationalist and folk culture frameworks, that American habits and appearance would be much more palatable if Americans accepted that they were a provincial people and stopped aiming for sophistication. If Americans were "disposed to assume the plain unpretending deportment of the Switzer in the days of his picturesque simplicity, . . . it would be in bad taste to censure him." Unfortunately, Jonathan insists on being a "fine gentleman," who "challenge[s] competition with the old world." In that case, the "old world" has no choice but to judge how "he supports his pretensions" (57). It is not the "old world's" fault if Jonathan doesn't like what he hears. We can speculate that the insults were all the more threatening because they hit at the heart of the white supremacist architecture that was increasingly coming into focus as the foundation of the U.S. national project: how did the United States justify itself to the world in the absence of the vaunted purity of its "people?"

One idea for renovating the American personage, according to anxious U.S. cultural nationalists, involved the renunciation of all "pretensions." Many believed that it was in trying to be a "fine gentleman," as Trollope put it, that Jonathan made himself vulgar and ridiculous instead of charmingly quaint and "picturesque," as one expected of objects of the touristic gaze. Accordingly, the antebellum period witnessed a cry among U.S. cultural nationalists for a rejection of sophisticated finery and a return to the days of republican plain dress. Writers from Anna Cora Mowatt and Henry David Thoreau to Walt Whitman, Horace Bushnell, and Ralph Waldo Emerson rejected consumer fashions and extolled the virtues of plain, sturdy clothes as the proper dress of a modern democratic citizenry. In his 1851 lecture "The Age of Homespun," Bushnell condemned "dress made of factory cloths" and celebrated "dress made of homespun"; he praised the kind of woman "who cloth[es] her family in garments prepared by her industry."[106] Mowatt's 1845 hit New York comedy *Fashion* satirized American fashion excess with New York characters done up in an orgy of wild colors and sparkling trim; one male character appears in "blue Albert coat," another in "brass buttons, yellow vest, red and black cravat, broad plaid trousers"; still another in "light blue trousers, patent leather boots, gay coloured vest and scarf, profusion of jewellery." Mowatt urged audiences to reject "foreign dross" that glimmers like "gold" and to dress instead in clothes that were "rough" and "very simple."[107]

Yet these admonitions to return to plain clothes and homespun were not alone in trying to address the problem of the American image. Ethnic nationalism relied on a certain semiotic ideology in which clothes acted as infallible sites of transmission. In this ideology, the surface of the body acted as a conveyance system for information about the wearer and their culture. But precisely to the extent that this system counted on the infallibility of the signal sent from subject to viewer, it also contained the possibility of signal glitch or blockage. In the following pages, accordingly, I look at the extent to which certain branches of U.S. nationalist and entertainment culture engaged in the reconfiguration of the "American" subject in the ethno-racial visual array not through a change of costume or body but through the unexpected intensification or disruption of the body's visual signals. In this scenario, the viewer met a kind of flare or sudden blockage that prevented information about the subject from being transmitted, making the identification of ethnicity and race impossible. As I will show, this counternationalist culture developed not inside familiar U.S. cultural nationalist writing, where the United States was earnestly celebrated or lamented, but in the transatlantic entertainment circuits and Europhilic culture that in the first place did so much to feed early nineteenth-century nationalist mania.

TWO

RESTYLING AN OLD WORLD

METROPOLITAN FASHION IN THE ANTEBELLUM UNITED STATES

Whenever we are dealing with imitation, we should be very careful not to think too quickly of the other who is being imitated.

JACQUES LACAN, "THE LINE AND LIGHT"[1]

In the opening pages of *Walden, or Life in the Woods*, Henry David Thoreau associates a "free" and "manly" United States citizenry with the renunciation of sartorial luxury. Clothing, according to Thoreau, has a fundamental purpose: "to retain the vital heat" and, "in this state of society, to cover nakedness." Anything beyond that is superfluous and threatens the subject's self-sufficiency and integrity. "[L]uxury," warns Thoreau, "enervates and destroys" nations.[2] Americans' love of finery is edging them toward corruption and destruction. "We worship not the Graces, nor Parcae, but Fashion. She spins and weaves and cuts with full authority. The head monkey at Paris puts on a traveller's cap, and all the monkeys in America do the same" (29). As an antidote, Thoreau recommends plain, sturdy clothes. A "thick coat can be bought for five dollars, which will last as many years, thick pantaloons for two dollars, cowhide boots for a dollar and a half a pair, a summer hat for a quarter of a dollar, and a winter cap for sixty-two and a half cents, or a better be made at home at a nominal cost" (28).

In one sense, Thoreau's admonitions against luxury summon an ideal of American appearance and subjectivity popularized in the years of the American Revolution. In their struggle against British tariffs in the 1760s, the residents of the thirteen colonies boycotted the consumption of British goods. Most famously they rebelled against the buying and wearing of the rich and colorful cloths that had formed a staple of the colonial import economy. Shedding their finery for plain garments made of the rough, locally woven cotton cloth called "homespun," the American patriots helped to generate an enduring connection between plain, unadorned clothes and modern values of liberty, social equality, and self-governance. Writing several decades later, cultural nationalists like Thoreau revived this rhetoric of "homespun" as part of a new, updated battle against social inequality. Instead of being waged against British "monarchy" and "aristocracy," Thoreau's battle was waged against the United States's increasingly powerful moneyed classes, which in Thoreau's account thrive on expansionism, manic financial speculation, and entrepreneurial competition. American entrepreneurial culture, Thoreau and his generation believed, venerated new and fashionable clothes as the signs of success. Accordingly, Thoreau is especially fierce about condemning new clothes. "I say, beware of all enterprises that require new clothes, and not rather a new wearer of clothes" (27). Recommending that men wear their "old coats until they are "actually worn out, resolved into [their] primitive elements" (27), Thoreau associates old clothes, plain clothes, and nakedness with conditions of social equality. "It is an interesting question how far men would retain their relative rank if they were divested of their clothes. Could you, in such a case, tell surely of any company of civilized men, which belonged to the most respected class?" (26).

At the same time, there are many odd properties of clothes in *Walden*. Plain, sturdy, and worn-out clothes, for example, do not always transmit or organize social equality. At one point, Thoreau observes poor Irish laborers cutting ice on Walden Pond in the dead of winter. At first, he is "wont to pity the clumsy Irish laborers who cut ice on the pond, in such mean and ragged clothes, while I shivered in my tidy and somewhat more fashionable garments" (82). But one day, one of the workers accidentally falls through the ice into the pond and arrives at Thoreau's hut to warm himself. Thoreau is repelled to see that the man wears not just old clothes but layers of old clothes. "I saw him strip off three pairs of pants and two pairs of stockings ere he got down to the skin." Something about these layers disgusts Thoreau. His pity vanishes and he resolves not to lend the Irish worker any dry clothes, presumably on the principle that he will only use them to make more layers. In this instance, plain and old clothes are not in and of themselves the agents or signs of equality among their wearers. On the contrary, the layering of clothes by the Irish laborer speaks to Thoreau of some character flaw, some insufficiency. Observing these layers, Thoreau is driven to muse, "Often the poor man is not so cold and hungry as he is dirty and ragged and gross. It is partly his taste, and not merely his misfortune" (81). For Thoreau, layering is "ragged and gross" and shows a lack of "taste." Presumably, Thoreau can count himself among the enfranchised in his hypothetical sartorial utopia not because his clothes are plain but because his clothes make a certain statement: they bear the imprint of a superior "taste" and sensibility; they are thin, "tidy," and "fashionable."

Thoreau is struggling here, I would suggest, not with the paltry issue of whether or not to wear layers but with a vast and invisible conceptual system that had intervened in liberal political thought about nations and bodies between the time of the American Revolution and the late 1840s. In the previous chapter of this study, I argued that in the 1810s and 1820s, the rise of ethnic and racial nationalisms in the Atlantic world permanently transformed the perceived relationship between the human body and the nation-state. American patriots had hypothesized a body scrubbed of its social and cultural signifiers, a blank slate upon which the subject wrote its own character and destiny. In ethnic nationalism, by contrast, as in the new visual regimes of racialist discourse, the existing surfaces of the body were transformed into ontologically and epistemologically revealing components. Hair, eyes, dress, jewelry, shoes, skin, were all assumed to transmit infallible information about the wearer's heritage, character, and intellectual abilities to observers in a way that escaped the wearer's control. The ethnic or racial body could not be altered or purged of its signifiers. In this formulation, the nationality of wearers of clothes merely preceded and impressed itself upon the visible form of the clothes themselves.

This is the conceptual structure that appears to intervene in Thoreau's attempt to imagine equality as an absence of meaningful sartorial and bodily signifiers. When Thoreau tries to imagine the plainly clothed body as the foundation of equality, he cannot overcome a predisposition to see the body as already produced by an indelible, invisible pre-existing spirit or character. Not coincidentally, this impediment is encountered in Thoreau's attempt to imagine the plain clothes of the Irish as an unwritten script, as the same or equal to his own clothes and body. What Thoreau unconsciously discovers when he tries to insert the Irish into the schema of revolutionary personhood is that Irishness, the condition of ethnicity, seemingly precedes his efforts to efface pre-existing signification. According to the logic of ethnicity and its sartorial regimes, as these had developed by the mid-nineteenth century, the clothes a person with Irish ancestry elects to wear can only ever transmit the Irishness of the wearer. This essential Irishness cannot be removed.

Laura Dassow Walls has recently argued, convincingly, that Thoreau was not anti-Irish, that his views about the impoverished Irish immigrants who flooded the region of Concord in the mid 1840s in the wake of the famine in Ireland were complex and politically fraught and involved Thoreau's empathetic projection of himself into their lives.[3] What I wish to note here is that however complex his feelings might have been, in describing the Irish, Thoreau reaches into what by the 1840s was a standard toolkit of tropes for the description of ethnoracial peoples. It is no accident that the Irish, in Thoreau's eyes, are distinguished by *layers* of clothes. As I showed in chapter 1, sartorial profusion was the sign of nonmetropolitan identity.

Like the lavish, colorful, overly decorated clothes of the ethnoracial peoples documented in contemporary costume ethnographies, Thoreau's Irish people are defined by their excessiveness and failure to grasp simplicity; their clothes, although mere rags, are marked by profligacy. Most important of all, the Irish do not understand their sartorial missteps. They do not control the arrangement of the surfaces of their bodies.

As Thoreau's struggles to create a democracy of dress suggest, in the middle decades of the nineteenth century, plain clothes lost their early connection to the absence or evacuation of positive identity and became instead foundational signs of a new kind of modern, white metropolitan subject, one marked not by its freedom from past inscription but by what was now seen as an immemorial character inherited from a superior "tribe." Plain clothes, in other words, had become a kind of ethnic clothes. Even as Thoreau struggles to reinstate the egalitarian possibilities of plain clothes, plain clothes appear in his work as symptoms of a racial unconscious. They function as both sign and evidence of the civilizational achievements of white western Europeans and their settler descendants, transmitting Thoreau's belonging not in a democracy, as he hopes, but in a regime of inherited "taste," of instinctive and superior "fashionability" that does not include other white ethnic groups. The presence of this regime in the U.S. nationalist imaginary undercuts Thoreau's idea that democratic social equality might be achieved if only the contrivances of industrial capitalist modernity, like mass-produced new coats, were stripped away. Instead, Thoreau's attempt to revive the sartorial logic of the revolution reveals his entanglement in a powerful nationalist symbol system that has replaced hierarchies of wealth and rank, in which clothes were seen as an addition to or ornament of the body, with hierarchies of ethnicity and race in which clothes were seen as inseparable from a pre-existing tribal heritage that inexorably shaped the clothed body's appearance.

Thoreau was not alone in trying to imagine his way out of the systems of ethnic nationalism. In the 1830s and 1840s, as arguments around slavery and capitalism exploded on the domestic scene and as transatlantic travelers attacked the appearance and habits of what was now identified as a degenerate "American race," many members of the U.S. intelligentsia echoed Thoreau in calling for a return to American plainness. Plainness, it was believed, would return the United States to its original republican values, curbing the consumer extravagance and gratuitous "aping" of metropolitan cultures that seemed to lie at the heart of U.S. problems. Anna Cora Mowatt, Carolyn Kirkland, Horace Bushnell, and Ralph Waldo Emerson were among the many U.S. intellectuals and artists who advocated a renunciation of consumerism and return to revolutionary values. But plainness, it turned out, was only one way to go. There was another. Over these same years, there developed in the United States a counterdiscourse of national appearance, one that celebrated rather than renounced luxury and that embraced the slavish imitation of foreign fashion that Thoreau attacked. This was the antebellum culture of Europhilia.

In the 1840s and early 1850s, northeastern U.S. bourgeois society was gripped by a thirst for anything remotely linked to the culture of the "Old World." For them, the Old World meant lavish dress, courtliness, pomp, ritual, ancient civilizations, and the mysterious sanctity of aristocratic privilege. The material artifacts to which these connotations clung—clothes, furnishings, manners, architecture, literature, histories, actors, opera singers, and even heraldic devices—surged as objects of consumer yearning and indices of polite caché. Romantic and Orientalist fascination with Europe and the Middle East, which had ebbed in the years after the War of 1812, now reappeared in full force and were joined by a breathless fascination among U.S. audiences with the contemporary English *ton*, the London celebrity aristocrats and authors who wrote and starred in Silver Fork novels. Magazines like *Godey's Lady's Book*, which advertised themselves as emissaries of refinement, routinely featured announcements of the clothes and "doings" of distant royal families, tales of amours between foreign princes and New York debutantes, serial articles on European folk costume, and lush illustrations of Mediterranean monuments and interiors. Even new styles of shawls for women were advertised with European aristocratic names: "La Comptesse Walewski," the "Princess Wagram."[4] An 1848 short story in Godey's summed up the rage for things European in the protagonist's remarks on one of its female characters: "[L]ike . . . most of our fashionable belles, she has a mania for everything foreign. Her manners, her dress, her servants, all come from abroad, and she has declared to me repeatedly her resolution never to marry an American."[5]

Both at the time and ever since, commentators have understood the aristocratic revival as a negation of U.S. nationalist aspiration and autonomy. Appearing in the same years as the travelogues of Trollope and Dickens, the aristocratic revival was reviled by cultural nationalists as a terrifying confirmation of everything that Europeans claimed about the United States. Indeed, as Thoreau's references to the "head monkey at Paris" suggest, the clothing sections of *Walden* seem to have been inspired by this vogue for foreign dress. Only when "clad" in a suit of his own, says Thoreau, will the U.S. citizen find "wise men to do him reverence" (28). For Thoreau, Americans wear false colors when they copy the clothes of Paris. Thoreau argues that it is only "the serious eye peering from and the sincere life passed within" that "consecrate the costume of any people" (28).

Modern scholars tend to follow Thoreau in seeing antebellum Europhilia as a negation of nationalist subjectivity, often pegging it as a leftover of European imperialism. In mid-twentieth-century histories, bourgeois Europhilia features as a betrayal of linear national unfolding. Richard Bushman identifies the midcentury vogue for foreign fashions as the reversion to an earlier, pre-revolutionary cultural state; genteel Americans "could not break the colonial and provincial habit of looking upward and outward for leadership."[6] In some studies, antebellum Europhilia appears as the antithesis of what are thought to be emerging local or vernacular cultures, like blackface minstrelsy. Eric Lott's study of minstrelsy casts "Ethiopian drama" as a "recognizably national cultural form for the American stage," a form that explicitly contested the "parvenu Whig fashioners of bourgeois taste such as Nathaniel P. Willis" and their promotion of "European talent, including Ole Bull and Jenny Lind."[7] More recently, Leonard Tennenhouse and Elisa Tamarkin argue that fascination with the Old World was not "regressive," precisely. Instead, it gave U.S populations of all classes and political persuasions a chance to fantasize lost continuity with a seemingly older, wiser power, one that had seen fit to abolish slavery. Worshiping England especially, according to Tamarkin, U.S. Anglophiles surrendered themselves to things that seemed unavailable in their present world. Anglophilia helped generate "an aesthetics of return to colonial structures of feeling." Americans could look back from beyond independence and "remember their experience of empire as an elegiac fantasy of rank, stability, and paternal authority where the life of the metropolis was reproduced in the society of Britons overseas." In these fantasies, Britain was imagined "as a reliquary of tradition, ornament, and ritual" that gave rise to "retrospective love of its imperial forms." In Tamarkin's words, "Amid the threats of political disunion" in the 1850s, "the monarchophilia of the masses . . . became the basis of a new patriotism that linked national preservation to the sentiments of obedience and reverence that monarchy inspires."[8]

And yet it is not entirely clear that the bourgeois mania for Old World fashion had much to do with actual British and European culture. In the early nineteenth century, clothes emerged as powerful racializing mechanisms, offering to extend the possibilities of ethnoracialization across a range of sartorial and material artifacts, including bodily coverings, hair, jewelry, tattoos, shoes, manners, and habits. In the tenets of ethnic nationalism, clothes functioned not as transient adornments but as powerful actualizations of the dressed subject's moral, intellectual, and genetic character. But it was precisely this belief in clothes as a site of transparency—a window through which the "serious eye" and "sincere life" passed unmediated—that bourgeois Europhilia, I would suggest, challenged. Following Thoreau, modern scholars assume that Old World worship necessarily describes a colonial relation. But this insistence potentially obscures a vital link between the midcentury mania for Old World fashion and the consolidation of an American "folk" or vernacular culture, arguably the same vernacular established by blackface minstrelsy. Indeed, suggested by Old World mimicry, with its seeming emphasis on racial sameness (whites imitating whites) and its invocation of a prenational or metropolitan identity, is the idea that such factors as race, class, and settler colonial history played a different part in the manufacture of vernacular cultures than is generally suggested by the scholarship on colonial imitation. Scholars of colonial imitation follow cultural nationalists like Thoreau in equating an "authentic" vernacular or local American culture with non-European culture. But made visible in the bourgeois mimicry of aristocratic Europeans is the extent to which this search for authenticity could interface with a claim that fakery was authentic, that the showy display of costumes or "masks" borrowed from other cultures was in itself a mark of originality, and was thus paradoxically indigenous to the United States.

Nowhere was this paradoxical fake-but-authentic appearance for Americans more cogently expressed than in the celebrity of the writer mentioned by Lott as this era's chief purveyor of imported taste, poet and travel writer Nathaniel Parker Willis. Unique among literary men of his generation, Willis overtly embraced and celebrated London and Paris fashion. Contemporaries dubbed him "the American D'Orsay" for his seeming to mimic the style of famed London dandy the Count D'Orsay; James Fenimore Cooper scornfully called him an "American in a European mask."[9] But Willis was linked in contemporary accounts not to old-style patrician Anglophilia, with its earnest attempts to embody and exude metropolitan polish, but to a popular antebellum culture that celebrated false costumes and painted-on faces. Whereas in prevailing formulations of colonial or racial mimicry, mimicry is said to be founded on a longing for or engagement with an object of imitation, the idiom of costumes and faces that Willis exemplified repudiated its objects, declaring that copies were independent from originals, that they were in fact more original, more truly authentic. Instead of suggesting his parochial longing for Europe's vaunted essence and authenticity,[10] Willis's dandyish mask did not really invoke Europe. It rather materialized the central figure of Jacksonian myths of spontaneous creation, the self-made man, a figure that seemed to spring, in a proleptic loop, from his own sartorial vision of himself.

I began the previous chapter by drawing a distinction between the antebellum United States's ideology of self-making and its reputation as a place whose population dressed in unconventional, colorful clothes. In that chapter I argued that reports of Americans wearing bright, multicolored clothes and curious boots and hats are not necessarily empirical or objective. To be sure, the United States was an early mass producer of ready-to-wear clothing. Local ideology advertised the United States as a place of equal opportunity and social mobility where the consumer objects that broadcasted wealth were in plentiful supply. But American clothes were also closely enmeshed in a Western symbolic order in which colorful bodily adornments were inseparable not from class mobility but from a variety of racialized properties: moral degeneracy, violence, and an inability to move forward into modern teleological time. But in this chapter, I want to propose that in the 1830s and 1840s, when U.S. nationalists began to "write back" to the insults of those like Frances Trollope, they experimented with new nationalist sartorial scenes by summoning up fantasies of miraculous entrepreneurial success, using urban myths of radical self-creation to reorganize how clothes worked in the larger global symbolic scene. It is important to stress that this reorganization did not always involve a material change in what U.S. populations actually wore or wanted to wear. Rather, cultural nationalist fantasies and experiments worked purely in the realm of signs, exploiting the certitude of ethnic and racialist belief to tinker with its premises as a regime of visual signals.

In the following chapter then, I begin by looking at Willis and his dandyish, Old World clothes as these appeared in the 1830s and 1840s via his considerable celebrity, writings, and public persona. In this section of the chapter I argue that the figure of Willis coalesced a fantasy of escape from conventional national ascription that was based not on the cleansing of a racialized white subject, which is what Thoreau imagined, but on the formal reconfiguration of the symbol systems through which race and ethnicity were thought to materialize themselves in the clothed body. Even while Willis was always imitating his social and national betters, whether it was the Boston elite at home or renowned aristocrats abroad, the peculiar imitative properties of his clothes allowed him to feature in the popular imagination of the day as an eerily uncanny, "original" figure. In this part of the chapter, I not only consider Willis and his "imitative originality" but I also look at similarities between his celebrity and other popular U.S. performance forms and tales primarily about uncanny clothes, including Nathaniel Hawthorne's *The Scarlet Letter* and Herman Melville's *The Confidence Man*. In all these instances, the oddly clothed figure in the "American" scene not only escapes positive ascription but he or she also acquires a kind of surreal power over the community of the conventionally dressed. I then go on to argue that it was precisely this hypothesized power, which seemed to issue from the superior authenticity of the imitation over the original, that was enacted in Willis's famous 1830s letters from London. A kind of revenge travelogue, in which Willis turns the tables on the mother country while touring it in metropolitan garb, Willis's writings from Europe evolve a fantasy of U.S. imperial supremacy in which "Americans," now perceived as a nation not of positive ethnic subjects but of mysteriously empowered painted faces and deceptive unembodied coats, conquer the British. Finally, in the third part of this chapter, I turn back to Thoreau and Emerson, who both wrote extensively on and celebrated plain clothes. Instead of seeing this celebration as indication of their cultural independence, I suggest that by the middle of the century, plain clothes, far from signifying a release from the colonial condition, were linked indelibly to white gentility and the supremacy of the "Saxon race," something that is made clear in Emerson's 1856 *English Traits*.

It is important to state from the outset that the seriousness of some of the documents I discuss is unclear. Willis himself is a protean figure who both avidly participated in the production of his sensational celebrity self and, on many occasions, watched it careen out of control in the face of vicious critics. Moreover, the antebellum entertainment field itself did not produce clarity. Teeming with advertising gimmicks, publicity stunts, hoaxes, and intellectual property theft on a global scale, the U.S. entertainment scene generated outsized personalities of dubious reality on a routine basis. But it is this consequent pastiche of images, voices, and narratives that interests me, partly because it draws a picture so similar to fantasies of sartorial renovation enacted on the antebellum stage or in books like the *Confidence Man*, and partly because the medium of celebrity itself, with its imperative performativity, its feedback chambers, its flickering, surreal relationship to truth, helped to consolidate a new kind of "American" national personage that parted company with sincerity and sartorial transparency. What was hypothesized in these scenes, I argue, was not a positive national character, a recognizable personality whose appearance speaks of regional group, lineage, religion, or geographical origin, but a kind of uncanny, almost eerie power that cunningly manipulates symbol systems to exempt itself from inclusion among raced and ethnic bodies.

Nathaniel Parker Willis in Boston

Although infrequently included in modern literary histories, Nathaniel Parker Willis was a central figure in the antebellum literary marketplace, a widely known poet, travel writer, essayist, and playwright.[11] Part of a new generation of shrewd and market-savvy U.S. journalists and magazine entrepreneurs who would permanently change the U.S. publishing industry in the 1830s and 1840s, Willis was the editor of a string of popular magazines and gift books, including the *Token*, the various *New York Mirrors* and *The Home Journal*, which he founded and which still survives today as *Town and Country*. As an editor and friend, he was mentor to dozens of writers, including Edgar Allan Poe, James Russell Lowell, and Bayard

Taylor. And Willis was more than just a literary figure. His biographer, Thomas Baker, calls him the United States's first celebrity in the modern sense of that term, a writer whose ability to anticipate and embody the fads of emerging print and consumer culture made him into a proto-Hollywood star, complete with legions of adoring fans and disgusted critics. Although attractive to antebellum audiences for many reasons—his quirky, sensational journalism and sappy poetry, his combination of slickness and innocent charm, and his promotion of remote and romantic lifestyles—Willis's initial fame rested on his incarnation of this era's favorite fable, the rags-to-riches story of self-made success.[12] The son of a Boston printer, Willis made a name for himself by "climbing into society," as he called it. He achieved fame by insinuating himself into the circles of the loftiest aristocrats and celebrities in Britain and Europe and then writing titillating accounts of his adventures.

Tangled from the first with his "climbing" and self-transformation, the politics of Willis's celebrity as a foreign dandy extended and amplified the politics of the entrepreneurial fantasies he encapsulated as a celebrity at home. These fantasies first started to collect around Willis's early efforts to resemble his American social betters, the Proper Bostonians whose circles he penetrated as a precocious young author in the late 1820s. As a young man raised in a middle-class household that followed strict Congregationalist teachings, Willis longed to be accepted by what was then called "Proper Boston," the elite families whose sons went to Harvard, toured Europe, and belonged to the Unitarian church. With neither wealth nor rank behind him, Willis relied for his high-society claims not just on his literary talents, but on his attractive looks, his charm, and, most importantly, his genteel costume. In the 1820s in New England, luxurious clothing was still considered the exclusive right of the rich and was thought transparently to reference superior rank and breeding. Indeed, such reference was usually accurate. At a time when only the wealthy could afford to buy genteel items of dress, which were marked by their fine cloth, their bespoke tailoring, delicate stitching, and use of high-quality buttons and trim, clothing, perhaps more than any other feature of personal appearance and manners, announced one's access to wealth, good family, and training in the nuances of an elite life.[13]

Yet what seems to have made Willis an icon for the culture of entrepreneurial self-making was not, as one might expect, the extent to which he successfully blended in with Proper Boston, but the extent to which he stuck out. Whether because of his "naturally extravagant animal spirits,"[14] as he put it, or a secret suspicion that his acceptance by the gentry was strictly provisional, Willis brought to his strategies of resemblance a conspicuous flamboyance, an affectedness, that for observers gestured less at any sincere relationship with Boston elites than at its own strange lack of substance. The northeastern gentry of the 1820s itself engaged in colonial mimicry, drawing for its models of refinement on the latest British and continental fashions. But it did so to capture a continuity with the mystical authority and prestige of the originals. Willis's imitations, by contrast, seemed neither to point to Proper Boston nor beyond it to the culture of the metropolis. They seemed merely to assert their own stylish emptiness. From the time of his earliest fame in Boston, Willis seems to have presented in uniquely material form a figure familiar to modern historians but wholly absent from discussions of antebellum colonial nostalgia. Typified in popular accounts as little more than the sum of his lavish garments, Willis encapsulated for his audiences a common antebellum myth about a laissez-faire, consumer society: that a fluid social order dangerously breeds a populace whose appearance becomes unreliable as a gauge of character. In this myth, the subject of social mobility appears contentless to the extent that his or her surfaces fail to convey pregiven rank and hereditary character. Yet Willis's clothes were not solely about a lack of content. While Willis seemed to contemporaries to incarnate a new entrepreneurial type whose signature was a hollow core, both he and the discourse he generated insisted on the authenticity this hollowness enabled. Construed as fundamentally empty, Willis's imitative costumes were also construed as the repository of a mysterious unreadable fullness that endowed them with originary value.

Like other young men in Boston's fashionable circles, Willis dressed in the latest fashions, though unlike the scions of Proper Boston he incurred enormous debts to do so. He owned a costly "bottle green coat" and a "beaver." His younger sister, Sara Willis, who would later become famous as the author Fanny Fern, recalled (with a heavy dash of acid) how his visits impressed the teachers at her school, who remarked on "what a very *distingué* looking person he was."[15] And yet for observers of the day Willis's clothes invariably had about them a whiff of theater, of something overtly artificial and pasted on. Years later, George Ticknor Curtis remembered his conspicuous appearance at a Harvard commencement:

> The last vehicle in the procession, and as if a part of it, contained Willis, seated alone in his gig, dressed in a green frock-coat, white waistcoat, buff-coloured nankeen trousers, all supremely fine; his broad-brimmed Leghorn hat lay on the seat by his side. With an air of supreme nonchalance he tossed his reins to a hostler who stood there waiting for such chances, put a quarter into the man's hand, and told him to take Thalaba to a certain livery-stable. He then passed up the broad aisle in the wake of the procession, and if he did not ascend the stage and seat himself among the dignitaries, it must have been because there was no room.[16]

Whether Willis's clothes and manners were actually as ridiculous as Curtis's description suggests is difficult to know. Willis, however, did nothing to discourage such descriptions of himself. Declaring "There is many a fine thought lost to the world, like many a fine spirit, for want of a modish dress," he explained to his sister Julia, "[T]he *ornamental* is my vocation."[17] While the pages of Willis's first solo editorial venture, the *American Monthly Magazine*, paid lip service to what Fredric Cople Jaher calls the "Olympian posture" of such organs of elite Boston as *The North American Review*,[18] they also delighted in celebrating the superficial. A fan of the late-Regency dandyism popularized by Lord Bulwer-Lytton's 1829 novel *Pelham*, Willis filled his magazine with images of dandyish style accessories intended to augment his fashionable editorial self.

In his "Editor's Table" essays, for example, Willis pretends to write in a crimson-curtained study where he reclines in a great gilt chair, a relic of Versailles. He sips a glass of *Margaux* or sherry with a bowl of olives at his elbow. Nearby are his pet spaniel, "L.E.L.," who makes her bed in a pile of rejected manuscripts, a servant, "Alphonse," who sees to his comforts, and his "japonica," with its white flowers drooping lazily in the summer heat.[19] Writing his editorials, Willis rarely finds a metaphor that is not related to clothes and consumer luxuries. Remarking on beautiful new editions of classic books issued by London booksellers, Willis imagines they are in their "holiday suits." "It is really curious to take up a dainty, silken-covered, fashionable-looking volume, in linen paper and fair type, and find under it some old friend whom one has known, time out of mind, as an antique gentleman, venerable in worm-eaten parchment, and illuminated Roman." Willis goes on to describe how tempting these volumes are, listing them among other luxurious frivolities. "We can pass very heroically by your rare cameo, or your *recherché* bosom studs. A beautiful print is sometimes not irresistible. A dog, or a knowing whip, or a curiously set eye-glass, nay, a wine from Herculaneum even, or a thrice proven *Margaux*, may be let slide with philosophy. But a book—dear glorious old author whom you have hugged to your heart with delight . . .—to find *him* in silk and linen, his inner man not altered, and his outer as kindly as eye-water to your weakly optics—that is what we call a temptation!"[20]

Like Willis's buff-colored trousers and Leghorn hat, which through their sheer ostentation drew attention to the fact that he had no seat among the Harvard elite, these literary fopperies, which seemed to focus on fashion for the sake of fashion, emphasized for contemporaries not Willis's resemblance to the patrician circles to which he aspired but some fundamental difference from them. Instead of conceptualizing Willis as a failed approximation of Proper Boston, commentators pegged him as the pure accretion of the sartorial signifiers conjured in his apparent celebration of style for its own sake. Critics quickly shortened his first names, Nathaniel Parker, to the more sartorially relevant "Natty P." He was the target of dozens of lampoons and pamphlets that highlighted and laughed at his curling hair and "bandbox trim."[21] Imitation denotes a reference to some original, but Willis's exaggerated performance of New England upper classness was figured by observers—with Willis's help—as a failure of reference, less the representation of some prior authenticity than the assertion of a blank. The titles Willis chose for an early series of stories and essays, "Unwritten Poetry," "Unwritten Music," "Unwritten Philosophy," for all the earnestness of their contents, seemed designed to hint at his vacancy. When the editor of *Harvardiana* purported to have difficulty filling his pages, he comically imagined filling them with the nothing that was Willis. He could "severely criticise Willis's *unwritten* poems," he said, "and compare them with those which might as well have been unwritten."[22]

The tropes of nothingness, of meaningless suits of clothes that had no reference to a prior social order, were not peculiar to Willis. In transatlantic ethnic nationalism, clothes were hypothesized as indelible signs of a people's character; they transparently transmitted the moral and intellectual capacities of their wearers. But among middle- and upper-class urban populations in the United States, clothes also featured as sites of uncertainty. In the 1810s, as we have seen, the United States became the site of the world's first ready-to-wear men's clothing industry. Beginning as small shops and taking advantage of the voluminous transatlantic traffic in cloth, ready-made clothing establishments in New York and other major urban centers multiplied by the hundreds over the course of the 1840s and 1850s. By the mid-1850s, there were roughly a thousand ready-made clothing establishments in New York alone, including giant emporiums on Broadway that featured plate glass windows.[23] These were presumably the clothes that tourists pegged as gaudy and grotesque, their varied surfaces seeming to speak of their wearers' backwardness and lack of metropolitan pedigree. But in local urban myth, these clothes became not objects of scorn but objects of anxiety, places where character, instead of being openly announced, might be disguised. Especially after 1830, when cities in the northeast ballooned with new working- and middle-class populations, white middle- and upper-class U.S. society fixated on clothes as potential sites of effacement.

On the one hand, this fixation had a dark, anxious side. Historians agree that the northern United States underwent a radical transition in the antebellum period. Traditional societies had relied on networks of kinship and patronage to verify the identity of strangers. In a society governed by rank, the appearance of the body tended to reflect fairly accurately an individual's social station, wealth, and education. Genteel manners, a knowledge of modern literature, and an intimacy with the mysteries of expensive tailoring were not easy skills for traditional poor or middling classes to attain. But with its newly crowded urban landscapes, its freewheeling capitalist economy, its unstable banking systems, its early adoption of modern commercial sales tactics, like advertising, and its revolution in clothing accessibility, the antebellum north saw the disintegration of these old, fail-safe techniques of divining character. In Michael Rogin's words, "Status, family, historically rooted relationships, and the insignias of dress [had] marked a person's identity in traditional, stable societies. Modern strangers who came together to buy, to sell, and to persuade revealed themselves by their performances."[24]

For conservatives and religious moralists, clothes and the visible appearance of the face, now potentially detached from easy legibility, emerged as new sites for anxiety.[25] Writing in 1851, popular novelist and advice author Timothy Shay Arthur idealized a "Golden Age," before the age of modern hypocrisy and deception, in which people's thoughts and feelings were faithfully transmitted upon their faces. In those days, "[Man's] face was the index of his mind—the table upon which all he felt and thought was written." Man's "eye" was "the perfect mirror of his mind, at a single glance sealing his lips into silence."[26] Now, however, the American landscape was contaminated with "false appearances." "Instead of acting in open daylight, pursuing the direct and straight-forward path of rectitude and duty," said advice lecturer Joel Hawes, "you see men, extensively, putting on false appearances; working in the dark, and carrying their plans by stratagem and deceit."[27] For moralists, those who pretended to gentility and high rank were a particular danger. According to Henry Beecher, the genteel impostor easily escapes detection among those who trust stylish forms. He "has a fine form, and manly beauty. . . . With notable diligence he ransacks the market for rare and curious fabrics, for costly seals, and chains, and rings. . . . Thus caparisoned, he saunters in fashionable galleries, or flaunts in stylish equipage, or parades the streets with simpering belles." Soon innocent young men can be seen imitating this suavely dressed imitator. "Copper-rings, huge blotches of breast-pins, wild streaming neckerchiefs, jaunty hats, odd clothes, superfluous walking-sticks, ill-uttered oaths, stupid jokes, and blundering pleasantries—these are the first fruits of imitation!"[28] Mere "animated puppets,"[29] "phantoms" whose lives are "a blank," these figures, like so many disembodied suits of clothes, walk the streets.[30] "We know but few men," Thoreau complained in *Walden*, "but a great many coats and breeches."

These fears of fraudulent appearance were famously crystallized and satirized in Herman Melville's 1857 novel *The Confidence Man: His Masquerade*, in which a swindler wearing various disguises amiably strolls the decks of a Mississippi riverboat, utterly undetected, looking for victims for his financial scams. Highlighting the logical extremes of a world in which clothes have become unhinged from any relationship to the character of their wearers, Melville's novel replicates for the reader the experience of moving through a world of "false appearances." In the course of the novel, we are presented with descriptions of the surface appearance of a long series of seemingly unrelated figures—a disabled Black performer, a blonde man in a fleecy hat, a man in a widower's weed, a man in a mustard coat. The reader eventually guesses that these must all be the same confidence man in various disguises. Disorienting in its formal insistence on the withholding of positive character, the *Confidence Man* literalizes the world of empty, phantom clothes projected in moralist cautionary tales.

At the same time, the ability of clothes to potentially efface one's identity was treated by some antebellum commentators as a positive, revolutionary development, one that was absolutely critical to the growth of a healthy democracy and meritocracy. In the revolutionary era, U.S. patriots had famously politicized British consumer imports, especially luxury cloth. In U.S. republican discourse, the renunciation of luxurious clothing was a sign of a dawning democratic modernity. Rejecting the "bloated pomp" of aristocratic and monarchical tradition and dressing instead in plain, undecorated homespun, late eighteenth-century revolutionaries declared their affinity for a new civic order based on equality of appearance, an equality guaranteed by the divestment (both symbolic and literal) of costly sartorial ornament and decoration. In the new democracy imagined by nineteenth-century proponents of widespread ready-to-wear clothing, dress would still be a sign of equality. But in this case, men, whatever their class, would all be dressed well in silk waistcoats and fine broadcloth coats. In these fantasies, the effacement of identity effected by the replacement of traditional intimate encounters with atomized marketplace relationships was a necessary element in the evolution of free-market liberal democracy with its goal of self-made selves. If the modern urban world was filled with mysterious strangers and anonymous suits of clothes, this was all to the good. To be sure, as both symbol and urban myth, the confidence man, in Rogin's words, "calls attention to the fictionalized, self-constructed character of American life. The confidence man exposes the absent core of marketplace reality itself."[31] But linked to the ideal of individuals and identities floating in a mobile economy, the mythically absent core of the marketplace subject conjured the possibilities of a citizenry equitably constituted by clothes alone. This ideal of a "democracy of dress" was trumpeted forth in new urban menswear magazines. In Zakim's words, "[I]n an industrial age devoted to artifice and material abundance and to the consequent weakening of fixed hierarchies, fashion presented a unique opportunity to create a common ground. Its ability to elicit voluntary compliance—to bring an individual to easily forfeit some of his hallowed independence in order to join the reigning mode—made fashion a form of governance: a system of majority rule for a polity that located sovereignty in the free will of every citizen."[32]

Not surprisingly, Willis was among those who celebrated the democratic potential of clothes. An early arbiter of urban U.S. taste, Willis was a bold champion of the culture of self-making and social mobility. He observed in 1843, "the age is, perhaps, forever gone by, when a privileged class could monopolize finery of garb; and, of all the civilized nations, it were least possible in ours."[33] But precisely because he materializes so perfectly the urban myth of empty clothes, Willis also illustrates some important features of this myth that historians typically miss. For both nineteenth- and twentieth-century commentators, the democracy of dress involved the emptying out of positive characteristics such as ancestry, inheritance, religion, and tribe; the clothes come to speak for a wearer divested of positive identity. Willis's case suggests, however, that what remained after this divestment or emptying of positive substance was not a strictly empty husk.

It is worth emphasizing here the extent to which Willis, not only in the 1820s but throughout his career, featured in the antebellum imagination as a kind of crystallization of evacuated substance. Indeed, as if he couldn't be imagined as anything other than a shell, he is rarely represented in antebellum discourse in anything *but* sartorial rhetoric; almost no account exists of him that does not contain, whether benignly or maliciously, some reference to his dress. From Oliver Wendell Holmes, who recalled Willis and his brand of dandyism as "something between a remembrance of the Count D'Orsay and an anticipation of Oscar Wilde," to John Moncure Daniel, who pronounced Willis "the man milliner of our literature," from Lydia Maria Child, whose memories of her brief flirtation with Willis singled out his "tall white hat, buff vest and new light-colored French gloves; all in the pink of the mode," to James Parton, who remembered his first glimpse of Willis and the impression made by his "extremely peculiar jacket," "a remarkably pretty garment of dark blue and white stripes," Willis's contemporaries thought of him as the shallow sum of his sartorial surfaces.[34] Indeed, so indebted was Willis to his clothes, according to James Russell Lowell, that even naked he would seem fully dressed. "He's so innate a cockney, that had he been born / Where plain bare skin's the only full-dress that is worn, / He'd have given his own such an air that you'd say / T'had been made by a tailor to lounge in Broadway."[35]

Members of Willis's family were no less convinced there was nothing to him but his clothes. Ruthlessly satirizing her brother in *Ruth Hall* in the wake of their permanent falling out, Fanny Fern asked the public, "Do you suppose . . . there *can* be anything to a man who wears fancy neck-ties, a seal ring on his little finger, and changes his coat and vest a dozen times a day? No; he's a sensuous fop, that tells the whole story."[36] To this, Willis himself might have agreed. To an extent that is unusual for this period, his private letters to friends are full of descriptions of his clothes, his "bottle green coat," his "opera gloves," his "Christmas vest." In one of his *American Monthly* editorials, Willis imagines what it would be like to review his own book. The published book, Willis decides, is the author dressed up in alien clothes, so that looking at it "He is like the peasant child taken and dressed richly; he does not know himself in his new adornments."[37]

And yet, while not precisely evincing a positive social identity, Willis's clothes did not at the same time give the sense of an utter lack of habitation. To the extent that the mythical go-getter as early antebellum traditionalists represented him could not be mapped within existing networks of signification, he featured in antebellum urban myth as a blank, a "suit of clothes," in Thoreau's words. But rather than depicting the self-maker as a failure of signification precisely, antebellum traditionalists tended to characterize the flatness and emptiness of his purely visual surfaces as potentially *too* significant. Offering nothing in the way of positive meaning, they created space for the proliferation of fantasy and interpretation. Warning innocent citizens of the influence of the confidence man's near relative, the demagogue, Henry Ward Beecher specified that the demagogue was utterly without substance. "For a profitable popularity he accommodates himself to all opinions, to all dispositions, to every side, and to each prejudice." But what makes the demagogue frightening in Beecher's mind is the extent to which his emptiness provokes observers into projecting their own meanings onto him willy-nilly. "He is a mirror, with no face of its own, but a smooth surface from which each man of ten thousand may see himself reflected."[38]

A similar provocation to interpret, fantasize, and project seems to have been energized by contemporary typifications of Willis as an empty suit of clothes. For even while contemporaries deplored Willis and used his example to warn of the moral dangers of embracing empty form over positive social content, these very condemnations, with their emphasis on Willis's flatness and emptiness, seem to have generated the meaning-making activities that traditionalists feared. For Willis himself, by extension, his emptiness ultimately formed a site of identity and self-affirmation. However flat and reflective, the "mirror with no face of its own" was endowed by virtue of the powers of interpretation and projection with a mysterious, almost magical, depth that enabled the postulation of a self behind the costume. And to the extent that this hypothetical self was premised on a blank, on the failure of fixed cultural references, it could be pegged as culturally original.

Even as Willis's contemporaries imagined that he was nothing but the sum of his clothes, this idea seems to have provoked a conviction that there must be more to him than meets the eye. At the most general level this conviction manifested itself in the extraordinary quality of Willis's celebrity itself. Even while in Boston and a figure of minor renown, Willis was constantly talked about, gossiped about, publicly lampooned, satirized, critiqued. Later in his career he was distinctive for the legions of fans he collected, the feverish adulation, condemnation, and obsession he inspired. By the end of his life, despite that he was considered a mediocre literary talent, he had been more written about than any other author of his generation. But apart from this general sense that Willis was a topic needing constant inquiry, the conviction that he was the sum of his visual surfaces produced the powerful suspicion that he led a secret life beyond the visual realm. When Poe satirized Willis in "The Duc de L'Omelette," he represented him as a man who would not—because, by implication, he could not—take off his clothes. Sent to the fiery mansions of hell and ordered by the devil himself "to strip," the Duc cries, "Strip, indeed! . . . no, sir, I shall *not* strip. Who are you, pray, that I, Duc de L'Omelette, Prince de Foie Gras . . . should divest myself at your bidding of the sweetest pantaloons ever made by Stultz, the daintiest *robe de chambre* ever put together by Rombêrt—not to mention the taking my hair out of paper—and all to gratify your bloodthirsty propensities!"[39]

But as if this fantasy of impossible striptease only provoked the suspicion that something must lie beneath Willis's unremovable "pantaloons," the idea that Willis was nothing but his clothes was complemented by an equally compelling conviction that when no one was looking Willis removed his clothes easily and too often. Not only during his tenure in Boston, but throughout his career Willis was the subject of an endless stream of furtive gossip and not so furtive scandal that focused on his sexual and erotic life. Some of this seems to have had its origins in fact, for Willis was known in Boston for his affairs with women. Willis also sometimes writes as if to seduce his readers. In the Editor's Table of the *American Monthly Magazine*, he invites readers to take off their metaphorical coverings in his company. "We are sure you are no *precieuse*, and there can be no earthly harm in our stopping aside this stiff, masquerading world, and taking off our dominos for a quiet half hour together. Our brief calendar of years has been written too much 'in red letters' to have made this buckram suit sit easily upon us."[40] But the sheer size and numerousness of the scandals—the accusations of adultery, libertinage, seduction of female readers—went well beyond objective evidence.

Unmoored from facts, the commentary on Willis's sexual life intimated that he worked in realms that escaped the factual. One lampoonist, in tropes that suggest the fantastic quality attributed to Willis's secret life, likened him to "Shakespeare's ass" who earned by magic the "kiss" "of "many a half-bred miss."[41] Associated not with positive cultural attributes but with the unknowable realms posed by his overornamented clothes, Willis's sex life was characterized as something that escaped language, even the language of the gutter. As Horace Mann put it, Willis's "wickedness must, perforce, remain unpublished, because common depravity has neither organ nor emblem to communicate it."[42] In their very exaggeration, contemporary accounts suggest the potency of the fantasy of mysterious meaning that Willis's unadulterated surfaces inspired. To the extent that he was imagined as all clothes, Willis offered to contemporaries a teasing intimation that he existed in some ineffable region beyond them, in what one critic suggestively called a "twilight of decency."[43]

There is much to suggest that Willis himself harbored a similar fantasy. Like his contemporaries, he characterized style for its own sake as a referentially empty surface that gestures at an unseen mystery beyond it. Modern democracy, according to one of Willis's early essays, had undone traditional terms of legibility. In earlier times, in Sir Walter Raleigh's day for instance, "the love of letters was another name for *humanitas*—gentle breeding." Modern writers like Willis, however, do not in his opinion evince this same transparency between "gentle" literary pursuits and "gentle breeding." They are "moulded" of "coarser clays." If their "gentle" pursuits are empty, in the sense that they no longer point to legible social categories, they are also significantly opaque. They have an "inward light" that "does not now, as in [Raleigh's] time, shine through."[44] That Willis characterizes the "inward light" of the modern author as a property not so much imputed as concealed by the "coarse clay" of the subject's surfaces suggests the extent to which for him the projected region behind the author's surfaces has a kind of autonomy and consistency of its own; however culturally inchoate and illegible, it forms the site of a subjective "inwardness." Willis's idea that surfaces not only imply but, in some sense, actualize interiority explains the peculiar personal investment in clothes displayed in his private correspondence. By offering himself even to friends and family as the sum of his "ornament," Willis may insist on his own vacuity, but insofar as that vacuum invokes the powers of imputation, Willis also, in a manner of speaking, fills himself up. He endows himself with the richness and dimensionality that seem to hover just behind the flatness of style for its own sake.

While Willis's imitation of his social betters vaguely conjectured his consonance with early antebellum elites, it also had the more dramatic effect of scripting his distinctiveness and difference. To the extent that Willis's imitative clothes, in their failure to convey the culturally instituted essence of upper classness, only posed their own superficiality, they offered the possibility of a mysterious self beneath the superficial surface, a self that was distinctive precisely because it seemed to have been born in a cultural and linguistic blank. Imitation, according to this logic, was not necessarily a capitulary gesture, nor was it a nod to an existing norm or prior authenticity. Imitation could postulate a kind of alternative or counterauthenticity—an other-realness—premised on the purely intuited presence haunting the hypothetical space behind the bubble of surface appearance.

The Imitation Game

Now it is useful to look more closely at the notions of cultural imitation at work in Willis's celebrity, especially given my emphasis here on the operations of costumes and imitations. Scholars of mimicry and imitation, from Homi Bhabha and Judith Butler to Monica Miller and Michelle Ann Stephens, tend to focus on the likeness or play of resemblance between imitators and the objects of their imitation. In these studies, the political energies of any given scene of imitation lie in the ambiguous places where the imitation fails to capture the idealized authenticity of the object. In Homi Bhabha's "Of Mimicry and Man," the colonial "mimic man" is the subject of a difference that is "almost the same but not quite."[45] Captive in the colonizer's gaze, he aspires to blend into the symbolic order, the order of the "Other." The condition of his subjectivity is that he can never blend in; he is, in Bhabha's famous turn of phrase, "*Almost the same but not white*."[46] But the political energy of mimicry, these scholars argue, comes from this same failure. Writing on the figure of the black dandy, another kind of mimic figure, Miller argues that it is "in this slippage, the space between repetition and difference, that the dandy finds and accrues power."[47]

But, leaving aside the question of racial difference, which I will address shortly, Willis's celebrity suggests that something other than resemblance or repetition was at work in his imitation of local elites. In Bhabha's account, the surface of the body is understood as a site of transmission where the colonial subject's failure to attain perfect oneness with the metropolis is made legible in an ongoing imperfect performance of metropolitan whiteness. What seems to have been exploited in Willis's celebrity, by contrast, is the question of what happens when the transmission of imperfection from the mimic to the viewer is short-circuited or led astray. In Willis's case, the viewing eye does not comprehend Willis as part of a larger class or national scene in which subjects strive to model themselves on a civic or class ideal; commentators never mention Boston elites when they discuss Willis. Instead, the eye of the viewer stops at the surface of Willis's body—his peculiar jacket, his seal rings, his tall white hat—unable to establish the play of likeness and ambivalence that makes the act of imitation possible at all.

The work of scholars like Bhabha and Miller, as well as more traditional historians of gentility and refinement, assumes that minoritized class, race, and gender imitators seek to belong to a stable social group from which they are excluded. It is unclear, however, that Willis and the other figures in the mythical landscape of American self-making had "fitting in" in mind. As the term "self-made man" acquired currency in northern popular culture in the 1830s, it postulated the existence not of a recalcitrant social hierarchy into which the self-made man, once having achieved wealth, slotted himself, but rather a whole society of radical nonconformists. The chief metaphors used to describe a social scene of radical self-creators tended to involve not pretension and imitation, which suggest hierarchies already in place, but, as we have seen, imposture, theater, and masquerade. Antebellum entrepreneurial and self-making figures, according to one contemporary, all acted in an urban "theatre of humbug."[48] Willis's form of imitation thus appears to have seemed for contemporaries like the equivalent of a stage or masquerade costume. Willis, his contemporaries seemed to conclude, was like someone *dressed up as* a gentleman. In this context, the costume conjures a generic type without being burdened with expectations of verisimilitude.

Now it is important to stress that the stage performance or masquerade has a very different set of semiotic conventions underpinning it than does sincere self-presentation or sincere imitation. Most obviously, there is no expectation that costumes are signs of their wearer's inner character or birth. On the contrary, as Jirí Veltruský underlines, theater costumes tend to be uncomplicated, to utilize only two or three signs—say, the crown of kingship, the robes of a priest, the disheveled hair of the clown—according to the needs of a "given dramatic situation."[49] What is fascinating to viewers about the person wearing a theater or masquerade costume is not the play of resemblance between the costume and some authentic prior image; no one at a costume party stops to wonder whether a person in a vampire costume actually resembles a vampire. In these cases, fantasy space is generated not around ambivalent resemblance but around a mechanism of blocked or distracted perception, in which the viewer's eye is stopped by cosmetics or costume from comprehending the person in their unmediated sincerity.

Unlike Bhabha's mimic men, who remain peripheral figures struggling to fit in, the masked characters who peopled the landscape of antebellum self-making culture were arguably figures of power, their dominion contained precisely in their ability to distract or thwart perception within an accepted semiotic scene. Indeed, as I will show, these figures were associated not just with metaphorical masquerades and impostures but with the literal theater and with popular entertainments that schooled northern U.S. populations in the instability of class, illustrating through illusions and sleights of hand the power to be had from self-creation, which was offered in these shows as a kind of visual trick. In this sense, Willis did not seek to approximate Proper Boston but to develop an alternative mode of imitation based on the originality made possible when perception was blocked.

Tricks with Clothes

We can better understand how exactly this mechanism of broken perception might have operated to establish Willis's autonomy if we look for a moment at two works by Nathaniel Hawthorne, his 1836 short story "The Minister's Black Veil" and his 1850 novel *The Scarlet Letter*. Hawthorne's tales do not feature imitation, but they both have at their center a garment—a black veil in the one story and an "A" made out of red cloth in the other—that blocks or inveigles the viewing eye in much the same way that Willis's overelaborate clothes were purported to do. Small and seemingly unimportant, these garments feature in the tales as unnecessary or ornamental additions to suits of clothes normally worn. Apparently because they do not fit any prior norm or expectation, these sartorial items have an inordinate effect on the intersubjective network of viewers, causing a warp or distortion of the symbolic field as soon as they enter it. In both stories, the entry of the sartorial item into the intersubjective scene is depicted as a sudden, unexpected visual blockage or distraction that beguiles the look of the viewing subjects and prevents them from making positive judgments about the wearer. In both stories, moreover, the wearers of these pieces of clothing suddenly acquire surreal dimensionality, becoming altered, eerie, and even revolutionized entities, as fantasy space dilates around them. Although not directly related either to class or ethnic and racial systems, the black veil and scarlet letter offer an introductory insight into the mechanisms of thwarted viewing and radical autonomy activated in Willis's celebrity and, as I will show, ultimately repurposed for ethnic and national designs.

In the first story, the "Minister's Black Veil," an ordinary, unassuming minister in a little New England town turns up to church one Sabbath with what Hawthorne calls a "slight" alteration to his clothing.[50] The Reverend Mr. Hooper is "dressed with due clerical neatness," but he wears a strange piece of clothing. "Swathed about his forehead, and hanging down over his face, so low as to be shaken by his breath is a black veil" (38). The veil is nothing extraordinary in and of itself. It "consists of two folds of crape" (38), "such as a woman might wear on her bonnet" (41). But it hangs over Mr. Hooper's face so as to "entirely conceal[] his features, except the mouth and chin" (38). The townsfolk are "wonderstruck." "Few could refrain from twisting their heads towards the door: many stood upright, and turned directly about; while several little boys clambered upon the seats, and came down again with a terrible racket" (39). The townsfolk set about immediately coming up with theories about the veil's meaning. Why is he wearing it? Has the Reverend Hooper lost a loved one? Has he acquired a disfiguring feature on his face or lost his virginity or gone mad? Neither the villagers nor Hawthorne's readers ever learn. Hooper goes to his grave decades later, still inexplicably wearing the veil.

With his facial features hidden beneath a piece of black cloth, Mr. Hooper undergoes a transformation. In the opening scene of the tale, as he describes the little town on an ordinary Sabbath morning, Hawthorne emphasizes the socializing function of clothes. "Children, with bright faces, tript merrily beside their parents, or mimicked a graver gait, in the conscious dignity of their Sunday clothes" (37). Clothes here are instruments through which emerging subjects "mimic" or perform a social role; clothes weave the children into a unified symbolic scene of prospective adult citizenship. But it is precisely this scene of clothing as performance of social identity that Mr. Hooper's black veil suddenly disrupts. Inserting itself between viewer and object, the veil thwarts perception, blocking the transparent transmission of character that is supposed to obtain in a regime in which clothes function as signs of the self. Moreover, instead of resulting in a scene of social incoherence or the ejection of the overclothed subject from the social fabric, as we might expect, the blockage of sight issues in a dilation of fantasy space and an enlarging of Mr. Hooper's power and presence. In the words of one observer, "He has changed himself into something awful, only by hiding his face" (38).

Like Willis, who seems to lead a life of profligacy behind his overornamented clothes, Mr. Hooper acquires a kind of surreal hidden life behind his veil. The first time Mr. Hooper delivers a sermon while wearing the veil, "[a] subtle power was breathed into his words." Watching him, "Each member of the congregation . . . felt as if the preacher had crept upon them, behind his awful veil, and discovered their hoarded iniquity of deed or thought." "So sensible were the audience of some unwonted attribute in their minister, that they longed for a breath of wind to blow aside the veil, almost believing that a stranger's visage would be discovered, though the form, gesture, and voice were those of Mr. Hooper" (40). Like Willis, who is thought to lead a magical, "twilight" life out of the public eye, Mr. Hooper seems haunted and otherworldly, filled with unfamiliar powers and energies. His presence in a room is "like a sudden twilight in the air." Enclosed behind his black veil, he is a person, seemingly, of "awful power" made "ghost-like from head to foot" (43–44).

Whereas the minister's black veil stages the blockage of perception—the literal blocking of the line of sight between viewer and face—the *Scarlet Letter* stages a subtler but still potent interference in the intersubjective array of visibility. Like "The Minister's Black Veil," the *Scarlet Letter* is about the powers of clothing to radically derange a social or political scene, insofar as that scene depends for its coherence on a belief that clothing transmits reliable information about its wearer. In this case, the scene is the Puritan Massachusetts Bay Colony in the late seventeenth century. The novel opens with a picture of garments. "A throng of bearded men, in sad-colored garments and gray, steeple-crowned hats, intermixed with women, some wearing hoods, and others bareheaded."[51] The Puritans, whose drab clothes match their sour personalities, are obsessed with a transparent correspondence of garments and moral character, hence their branding of Hester Prynne, an adulteress, with a large letter "A," an item made out of red cloth and permanently pinned to the front of her dress. Defiant of the Puritan community, Hester spends her time in prison changing the appearance of the stark red piece of cloth, adding to it "fantastic flourishes of gold thread," which she contrives with a "gorgeous luxuriance of fancy" (53). When she confronts the Puritan community for the first time, it is this new glittering, red and gold "A" that is emblazoned on her breast.

Here again, as in the "Minister's Black Veil," the unexpected addition of a decorative item to a suit of clothes—in this case, the fanciful gold embroidery across the face of what should be an unornamented red "A"—suddenly deflects and distracts the interpreting eye. At the start of the novel, Hester is forced to stand with the "A" on her breast in the "market-place" so as to display her sinfulness (which has been made living flesh in her newborn baby). Instead of transmitting a transparent moral lesson, the newly embroidered "A" obtrudes itself upon the sight of the villagers. "But the point which drew all eyes, and, as it were, transfigured the wearer,—so that both men and women, who had been familiarly acquainted with Hester Prynne, were now impressed as if they beheld her for the first time,—was the SCARLET LETTER, so fantastically embroidered and illuminated upon her bosom" (53–54).

"Glittering in its fantastic embroidery" (160), the embellished letter is a distraction to the eye, short-circuiting the transmission of information about Hester's morality and initiating instead a proliferation of fantasy space, of vertiginous meanings and possibilities. The spectacle of Hester's shame is invested with "awe" (56). Finding the letter in the 1840s, two centuries later, the narrator of the *Scarlet Letter* reports, "My eyes fastened themselves upon the old scarlet letter, and would not be turned aside. Certainly there was some deep meaning it, most worthy of interpretation, and which, as it were, streamed forth from the mystic symbol, subtly communicating itself to my sensibilities, but evading the analysis of my mind" (31). And here again, as in the case of Willis and Mr. Hooper, the wearer of obtrusive or distracting clothes acquires surreal dimensions, seeming to live an otherworldly existence; the scarlet letter "had the effect of a spell, taking [Hester] out of the ordinary relations with humanity, and inclosing her in a sphere by herself" (53–54). In later years, as the town grows accustomed to seeing Hester while remaining estranged from her, "the scarlet letter had the effect of the cross on a nun's bosom. It imparted to the wearer a kind of sacredness, which enabled her to walk securely amid all peril" (163).

Moreover, in both the "Minister's Black Veil" and the *Scarlet Letter*, Hawthorne intimates that these tricks with clothes do more than simply thwart perception of the wearer by a viewer. They inaugurate new signifying circuits and thus new subjectivities, retroactively actualizing a new subject, transforming the interior psychical composition of the wearer in radical and unpredictable ways. Thus not only is the town transformed by Hooper's veil, but so is Hooper himself. The veil "involved his own spirit in the horror with which it overwhelmed all others." The effect of the scarlet letter on Hester is "powerful and peculiar." "All the light and graceful foliage of her character had been withered up by this red-hot brand, and had long ago fallen away, leaving a bare and harsh outline, which might have been repulsive, had she possessed friends or companions to be repelled by it" (163). In her lonesome cottage, under the "lurid light" of her letter, Hester entertains "shadowy guests," "such as dared to enter no other dwelling in New England." She assumes "a freedom of speculation": "The world's law was no law for her mind" (164). In Hawthorne's work as in Willis's celebrity, in other words, trivial and meaningless garments contain powers of self-origination, in which new clothes really do in some sense issue in radically new selves.

In Bhabha's formulation, the mimic man, who must stand as a partial embodiment of Western presence, doomed to inferiority, remains subordinate to a symbolic and ideological reality determined by the colonizer. He is an "authorized version of otherness."[52] To be sure, his inability to perfectly personify the colonizer is also the instrument through which he threatens the colonial apparatus. "Under cover of camouflage, mimicry, like the fetish, is a part-object that radically revalues the normative knowledges of the priority of race, writing, history. For the fetish mimes the forms of authority at the point at which it deauthorizes them."[53] But still he remains the "fetish" of the colonizer. But in Hawthorne's stories this is not the case. Jacques Lacan's lecture "The Line and the Light," from which Bhabha takes the epigraph for his essay "Of Mimicry and Man," offers a more expanded version of mimicry, one that comports more with the operations of vision and surface we see in Hawthorne and ultimately, I will suggest, in Willis.

In fact, Lacan's essay is not about imitation or even mimesis but about the technical operations of vision in intersubjective communities based on signs. Lacan makes the case that what we see when we look at a particular scene is not the actual material world in any transparent or direct sense. We see instead a mise-en-scène arranged through reference to a "point of light." Lacan explains what he means with an anecdote. One summer, when he is a "young intellectual," he joins a working-class fishing crew, helping to harvest food for a nearby cannery. At one point, one of the fisherman points to a sardine can floating alone in the sea, "glitter[ing] in the sun," and says, "*Do you see that can? Do you see it? Well it doesn't see you!*"[54] The fisherman laughs but Lacan goes on to conclude that although the can doesn't see him, "it was looking at me, all the same." Lacan goes on, "It was looking at me at the level of the point of light, the point at which everything that looks at me is situated—and I am not speaking metaphorically."[55] What Lacan is saying here is that the subject's relationship to the visual field is organized by the illusion that something in the visual field looks back at him. In this anecdote, it's the sardine can glittering with light that looks back. Of course, the sardine can doesn't literally see Lacan. But at this particular moment, it forms what Lacan elsewhere calls a blot or "*objet a*" or anamorphic spot, the pure signifier around which both subject and intersubjective network are arranged. In Lacan's allegory, the sudden awareness that the sardine can, a "point of light," is potentially looking at him, creates the conditions for subjectivation. Seeing it, Lacan acquires consciousness of himself as an uncanny, dimensional self. At the same time, because of the incident with the sardine can, the whole scene Lacan describes—the dilapidated Brittany coast, the declining fishing industry, the tubercular fishermen, the "young intellectual" looking for authentic experience—suddenly acquires, for both Lacan and his readers, a set of layered political and aesthetic meanings it did not have before.

This seems to be the operation put into place by the black veil and scarlet letter in Hawthorne's tales. Indeed, Hawthorne's "The Minister's Black Veil" provides a powerful corresponding allegory to Lacan's tale of the sardine can. Nothing in and of itself, the veil is suddenly obtruded into the visual field of the New England parish and radically reorganizes the social and spiritual world of the community. Under the regime of the veil, the town funerals, christenings, weddings, and Sabbaths are all made more terrifying but also more meaningful, more spiritual by its presence. At funerals, the townspeople imagine that Mr. Hooper behind his veil is communing with the recently dead. At weddings, the veil, by reminding everyone of death and the afterlife, brings a kind of hallowed joy to the proceedings. The veil does not stand for anything. It is not a discernible symbol for anything. Nevertheless, in this tale it plays the role of the "point of light," the distracting warp in the symbolic order where the eye doubles back on itself. Like the sardine can, glittering in the sun, the veil suddenly organizes and produces a reality and subjectivity that did not previously exist. It seems haunted, filled with unseen meanings and dimensions.

In these accounts, accordingly, the question of fitting in, of the exclusion or insertion of the subject into an existing symbolic schema is irrelevant: the subject is originated at the moment the extraneous article of clothing attaches to their face or body and blocks or distracts the social world's conventional lines of sight. Moreover, what Hawthorne's tales intimate is that the fetishizing gaze is not located somewhere outside the subject in an ideological reality that subordinates the subject to itself. Rather, the gaze is built into the mise-en-scène. Hooper and Hester do not change the worlds they live in by trying to change the minds of the viewing public. They rather change the point of the gaze by changing what the public is looking at, and they do so in both cases by blocking or distracting the viewer's line of sight. The gaze, the thing that looks back at the viewing public, shifts to sit precisely in that spot that the eye of the public cannot penetrate.

These fantasies of spontaneous self-creation through the technical manipulation of signs and symbol systems were, as scholars have long understood, a central feature of antebellum mass entertainments. Crystallized in the shows of self-made impresario P. T. Barnum, antebellum entertainments offered audiences a chance to imagine themselves at the center of scenes of radical social alteration. Indeed, Hawthorne himself was one of many antebellum authors to make the popular connections among clothes, self-making, and the rehearsal of episodes of altered and revolutionary vision. Hawthorne's 1852 novel *The Blithedale Romance* features another "veiled" personage, "The Veiled Lady," a young woman "enveloped" from head to foot in a long veil of "silvery whiteness."[56] Instead of being a town worthy, like Minister Hooper, or an outcast, like Hester Prynne, the Veiled Lady is part of a traveling show. She appears in the town hall, along with "a rich and varied series of other exhibitions," including "the ventriloquist," with his mysterious voices, "the thaumaturgist . . . with his miraculous transformations of plates, doves, and rings," the "itinerant professor" with his "mannikins in wax, from Paris," "the choir of Ethiopian melodists," and the "diorama of Moscow or Bunker Hill."[57] In this passage, mysterious veiled or overclothed figures belong to the same scene of optical stimulation and illusion as the panoramas, wax figures, ventriloquists, and magicians who populated the world of antebellum entertainment. When the Veiled Lady appears on stage wearing a white veil over her entire head and body, she is an object of awe. As in "The Minister's Black Veil," the entry of a veiled figure into the conventional world and its audience causes at first a short-circuiting of information as the viewer's eye is stopped in the act of perception by the wall of the veil, and then a breathtaking, surreal expansion of fantasy space. The Veiled Lady comes to rest in a chair on stage. "Sitting there, in such visible obscurity, it was perhaps as much like the actual presence of a disembodied spirit as than anything that stage trickery could devise." Behind her veil, the Veiled Lady seems to her audience to vanquish traditional time and space; she can "hear the desert wind sweeping over the sands as far off as Arabia; the icebergs grinding one against the other in the polar seas; the rustle of a leaf in an East Indian forest."[58]

In this novel in particular, the veiled figure in her theatrical setting is expressly posed as an agent of social transformation. The Barnum-like "professor" who introduces the Veiled Lady speaks of "a new era that was drawing upon the world; an era that would link soul to soul, and the present life to what we call futurity, with a closeness that should finally convert both worlds into one great, mutually conscious brotherhood."[59] As in the case of the minister's black veil and the scarlet letter, unconventional bodily coverings, with their ability to upset conventional audience perceptions and create original subjectivities, here inaugurate new social experiments. Speaking on the intersection between clothes and radical social mobility in his famous book *The Art of Money Getting*, P. T. Barnum opined, "In this country, where we believe the majority ought to rule, we ignore that principle in regard to fashion, and let a handful of people, calling themselves the aristocracy, run up a false standard of perfection, and in endeavoring to rise to the standard, we constantly keep ourselves poor. How much wiser to be 'a law unto ourselves.'"[60] In Barnum's vision, the commission of "lawless" fashion decisions with their ability to perform a kind of magic on intersubjective scenes is the first step to class and personal autonomy.

Writing on the "cultural logic of the hoax" in the antebellum United States, Jonathan Elmer argues that Barnum's entertainments relied on the exploitation and exposure of the technical workings of visual and verbal sign systems. They developed what Elmer, quoting Barnum historian Neil Harris, dubs an "operational aesthetic." Reflecting "a culture-wide fascination with the technical," the "operational aesthetic" revolved around the contemplation of "how things worked."[61] Turning the era's often terrified fascination with fraud into what he called a "money-getting" enterprise, Barnum openly advertised exhibits as potentially fraudulent—was his "Feejee Mermaid" real or just a composite of fish and monkey parts?—daring audiences to spend money to judge for themselves. In paying money to see the Feejee Mermaid, antebellum audiences were not just invited to contemplate a mysterious pseudo-object and to develop fantasies about its provenance, but they were also indirectly paying to see the workings of their judgment itself, imagining themselves as spectators contemplating wholly original objects and being asked to decide on their veracity and merits. Introduced to the delightful contemplation of an object whose true nature was undecidable, audiences were asked to see themselves as judges seeing themselves.

Like Hawthorne, who draws attention to the eerie, almost transcendent quality of the Veiled Lady's presence on the stage, despite the creaky nature of the apparatus, Elmer emphasizes the overtly fraudulent nature of the object in many Barnum shows. In a famous episode that took place in Barnum's Museum on Broadway in the 1840s, Barnum, hoping to make more money by moving viewers through his museum more expeditiously, hangs a sign above a door that says "To the Egress." Thinking they were about to see an exotic creature called the "Egress," visitors would eagerly push through the door, only to find themselves in the museum's back alley, their tour over for the day. Elmer describes the fundamental trickery at the heart of this hoax. "The important thing to recognize in this operational aesthetic is the precarious status of the technological object itself. The accent is in fact not so much on the object as on its mechanism or mode of operation, and this is because the object's function is ultimately only that of a necessary complement of the process of judgment in which the spectator is engaged."[62] The pleasure taken in Barnum's exhibits turns on "a naïve assumption of reference: signs point to things, we imagine. . . . When we discover a void where there should be an object, we do not necessarily experience frustration; we may also experience a pleasure, arising from this circular motion in which we return to ourselves as both ourselves and other. This circular movement around an essentially misrecognized and voided object is the rudimentary trajectory of the cultural logic of the hoax. The object of representation is severely subordinated to its effect; the object—feejee mermaid or buffaloes in Hoboken—becomes disposable and of no interest once the representational logic in which it figures has come to visibility."[63] What was ultimately on display in Barnum's shows, in other words, was not the object but the representational logic of the exhibitionary scene itself.

What was emphasized in Willis's celebrity and Hawthorne's tales, correspondingly, was the ability of minor objects that distract the eye (gentleman's coat, black veil, scarlet letter) to overpower a viewing scene purely through their technical placement in the line of vision, insofar as vision itself was only contingent upon the symbolic circuits of the intersubjective network. Indeed, Barnum himself described his art in a way that coincides with these outsized sartorial techniques. Defining what he famously called "humbug," Barnum wrote, "[A]s generally understood, 'humbug' consists in putting on a glittering appearance—outside show—novel expedients, by which to suddenly arrest public attention, and attract the public eye and ear."[64] Willis's imitations of the Boston gentry, then, made use of these technical features of the early nineteenth-century semiotic field. Instead of mimicking the Boston patriciate and signaling his desire to belong to the dominant class, Willis's clothes, which announced their own excess and inappropriateness, suggested his distinctiveness from Boston's elites. By offering himself as a figure so artificial and distracting that he couldn't possibly hope to pass as the real thing, Willis effectively eschewed the time-honored grail of class aspiration—membership in the dominant class—and established himself instead as a distinct and separate entity. Inflated by the fantasy projections and surreal hidden lives purportedly generated by empty clothes, Willis offered himself as an entity independent of genteel approval and potentially mythical on its own terms. His clothes vaguely summoned up the gentry only so as to suggest that he had nothing to do with the gentry.

The Mask of the Folk

Now we need to stop here and ask how any of this might have interfered in what by this point were more powerful ideologies of biovisual race, ethnicity, and nationality. What difference did a mere badge or veil make in the visual arrays that elaborated ethnic and racialized subjects? As we saw in chapter 1, within ethnic nationalism, the clothes that any given people wore could only ever convey their existing national character. As a peripheral population, Americans were assumed to make clothing choices in accord with their inherent inclinations as an inferior people; they were similar to Thoreau's Irish, who instinctively choose "more" clothing. Americans were thought to love gaudy clothes, gold tinsel, ruffles, colors, and patterns. In this formulation, the addition of something like a black veil or gold-embroidered red badge to a given outfit would only have signified a more complete exemplification of the debased character of the American people. Indeed, within the rubrics of Western ethnic nationalism the sporting of seemingly superfluous items of clothing like veils or badges was precisely the sign of an inferior provincial people. And yet both *The Scarlet Letter* and other performance forms of this period suggest a mechanism through which this very addition of sartorial items produces a blocking and repositioning of the gaze, not just in the scene of relations among Americans at home but also in the scene of relations between Americans and other nationalities abroad.

The Scarlet Letter, for example, is often conceived not just as a vernacular drama but as a meditation on "America" as mythical entity. To be sure, *The Scarlet Letter* does not appear at first glance to have significant "ethnic" content. But if we remember that the English, along with other white populations in Europe, were defined as an ethnicity or "race," the novel's commentary on ethnic nationalist personality is not insubstantial. In fact, Hawthorne goes to great lengths to establish Hester as a model of English embodiment. Hailing from "Old England," Hester grew up in "antique gentility" under "a half-obliterated shield of arms." The English, according to Ralph Waldo Emerson, are a "robust race," typified by a "fine physique" and "personal rigor."[65] Hester has a strong frame and "dark and abundant hair." Her face has "the impressiveness belonging to a marked brow and deep black eyes" (59). Indeed, Hester's "ethnic" stamp is part of the genre convention here, for Hawthorne's Puritan tales, with their unfurling of romantic "legends" from the misty past and their "dark" heroines, were directly indebted to Scott. Hester is modeled on the defiant, dark-haired Flora from *Waverley* and the spirited, beautiful, Jewish Rebecca in *Ivanhoe*. In Hawthorne's words, Hester has "in her nature a rich, voluptuous, Oriental characteristic" (83). If Hester is also "American," then this "Oriental characteristic" in her presumably corresponds to what tourists saw as the regressive, primitive side of the American character.

What is important about the novel from my point of view, however, is that it dramatizes the failure of this transparent ethnic personality to materialize itself in the Puritan settler community and, by extension, in the transatlantic nationalist visual array that defines Hester's journey. The agency of this failure is, of course, the ornate scarlet letter. Intruded into the scene of Hester's first appearance before the Puritan community, the letter, with its strange "illumination," not only distracts those who see it, but it also implicitly short-circuits the transmission of ethnic signals from Hester to the viewing eye. Thus the moment in which Hester might be understood as an ethnic national subject on the model of Flora or Rebecca—the moment in which her appearance might faithfully transmit her character to onlookers—is disabled by the distracting glitter of the letter's gold thread. The letter assaults the viewing eye, stopping perception, making Hester strange and surreal. Moreover, as the novel proceeds, Hester's Englishness and "Oriental" character cease to exist. Lit by the "A," which stays pinned to her breast and casts a "lurid gleam" over her existence, Hester's original character, in its lush physicality, fades away. She loses her "robustness" and becomes a faint, spectral creature, pale and gray, a mere "bare and harsh outline" (163). Her "Oriental" qualities are not just blotted out in the scarlet letter's initial dazzle; they are vanquished and remain imperceptible as long as she continues to wear it.

We can better understand how this mechanism of blockage and distraction might have worked in a transatlantic scene in which Americans appeared as imitators of the British if we look for a moment at the many genres of antebellum entertainment that expressly featured the imitation of ethnic and racial populations. Most notorious, of course, is blackface minstrelsy. Among modern scholars, blackface minstrelsy is, justifiably, inseparable from the history and legacy of race-based slavery in the United States. But, as many scholars of early U.S. and British theater have pointed out, the first modern blackface characters came out of ethnic nationalist comedy theater, the same theater that gave birth to the "Yankee." Scholars generally hold that the first specifically *American* blackface character was Agamemnon in the British comedian Charles Mathews' *Trip to America*, developed from 1822 to 1823.[66] Precisely because the blackface genre had its roots in ethnic nationalist visual culture, it provides an important way of understanding how this culture's optics, which were organized not around bodies and skin surfaces but around clothing and adornment, could be manipulated to produce unconventional ethnic and racial hierarchies. Indeed, the existence of antebellum ethnic and race imitation genres allows us to understand how the distraction of perception might have been used to counter not just the viewing experience of U.S. entertainment's popular audiences, but also the more recalcitrant vision of the European touristic eye. For here again what we see if we look more closely at genres of race imitation is not the alteration of the object of the white ethnographic eye but an interruption or blockage in the field of vision that disables the clarity of the eye's perceptions and proliferates fantasy space.

Not surprisingly, given the often fierce intractability of biovisual racial ascriptions in the early nineteenth-century United States, clothing and costume, which are central to our analysis of class and metropolitan imitation, are not usually considered important aspects of race imitation.[67] Almost without exception scholars of race imitation focus on political and hierarchical relations that exist between the object and imitator *prior to* the addition of costume and makeup. Thus, for the majority of scholars, blackface minstrelsy, which features the literal blacking of the white performer's face with black, burnt-cork greasepaint, echoes and extends the already existing hierarchical relationships between the white performer and the Black body in the real world. In a sense, the paint in this scenario is incidental except as a kind of punctuation on what is already a densely racialized and hierarchized scene.

Yet one of the chief characteristics of blackface minstrelsy as it developed in the United States over the course of the early nineteenth century was that it was perhaps the one performance form in which the actual ethnic or racial descent of the performer was deliberately blocked from view. Although performed predominantly by white performers and musicians, blackface minstrelsy allowed for the possibility that performers of any ethnicity or race might be on stage instead. Indeed, at the end of the nineteenth century, Black performers like Bert Williams entered the segregated mainstream U.S. entertainment industry by painting their faces with the minstrel mask and starring in minstrel shows where they could not be detected among their white peers. Moreover, evidence suggests that this element of uncertainty—of the hiddenness of the performer—was helped by an elaborate costume, the artifact of the genre's roots in folk nationalism. The result was a scene not unlike that produced in "The Minister's Black Veil" or the *Blithedale Romance*, in which audiences watched a performer whose facial and bodily features were blocked from their view. As in Hawthorne's tales, the blackface performance involves the eye of the audience suddenly hitting a site that foils perception. Thus, one of the features of blackface performance, according to contemporary accounts, was the proliferation of fantasy space around the performer in a way that mirrors the operations at work around Willis's clothes. In this scenario, the imitator and the object of the imitation, instead of the one being an inferior echo of the other, change places, the imitator becoming a repository of eerie power.

One of the most famous accounts of blackface minstrelsy, penned by Robert P. Nevin and published in *The Atlantic Monthly* in 1867, begins with the performer's acquisition not of a black mask, precisely, but of an elaborate costume. Purporting to remember T. D. Rice's inaugural performance of the blackface genre in the early 1830s, Nevin recounts how Rice, taken with African music heard in the street, lured a Black man named Cuff to the theater and there, "having shaded his own countenance to the 'contraband' hue, ordered Cuff to disrobe and proceeded to invest himself in the cast-off apparel." Modern critics focus on Rice's blackened "hue" so as to investigate his relationship as a white performer to the north's Black population. But mentioned only once, Rice's make-up is not a special focus in this account. Rather, the account is preoccupied with Rice's clothes. Rice is "habited in an old coat forlornly dilapidated, with a pair of shoes composed equally of patches and places for patches on his feet, and wearing a coarse straw hat in a melancholy condition of rent and collapse over a dense black wig of matted moss." Suggested here is the idea that the burnt cork paint is merely one part of a larger project of sartorial bravado, of masking and over-ornamenting the body. And like Willis, whose overdone clothes produce the fantasy of his "twilight life," Rice is made magical by his clothes. Dancing out on stage in his elaborate costume, he is an "extraordinary apparition," his effect on the audience "instant" and "electric." Cuff, meanwhile, remains in this scene, not to show that he is "blacker" than Rice but that he is not as covered up. As Rice dances, Cuff runs onto the stage in "ludicrous undress" and demands the return of the clothes responsible for launching Rice's new career. "'Massa Rice, Massa Rice, gi' me nigga's hat,—nigga's coat,—nigga's shoes—give me nigga's t'ings!'"[68] Cuff serves to illustrate the fashion principle that, in this instance, more is more, that one of the figures in this scene is overdressed, made magical by his costume, while the other must make do with what nature gave him.

Now Nevin's account clearly resorts to conventional notions of the racialized subject as naked, and I do not want to suggest that blackface minstrelsy was not centrally about the mockery of a minoritized group. What interests me about this scene, however, is the way it produces a hierarchy that is not based on a black/white polarity, as we might expect of a show grounded in racial imitation, but on an undressed/dressed polarity created in the moment of the performance. It isn't just that Rice is an imitator. The stage and costume work a magic on Rice, transforming him into an unexpected figure of power, an "apparition." In this sense, nakedness does not necessarily issue from a larger ideological array in which Cuff's inferiority is already decided prior to his arrival on stage. Rather, the mask and costume produce their own sites of power and hierarchization. Eerily *more* than the visible total of their signifiers, masks and empty costumes can theoretically demote the status of the object simply by making it seem to contain something *less* than the imitation. Of course, in this instance, Cuff's inferiority is already decided, but it is important to stress that nakedness—unlike, for example, "blackness"—is offered here less as a function of prior biological attributes than as a formal or technological creation that takes place in the moment of the performance.

The workings of this imitative complex are likewise illustrated by James Fenimore Cooper in a comparable scene of imitation involving Indigenous people, the imitator in this case being Cooper's exemplary frontier hero, Natty Bumppo. Introducing Natty in *The Last of the Mohicans*, Cooper presents him not in a refreshing state of dishabille, as one might expect of someone who has left behind the trappings of civilization, but covered up to the eyes in the "rude and nearly savage equipments" of the native peoples he visits: a forest green "hunting shirt," a "summer cap of skins," a "knife in a girdle of wampum," "buckskin leggings that laced at the sides," a "pouch and horn," and moccasins, "ornamented after the gay fashion of the natives." The Indigenous people themselves, meanwhile, stand beside Natty "nearly naked." More than Nevin's account of Rice, Cooper's description of Natty (and one can't help but remark on the sartorial reference of Natty's name) suggests that nakedness is not so much a function of the absence of clothing as it is a function of the absence of interpretive opportunities. Natty's dress, says Cooper, is a "mask"; to assess him one must "judge" by "such parts as [are] not concealed by his clothes."[69] The Indigenous characters don't need to be conventionally naked (primitive, savage, etc.) to be naked. They can merely seem so next to the impenetrability of a "mask" that elicits "judgment" and produces mystery.

What these scenes elaborate, in other words, is a principle that potentially circumvents the pregiven hierarchies in a scene in which both subject and the object of imitation are, in fact, white. Precisely because masks and empty clothes intimated meanings in excess of mere appearance, they potentially had the power to bestow deficiency on even exalted objects. Next to empty clothes anyone could seem naked. It was Willis's opinion that while his own ornate and trumped-up narrative persona exposed nothing but implied much, the fashionable objects of his imitation revealed "the undress of the mind."[70] Empty clothes, in other words, could be marshaled in scenes of class and colonial imitation not as aspirational tools that express the longing of the subject for the purity of a dominant group but as a mask and cover-up whose lack of disclosure and uncanny magic confer power on the imitator.

It was this performance of radical self-creation, then, that Willis would embody in his transatlantic celebrity. In the 1820s and 1830s, Willis was a local phenomenon, one of many young men and women in the United States who sought to take advantage of the new transatlantic craze for literature by becoming famous authors themselves. Working in Boston in the late 1820s, Willis was connected to an extended network of writers, editors, and publishers who would go on to be the architects of U.S. mass print culture and who would help develop some of the mechanisms in the "operational aesthetic" that showmen like Barnum exploited. Willis was not only friends with elite writers like Henry Wadsworth Longfellow but also with more obscure writers: Park Benjamin, founder of the "mammoth" newssheets in New York in the late 1830s, and Joseph Snelling, a creator of the scandalous "flash" genre of sporting magazines. By the 1840s, Willis would be writing plays for the New York stage, employing Edgar Allan Poe on his magazine, *The Evening Mirror*, and colluding with Barnum on the promotion of transatlantic musical entertainment.

Willis's travels to Europe and England in the early 1830s helped to extend the fantasies of local entertainment to the realms of transatlantic tourism. Embarking for Europe in 1831 and alone among middle-class travelers of that period to attempt a genteel-style grand tour, Willis in one sense reorganized European travel and fashion for a bourgeois consumer constituency destined to balloon over the next two decades. What he offered this constituency was the freedom to indulge in fantasy and consumer desires. Unburdened of the oppressive weight of elite judgment, Willis modeled a subjectivity based on style for its own sake. Whereas patrician travelers and cultural nationalists looked upon European literary and material culture with both reverence and a fear of indebtedness, Willis and his clothes posed a model of imitation that handily circumvented class and national debts by insisting on its own surreal originality. At the same time, Willis's travels did more than simply sketch out a new regime of consumer appetite. The power of empty clothes to meddle with the ascribed identity not just of the imitator but of the object had a special relevance to what Cooper called Willis's "European mask." Although antebellum fads for imitating Old World culture get typified by historians as a regressive, still-colonial allegiance to Europe's authority, Willis's travels suggest that the reverse could be true. As the first traveler to export the vernacular rhetoric of costumes and masks to transatlantic scenes, Willis introduced the possibility of reorganizing existing political hierarchies between metropolis and settler colony in a way that not only refused cultural dependency but that figuratively reassigned the roles of Europe and America on what Willis liked to call the world "stage."

In the early nineteenth-century ethnographic imagination, metropolitan Europeans were distinguished by their elegant plainness and simplicity. Dressed in their monotone garments, they represented the apex of teleological history, their plain bodies the fail-safe transmitters of an alleged exalted purity, of human intelligence and civilizational refinement in their highest form. The ethnic or racialized body, by contrast, was doomed to explosions of color and garish ornament, its attempts to mimic the superior polish of the metropole fated to excess and overstatement, bound to transmit inferiority. But it was precisely the scrubbed clarity of metropolitan people that Willis denigrated. Equipped with a rhetoric and style of person that produced the unseemly nakedness of the other as much as the shimmering impenetrable mystery of the self, Willis's European "mask" drew on the traditional sartorial codes of empire to write back to the metropole, refiguring Europe as a backward, primitive world, destined to give way before what Willis depicted as a newly empowered United States. The site of this empowerment was the overdressed provincial subject. Armed with a local culture of radical self-creation that depended on the rearrangement of semiotic conventions in the visual field, Willis challenged the way Americanness was perceived. He helped to turn the traditional liability of the flawed imitation and overdone surface into an asset, transforming the ethnic and racialized body into the haunted mask of the culture of self-creation.

Willis in Europe

When Willis crossed the Atlantic in 1831, he sailed to a mythical "Europe," a place of grandeur and fearful authority that was very much produced for his generation by the sensibilities of the U.S. domestic patriciate. At a time when European travel was a luxury, only Americans with wealth, education, and leisure could afford to make the journey. The Old World of early republican gentry fantasy was a source of both deep anxiety and immense consolation. Members of the gentry revered the Old World with what Washington Irving described as "a hallowed feeling of tenderness and veneration, as the land of our forefathers—the august repository of the monuments and antiquities of our race—the birth-place and mausoleum of the sages, and heroes of our paternal history."[71] Developing a sort of genetic continuity with this history, Irving held that the great European cultural "fathers" had transmitted to their American "progeny" a "vital principle," like that essential for continuation of a "species."[72] Even those patricians less committed to Europe as an ancestral origin related their authority and prestige in their own country to their ongoing continuity with the English upper classes. As James Fenimore Cooper phrased it in his own 1830s travelogues, "Nothing is more natural than that one educated in American society, should feel a curiosity to see the higher classes of a country like England. Such a feeling would, under ordinary circumstances, be stronger perhaps, in the American accustomed to the really good company of his own country, than in another, for it would, in a degree, be necessary to his habits."[73] On the other hand, those like Cooper who had been weaned on the fierce iconoclasm of post-1812 U.S. nationalism tempered their adoration of Europe and England with a horror of cultural dependence, what Emerson would shortly call "our long apprenticeship to the learning of other lands."[74] Painfully aware of their provincial status and believing that true nationhood was impossible without an autonomous national culture, patrician nationalists, especially in the wake of the scorn of English critics like Sydney Smith, longed to create a dazzling homology of what Europe itself had produced.

But if Willis embarked for Europe burdened with these accepted models of response, he lacked the wealth and social position that formed their basis. Indeed, his trip was launched under the shadow of his exile from whatever social position he had managed to gain. In 1830 Proper Boston finally galvanized and effectively drove Willis from the city, fittingly citing crimes related to his clothes: the excessive debts that went with keeping them on his body and the "dissipations" that went with taking them off. Disgraced and deeply bitter at his treatment by what he called "naked America,"[75] Willis escaped to Europe in 1831 as the foreign correspondent for George P. Morris's *New York Mirror*. Not only did he arrive there with a revivified sense of his own lowliness, dubbing himself "a sometime apprentice at setting types," but, as he wrote his sister Julia, he arrived "without a *sou* in the world beyond what my pen brings me, and with not only no influence from friends back home, but a world of envy and slander at my back."[76] Unfortified by the essential materials of patrician tourism—rank, wealth, letters of introduction to influential people, and a lofty sense of entitlement—Willis's letters to the *Mirror* veered significantly from traditional responses to Old World scenes and personalities. His letter describing his arrival in England after a bad bout of seasickness might easily describe the revisionist work of the letters as a whole. "[I] had neither eyes nor disposition to indulge in the proper sentiment on approaching the 'white cliffs' of my father-land."[77] What Willis had in lieu of pedigree and "proper sentiment," however, were his extravagant clothes, good looks, and unflagging ambitions. And against all odds Willis managed to parley these into a social success that dazzled even him.

In some ways, Willis's success among European and British "notables" was not unlike his success among the Boston gentry, not least because Willis mounted a similar performance. Anxious to win double acceptance as both an American "gentleman" and a worldly "man of fashion," Willis paraded himself in the guise of a dandy poet and man of means. And possibly because he was more than ever aware of his own lowliness, Willis more than ever made a point of his mysterious "inwardness," a maneuver made possible in this case not just by a trick of fashion but by a trick of rhetoric, the screen of his correspondence. Even while Willis's letters to the *Mirror* constructed his spurious consonance with his European hosts, they situated his specular appreciation of them in the mysterious region beyond the visuality of his simulation. From this vantage point, Willis did more than simply admire the glamour of the Europeans. He undressed them. Drawing not only on what Willis candidly called his "milliner['s]" eye[78] but on the relatively new languages of scandal and exposé, Willis's letters postulated the power and supremacy of his own overdressed person over the naked legibility of those they purported to expose.

Whereas Washington Irving discovered in Europe the recovery of what he called his "cast" [*sic*],[79] Willis arrived there with the much more humble hope of merely worshipping at the feet of its luminaries, the group of literary, political and social celebrities who made up, in Willis's words, "the world of fashion and genius."[80] Armed with the nominal title of attaché to the American legation at Paris, a title procured for him by the Marquis de Lafayette whom he befriended in France, Willis quickly worked his way into Europe's most exclusive circles, attending the balls of the Grand Duke of Tuscany and the parties of the former king of Westfalia. But it was in England that Willis flourished most. Introduced by Walter Savage Landor to Marguerite Gardiner, the Countess of Blessington, one of London's leading hostesses, Willis was instantly nominated her protegé and became a regular guest at her famous and intimate parties, where he dined with all the global celebrities of Britain: Edward Bulwer-Lytton, Benjamin Disraeli, Thomas Moore, John Lambton, Earl of Durham, James Smith, Albany Fonblanque, John Galt, Lady and Sir Leicester, and, of course, the foremost dandy of the age, the Count D'Orsay, who was Lady Blessington's son-in-law.[81] These friends introduced Willis to others; he breakfasted with Henry Crabb Robinson and Charles and Mary Lamb, and he met with Lady

Byron and Augusta Leigh. He spent time not only with society in London, but at the country homes of men like the Earl of Dalhousie and the Duke of Gordon.

Perhaps even more than in Boston, where his well-known origins impeded his performance of upper-classness, Willis's success in England turned on his impersonation of the cosmopolitan man of fashion. Apparently devoid of the lofty expectations that soured Cooper, possessed of the exoticism of the foreigner, and outfitted in the dandy persona—complete with "high-heeled French boots"[82]—he had in the first place borrowed from Bulwer, Willis slipped with ease into fashionable circles. Blessington's friend and biographer, R. R. Madden, remembered him as "an extremely agreeable young man," "degagé in his manner, and on exceedingly good terms with himself and with the élite of the best society wherever he went."[83] Willis himself wrote his sister, Julia, "[A]ll the world in France, Italy and England treat[s] me like a son or a brother."[84] In an important way, moreover, the dandy persona chosen by Willis was not incidental to his success. As Ellen Moers underlines, the Regency dandy, born in the person of Beau Brummell in the giddy aftermath of the French Revolution, postulated a world governed by fashion instead of by titled aristocrats.[85] Years later, Willis himself paid tribute to this connotative insurgency. "Fashion, in England," he said, "should be named as a power, after King, Lords and Commons. It is . . . a class . . . formed exclusively from no other class—capable, as was shown in Brummell's time, of giving a slight to the blood royal, and in the constant habit of putting down rank that does not look like rank, and selecting nature's favorites from the people."[86] In a way that would shortly be made apparent, however, there was an important difference between the way Willis wore his dandyism and the way the men in the Blessington circle wore theirs.

Modern scholars of dandyism emphasize that while the Regency and Victorian dandy revised traditional standards of exclusivity, he did not revise the notion of a transparent correspondence between clothing and superiority. Like his earlier counterparts among the titled nobility, the European dandy's superiority was conveyed in the splendor and nuances of his dress, though these had ceased to refer to things like lineage or lands and now referred to the dandy's innate or natural supremacy. As Domna C. Stanton argues in her survey of dandyism in France, the details of the dandy's dress "fill an essentially synecdochic function. They do not only convey connotational and esthetic information; they reveal the nature of the emitter. To the informed receiver, the part announces the whole."[87] Or, as Balzac put it, "A man's mind can be divined by the way he holds his cane."[88] Touring Paris in the early 1830s, Frances Trollope noted how certain classes of Parisians self-consciously arranged their bodies as signal systems. "These gentry choose to leave no doubt upon the subject of their *clique*, but contrive that every article contributing to the appearance of the outward man shall become a symbol and a sign."[89] Like other bohemians before and since, men like Disraeli and even D'Orsay took their lavish clothes seriously as transparent signals of their supremacy as socialites, artists, and thinkers. While they asserted the theatrical dimension of clothes, for them theatricality meant an especially striking broadcasting of character, a form of self-display in which, as James Eli Adams writes, "a charismatic subjectivity or interiority . . . is bodied forth in verbal and visual disruptions of social decorum."[90]

Willis's dandyism, by contrast, while implicitly offered in his letters to the *Mirror* as the source of his ability to blend into fashionable circles, was also overtly scripted as a form of pretense that bore no relation to the "nature of the emitter." His letters gave the impression that even in the midst of the most intimate events he attended—even when he seemed most at one with his hosts and most at home in their company—he remained detached from his merely visible oneness with the occasion, secure in some region behind his impersonation, less an intimate of British socialites than a kind of spy among them. Breeching the codes of sociability and friendship, his letters cited verbatim confidential conversations he had heard or had. In one of his letters Thomas Moore is reported calling his absent friend Daniel O'Connell a "coward"; in another, Willis recites his conversation with John Wilson ("Christopher North") about the *Quarterly*'s editor, John Lockhart. "Do you know Lockhart?" Wilson asks. "No I do not," says Willis, "and . . . I have no wish to know him. . . . I probably have met a hundred of his acquaintances, but I have not yet seen one who pretended to be his friend."[91] Posing Willis's imitative mask as the generative instrument of a secret gaze the British could neither detect nor deflect, Willis's letters equally posed a contrast between Willis himself, securely locked behind the screen of his visual surfaces, and the legible transparency of his British hosts.[92] To the extent that the British were not the sum of their surfaces, to the extent that their gorgeous appearance was a mere synecdoche for the reality beneath, their glamourous clothes, Willis implied, could be removed.

Thus, while Willis's letters to the *Mirror* lovingly detailed for readers back home the exclusive balls and dinner parties he attended, while they exclaimed over the fame of the lions and notables he met, they also provided a running commentary on Old World luster as a thin veil on a disappointing truth. Staying at Gordon Castle, Willis noted that last night's "*soigné* man of fashion," "faultless in costume and distinguished in his appearance—in the full force of the term" showed up the morning after "in a coat of fustian, with a coarse waistcoat of plaid, a gingham cravat, and hob-nailed shoes . . . and in place of the gay hilarity of the supper-table, wore a face of calm indifference." Stripped of their evening dress, these aristocrats are a "plain party," many of their clothes "amounting almost to want of style."[93] If Willis was typified by his contemporaries as all style, his profligate body a phantasmal entity merely conjured by the ornamented surface of his appearance, Willis implied that his British hosts, with their removable style, were emphatically bodied beneath it.

Not only did his descriptions dwell on the "plainness" of the British, they emphasized the unfortunate physicality that plainness entailed. Describing Bulwer, author of *Pelham*, the "hornbook of dandies," Willis noted that he was "as ill-dressed a man for a gentleman as you will find in London," and, worse, he was "short" and "knock-kneed."[94] On his trip to visit the famous John Wilson who wrote for *Blackwood's* under the pseudonym, "Christopher North," Willis was surprised to discover "a large, muscular man, something slovenly in his dress" with an "exceedingly ample head."[95] He thought the queen "the plainest woman in her dominions, without a doubt" and observed that Lord Brougham had "a convulsive twitch" and an "unsightly pug nose."[96] Of the famous editor Albany Fonblanque, he wrote, "I never saw a much worse face—sallow, seamed, and hollow, his teeth irregular, his skin livid, his straight black hair uncombed and straggling over his forehead. . . . A hollow, croaking voice, and a small, fiery black eye, with a smile like a skeleton's, certainly did not improve his physiognomy."[97] Implicitly contrasted in such commentary was not just the distance between glossy reputation and grim reality, but the distance between Willis, empty, insubstantial, mysterious, and the members of fashionable society, stripped down to their naked essentials.

While the English thus appeared in the *Pencillings* in embarrassing undress, Willis's contrasting emptiness was emphasized not just by his rhetoric but also by the scandal he provoked. This scandal issued from the fact that Willis's characterization of himself as an imposter turned out to be more than merely rhetorical. While writing his letters to the *Mirror* Willis justified his candor by claiming that since he was publishing his letters in the far-off United States there was no harm in saying things he supposed the English would never read. But the English did read them. When Willis's letters were published in expurgated form as *Pencillings By the Way* in 1835, reviewers like Lockhart looked up the offensive originals and cited them in the British journals. The subjects of Willis's thoughtless observations, not only Lockhart, but Bulwer, Moore, and Fonblanque, were outraged, the more so because none of them had known that Willis was a journalist nor that he was publishing a diary of his travels; they had assumed he was an *attaché* and Willis had not informed them otherwise. Adding insult to these various injuries was an incident involving Captain Frederick Marryat that seemed to epitomize Willis's duplicity. In a letter to the *Mirror* in 1835, Willis included a postscript about the London book trade meant for George Morris's eyes only in which he noted, "Captain Marryat's gross trash sells immensely about Wapping and Portsmouth, and brings him five or six hundred the book, but that can scarce be called literature."[98] Morris accidentally published the letter in its entirety, postscript and all. This material evidence of the gap between what were now revealed as Willis's contradictory and potentially equally spurious public selves—dandy poet and low-rent journalist—contributed to the more general impression of the fraud he had perpetrated.[99]

Willis's exposés of the British centered on precisely those qualities that in conventional ethnographic discourse signified their superiority: their sincerity, their unvarnished plainness, their disregard of the rules of mere fashion. "The Frenchman," Ralph Waldo Emerson would observe in 1856, "invented the ruffle, the Englishman added the shirt" (89). Included in Emerson's admiring list of "English Traits" were "Plain rich clothes, plain rich equipage, plain rich finish throughout their houses and belongings"; these, says Emerson, "mark the English truth" (122). As we saw in chapter 1, this was the opposite of American "truth." Writing about her travels in the United States in the late 1820s, Frances Trollope dwelt on the garishness of American appearance. "The ladies . . . powder themselves immoderately, face, neck, and arms, with pulverized starch"; they are "partial to false hair, which they wear in surprising quantities"; they love expensive clothes but have no "taste" and "do not consult the seasons in the colours or in the style of their costume." Trollope reports, "I have often shivered at seeing a young beauty picking her way through the snow with a pale rose-coloured bonnet, set on the very top of her head."[100] Devoted to facial cosmetics, false hair, and random colors unrelated to seasonal propriety, Americans betray their parochial roots and inclinations. As a consequence, the U.S. intelligentsia invested in plainness as an ideal all the more, not merely for its connections to eighteenth-century republicanism but for its ties to what they believed were the highest orders of European civilization, orders easily attainable, the theory went, for select white Americans. In Emerson's opinion, the best Americans were those with English heritage. And because "It is in the deep traits of race that the fortunes of nations are written," Americans would soon be the equal of their "fathers" (137).

Willis's *Pencillings* clearly rewrote these polarities, turning English plainness into a sign of degradation and mysteriously withdrawing the "American" from familiar scenes of transatlantic interpretation. He did not offer himself to revelation and undress; he made it impossible for the British to say, as they said of Cooper, that he was merely a jealous, insecure colonial.[101] Indeed, the thing that mesmerized contemporaries, who scrambled to talk about what Willis meant, was his apparent immunity to classification. As was the case with Willis's celebrity generally, British and patrician U.S. commentary on his travels, which fixated on his "masked" form, generated the same fantasies and apparitions that haunted his local celebrity in

Boston, helping in the process to create the thing they feared: an empty, unscrupulous Willis, dangerous, unaccountable, voracious.

Patrician U.S. responses to Willis were the most straightforward in that they disowned him outright, claiming he was better seen as a European. As the *North American Review* put it, his writings "breathe a worldly and voluptuous spirit" that is "out of keeping with American thought, American morals, and American life."[102] The British press argued over whether Willis was a class or a national phenomenon. British journalists called him the worst sort of "toadeater" and drew attention to his degraded "birth, parentage and history."[103] Lockhart decided that Willis was "a just representative—not of the American mind and manners generally, but only of the young men of fair education among the busy, middling orders of the mercantile cities."[104] Marryat, on the other hand, thought that Willis, while granted of low birth, was the product of an American linguistic and political malaise. "In England, being attached to an embassy implies that the parties so employed are of high connexion, or of acknowledged talent." The American government, on the other hand, "allows what may be termed *spurious attachés*; that is the permission to their countrymen so to call themselves, for the '*convenience of travelling*.'"[105] Indeed, so American was Willis, according to some, that certain rumors around London had him patronized by Andrew Jackson personally.[106]

Accompanying these attempts to locate Willis in class and national categories was a more profound obsession with his surface "face," with the odd way he had slipped through the fine net of London society standards undetected. Thus, John Lockhart, who claimed he had the gist of Willis when he labeled him a bland American middling type, was also driven to pronounce him a dangerous, ambiguous power, "an unsafe traveller." "[A]s far as we are acquainted with either English or American literature, this is the first example of a man creeping into your home, and forthwith printing—accurately or inaccurately, no matter which—before your claret is dry on his lips—unrestrained *table-talk on delicate subjects, and capable of compromising individuals*" (emphasis in original).[107] Such commentary animated the political dynamics it wished to nullify. When rumors of Willis's dalliances—of his "twilight" life—began to circulate in London, they reproduced the *Pencillings*' images of English grotesqueness and vulnerability while describing Willis as empty yet potent text. *Fraser's* dubbed him a "namby-pamby writer in twaddling albums, kept by the mustachioed and strong-smelling widows or bony matrons of Portland Place or Curry Row."[108] William Thackeray pictured Willis "elbow[ing] his way through royal palaces" with "all womankind" sighing after his "famous *Free Pencil*." "He must have whole mattresses stuffed with the blonde, or raven, or auburn memories of England's fairest daughters."[109] Willis eventually featured in chapter XLIX of *Vanity Fair* as Mr. John Paul Jefferson Jones, correspondent not for the *New York Mirror*, the paper for which Willis actually worked, but for Thackeray's imaginary *New York Demagogue*, his slick surfaces and dangerous powers of entrancement interchangeable.

The Power of the G(l)aze

The fact that Willis entered British discourse as an empty pretense that transformed Britain's very amplitude—its charismatic authenticity and transparency—into a degrading liability was apparently the feature of him that chimed with popular moods in the United States. Although conservative U.S. readers were appalled by Willis's behavior in England and smarted keenly under the slights of those like Lockhart, Willis's popularity soared. While he was writing them, his London letters to the *Mirror* were reprinted in dozens of U.S. journals and newspapers.[110] The *Pencillings* were subsequently enshrined as *the* guidebook for U.S. travelers, so auspicious in status that when Daniel Webster embarked for Europe he kept a copy ready in his pocket.[111] By the early 1840s Willis was the United States's highest paid professional writer and a reigning authority on European travel and fashion. In 1842, the *Spirit of the Times* announced, "N.P. Willis is now recognized as the head of the new and popular school of lively and graphic sketches of fashionable and romantic life, which he in a great measure founded, and of which he is the Coryphaeus."[112] Willis's popularity helped usher in the mania for Old World travel and fashion that gripped the U.S. bourgeoisie until well after the Civil War.

To be sure, some of this mania was sincere. Like Emerson, many people in the United States were enamored of England as the model for a fantasy United States that might have been, for a nation cleansed of slavery and still enmeshed in the familial web of the Old World. But a significant slice of the Europhilia produced by U.S. intellectuals and entertainers took delight in its own fakery and production of surreal energies. In her study of fraudulence in antebellum literature, Lara Langer Cohen argues that the blackface minstrel and the frontiersman, when they emerged as prominent stage and literary characters in the early part of the century, were considered crass, "fraudulent," and improperly "American." But precisely because they were low-class, cultural "frauds," these figures became celebrated in the 1840s as uniquely vernacular figures, their very fakery central to their appeal as nationalistic icons.[113]

The same is true, I am arguing, for a certain branch of Europhilia. Like race imitation, Europhilic imitation announced itself overtly as a form of trumpery;

instead of being gaudy colonials whose imitations failed to reproduce the exalted spirit of metropolitan Europe, Americans in this scenario were merely dressed up in European clothes. But it was precisely this imitation, which thwarted the view of the "sincere eye," that emerged as a new definition of Americanness, one that allied itself not with an earnest desire to resemble metropolitan populations but with flashy entertainment, with U.S. capitalist empire, manifest destiny, and even the conquest of Europe itself. As this new idea of "America" took hold, moreover, it presented the "American" as free of positive racial or ethnic ascription, a mere trick of light in the global panoply of nations and peoples. What we find in the language of the "aristocratic revival," accordingly, are not gestures of obeisance but the sense that Europe is a dull plenitude, destined to bend to the imperial possibilities of the gaudier United States, a nation of imitators whose global emissaries are masked figures of power and potency.

According to an 1855 article in *Putnam's* titled "The American Traveler," "The American is the great national eclectic . . . in the sense of adaptability." "While in Paris, Mr. Bull has his shoes a little thicker in the sole, and his waistcoat a little shorter, and his checks a little more pronounced, lest he should seem to succumb to Gallic corruption, [but] his cousin Jonathan arrives without a wardrobe, that he may appear in the very last French fashion." Dressed up in foreign fashions, "Cousin Jonathan" is like Beecher's "mirror with no face of its own"; he is "all things to and with all men." Yet neither is "Jonathan" the same as "all men." His clothes house "a certain rank independence and secret sense of superiority." Armed with this ineffable something, the imitative American not only resembles the populations of the countries in which he travels, but he represents an actual improvement on then. "In Paris, [the American] is more French than the Parisian; in Rome, more Italian than the Roman; and in Britain, more English than the Englishman." As *Putnam's* shortly specifies, the logic behind an impersonation that improves on as it replaces metropolitan authenticity, is appetite. "[F]ed for years upon the splendid literature of all time, and the pompous history of the nations that have occupied and moulded the earth, and yet separated from those nations and that history," the American "goes out to take possession of his dreams and hopes, and boundless aspirations." It hardly comes as a surprise, given these sentiments, to discover that *Putnam's* favorite traveler is Willis, who, granted, is "artificial" and wears the "air" of foreign "drawing rooms," but who is nevertheless "vivid and individual" behind his "airs" and pronounces "the judgment of the New World upon the Old."[114]

But perhaps nowhere is this imitative, yet eerily empowered, American traveler more cogently set out than in Melville's *The Confidence Man*. As we have seen, *The Confidence Man* not only lays out a comprehensive panoply of American "types" but it also stages the constructs of U.S. urban myth and entertainment in peculiarly condensed ways, crystallizing the notion of the American as masked, inscrutable trickster. What is notable about *The Confidence Man* is that it also situates itself inside the larger Western panoply of ethnic and national personalities. Journeying aboard the riverboat, the *Fidèle*, are "Northern speculators and Eastern philosophers; English, Irish, German, Scotch, Danes; Santa Fe traders in striped blankets, and Broadway bucks in cravats of cloth of gold; fine-looking Kentucky boatmen, and Japanese-looking Mississippi cotton-planters; . . . slaves, black, mulatto, quadroon, modish young Spanish Creoles, and old-fashioned French Jews."[115]

On the one hand, as so many scholars note, the Confidence Man disguises himself as a variety of recognizably "*American*" figures, such as the blackface minstrel Black Guinea, the Missouri frontiersman, and the capitalist land scheme swindler. But, to a degree not often recognized by modern readers, Melville's Confidence Man also wears pointedly ethnic costumes. In the second half of the novel, the Confidence Man appears as the "Cosmopolitan," a seemingly benign, "catholic" personage dressed in a loud and colorful array of overt ethnic and folk costumes, his whole person seeming to materialize in one act the successive imitations of the travelling American imagined by *Putnam's*. The passage is important to my argument and is worth quoting in full:

> [T]he stranger sported a vesture barred with various hues, that of the cochineal predominating, in style participating of a Highland plaid, Emir's robe, and French blouse; from its plaited sort of front peeped glimpses of a flowered regatta-shirt, while, for the rest, white trowsers of ample duck flowed over maroon-colored slippers, and a jaunty smoking-cap of regal purple crowned him off at top; king of traveled good-fellows, evidently. Grotesque as all was, nothing looked stiff or unused; all showed signs of easy service, the least wonted thing setting like a wonted glove. That genial hand, which had just been laid on the ungenial shoulder, was now carelessly thrust down before him, sailor-fashion, into a sort of Indian belt, confining the redundant vesture; the other held, by its long bright cherry-stem, a Nuremburgh pipe in blast, its great porcelain bowl painted in miniature with linked crests and arms of interlinked nations in a florid show. As by subtle saturations of its mellowing essence the tobacco had ripened the bowl, so it looked as if something similar of the interior spirit came rosily out on the cheek.[116]

In these passages, the Confidence Man, with his predominantly "cochneal" or red clothes, his Highland plaid, his Emir's robe, his French blouse, is like a compendium of the costume albums I examined in chapter 1. What is important to note here is that the "confidence" figure is not just elaborated in the U.S. domestic context. He is intended as a symbol of a certain kind of "American" in a global scenario. With his collocation of ethnic sartorial signs, the Cosmopolitan is a kind of equivalent of the *Putnam's* traveler, whose Americanness is encapsulated by the fact that he wears the clothes of whatever peoples he visits.

James Salazar argues that the Confidence Man's "capacity for construing the signifying marks of the body and making them into the expressions of origin . . . is . . . the ground of the hermeneutic capacity that empowers his mastery of character." In Salazar's reading, the Confidence Man formulates the grounds of the racial and ethnic differences that then authorize his benignly pluralist, federating power.[117] But in my reading, Melville is not arguing that ethnicity is an unstable, shifting quality in and of itself but that insofar as it relies on the transmission of information through the medium of the sartorial and biovisual surface of the body, the transmission is open to blockage and the short-circuiting of signals. Like *Putnam's* traveler, the Cosmopolitan exists to underline that the "American" is not a positive presence but a surreal, flickering figure beneath a bright, bewildering surface of imitative clothes and ornaments. Indeed, the signal feature of the book is that the Confidence Man lacks any discernible positive presence whatsoever. He is the ghostly nothing behind a series of vivid costumes.

In this context, the Nuremburg pipe the Cosmopolitan smokes features in this scene to draw attention to the transgression of the rule of transparency it seems to invoke. Like the Nuremburg pipe, whose inner heat blazes forth in a "florid show" on its rosy white porcelain cheek, ethnic clothes and racialized complexions are supposed to transmit to viewers the character of their owner. As with the "ripened bowl of the pipe," which shows its "interior spirit" on its outside surface, racial and ethnic character should come "rosily out in the cheek," announcing themselves in the appearance of the body and its adornments. But the pipe exists in this novel in order to illustrate that this process is *not* working in the case of the Confidence Man, whose inner motives are closed off to the perceiving eye. The viewer cannot penetrate the mask of the body's surface. The "American" in this novel, by extension, is a figure identified not in the "florid show" of his inner life but in the operational trick of sartorial and racial signs that block or confuse perception, whether these signs are recognizably vernacular in origin, as in the case of the blackface performer or frontiersman, or "European" and "global," as in the case of the Cosmopolitan. The Confidence Man is like Willis or the *Putnam's* traveler, an entity who is unseen and magical behind his imitative clothes and who, correspondingly, acquires power over the passengers aboard the *Fidèle*.

The revised relationship between the United States and Europe postulated in midcentury scenes of American travel, in which Americans appear as impostors and masked imitators, would come to feature large in the midcentury bourgeois mania for Old World fashion. On the one hand, the stagy foreignness of Old World style corroborated the nationalist fantasy of a community of persons distinguished by their surfaces alone. When the "new science of heraldry" became a fad in the late 1840s Willis optimistically predicted a future in which "any Yankee" might claim a coat of arms.[118] In another sense, the vogue for foreign fashions corroborated the national narrative parleyed in the literature of European travel. Like the exportation of "masked" American travelers to foreign climes, the importation of "artificial" Old World courtly culture to the urban northeast evolved a narrative of U.S. extension and supremacy. According to George Foster in *New York in Slices*, American dandies handily surpassed as they copied all the dandies of the world. "New York is the only city and Broadway the only street in which any thing like a respectable assortment of live Dandies can be found.–As to the bucks of Bond-street and the swells of St. James. . . . They must be regarded as monstrosities." In New York, by contrast, "we have . . . the true mixture—the French sparkle, the Italian grace, the Spanish impudence, and a pretty considerable tall sprinkling of the true 'native American nerve.'"[119] Importing "French sparkle," "Italian grace," and "Spanish impudence," the United States itself can become all things to all men. Or, as Willis puts it, "The truth is that the world is not a globe, as is erroneously represented, but an amphitheatre whose civilized radii have an irresistible declivity toward one centre." New York, he says, is about to become that center. It will achieve its destiny not by war, commerce, or industry necessarily, but by expediting the "overtaking of Paris in *Luxurious habitableness*" (emphasis in original).[120]

It is worth emphasizing, as I conclude this discussion, that what is made evident in Willis's European mask is not the extent to which the mask conjures a superior untarnished whiteness, as Michael Rogin suggests is the case with blackface minstrelsy, but that it conjures the idea of a subject impervious to positive racial and ethnic classification, including whiteness, by creating a block to perception. Thus Willis was able to evolve a standard of national distinctiveness that drew upon differences between British "Anglo-Saxon" and white "American" complexions based on the principle that whereas the English had pure white skin, Americans had a coat of paint. The English, he said, live in a moist climate that transmits itself from the inside out in the famous facial "bloom." Americans live in a dry climate that "produces a feeling, if I may so express it, like that of being *glazed*" (emphasis in original).[121] Precisely to the extent that the vernacular culture of masks and imitative costumes was able to turn Britain's enduring trump cards—its self-proclaimed civility, sophistication, and what Bhabha calls its "whole undifferentiated white body"[122]—into things of negligible appeal next to the flickering mysteries of pure surface, it provided a way of imagining a United States that might itself be empowered by artificiality and masks alone.

The American

In the 1830s, Willis's brand of nationalistic performance, with its outlandish surfaces and tricky, apparitional subject, represented a minor challenge to an otherwise overwhelming cultural nationalist focus on Americans as a plain, transparent people. Most U.S. cultural nationalists, from Emerson and Thoreau to Caroline Lee Hentz, Anna Cora Mowatt, Walt Whitman, and Horace Bushnell, celebrated sincerity and advocated for a return to homespun values, a fantasy in which white Americans appeared in plain faces and unadorned outfits. As I have indicated, Emerson's travelogue *English Traits*, which appeared in 1856, is full of admiration for the English and their "plainness" and sincerity. "The Englishman wears a sensible coat buttoned to the chin, of rough but solid and lasting texture. If he is a lord, he dresses a little worse than a commoner." Emerson continues, the English "have diffused the taste for plain substantial hats, shoes, and coats through Europe. They think him the best dressed man, whose dress is so fit for his use that you cannot notice or remember to describe it" (89). The goal of clothes for Emerson is the transmission of the true character of the wearer. Plainly dressed, the English are "the nationality of veracity" (123). And here again, these plain clothes are linked to racial constructions, in this case white northern European heritage. In Emerson's mind, the English transmit in their appearance and culture "Old Norse power" (211).

As Reginald Horsman points out, the identification of some branches of English people as "Anglo-Norman" instead of "Anglo-Saxon" was a favorite gambit of white southerners in the years leading up to the Civil War. Hoping to sever themselves from white populations in the northern United States, they began to divide North and South people of English ancestry into Saxon and Norman, the idea being that the English "Norman" races, from whom white southerners were allegedly descended, were the loftier and purer of the two.[123] The plain clothes in Emerson's *English Traits* are barely concealed code for racial supremacy of this peculiar type. Emerson promotes this racialized wardrobe for U.S. populations generally, regretting that America is all painted up and inappropriately clothed, "whitewashed all over by unmeaning names, the cast-off clothes of the country from which its emigrants came" (181).

Yet it would be the glittery Barnumesque figure of the "con man" that would come to prevail over these plain national stereotypes by the late nineteenth century, not necessarily in this figure's nefarious aims but in its shining surfaces. In these portraits, the American was not offered as a sturdy, plain type, as Thoreau and Emerson recommended. Rather, the "American" appears as a kind of empty shell, an unformed nothing wrapped in a flashy suit. I will have more to say about these personages in upcoming chapters, but I want to pause briefly to mention Henry James' gently humorous portrait of Christopher Newman, the quintessential American protagonist of his 1877 novel *The American*. At first glance, Newman, who is visiting Europe for the first time, is the stereotypical American of midcentury British and European travelogues, fond of shiny clothes and gilt and varnish, lacking completely any aesthetic judgment. In Newman's clothes, "an exposed shirt front and a cerulean cravat played perhaps an obtrusive part."[124] Untutored in aesthetic nuances, Newman likes the copies of paintings in the Louvre better than the originals, privileging ornament and gilt for their own sake. He is especially enthusiastic about a copy of a Renaissance masterpiece when it arrives at his apartment "endued with a layer of varnish an inch think," with "its frame, of an elaborate pattern . . . at least a foot wide." The painting "glittered and twinkled in the morning light and looked, to Newman's eyes, wonderfully splendid and precious." Newman's "idea of grandeur was a splendid façade, diffusing its brilliancy outward."[125] But the difference between this and earlier portraits of the American is that behind these glittering surfaces, Newman himself lacks positive qualities. His face "had that typical vagueness which is not vacuity, that blankness which is not simplicity." In his eye "you could find almost anything you looked for."[126] It would be this vacuous personage, a pure surface with no definable center, that would come to dominate stereotypes of the American subject and its habitats by the end of the century.

In the next chapter, I look at the processes through which this dissemination of the American as a set of flashy surfaces occurred, particularly in the creation of new settler colonial personages and landscapes. It is not irrelevant to my topic that Christopher Newman bears the name of the ur-colonizer of North America, Cristoforo Colombo, that he is from the "American West," that he served in the Civil War, and that he made a fortune in copper and railroads. Newman's name and biography map onto a long record of colonial violence interspersed with a war around slavery and expansion. But James does not tell us much about this history. Indeed, we learn almost nothing about Newman's past beyond a vague summary of his efforts at making money by "working hard." In an important sense, we might speculate, Newman's emptiness, overlaid by glittery gold and varnish and an obtrusive suit, sits at the spot where his true history as a white settler "American" should be fully visible but isn't.

In the next chapter, I look more closely at how the deflective surface, which was a novelty in the antebellum era, came to help in the narrativization of U.S. colonial and imperial wars in the second half of the nineteenth century. In one sense, this period saw the precipitous magnification of white ethnic and racial ideology in U.S. nationalist thought. The years following the Civil War and Reconstruction are notorious for their expansion of white supremacy and proliferation of racism against Mexican, Black, and Asian populations, as well as genocidal wars with Indigenous Plains people. Racist stereotypes flourished both in popular fiction, such as dime novels, and in the new illustrated magazines that blossomed all over the United States in the 1860s and 1870s. But these powerful ideologies produced their own fears and problems. Eager to compete with European empires in a new global arena but dogged by controversy and worries over the reappearance of slavery in faraway lands, U.S. nationalist projects at the end of the century turned to the figure of the empty, overclothed American as a deflective, compensatory structure, one that protected the history of the United States from too much visibility.

THREE

"CLOTHES UPON STICKS"

THE SETTLER COLONIAL SARTORIAL EYE

The many satires of James Fenimore Cooper's Leatherstocking novels that circulated in the United States in the second half of the nineteenth century are unified by their insistence on Cooper's problems with depth. From James Russell Lowell, who decided that Cooper's characters are as flat as a prairie, and Francis Bret Harte, who shows Cooper heroes getting mortally confused by false hair pieces, to Mark Twain, who demonstrates that Cooper was the king of wonky landscape perspectives, Cooper's satirists attacked him on his seeming refusal of proper dimensionality. Tempting as it may be to conclude that Cooper's satirists had a good point, I wish to suggest that this later nineteenth-century preoccupation with Cooper's depth offers an important clue about the way certain concepts of white racial destiny, popularized by Cooper in the 1820s, were being experimentally remodeled by U.S. constituencies in the decades surrounding the Civil War. Indeed, Cooper himself participated in this remodeling project by taking issue, late in his career, with his own notion of racial destiny as something deeply and immutably fixed in the depths of the body and soul.

As many critics note, Cooper's 1820s' Leatherstocking Tales had sought to authenticate and romanticize white settler colonialism by freely (if sometimes contradictorily) drawing on the two prevailing racial theories of his era, both of which understood race and ethnicity as properties inherent in a people's character and destiny. On the one hand, as James D. Wallace argues, Cooper was committed to older monogenetic theories of race, which held that all the world's peoples were descended from Adam and Eve but had been shaped into diverse populations by their different environments. Holding that individuals are like plants and once having taken "root" in a certain "soil" became one with the land, the theory of monogenesis naturalized colonial settlement by illustrating the organic intertwining of people and land once settlement occurred.[1] According to early nineteenth-century stadial historiography, Indigenous North Americans were an ancient, exhausted people who would soon to die out. White settlers were destined to replace them as the new shepherds of nature, becoming themselves powerfully linked to the land, now reconceived as virginal and waiting to accept them. On the other hand, as Jared Gardner shows, Cooper embraced the newer polygenetic theory of racial origins, according to which the human races, instead of being descended from common parents, had been created by God as distinct and already hierarchized entities.[2] Each race had what Cooper called its own "gifts" and its own destiny on the North American continent. By depicting Indigenous peoples as a group whose coherence was incidental to geographical location, this theory conceptually vacated the continent for use by white settlers by insisting on the alienability of Indigenous land and on the priority of those who undertook the land's "cultivation" and "improvement," or what proponents of expropriation often called the right of "use."

Cooper was ultimately unable to decide which of these theories was correct, and we might speculate that he did not need to, that he embraced these contradictory positions precisely because they covered all bases. In the mid 1830s, however, Cooper found himself confronting a situation that made both theories curiously unworkable. During the nearly twenty years that Cooper had lived among his wife's family or traveled abroad, the inhabitants of Cooperstown had taken to picnicking on a wild, picturesque spot on Otsego Lake, called Three-Mile Point, that legally belonged to the Cooper estate. When Cooper moved back to Otsego Hall in 1837 and announced that Three-Mile Point was off limits, Cooperstown villagers were outraged and insisted that the property belonged to them. The arguments they used conjured both views of the racial question. On the one hand, the villagers claimed they had set down roots and formed an organic relationship to Otsego's natural world. In this formulation, Cooper and his family had abandoned North American land and had been off forming an organic relationship with Europe. Villagers called on the evidence of Cooper's Swiss servants, of Otsego Hall, which Cooper had elaborately refurbished in the Gothic style, of his daughters who spoke more French than English, and even of the Cooper family cat, which was French. On the other hand, popular legend held that Cooper's father had simply ceded Three-Mile Point to the public, much as its original Haudenosaunee inhabitants had allegedly ceded it to the colony, a point echoed by the Whig press, which took to calling Cooper a "savage" for his treatment of villagers. Even in the absence of legal claims, villagers asserted squatter's rights. They claimed that the land was alienable, that it did not belong in any fundamental way to Cooper's family, and that it was theirs by right of "use." This argument carried additional weight because Otsego Hall and its estates had earlier been sold by Cooper to cover family debts, and while the estate languished uninhabited between 1823 and 1834, Cooperstown residents had made various improvements to the Three-Mile Point grounds at their personal expense, effectively demonstrating their "cultivation" of an unclaimed and vacant precinct.[3]

While critics debate the extent of Cooper's commitment to either of the two prevailing racial theories of his era, then, I wish to suggest that Cooper's confrontation with the logic of contemporary race science as applied to himself led him to look for different and ultimately surprising ways of defining racial character and its relationship to place. Between 1837, when the Three-Mile Point controversy first flared, and 1841, when it finally died down, Cooper devoted an astonishing amount of anger and energy to his side of the debate, especially given that the actual legality of his title was never in question. Publishing hotheaded cards in the local papers, launching a series of libel suits against Whig editors, and producing no less than three hefty novels and two books of prose devoted expressly to this topic (four of them published in 1838 alone), Cooper was initially determined to defend the principle of his sovereignty through the conventional languages of private property and landed privilege.[4] But in the end Cooper pulled out the big guns and tackled the romantic mythology of white settler colonialism itself, rewriting the history of Otsego Lake's past in what would be the final installment of his famous Leatherstocking series, *The Deerslayer*, which he published in 1841.

What is remarkable about this novel is that it represents race in a highly unconventional way, not as something that inheres in the depths of the body and soul, as was commonly believed in this period, but as a flickering, spurious construct—like a theatrical costume or a mask—that has no definable relationship to either geographic locale or hereditary character. In *The Deerslayer*, Cooper resorted to the strategies for representing nation, ethnicity, and race being developed in these same years in the popular U.S. press. Indeed, in the mid-1830s, as he waged his war against Cooperstown, Cooper was drawn into the violent echo chamber of U.S. news and entertainment, the same world that at this moment was giving birth to Willis and Barnum. He found there, I will suggest, strategies for undermining the mythical settler land claims that he himself had done so much to shape the decade before and which now stood in the way of his own perfect title. Drawing on a set of visual tricks made possible by the early nineteenth-century racial and sartorial semiotic fields, Cooper developed a logic of land ownership that escaped early nineteenth-century notions of racial and national destiny, allowing him to formulate a highly specialized proprietary relationship to Otsego Lake and its surrounds. Cooper concocted a kind of "confidence man" theory of land possession.

Dispensing with biological theories of race, Cooper was able to imagine his own peculiarly exclusive ownership of the Otsego world.

Cooper's unorthodox treatment of settler mythology in *The Deerslayer* had little effect on U.S. settler colonial ideology in the 1840s and 1850s. On the contrary, U.S. settler colonial mythology continued to rely more than ever on doctrines of racial destiny, doctrines that were themselves increasingly biologized in the pseudoscientific disciplines of this period. What is significant from the point of view of this study is the extent to which Cooper's escape of biological imperatives, however unconventional it was in 1841, was paradoxically normalized as part of white U.S. racial and national destiny in the second half of the nineteenth century. Cooper's shifting reputation in the late nineteenth century, in particular his reputation as a maker of empty mechanisms, allows us to trace the mainstreaming of the flickering, hollow American personages sketched out in Hawthorne and Melville. Formulated originally as a challenge to conventional ethnic nationalism, with its biological imperatives and narratives of racial destiny, these overclothed "American" figures emerged as central to nationalist visions of the United States as a continental and overseas imperial power in the decades after the Civil War.

In previous chapters of this book, I looked at U.S. nationalism from within the context of Anglo-European ethnic nationalism. This chapter emphasizes the extent to which transatlantic ethnic nationalism mapped onto and merged itself with developing racial theories inside the United States, especially as these related to settler ideology. In formulating his romantic tales of frontier conflict, Cooper copied the ethnic nationalist novels of Walter Scott. Indeed, what becomes clear in Cooper's novels is the ease with which Scott's theories of Anglo-Saxon supremacy and his depictions of the struggle of minoritized peoples in England and Scotland repurposed themselves for a settler colonial mythos already rooted in transatlantic doctrines of Anglo and Germanic supremacy. While Cooper was not as vocal a champion of Anglo-Saxonism as some of his contemporaries, his ideas of a superior, climatically and biologically formed white race comported exactly with early nineteenth-century race pseudoscience as it moved through its various phases.

But the focus of this chapter is the extent to which Cooper, having held these beliefs, also replaced these seemingly immovable "scientific" notions of race with the ephemeral, hallucinatory figures of "Americans" developed in antebellum popular entertainment. Like Willis, whose dandies represented a challenge to narratives of Anglo-European white racial superiority in the transatlantic frame, Cooper launched his odd, empty frontier personalities as a challenge to the hegemony of narratives of white racial destiny within the frame of the internal United States. In both cases, the aim was to undermine and empty out a master trope by exploiting the tricks made possible by an ethno-racial visual regime in which the surface of the body was thought to transmit to the viewer without flaw the character and destiny of the clothed subject. What we see in Cooper's late career is the hinge by which this trickery itself could, in turn, become a symbol of authentic Americanness as the century wore on. The surreal hollowness and superficiality of the frontier that Cooper imagined in the *Deerslayer*, its lack of connection to any kind of "scientific" or biological racial bedrock, would become an object of attraction for U.S. settler and imperialist culture at the end of the century.

In the first part of this chapter, accordingly, I offer a detailed a reading of *The Deerslayer*, partly because scholarship on this novel, while recognizing it as a distinct anomaly in the Cooper canon, has generally been content to follow D. H. Lawrence in regarding it as one of Cooper's most impassioned if embattled expressions of the "myth of the essential white American."[5] In my view, however, *The Deerslayer's* numerous oddities, in particular its depiction of "essential" whiteness, have not been sufficiently considered by critics and cannot, if we look at them carefully, simply be construed as a more high-pitched or defensive version of beliefs about national and racial destiny Cooper expressed in his other writings. Moreover, I look at the extent to which Cooper's decimation of the foundationalist terms of white settler mythology was predicted in his earlier work, *The American Democrat*, published in 1838, in which Cooper both takes to task and sides with the U.S. media industry for its ability to subvert conventional race and ethnicity.

In the second part of this chapter, I expand to consider some of *The Deerslayer's* wider implications, chiefly by looking at the trajectory of Cooper's reputation in the second half of the nineteenth century. In chapter 2 of this book, I looked at how in the 1830s and 1840s, U.S. cultural nationalists developed alternative theories of Americanness whose chief feature was their short-circuiting of the visual relays of Eurocentric racial and ethnic meaning. In this chapter, I follow this early development through to its popularization in the late nineteenth century, when the figure of the gaudy, costumed American achieved paradoxical hegemony as a national and racial stereotype. In this formulation, the very failure of the American to signify as a normatively racial and ethnic subject emerged as an ethno-racial characteristic, a peculiar feature of the American personage in the scene of global peoples. Not only evident in Cooper's reputation but also in late nineteenth-century U.S. expansionist propaganda and in the redevelopment of the "frontier" itself into a kind of transient stage show, the fleshless yet ethnicized American came to serve a central role in U.S. imperialist campaigns.

Skin Traders and *The Deerslayer*

Perhaps one of the most notable features of *The Deerslayer* is that unlike most tales of frontier exploration and settlement, including Cooper's own previous efforts, its central events chronicle a process of *de*-settlement.[6] Cooper sets his novel on Otsego Lake in the 1740s, almost half a century before his own father arrived to take possession of the region, and he emphasizes again and again that at this early date the lake is completely unclaimed; it is uncharted, uninhabited even by Indigenous people, and nameless except for the merely temporary designations bestowed upon it by a series of migrants. Indeed, in Wayne Franklin's words, the opening of the book in that beautiful isolated spot seems "redolent of Creation itself."[7] At the start of the novel this seems about to change. Mohicans and Mingos (Cooper's name for a generic evil Indigenous group) are frequenting the territory to hunt and fish, while a lone white squatter named Tom Hutter, who settled on the lake fifteen years before, is claiming ownership of the entire region. Although the main plot of the novel revolves around the brutal skirmishes between Hutter and the Mingos for pre-eminence over the "Glimmerglass," as the lake is currently called, this swath of land, Cooper makes clear, is destined for vacancy. The Mingos are routed and slaughtered by colonial troops who show up briefly and then retreat to the distant garrisons. Tom Hutter and his younger daughter, Hetty, are killed; the surviving daughter, Judith, follows the colonial troops back east. When Cooper's famous frontier hero, Natty Bumppo, who helps Tom Hutter in his fight for the Glimmerglass, briefly returns to the lake fifteen years later, it not only remains unclaimed, it is now utterly unpopulated, and remarkably has remained unvisited by any humans in all the time since Natty last saw it.[8] Reposing in "magnificent solitude," the lake is so immune in its sublime loveliness to the imprint of human lives that even the graves of its former sojourners "could not be found" (546).[9]

Many critics have argued that this drama of "extinction," as John McWilliams calls it,[10] is designed to clear Otsego Lake of all human claims until the time Cooper's own father will arrive to "found" the region in the early 1790s, thus conferring this originary possession upon Cooper himself. In this sense, the novel seems to fit with what Stephen Germic calls the "crises of identity associated with land and legal entitlement" that haunted the Cooper family legacy.[11] We can speculate, however, that more urgent for Cooper in the late 1830s than establishing his hereditary claim to Otsego Lake was developing a principle by which his land would be impervious to new "settlement" by Cooperstown residents in the present day, its "magnificent solitude" assured in perpetuity. Whereas Cooper's earlier Leatherstocking Tales had orchestrated as they lamented the conventional melancholy "vanishing" of Indigenous peoples before the advance of white settlement, *The Deerslayer* sets itself the more unusual task of arguing that this piece of wilderness is, in fact, unsusceptible to white settlement. It wants to argue that white settlers, much like Indigenous populations, are doomed to vanish from Otsego's precincts, and that the only inviolable claims to Otsego land, whether in the past or the present, are Cooper's alone.

We can better understand the difficulty of arranging the logic of white settler disappearance if we consider for a moment the powerful links that were theorized in this period between race and land. In Johann Gottfried Herder's *Outlines of a Philosophy of the History of Man*, humans, who were all descended from Adam and Eve, were solely the products of the lands they inhabited. "Adam was formed of the dust of all the four quarters of the Globe, and animated by the powers and spirits of the whole Earth."[12] Thereafter, whatever geographical location Adam's various descendants made their homes determined their entire character, appearance, and culture, all of which were infused with an essential "spirit" appropriate to the region and climate. "The constitution of their body, their way of life, the pleasures and the occupations to which they have been accustomed from their infancy, and the whole circle of their ideas are climatic. Deprive them of their country, you deprive them of everything."[13] In Herder's view, "The arab of the desert belongs to it [the desert], as much as his noble horse, and his patient, indefatigable camel." Part of a people's essential spirit, these attributes were "imprinted" on the racial and national subject in virtually indelible form. The Arab's "simple clothing, his maxims of life, his manners and his character, are in unison; and, after the lapse of thousands of years, his tent still preserves the wisdom of his forefathers."[14]

These ideas were widely known among intellectuals in the United States. Writing in 1810 on the different attributes of the world's various social and racial groups, U.S. ethnologist Samuel Stanhope Smith argued that climate and region accounted not just for cultural differences, as we might expect, but also for morphological differences among the world's inhabitants. In Smith's view, phenotypical features of race—he concentrates on shades of complexion but also mentions "the hair," "the figure of the head," "the proportions of different parts of the body," and "the features of the face"[15]—are the result of a given people's long habitation of a single geographical space and habitat. These features of the body are "habits," but they are also irrevocably "fixed." Once a people occupies a certain place for a sufficient length of time, they acquire "a permanent character" and this character "becomes a hereditary property of the race."[16] Formed in certain regions and climates, each nation acquires "that complexion, as well as that peculiar expression, which go to form what is called a national countenance."[17]

In addition to being central to monogenesis race science, the matched destiny of a people and their land was also a central tenet of Western settler colonialism; not only was the "frontier" imagined as an entity waiting for settlers to arrive but it also conferred a mystical legitimacy on the settler project, promising to transform migrant populations into a retrospectively indigenized "people." In Lorenzo Veracini's words, the "frontier" or "outback" in settler colonial idiom "provides a mythical reference for 'indigenisation' processes, allowing for crucial settler investment in place and landscape."[18] In this case, land and people were not understood to be linked in a linear temporality, like a tree growing in a certain soil; rather, they were destined for oneness, linked together in a promised future that had not yet arrived. Veracini calls the signature narrative structure of settler colonialism a "palindrome." The settler colonial collective's arrival and settlement in a certain locale does not speak of a continuity with the past; it rather anticipates a utopian destiny: "settler colonialism mobilises peoples in the teleological expectation of irreversible transformation."[19] Settler colonialism operates on the assumption that history is preplanned, that settlers are destined to arrive in a given locale, and their arrival is part of a providential design that will climax with a modern, perfected white humanity. Writing about the United States and its "democracy" in 1835, Alexis de Tocqueville spoke of the inevitability with which it moved across the continent. "One must not therefore believe that it is possible to stop the English race in the New World. . . . No power on earth can close off . . . this fertile wilderness, which is open on every side to industry and offers a refuge in all miseries."[20] In the 1840s in the United States, of course, this destiny was given a name: "Manifest Destiny." In the proleptic formulation of settler colonial narratives, the white settlers' relationship to the land is paradoxically new and retroactive; white settlers imprint themselves racially on a new environment that is already preparing for their group's arrival. In this narrative, the fantasy of a "virgin" or "empty" wilderness that forms the heart of settler colonial myth mirrors the settler collective's imperative to begin anew, to refresh themselves by taking a step toward a foregone future. The freshness of the land mirrors the freshness of the settler character, the "national countenance," as Smith would say.

In the 1820s Cooper subscribed absolutely to these common ethnic nationalist and settler colonial views. According to Cooper himself, whose well-known opinions on this topic in the 1820s very much echoed those of his fellow expansionists, from Thomas Jefferson to John Quincy Adams, the takeover of the "wilderness" by white settlers was part of a providential and proto-evolutionary design. Echoing stadialist and teleological history, Cooper believed that the "ancient" races, which included North American Indigenous populations, were due to exhaust their time on the continent and to become extinct, making room for what was alleged to be the younger, more modern white race. Often this extinction was imagined by Cooper to inhere in the vast diurnal rhythms of history; as Cooper put it in *The Last of the Mohicans*, Indigenous peoples are a "setting sun," the Europeans are a dawn.[21] At other times these late Enlightenment models of the inevitable rise and fall of civilizations were textured in Cooper's mind, as Gardner argues, by more recent scientific theories that argued for the equally inevitable mechanism of genetic enfeeblement, which guaranteed the gradual disappearance of certain biological populations as these aged or failed to adapt to rapidly changing environments and geographies, including changes wrought by removal and human transfers. "As a rule," Cooper wrote in his 1828 *Notions of the Americans*, "the red man disappears before the superior moral and physical influence of the White, just as I believe the black man will eventually do the same thing, unless he shall seek shelter in some other region." White populations, Cooper believed, were hearty and vigorous, capable of vast feats of migration. People of color were not. At one point in *Notions*, Cooper expresses his idea that former enslaved Black people who move north find themselves too sensitive to the cold climate, whereupon they cease to reproduce. Indigenous peoples who cannot adjust to changed conditions and who, instead of "removing" west before the onslaught of white settlement, linger in the lands of their ancestors, become infected by "civilization"; they become a "stunted, dirty, and degraded race," doomed to an excruciating decline.[22] But if Cooper had all along believed that the nonwhite races disappeared from North American history and land because they lacked the vigor and wanderlust of white settlers, it was now incumbent upon him to arrange for the more unlikely depletion of white settlers, of those whose superiority was contained precisely in their adaptability and their eagerness to migrate.

One of Cooper's signal strategies here, evident from the moment he started struggling with the Three-Mile Point controversy, was to attack the time-honored link between white migratory habits and white superiority. In his thinly veiled autobiographical novel, *Home as Found* (1838), for example, Cooper blames recent migrants to Cooperstown for the disrespect done to his land. It is not the longtime residents, those who have cultivated the "hallowed" "sentiment that is connected to locality," who are intent on defying Cooper's ownership of Three-Mile Point. It is "the birds of passage . . . a numerous and restless class, that of themselves are almost sufficient to destroy whatever there is of poetry or of local attachment in any region where they resort."[23] Indeed, Cooper goes so far as to cast a general blame on "the migratory habits of the American people," which "keep[] society more unsettled than might otherwise prove to be the case."[24]

Thus, in one sense *The Deerslayer* organizes its logic of evacuation by depicting all the various claimants to the Otsego region, whether white or Indigenous, as migrants, as haphazard settlers of insufficient "local attachment." But I would also suggest that Cooper goes much further, that he covers his bases not only by undoing contemporary links between white migration and white superiority, but also by pulling away the foundations of racial character that made such links possible. In this, Cooper does what Hawthorne and Melville were doing in these same years. To the extent that surface appearance was guaranteed, according to this period's racialist biovisual regime, to transmit moral character and historical destiny, surface appearance could also be transformed into a site of interference and noise, blurring instead of clarifying the identity of the subject. The difference between Cooper and Melville or Hawthorne is that in *The Deerslayer* this instability of appearance is extended into an ontological condition; the settler characters are elaborated in almost postmodern form as mere transitory constructs, hallucinations of culture that in fact have no grand destiny. Accordingly, in *The Deerslayer* the traditional markers of the racialized subject, which include everything from names and faces to kinship origins, complexions, and clothes, are themselves depicted as migratory and impermanent, the implication being that since none of these characters (and by extension no one living in Cooper's own time) can claim any ontological coherence or stability whatsoever, they can never enter into a permanent relationship with Otsego land.

One of the first things we learn about Thomas Hutter, the white squatter who seems to be a metaphor for the squatting picnickers on Three-Mile Point, is that he has no definable relationship to the category of race. Natty Bumppo calls him "an oncommon mortal; neither Mingo, Delaware, nor Pale Face" (24). Natty's inability to pin Hutter down to any definable social or genetic group is symptomatic of a lack of definition shared by pretty much every character in this novel, a point that Cooper elaborates by illustrating the failure of conventional markers of identity to convey stable or unproblematic information. Frequently noted by critics is the profusion and volatility of names in this novel.[25] To the extent that names would conventionally fix and make legible a person's regional and hereditary origins, anchoring local attachment, Cooper obviates this possibility by giving each character anywhere up to seven unrelated names, including Christian names, nicknames, sobriquets, and aliases. The situation is so exaggerated that when Hetty ventures to ask Natty his name it takes almost two pages of printed text for Natty to list all his titles. Paternal names, meanwhile, prove to be no indication of paternity. Tom's daughters believe themselves to be Tom's offspring but then discover that their father was someone else whose name they never learn, leaving them with Christian names and various nicknames alone. Although an emphatic but ultimately minor subplot involves Natty's change of sobriquet from Deerslayer to Hawkeye once he kills his first human being, the profusion of names overall is designed to back up Natty's personal intuition when he says, "I put no great dependence . . . on names" (67).

The instability of names in this novel supports more fundamental instabilities, beginning with the instability and incoherence of faces. In the early nineteenth-century tradition of physiognomic and craniological analysis, faces were, of course, taken as the transparent, fail-safe transmitters of inner character. Physiognomic description, accordingly, was something upon which early nineteenth-century novelists relied to fix a character's behavior possibilities and destiny in the plot. In his first Leatherstocking novel, *The Pioneers*, Cooper had exploited this convention to describe his genteel lead character, Judge Temple. The reader's first sighting of Temple offers an uncomplicated clue to the truth about him; we see "a fine, manly face, and particularly a pair of expressive, large blue eyes, that promised extraordinary intellect, covert humor, and great benevolence."[26] But as numerous critics point out, in *The Deerslayer* faces lie, not just to the other characters, but to the reader. Our introduction to Harry March in the book's opening pages, for example, signals that he will be the hero of the tale. "It would not be possible to find a more noble specimen of vigorous manhood, than was offered in the person of him who called himself Hurry Harry. . . . The stature of Hurry Harry exceeded six feet four, and being unusually well proportioned, his strength fully realized the idea created by his gigantic frame. The face did no discredit to the rest of the man, for it was both good-humoured and handsome" (20). But Harry's face, introduced here as if it belonged to the hero and later revealed to belong to a reprehensible character who has a fairly small role in the drama, turns out to be part of this novel's cautionary machinery on the danger of putting too much trust in faces.

This is a point further emphasized in Cooper's elaboration of his main characters, all of whom are given tricky faces, from Judith, with her extraordinary, unblemished beauty and blemished moral character, to Hetty, whose blonde prettiness transmits no sign of her cognitive and moral disability, to Natty himself, whose much-remarked ugliness bears an odd, imperfect relationship to the alleged nobility of his spirit. Indeed, the theme of unreliable faces that fail to transmit proper information is dramatized in the action (Hetty foolishly falls in love with Harry because he is handsome and Harry falls for Judith because she is beautiful); it is discussed by the characters (the opening conversation between Harry and Natty is about the reliability of facial beauty as an indicator of merit); it is repeatedly insisted upon by the Cooper narrator; and it is hammered home in Cooper's repeated introduction of physiognomically based character types he then foils, including the blonde and blushing Hetty, who seems at first to be a typical genteel heroine in her appearance, but who, we later discover, was born "feeble-witted."

That Cooper's aim here is not just a kind of general elaboration of the ephemerality of human names and appearances, but a much more specific undermining of the ability of racial heritage to adjudicate and foretell destined dominion over land is made clear if we consider more closely the relationship between faces and race. A phrase that gets repeated across all of Cooper's Leatherstocking novels is "*pale-faces and the red-skins*." Throughout all the Leatherstocking novels, Cooper and his characters use this phrase, "pale-faces and red-skins," on dozens of occasions to describe relations between settler and Indigenous people in soon-to-be colonized territories. When Harry and Natty first meet up in *The Deerslayer*, they have a discussion "concerning the respective merits of the pale-faces and the red-skins" (23). In this novel, however, the repetition of this phrase serves a disorienting purpose, partly because the "pale faces" are, as we have seen, unreliable and impossible to read with any clarity, but also partly because the racially loaded entity of "skin" turns out to be problematic and unstable as well. Cooper is obsessed with skin in this novel. Indeed, skin serves as a central organizing trope for the plot, which is about scalping. And just as "pale faces" cannot be counted upon to transmit the truths of inner character and destiny, "skin" is shown to be incapable of anchoring the supposed stabilities of racial and ancestral identity, stabilities that would, according to nineteenth-century racial theory, assure a legitimate intimacy with and claim over the land.

In one sense, Cooper's many meditations on skin in this novel merely echo what had long been his conflicted commitment to contemporary racial theories. Traditionally, as we have noted, Cooper was committed to monogenesis theories explored by those like Herder and Smith. Polygenesis theory represented a newly popular turn in early nineteenth-century race science, most famously touted by U.S. ethnographer and raciologist Samuel Morton, whose volumes, *Crania Americana*, published between 1839 and 1849, are widely regarded as a milestone in the development of this branch of pseudoscience. In this theory, such characteristics as skin color come to stand not for environment and climatic adjustment but for the disparate evolutionary destinies ordained for white people and people of color. At the time of Noah's flood, says Morton, God ensured that "each race was adapted from the beginning to its peculiar local context."[27] Each, Morton believed, was formed separately for its own separate homeland, its "spirits" and genetic material never to be mixed with other races.

Not coincidentally, given Cooper's hesitations about such notions, in *The Deerslayer* it is the boorish Hurry Harry who expresses faith in the idea of complexion as an indicator of species difference. Announcing to Natty that "skin makes the man," Harry goes on to explain, "This is the reason; else how are people to judge of each other. The skin is put on, over all in order that when a creatur,' or a mortal, is fairly seen, you may know at once what to make of him. You know a bear from a hog by his skin, and a gray squirrel from a black." Natty, however, answers, "True Hurry . . . nevertheless they are both squirrels," and adds that the same is true of "white men" and Indigenous men, who are, in the final analysis, both "men" (59). Such sentiments, which flicker in and out of Cooper's earlier novels, give voice to the older monogenesis theory of race of Herder and Smith: race is something that, rather than being determined in a prior creationist moment, happens to human groups when they are long-accustomed to a specific locale. But the important thing to note here is that while Cooper, in his earlier novels, dislikes the idea that skin denotes impassable differences, skin still stands in these texts as a relatively stable indicator of a character's heritage and environment.

In *The Deerslayer* this is not the case. Cooper not only insists upon the deceptiveness of "pale faces" and has Natty insist upon the irrelevance of complexion when it comes to classifying human beings, but he also illustrates that skin itself is, quite literally, an unembodied property. It features in the novel as an insubstantial, migratory item that refuses to stick to either persons or places. The white characters in this novel are all fur trappers, most of them working as what Harry, at one point, calls "skin-traders" (28). Both the novel's main action and all the tragic events that befall the characters are precipitated by and revolve around episodes of scalping. Contradicting Harry's idea that "skin makes the man" is Harry's simultaneous belief, more firmly endorsed by Cooper's drama, that all skins are, in fact, items of "trade" whose meaning is defined neither by genetics nor by long exposure to "locality" but by the far less stable exigencies of the colonial economy. "As for scalping, or even skinning a savage," says Harry, "I look upon them, pretty much the same as cutting off the ears of wolves . . . seeing that the very Colony has offered a bounty for the job, all the same as it pays for wolves' ears" (50).

Many scholars have argued that in emphasizing the contingent, commodity status of skin, Cooper is not actually critiquing the notion that race is inherently stable—an idea upon which readers of this novel, understandably guided by Cooper's open opinions on this matter, have not ventured—but is rather attacking a modern colonial economy that upsets this stability by offering gold for body parts and thus encouraging the transgression of the boundaries established by God for his various creatures.[28] This is the argument loosely put forward by Natty, who believes that the races are each endowed with their special "gifts" (spiritual, moral and behavioral imperatives), and that by engaging in what Natty calls "savage" behavior, like scalping, the white men are wreaking havoc on this perfected organization. "Savages," in Natty's racial morality, are allowed to scalp; white men are not. That Cooper is less interested in establishing the transgression of racial boundaries than he is in obscuring and confusing their existence, however, is suggested by his extension of the whole issue of skin to the issue of clothes.

Now, as I showed in chapter 1, clothes and the biovisual or phenotypical body tended to be coextensive and easily confused in early nineteenth-century racial and ethnic theory. Cooper himself often exploited clothing as a window into character. In the third Leatherstocking Tale, the *Prairie* (1827), for example, the moral shoddiness of the squatter Ishmael Bush is immediately transmitted not just in "the inferior lineaments of his countenance," which are "low, receding, and mean," but in his clothing. As in the case of the peoples described in ethnic costume geographies, Bush's "low" and "mean" character is materialized with fail-safe accuracy in his taste for "a singular and wild display of prodigal and ill judged ornaments," including a "tarnished silken sash of the most gaudy colors," buttons made "of the glittering coinage of Mexico," and "no less than three worthless watches" dangling from his waistcoat (5). By contrast, the chief feature of both clothes and skins in *The Deerslayer* is that neither produces reliable information. On the contrary, it is by confusing skins and clothes that Cooper is able to revise the whole idea of racial "gifts" as a kind of arbitrary contrivance, indicative of merely superficial and temporary habits and arrangements, and thus proving as impotent as names, faces, and complexion color to produce an authentic relationship to the land. Indeed, Cooper's sartorial tropes are worth special remark, for it is by insisting on the sameness of "gifts" and "garments" that he advances his most aggressive renunciation of the foundational premises of racialized land dominion.

Cooper's extension of the properties of skin into the arena of clothing is most obviously illustrated by the fact that he dresses most of his characters literally in skins and other organic body parts, from Natty's suit, "which is composed in no small degree of dressed deer skin" (21), to the skins, furs, bones, shells, and feathers that dress the various other characters. Indeed, Harry worries at one point that even human skins, namely his own scalp, will become some Indigenous person's "nightcap[]" (75), and, fittingly, when Hutter is scalped no one notices at first because the Indigenous warriors have put his "cap" back on his head. Most prominently, Cooper's illustration of the interchangeability of clothes and skin allows him to emphasize the instability and even the nonexistence of the boundaries separating Indigenous people from white people and the savage state from the civilized. Thus Cooper's literal equation of clothes and human or animal organic matter is also metaphorically extended to encompass the white colonial officers, who are several times referred to as dressed in bright "flaring coats and fine feathers" (69), as well as to the Indigenous characters: Chingachgook tries on a scarlet gentleman's coat and dresses in a "white man's" shirt to fool his enemies into mistaking his identity. *The Deerslayer* is filled with such episodes of misdirection and misinformation, in which clothes and organic bodily parts feature as mutually alienable and mutually unforthcoming contrivances, from the officers' "fine feathers and scarlet coats," which, for Judith, serve as cover for "deception" (136), to the lone floating moccasin Natty finds, which puzzles him by refusing, against all expectation, to divulge the tribe of its origin.

In the 1830s, as we have seen in chapter 2, even as transatlantic ethnic nationalism increasingly fetishized clothes as the fail-safe indicators of moral and intellectual character, clothes and other bodily coverings were also being redefined in some quarters of U.S. culture as potentially unreliable surface formations—costumes, disguises, masks—that could easily form a barrier to knowledge. Indeed, we might speculate that as U.S. racial ideology changed focus from monogenism to polygenism, thus placing more emphasis on cranial and skeletal structures and their alleged manifestation in the naked body, the widespread preoccupation with clothes as a site of racial transmission waned. Clothes emerged as more unstable symbol systems than they might otherwise have been. What seems to be important for Cooper's project is that he was able to exploit this instability in the sign systems of clothing in order to undermine the sign systems of the phenotypical body as well. That is, to the extent that the traditional phenotypical body and its outer coverings were considered identical, the instability of clothing could be shifted over to intimate a similar instability when it came to more conventionally embodied racialist features.

Accordingly, the confused, incoherent boundaries suggested by Cooper's emphasis on the homology of skins and clothes are confirmed in this novel's crucial redescription of the "laws" governing what he calls "racial gifts" as these were developed in his earlier frontier novels. In the fourth Leatherstocking Tale, *The Pathfinder*, for example, published in 1839, Natty Bumppo asserts, "Every skin has its own natur', and every natur' has its own laws, as well as its own skin"; consequently "red-skin knowledge doesn't come . . . easy to white-skin nature."[29] (27). But in *The Deerslayer* these "laws" have undergone explicit revision. When Judith questions Natty about what he means by the "gift" of race, she asks, "In what is a gift different from nature? Is not nature itself a gift from God?" Natty says no, gifts do not come from nature or from God; "gifts come of sarcumstances. Thus, if you put a man in a town, he gets town gifts; in a settlement, settlement gifts; in a forest, gifts of the woods." All human beings, he goes on to say in a pointed confusion of skins and clothes, are born the same, "just as a man who is clad in regimentals is the same as the man that is clad in skins. The garments make a change to the eye, and some change in the conduct, perhaps, but none in the man" (439).

These comments are often taken by critics to mean that the failure of settlement in this region is the consequence of disreputable habits and customs that have left these particular white settlers without an affinity for nature. Yet Cooper's emphasis on the sartorial dimensions of race is also, I would suggest, designed to make a more aggressive point: As far as these characters are concerned, there is no pre-given racial spirit that might meld itself with the land. The surface is all there is. In Herder and Smith, the racial subject is infused with a transcendent creationist "spirit," a spirit that both flows from and allows it to become one with the inspirited land. It is precisely this transcendent spirit that is absent from and unavailable to the characters in the *Deerslayer* world. The very idea of some kind of essential spirit inside these characters that might lend itself to an epiphanic fusing of humans and nature is revealed, via this novel's sartorial tropes, as a tautological hypothesis. The whole notion of white settler oneness with nature or the land is posited not as a providential dream grandiosely written in the book of nature but as a cheap surface illusion of "culture."

Nowhere is this surface quality of the characters more pointedly demonstrated than in eerie episodes where characters are introduced to the reader and to other characters through the evidence of their garments alone. Before Natty meets Judith and Hetty in person, for example, he treats himself to a lengthy tour of their respective wardrobes as he happens upon their uninhabited abode; it is from the close study of their dresses, hanging on hooks around the walls, rather than the study of their embodied attributes, that Natty deduces what they are like. To be sure, early nineteenth-century sartorial theory allowed for this kind of analysis, for it was generally believed that individuals spontaneously selected clothes that perfectly matched their inner character. Yet Cooper exploits a different side of this theory: not that clothing transparently ferries forth the true nature of the inner self, but that the inner self, interchangeable with clothing, is a superficial formation, retroactively brought into being by clothing's artful surfaces. The countless sartorial episodes that punctuate this novel do not offer clothes as sites that transmit a "deeper" or pregiven essentialist truth about the characters. They elaborate an ontological condition—what might be called a new set of natural "laws"—in which such truths are brought into being by trivial cultural arrangements alone. The essential selves of racial myth are here generated not through history, genetic lineage, or destiny but through a shifting field of visual surfaces, mediations, and cultural arrangements. Indeed, these new laws are evidenced in the physical and ontological dynamics of concealment and disclosure in *The Deerslayer* universe. Even as Cooper stresses that clothes are superficial, shifty, and deceptive, he does not, at the same time, endow them with powers of betrayal or concealment that might suggest the existence of something positive or truer "underneath" them. On the contrary, Cooper is at pains to show that when these characters attempt to look "inside" themselves or "underneath" their clothes to discover their redemptive affinity for nature, they find only the purely shallow, surface selves that prevent them from cultivating the "gifts of the woods."

Nowhere is this absence of essential racial spirit more cogently dramatized than in Cooper's brief introduction of a disguise plot that centers on Judith Hutter, the one character who at the end of the novel will attempt to secure title to the Glimmerglass region. The familiar nineteenth-century contrivance of the disguise plot, which Cooper had used to great effect in several of his earlier novels, tended to be hauled out by U.S. writers to verify the immutability of race and class identities. To the extent that operations of disguise depend upon the assumed stability of some pre-existing inner nature that the disguise can cover up and that can subsequently be revealed as the truth, the disguise plot often featured in this era's efforts to cement the verities of inborn character by purporting to contrast these with the artificial and purely fictitious status of the pretense. In *The Pioneers* Cooper relies upon a disguise plot to authenticate white settler dominion over Indigenous living spaces. The romantic hero, Oliver Effingham, pretends to be the mixed-race son of a local Indigenous leader and thus the true heir to the Otsego region. At the end of the novel he is miraculously revealed to be the son of a wealthy English loyalist who was Judge Temple's partner in the Otsego venture all along. His land claims, initially thought to derive from his Indigenous heritage, are here "revealed" to derive in proleptic fashion from the circumstance of his English heritage, a circumstance which by seeming to lie *beneath* his disguise can be asserted as primary. Having turned out to be a fiction, the Indigenous claimant can be forgotten in favor of the truth and solidity of the English claimant, whose possession is now understood as a destiny.

In *The Deerslayer*, on the other hand, the disguise plot is briefly introduced so as to illustrate the absence of its central principle. When Judith, wearing a gorgeous aristocratic gown, pretends to be a god-like princess who desires the Mingos to free Natty from captivity, the Mingos are not fooled for a moment; they instantly conclude that she is lying. Their conclusions are quickly confirmed by the truth telling Hetty, who announces outright, "That's my sister Judith, Thomas Hutter's daughter" (514). Not only does this episode imply that there is nothing stable and essential inside Judith that disguise can either cover up or expose, but it also corroborates the idea implicit in Cooper's more general collapse of racial and ethnic boundaries and categories: that racial character, far from being determined in biblical and evolutionary time, is merely inscribed in the flat surfaces of a field of cultural signification. Unlike Oliver Effingham's disguise, which ends up revealing a truth—that he was born an English gentleman and an heir to Otsego land—Judith's disguise ironically ends up substantiating a fiction, the belief that she *is* Tom Hutter's daughter, which in fact she is not. Moreover, consisting of a gown that had belonged to her mother, Judith's disguise, in a further twist, constitutes one of the few pieces of evidence Judith has about her "true" origins; in looking past Judith's disguise the Mingos miss the point that the disguise itself, in this revised scene of nature's laws, is the only truth.

Cooper's insistence on the absence of a transcendent or biological principle beneath the surface forms of clothing (which is also skin) accordingly fortifies the impossibility of a "lawful" bond for any of these characters with the natural "woods." The precise terms of this impossibility are important to note, for while Cooper allows the idea of inborn character, he does so tautologically, on the condition that it is always already a merely cultural trick. Thus, while Cooper hints that Judith's claims to Otsego Lake must be foreclosed because she is not a proper creature of the "woods," as her love of sartorial finery and the garrison life attest, he also underlines the fallacy of this line of reasoning. Rather, in accord with the "law" that makes nature and culture identical, Cooper insists that Judith's tastes for sartorial finery and for the gentlemen of the garrison are genetically inherited from her mother, that her implication in artifice *is* her "nature." At the end of the novel, when Judith wants to establish her own title to the Glimmerglass, it is only upon Hutter's fictional paternity—in effect a kind of origin in fiction—that she can base her claim. And not surprisingly, her attempt to bond with the land on these purely fictional, operational terms is a foregone failure, one dramatized through Natty's renunciation of Judith's marriage proposal on the ostensible grounds of her "nature" as a fallen woman.

Through these complex and carefully developed tropes, then, Cooper insists that because none of these characters can claim a racial destiny—or indeed even a racial provenance—they cannot enter into a settler relationship with the land. Does Cooper include Natty, his prized frontier hero, in this scene of fictions and surface scripts that dooms the white settler project to disappearance? Generations of Cooper readers, while allowing that Cooper's vision of the white settler dream receives unusually pessimistic treatment in this novel, have seen Natty as its one redemptive stability, a purified repository of Christian virtues and white supremacist ideals erected in triumphant opposition to the decadence of the European civilizing project. It is my contention, however, that precisely to the extent that Natty—in all his whiteness, his adventurousness, his transience, his adaptability, his violence, and his Christian purity—had served so well in the role of expansionist hero in the 1820s, he must in this novel be made to serve the opposite ends. Natty asserts at one point, "White I was born, and white I will die; clinging to color to the last" (125). It is precisely this quality of "clinging" to whiteness, as opposed to simply having it as a fact of nature, that Cooper elaborates as a central feature of Natty's character. Even while Cooper strives to maintain Natty's heroic stature, which was tied to Cooper's sales as a novelist, he also takes pains in *The Deerslayer* to ensure that Natty, for all his lofty claims of white racial purity, belongs to the same unstable ontological scene as the other characters in this novel, and is thus no more capable than them of "settling."

At the simplest level, Natty is grouped with the other characters through the many transient identity features they share, from his deerskin clothes, emphasized by Cooper for their "smartness," and his unrevealing face, to his numerous names and his nomadic lifestyle. Even the famous rifle that features in Natty's future adventures (and had always acted, in the opinion of many critics, as the prosthesis of white dominion) is here shown to be an item inherited from *The Deerslayer's* most degraded transient, Tom Hutter. But equally important is that Cooper assures Natty's ontological equality with the other characters—and thus his dubious intimacy with "nature"—by subtly hollowing out the divine architecture upon which Natty's proclaimed purity and whiteness are founded. Dogging Natty's frequent expressions of faith in Christian truths, for example, are the repeated analogies Cooper draws between Natty's Christianity and what he dramatizes as Hetty's dangerously simple-minded faith in and literal enactment of instructions she finds in the Bible. Before he meets her, Natty feels that Hetty will be a kindred spirit. Born "feeble-witted" (30) and without her "proper share of reason," Hetty, Natty believes, is especially "gifted" by God in the property of goodness (27). But Natty also remarks that "the great protector and guide [ostensibly "reason" but also potentially "God"] fails" these simple souls (30), and given the oft-remarked similarities between Hetty and Natty (honesty, simplicity, literal-mindedness, plain looks) the implication is that the "great guide" is perhaps not there for Natty either. Fittingly, when he gazes upon Hetty's empty clothes on their hooks, Natty is reminded of his mother, a scene that places him within the same empty sartorial genealogies that originate Hetty and Judith, whose parents are present in the novel in the form of a dress and a coat.

In a gently humorous episode that seems designed to underline these points, a mysterious chest in Tom Hutter's floating "castle" is pried open. Among the many obviously cultural objects it contains—the costly scarlet gentleman's coat worn by Chingachgook, the gorgeous lady's gown worn by Judith, as well as a nautical sextant and a pair of silver dueling pistols—is a set of exotic and ornately carved ivory chess pieces: knights, castles and pawns. The parochial and Protestant Natty, who doesn't know what chess is, immediately draws back in fear from these marvelous pieces because he assumes they must be "idols," that is, objects that stand in during worship for a divine agency. Although the conventional way of reading this episode is to see it as a corroboration of Natty's redeeming innocence—he is a "natural" creature, too unschooled in the ways of "civilization" to understand its "games"—the other way of reading it is as a subtle comment on the absence of divinity and righteousness in those objects Natty sees as divinely infused, including, potentially, himself. Literally white knights and castles made, like the clothes in this novel, of an alienated organic substance (bone), these chess pieces not only figure an arbitrary surface "game" of European imperial jockeying and racial typification, but they also suggest that the white knight Natty, engaged in the chivalrous defense of Tom Hutter's "castle," as the characters call it, is as disposable, as lightly made, and as bereft of the authorizing powers of god and race as the tokens in the chest. It is the fate of these pieces, moreover, not to sit upon the fixed grids of the chess board (we might say the land) discovered elsewhere in the chest—and in fact Hutter's castle floats on the lake rather than sitting on land—but immediately to be dispensed within the same circuits of trade as the skins and clothes, their transiency evocative of a general condition of metaphysical, as well as physical, placelessness.

The floating free of this board, which would confer a definitive organization of "black and white" upon the settler project, figures the inability of any of these characters, including Natty, to claim oneness with Otsego land. In *Home As Found*, Cooper had enlisted the mythical Natty's aid in his depredation of new settlers by imagining Natty himself, the defender of the wilderness, as a kind of timeless, originary presence in Otsego's "hallowed" world. Legend has it, says John Effingham (one of Cooper's mouthpieces), that the very echoes among the lake's rocks and trees "come from the spirit of the Leather-Stocking, which keeps about its old haunts. . . . [W]e all know that Natty did dislike to see a new settler arrive in the mountains." Indeed, there is a pine that Natty "notched at every new-comer, until . . . his honest old heart could go no further and he gave the matter up in despair." Now a symbol both of Natty himself and of the glorious, defiant persistence of the "nature" he sought to protect, this tree, called the "Silent Pine," is a "sublime," "lofty object" reposing in "solitary glory" and timeless verdancy with its "roots embedded in the earth." Upon reaching its summit, the Effingham family "hold a little communion with the spirit of the Leather-Stocking," while Effingham assures them, "[This] Point has been ours ever since civilized man has dwelt among these hills; who will presume to rob us of it?"[30]

In *The Deerslayer*, by contrast, the one tree to which Cooper draws attention has not only fallen and lost its purchase on the "earth," but it has also been hollowed out. "Decay . . . had attacked its centre, even while it stood erect, in the pride of vegetation, hollowing out its heart, as disease sometimes destroys the vitals of animal life, even while a fair exterior is presented to the observer" (34). Clearly symbolic of all the rootless, centerless objects and persons in this novel, from Floating Tom and his floating castle, to Hetty who lacks a "guide," and the aptly named Riven*oak*, the leader of the nomadic Mingos, this "giant trunk" equally figures Natty's significantly changed relationship in this novel to Cooper's land. Although Donald Pease argues that Cooper revives Natty's presence on Otsego Lake in *The Deerslayer*, as he does in *Home As Found*, in an attempt to cement his possession of Three-Mile Point through the fictional paternity of his most famous character, the concluding drama of *The Deerslayer*, in fact, features Natty's renunciation of precisely this role.[31] Natty turns down the opportunity to settle on Otsego Lake when he turns down the marriage proposal of Judith. It has been customary for critics to see Cooper's refusal to give Natty a marriage partner, both in this novel and in *The Pathfinder*, as the sign of a kind of infantile male fantasy of flight from domesticity and women. But in the context of the Three-Mile Point controversy, Natty's aborted love in *The Pathfinder* (the woman he wants to marry turns him down), and his lack of desire for the beautiful Judith in *The Deerslayer*, just as easily signify Cooper's refusal to allow his white settler hero to propagate himself. Natty's rejection of Judith, regarded by readers both at the time and ever since as painful and unnecessary, ensures that Natty himself, the land's most plausible white claimant, vanishes from its precincts as inexorably as the other migratory, patchwork selves in this novel, unable, like them, to reproduce and revitalize himself in a stable white racial lineage, and thus unable to set down "roots," unable to form anything but a spurious and temporary affiliation with the wilderness that Cooper claims as his.

But if Natty is no exception to the rules of this novel, if both he and the other characters are merely cobbled together in haphazard fashion from the culturally and economically contingent names, beliefs, costumes, habits, and forms of commodity exchange that form the basis of both race and community, then Cooper here seems to be making an ontological comment on human subjects generally. Cooper seems to be saying that no human beings are infused with special racial spirit, none are innately superior, and none can therefore establish some kind of transcendent, authentic relationship to a given piece of land. But, of course, the question arises how any of this helps Cooper establish his own dominion over the land. How does Cooper exempt himself from a condition that he attributes to all persons generally? It is important to stress here that, in fact, Cooper cannot exempt himself. Indeed, given that he was being flayed in the press for having returned from Europe lacquered over with foreign pretensions, Cooper could hardly have been unaware of including himself in the company of characters whose various surface coverings he so assiduously depicts.[32]

But rather than insisting on his own racial or dynastic affiliation with the land and thus cementing his own peculiar claims to the Otsego wilderness, Cooper adopts a different strategy, which is to represent the wilderness itself as a surface formation where ethnic and racial substances are short-circuited and lost. Cooper's choice of the name "Glimmerglass" for Otsego Lake, which forms the stage for all the action of the drama in this novel, is not coincidental. In an echo of the luminous veils and tinsel that misdirect the eye in the tales of Nathaniel Hawthorne, Cooper's land in this novel acts as a kind of reflective device—as the name of the lake suggests, it is a "Glimmer glass"—a shiny surface that foils the eye. In this case, it deflects not just the eye of the viewer but also the desire of the settlers wanting to settle, repelling their eyes and reflecting back to them a scene of racial incoherence. Chiming with the reflective, glitchy surfaces and objects being developed in U.S. nationalism in this same period to fend off problematic racial and ethnic ascription, the "Glimmerglass" functions as a kind of central organizing trope, its reflective hallucinatory surface blocking the development and circulation of normative ethno-racial transmissions and affects. Indeed, the lake literally functions as a reflective device: the characters frequently look into its mirror-like surface to assess their appearance.

Fortified, as many critics have pointed out, by Cooper's references to the "gala dress" (37) of the trees and by his reliance on the conventions of picturesque landscape painting in his descriptions of the natural world, these tropes of surface contrivance and reflexivity suggest Cooper's deliberate artificialization and operationalization of his land.[33] By rejecting the foundationalist frameworks of white settler nationalism, by insisting that human subjects are neither biologically galvanized nor shaped through a spiritual relationship to terrestrial environment, and by insisting, at the same time, that the value of the land itself is a trick of the eye, Cooper can advance claims to ownership on the basis of aesthetic mastery and invention. It is precisely aesthetic invention that Cooper emphasizes, not only in both of his prefaces to *The Deerslayer*, which highlight his capacities as a "painter" (16), but in Harry's observation that "Pen was never put to paper, consarning neither hill or valley" (24) in the Otsego region and in Natty's sense that to apprehend Otsego land requires the soul of a "poet."

To put this another way, Cooper is asserting his proprietary claims to Otsego Lake not by asserting his heritage or legal rights but by suggesting what many postmodern critics have said: that Cooper, as the United States's premier nationalist novelist, invented the "frontier" wilderness, that the area of Three-Mile Point could not exist as a desirable, picturesque spot for picnickers without Cooper having created its romantic and pastoral associations first.[34] To the extent that the prevailing racial theories of Cooper's day, which insisted on geographical environment or predestination as foundations of settler colonial destiny, interfere with Cooper's agenda, he gets rid of them; all human subjects and their habitats, he decides, are invented by humans, and ownership and authority thus fall upon the most potent inventor among them. Performing this potency, moreover, is *The Deerslayer* itself. It reinvents the frontier wilderness and the iconic white settler so as to nullify what Cooper himself had so often said was their inevitable companionability.

The Afterlife of the Cooper Frontier

In the early nineteenth century, ethnic and racial nationalism swept across the conceptual systems of Western modernity, redefining populations as biovisual racial groups locked into fixed environments and destinies. In these formulations, the white populations of the United States appeared like other white creole and provincial populations. They were typified as a laggard group, plodding in the wake of the progressive, cutting-edge peoples of northern Europe and England, people who illustrated their sophistication and potential by wearing only the plainest clothes. Addicted to trivial consumer objects, to glittery clothes and flashy colors, Americans were thought to exist in conditions of moral and intellectual underdevelopment. These attributes were defiantly embraced by working-class white nationalist constituencies in the United States, who celebrated their own imputed rawness and lack of sophistication, who proudly advertised their taste for shocking colors, slick hair, and gold watches. At the same time, these imputed attributes of Americans were rejected by the U.S. intelligentsia. A substantial number of U.S. cultural nationalists advocated, more loudly than ever, for plain clothes and homespun for Americans, not because plain clothes represented democracy but because they had come to represent racial and ethnic purity and supremacy. But it was also the case, as we have seen, that in the 1830s and 1840s certain branches of U.S. intellectual and entertainment culture fought back against the derogation of white U.S. populations by undermining the biological and providential designs of racial and ethnic nationalism. This fight involved a tricky manipulation of the visual sign and symbol systems upon which ethnic and racial nationalism depended. *The Deerslayer*, I am suggesting, belongs in this class of cultural objects.

In this chapter so far, then, I have argued that Cooper's obsessive desire to extend his powers over his land beyond the terms authorized by the language of white settler priority led him to devise a kind of highly unnatural "frontier." Overtly mediated and transitory and cast as little more than a vague cultural hallucination, the "frontier" in *The Deerslayer* is not only designed to obliterate essentialist continuities between human populations and the landscapes they inhabit or seek to inhabit—in this case so as to evacuate the Otsego world of all possible claimants—but also to instate cultural hierarchies as an alternative to providential and biological ones when it comes to questions of land disposal. If the "frontier" is cast as a highly unstable fictional construct, in other words, Cooper can make claims to his land not on the basis of racial priority, but on the basis of his superior powers as a writer of fiction. While Cooper's strategies in *The Deerslayer* were unusual for the time and were ultimately aimed at addressing a fundamentally local and idiosyncratic problem, his idea of a highly "artificial" frontier eviscerated of its debt to providential and biological frameworks would come alive in U.S. nationalist and expansionist thinking in the second half of the nineteenth century.

The Deerslayer is arguably unique among Cooper's novels for its evisceration of white settler mythology. What is uncanny about this novel is the extent to which its patterns reappear with a vengeance both in Cooper's reputation after his death in 1850 and in late nineteenth-century spectacles and entertainments involving "the Frontier." What Cooper's afterlife allows us to trace is the extent to which the ideas of Americanness as a site of short-circuited transmission that were introduced in the antebellum period were normalized and accepted as part of U.S. nationalist self-description by the 1880s. This is not to say that such descriptions of Americanness somehow undermined or sidestepped ethnic and racial nationalist structures. Rather, they emerged as part of a new idea of "Americans" as the sum total of their artificial, flashy surfaces. These ideas not only entered U.S. frontier mythology, but they also became internal to the new phenomenon of U.S. overseas imperialism, where settler colonial myth confronted the problem of its own extension into lands that could not be imagined as untouched, virginal, and waiting for cultivation. The new mythology of a kind of bodiless, artificial U.S. nation, severed from biological and providential organization and made up of glittering consumer surfaces, served the expanding dictates of U.S. aspiration. Cooper's refusal of biological imperatives, however unconventional it was in 1841, was paradoxically normalized as part of white U.S. racial and national destiny in the second half of the nineteenth century. Cooper's shifting reputation in the late nineteenth century, in particular his reputation as a maker of empty mechanisms, allows us to trace the normalization of nonbiological and nonbiovisual racial theory as it influenced representations of U.S. continental and overseas imperialism in the decades after the Civil War.

The Limits of Settler Colonialism

On the one hand, U.S. nationalist, settler colonial, and imperialist doctrine after 1840 relied more profoundly and zealously than ever on the logic of Anglo-Saxon supremacy. In *The Anarchy of Empire*, Amy Kaplan argues that within the theoretical "boundlessness" of the scenes of U.S. empire, the "self-contained white body" functioned not just as a rationalizing fable but as a crucial differentiating structure, in the sense that it was only this allegedly fixed, pregiven entity that was capable of distinguishing such concepts as "nation" or "American citizen" within the otherwise profligate, racially and nationally undifferentiated sprawl of what Kaplan describes as a process of proto-globalization. The superior white body, in other words, was not just an "enabling fiction," as scholars generally concur, but a delimiting principle. The United States was recognizable as a sanctified, bounded item within the vast eddies of global empire dominated by Europe by virtue of what were believed to be its divinely sanctioned white settler citizens, typified in midcentury theater and fable by such nationalist figures as the rugged frontiersman, the Anglo-Saxon citizen-soldier, the settler family, and the genteel "republican mother."[35] And yet as certain constituencies in the United States embarked on projects of formal imperialism in the second half of the nineteenth century, these settler colonial and racial mythologies, with their familiar personations, were put under significant pressure.

We can better understand the form this pressure took by looking at its articulation in some of Cooper's other Three-Mile Point writings. Not only in *The Deerslayer* but also in *The American Democrat*, a work of political critique published in 1838, Cooper sought to reimagine relationships between race, land, and nation in ways that severed their immemorial bonds. Drawing on antebellum popular entertainment's idioms of garbled or blocked visual transmission—of faces, clothes, skins, and masks that foil legibility—*The American Democrat* hypothesizes nascent versions of the mediated, highly artificial frontier constructs Cooper later fully realizes in *The Deerslayer*. These same patterns, moreover, appear in Cooper's posthumous reputation as the creator of stick figures. *The American Democrat* suggests that Cooper's posthumous reputation was not, as scholars generally assume, driven purely by the idea that Cooper was a bad writer or a votary of outmoded romantic traditions. Rather, by the end of the nineteenth century, Cooper's creaky, artificial frontier, which fantasized a land and people evacuated of their customary biological and providential depth, had become a norm within U.S. nationalist and imperialist symbol systems, their trickiness and lack of depth the tools of imperialist projects that sought to sever U.S. imperial aspiration from what were now conceived as the limiting structures of the biological racial and ethnic body.

It is important to keep in mind when reading some of these materials that in contrast to much recent scholarship, which stresses that U.S. conquest and expansion were authorized and enabled by essentialist racial beliefs and by the concept of a nation sanctified by natural and divine laws, the writers I look at here, including Cooper, make a different and more novel assumption: If you rid empire of the anchoring concepts of race and destiny you do not stop its progress; you rather encourage its indiscriminate, uncontrolled spread and foster conditions for the actualization of fantasies of omnivorous possession and control. Writing in *The American Democrat* in 1838, Cooper expressed profound ethical doubts about the idea of robbing the national scenery of its fixity in biological nature, and it is unclear that after his brief flirtation with such a scenery in *The Deerslayer* he returned to these models again. Outlined in *The American Democrat*, however, is the idea of an entirely mediated national landscape that conforms to what Kaplan argues was the end-of-century conflation in pro-imperialist culture of U.S. empire and "media empire," where fantasies of total control played themselves out on what was often called the "world stage."[36] The later insistence on Cooper's "flatness," generated as much by his defenders as his attackers, addressed the fate of the early nineteenth-century romantic settler frontier, which claimed to be rooted in "nature," within later extremist pro-imperialist doctrines that expressed their impatience with limits.

Written during the early leg of the Three-Mile Point controversy, *The American Democrat* is a passionate defense of the settler ideal of the Jeffersonian republican nation, while also being a kind of covert justification of the unimpeachable nature of manorial privileges and thus of Cooper's own sovereignty over Three-Mile Point. Cooper argues that his manorial privileges are an extension of his natural rights as a white male U.S. citizen, something he tries to assure rhetorically through constant reference to the laws of nature and to the anchoring force of the white body/subject whose biological integrity and interior (spiritual) depth Cooper calls upon to fix continuities between himself and Otsego's natural world. He argues, for example, that property (which he describes as a personal possession) exists as a bordered, sacrosanct entity because it is coextensive and interchangeable with the "natural" bodies and "natural rights" of those to whom it belongs. "It is not known that man exists anywhere without establishing rules for the protection of property. Even insects, reptiles, beasts and birds, have their several possessions." He goes on, "We may infer that the rights of property, to a certain extent, are founded in nature.[37] To trespass on property is to trespass on the "rights" of the creature as formed in nature and materialized in "natural rights." In *Home As Found*, similarly, Cooper insists that Three-Mile Point belongs to him alone—despite the fact that he has not lived on the land for twenty years, despite that he sold it, and despite that he has spent almost a decade traveling abroad—because the land is fixed in his interiority, in his childhood memories, and in his identity as a novelist.

Yet even as *The American Democrat* argues tirelessly for nature/property as the proper constitutive medium of U.S. citizens, it also hints at the possibility of an alternative. Along with being a defense of property, *The American Democrat* is a kind of vengeful, helpless tirade against the U.S. press and popular media, a tirade fueled by Cooper's fury at what New York's powerful Whig editors were doing to his public character and his own idea of himself. The terms of this attack are worth repeating for they were keyed to bar Cooper from his proprietary and spiritual claims to his land. Indeed, precisely because it exposed contradictions within what Alexander Saxton calls pro-expansion "white egalitarianism"[38] (the idea, in this context, that all white men enjoy equal rights to the "soil") the Three-Mile Point affair was exploited by Whigs to discredit Cooper not just as a "democrat" but as a proper citizen deserving of any property or privileges at all. Cooper, announced James Watson Webb, is a "*viper* so long nourished in our bosom"; he must "leave our shores never again to disgrace with his presence a land to which he has proved an ingrate and . . . been anything but a reputable, useful, or even harmless citizen."[39]

Watching himself being transformed, purely in the ether of the press, from a beloved national icon to an alien and foreign element—in a metaphor not irrelevant here, Thurlow Weed gleefully thought that the Whig papers were "skinning [Cooper] alive"[40]—Cooper sets out in *The American Democrat* to finger the U.S. information and culture industries for their production of a bogus, illusory national scene. At the simplest level, he pillories contemporary media on the principle that they serve the desires of "political adventurers," self-interested editors and writers, who are all "partisan[s] in politics, religion, or literature" and other charlatans too unscrupulous to not to trade in "Puffs, political, literary, personal and national."[41] More complexly, however, Cooper identifies this virtual realm as a kind of alternative to the coherent bodies and spaces imagined in his celebration of "property" and "nature." The idea here, as Cooper sets it out, is that if you deconstruct the racialized subject you may decimate the coherence and power of the white settler citizen, but you also devolve coherence and power upon tiny interest groups and individuals whose claims to dominion become a function of their facility in the manipulation of symbols. Cooper rails against this idea on ethical grounds and he condemns the contemporary press for promoting these bizarre hallucinatory conditions at the expense of "Nature," "Property," and the rights of U.S. citizens. At the same time, he indirectly hypothesizes a national scenery in which one simply eviscerates the cumbersome substance of the white Anglo-Saxon citizen, not to open up the discursive realm of property or nation to currently nonlegitimate persons, but to relocate control of what would hence be a purely surface national landscape, implicitly unbounded by any kind of limits, to those who command and can exploit symbol systems and media, a group in which Cooper includes himself.

Now it is not insignificant that the "press" so berated by Cooper was the one dominated by figures like Nathaniel Parker Willis. Indeed, Park Benjamin, one of Cooper's chief tormenters, was the founder of the penny paper *Brother Jonathan* and one of the architects of the midcentury cheap entertainment revolution, his gimmicky "mammoth" newspapers (several feet tall and crammed with pirated Dickens novels and inflammatory editorial commentary) anticipating Barnum's productions a few years later.[42] One historian calls Benjamin "the father of the cheap press in America."[43] Figures like Willis, Griswold, Benjamin, and penny paper magnates like James Gordon Bennett were transforming U.S. news and entertainment culture by birthing a kind of early "reality" press that sold papers by attacking writers, politicians, and other public figures, and generating echo chambers of invective. The point here is not simply that Benjamin was an influential figure, but that he represented and indeed helped to establish the highly mediated U.S. entertainment milieu in which the mythology and mechanisms of the Barnumesque "operational aesthetic" were emerging. When Cooper talked about the power of the press in the United States, he was talking precisely about this realm, which produced not only Benjamin but also Willis's masks and Hawthorne's tricky veils and badges.

Not surprisingly, considering what it was doing to his reputation, in *The American Democrat* Cooper typifies the realm of "the press" as the exact opposite of "nature." Unlike the solid realm of "property" and "nature," the realm of the contemporary media is all "simulation" and "artifice, an "industry of the designing" where "studied misrepresentations[] permanently take the place of facts" (158). On the one hand, Cooper stresses that print information is crucial to the coherence of a "vast and thinly settled country" (129), as well as being "indispensable to mental independence" (132). But precisely because the coherence of the national body is dependent on print and report, the national body, says Cooper, is currently a vast unbodied vapor of lies and illusions. The contemporary media constitute national coherence not as a finite, foundational phenomenon but as a shifting network of inaccuracies, fictions, and mystifications, an "admixture of truth and falsehoods," the falsehoods, generated by "passions, cupidity and [political] interests" forming "the majority of cases" (132), to the point where newspapers will "manufactur[e] 'news' . . . when none exists in reality" (185). It is a "terrible picture to contemplate," he says, "for when the number of prints is remembered, and the avidity with which they are read is brought into the account, we are made to perceive that the entire nation . . . breathes an atmosphere of falsehoods" (129). Unlike the world of "nature" and "property," where individuals are solidly materialized in visible substance, the world of the media makes and remakes persons without reference to corporeality in an endless prism of rhetoric and "rumour," "*ex parte* statements," "blind" "eulogium," and "vulgar report" (131, 132). Whereas the world of "nature" and "property" is productive of properly differentiated "individuality" (182), the world of the media is productive of a formless, raceless, sexless "body" that Cooper over and over again calls the "mass" and the "body of the mass" (see, e.g., 57, 93, 98).

At the same time, Cooper does not see this mass-mediated condition as one that fosters the breakdown of differentiation exactly, but as a birthing place for new kinds of differentiation that allow for the proliferation of new kinds of power and appetite. Even as Cooper lambastes the media for their arbitrary production of hallucinations, he also sees them, for this very reason, as an agency of almost unthinkable constitutive powers, "tyranniz[ing] over publick men, letters, the arts, the stage, and even over private life" (131), able to create or topple not only men but nations and empires. Eviscerated of depth and substance, the illusory realm of the media proliferates its own phantasmal population of power-hungry "demagogues," "visionaries," impresarios—men of "intrigue and deception, of sly cunning and management" (100)—who are at once creatures of the media's making and canny experts in the manipulation of its depthless symbols and contrivances, what Cooper calls the "theater" of the "arts of printing" and "cheap publications" (98). Cooper's overt and passionate concern is to expose the mechanisms of this ungrounded, unnatural power; and indeed large portions of *The American Democrat* are pure exposé as Cooper, in his expressly advertised capacity as a famous novelist, political essayist, and journal correspondent, enlightens the naïve public, who are wont to believe in the transparency of what they read, on how newspapers and other cultural organs really work, how editors will say anything for the sake of copy, how self-interested politicians pay the press to concoct lies.

Yet precisely in so aggressively establishing Cooper as an expert in the hidden mechanisms of information and culture systems (partly through its deliberate address to a gullible readership), *The American Democrat* not only condemns the press but it also implicitly sets out the advantages that these mediated conditions represent to those like Cooper; that is, those who understand how culture systems work. Indeed, in an important sense, *The American Democrat* is a kind of perverse warning to the "American people": Do not let go of your faith in fixed natural and proprietary hierarchies, it seems to hint, or you will license your exploitation by people like me. Cooper argues that because it forces his fixed, continuous relationship with his community and nation, property (and by implication the larger array of legal, social, and racial privileges that go with it), also impels his powerful sense of ethical responsibility and his commitment to truth and to communal well-being. Property, says Cooper, is "the base of all civilization," and it is through its ownership that humans come together as social beings all connected to a common goal of "social improvement" (135). What is implied here is that a Cooper loosed of the ethical limits and responsibilities enforced by the sanctity of property might easily rearrange this "atmospheric," surface national scene, transforming himself by virtue of his vast, intricate knowledge of cultural symbols and information mechanisms into whatever autocratic, self-deified creature he desires. Even as Cooper majestically insists that he would never stoop to this amoral expedient, *The American Democrat* closes with Cooper talking about his "higher intelligence" spreading itself over "the vast extent of the [nation's] surface" (185).

It has been my contention in this chapter that *The Deerslayer* goes forward at the place where *The American Democrat* and Cooper's other Three-Mile Point writings stop. It denies all the hallowed personages of the traditional white settler colonial dream—most notably the figure of the white frontiersman himself—their claims to innate racial spirit and property alike, not so as to critique the U.S. expansionist enterprise (which Cooper continued to support), but so as to alter the conceptual limits through which this enterprise is pursued. In this case he substitutes a cultural/information hierarchy for an ethnic or racial one in order to decimate a framework of white egalitarianism that Cooper experienced as a limit on his desire. By emptying the white settler project of its putative foundations in the realms of "nature" and "property," Cooper, according to his own formulation, frees himself of his responsibility to the concept of a coherent, equalitarian white republic whose claims can be made to vanish in the service of Cooper's own autocratic pursuits. It is important to stress, furthermore, that Cooper does not pretend to stand outside the newly hollow national scenery he promotes. On the contrary, he transforms himself as well, substantially revising the terms of his relationship to the Otsego region as set out in *The American Democrat*. In that book, Cooper's property had featured as the origin of himself as a fully dimensional white subject. In *The Deerslayer*, it is Cooper who originates his property as a canvas he "paints" or, to use *The Deerslayer*'s insistent stage imagery, a wonderful "theater" or "simulation" he designs, just like all the other simulations floating in the "atmosphere" of the contemporary media. As in *The American Democrat*, Cooper draws attention in *The Deerslayer* to the utterly constructed quality of this mediated world, but he does so in order to underline that he is the one doing the constructing as he inscribes himself as sole maker of the scene. Upon the scene of American fiction, said a laudatory 1832 review of Cooper, Cooper had "stood, like another Columbus, on the ground he had discovered, and perceived that it was untrodden."[44] Exchanging real for fictional "ground," *The Deerslayer* rewrites Cooper as "founder" in a scene in which the only real property is a hypothetically limitless expanse of fiction.

"His Little Box of Stage Properties"

In an important sense, Cooper's attack on his own regenerative frontier in 1841, which began as an attack on putative white settlers—the squatters who sought to co-opt Three-Mile Point—anticipated a powerful line not of imperialist but of anti-imperialist argument that would, ironically, be leveled at his own novels in the second half of the nineteenth century. The peculiar terms of this attack are important to specify. Within white settler ideology, the frontier was depicted as a site of white racial regeneration, self-actualization, and ultimately "national grandeur." Thus Cooper's Leatherstocking novels, said *The United States Democratic Review* in 1851, "depict with singular clearness and force the superiority of the white blood in its simple strength enamored of forest life, struggling alike with the wilderness and the savage—forcing a way for the advance of the more industrious and less adventurous settler—while the enduring natural nations of the forest perishes [*sic*] by the way."[45] In this writing, the "frontier" was a space not just of struggle but of sublimity and purity, of precisely those qualities so often celebrated by Cooper, of magnificent silence, solitude, and spirituality where the harassed soul, tired of civilized life, was replenished. Anti-imperialist groups, by contrast, offered a drastically revised version of the "frontier," one that is clarified if we take a moment to look more closely at the anti-imperialism movement itself.

"Anti-imperialism" signified a loose political position that came of age in response to the U.S. war with Mexico between 1845 and 1848, and was adopted by numerous constituencies in the United States between 1848 and 1900. Anti-imperialists did not necessarily object to traditional contiguous settler expansion over continental (Indigenous) lands, but they did object to the extension of the "slave empire" (in the pre–Civil War era) and, more violently, to the looming prospect of a formal European-style colonial empire from the late 1840s onward. On the one hand, this position was founded on undying beliefs in the United States as a republican entity that was itself a former colony and that had renounced empire and must act as an agent of liberty. On the other, anti-imperialism was both fueled by and exploited white racial xenophobia.[46] Thus, for example, anti-imperialist groups agitated (successfully) against the conquest and annexation of geographical precincts that contained significant non-Anglo populations who would either have to be admitted to the United States as full voting citizens or else administered as colonial subjects in a system of political dependency, including Mexico, the Caribbean, and the Pacific Islands. Mobilized during debates around the annexation of Mexico in 1848, anti-imperialist constituencies called upon the ideal of a free white republic (free of both racial others and of the tentacles of European influence) to defeat pro-expansionist agendas. The tropes of anti-imperialism clashed with the tropes of pro-expansion. Anti-imperialists believed that in distending itself beyond its organic continental limits or in attempting the colonization or the incorporation into itself of what were often called "mongrel races," the white republic was destined for disintegration, becoming both a racially undifferentiated nightmare and a blip on the makeshift landscapes of global empire, its independence and integrity dissolved within a scene engineered by imperial Europe.

In this framework, then, the "frontier" is evolved as a space not of national and personal actualization but of immanent dissolution. The essentialist fixity and organic rootedness of the white body/nation feature as barriers to profligate extension, while empire itself is understood as destructive of these bounded naturist depths and verities. In other words, anti-imperialists sought to decimate midcentury settler colonial visions of racial and national regeneration on the frontier, not by arguing that white supremacy was inaccurate or inequitable, necessarily, but by arguing that it could not properly actuate itself on a distending, moving border. The only hope for a properly coherent, purified white nation lay in the consolidation and fortification of national borders, not in their profligate extension. Thus one of the chief features of the long tradition of Cooper denunciation that started in the late 1840s is its insistence that the regenerative frontier depicted in his works is in reality a sprawling space of unnaturalness and disintegration, destructive of the very racial and national coherence it promises. Cooper also anticipated the terms of his own canonization, however, for by the end of the century it was precisely Cooper's "unnatural" frontier that was reclaimed as the exemplary expression of an empire that knew no "natural" limits.

In the tradition of attack and satire launched by abolitionist and anti-expansionist James Russell Lowell in 1848 in *A Fable For Critics* and taken up not only by Francis Bret Harte and Mark Twain but also by numerous midcentury reviewers, the Cooper frontier is not a space of naturalness, national possibility, or individuation but a kind of vast undifferentiated stew of unnaturalness. Far from breathing the pure spirit of the woods and lakes, the Cooper frontier is a space full of creaky aesthetic contraptions and unreal hallucinations in which all terms of boundedness and discrimination have ceased to exist. In one sense, of course, these writers, particularly Harte and Twain, lambaste Cooper for his affiliation with an outmoded romantic tradition associated with Walter Scott. In this view, Cooper's frontier is nothing more than a set of cheap medievalist tropes filtered through Scott and foolishly foisted onto American climes. But the very emphasis on Scott and other things "European" makes Cooper's frontier in these satires part of an indefinite geography that is destructive of coherence and borders. Thus, one of the first things we notice about the satires—apart from the fact that they are very funny—is their production of the same tropes that organize *The Deerslayer*'s project. Here again are the sartorial coverings, cosmetics, scalps, hollow contrivances, and proliferating artifacts of "culture," and here again their purpose is to eviscerate the romantic settler frontier as a realm of depth and promise.

Harte's parody, for example, begins with the description of a typical little cabin in the Cooper wilderness:

> Although the exterior of the cottage was humble and unpretentious, and in keeping with the wildness of the landscape, its interior gave evidence of the cultivation and refinement of its inmates. An aquarium, containing goldfishes, stood on a marble centre-table at one end of the apartment, while a magnificent grand piano occupied the other. The door was covered with a yielding tapestry carpet, and the walls were adorned with paintings from the pencils of Van Dyke, Rubens, Tintoretto, Michael Angelo, and the productions of the more modem Turner, Kensett, Church, and Bierstadt. Although Judge Tompkins had chosen the frontiers of civilization as his home, it was impossible for him to entirely forego the habits and tastes of his former life.[47]

Mulching together nature and culture, and even culture and culture in a wash of multiplication without distinction, the Cooper frontier in Harte's parody hilariously decimates all terms for differentiation and recognition. Judge Tompkins' lovely daughter, Genevra, gets engaged to Natty Bumpo [*sic*], "the celebrated Pike Ranger of Donner Lake" after he rescues her from simultaneous attack by "a monstrous grizzly, closely followed by a Californian lion, a wild cat, and a buffalo, the rear being brought up by a wild Spanish bull."[48] One night Natty is prowling around in the woods when to his utter horror he sees his best friend, Muck-A-Muck (Chingachgook), dancing wildly around a fire. On his face is war paint, on his chest are postage stamps, in his hand is a scalp—"the clustering curls of Genevra"! "Sickened," Natty shoots Muck-A-Muck on the spot and runs to Judge Tompkins' cabin with the scalp of his beloved Genevra clutched in his hand, only to find Genevra herself in her father's cabin alive and well. Natty is speechless. He holds up the "silken tresses" in bewilderment.[49] Genevra is embarrassed. Judge Tompkins tells Natty it's only Genevra's hairpiece. The parody concludes, "The famous Pike chieftain never recovered from the deceit, and refused to marry Genevra, who died, twenty years afterwards, of a broken heart. Judge Tompkins lost his fortune in Wild Cat. The stage passes twice a week the deserted cottage at Donner Lake. Thus was the death of Muck-a-Muck avenged."[50]

Not only do the scalp/hairpiece, the clothes/postage stamps, and the ridiculous cottage walls hung with European masters, chime with *The Deerslayer*'s scalps, circulating clothes, and its chest in the wilderness full of symbols of "culture," but also, more subtly, so do Harte's vanished inhabitants, capitalist economies, and broken reproductive lineages. The same is true of Lowell's and Twain's parodies, which are likewise filled with tropes of constructedness and hollowness. In a parodic inversion of the imagery of vital organic growth (often figured as a lofty tree or prairie grass) that typified the language of settler expansion, Lowell describes Cooper's compositional practices:

When a character's wanted, he goes to the task
As a cooper would do in composing a cask;
He picks out the staves, of their qualities heedful,
Just hoops them together as tight as is needful,
And, if the best fortune should crown the attempt, he
Has made at the most something wooden and empty.[51]

This same language of clumsy and unnatural contrivance dominates Twain's essay. Echoing Lowell, who says that Cooper's characters are just "clothes upon sticks,"[52] Twain concludes that Cooper "hadn't any more invention than a horse; and I don't mean a high-class horse, either; I mean a clothes-horse."[53] "In his little box of stage properties," says Twain, drawing upon yet another metaphor of constructedness, "he kept six or eight cunning devices, tricks, artifices, for his savages and woodsmen to deceive and circumvent each other with, and he was never so happy as when he was working these innocent things and seeing them go."[54] Like Harte, who suggests that Cooper's "nature" is utterly interchangeable with a set of "paintings" of landscapes hung on a wall, Twain pillories the Cooper frontier itself as a bizarre, unreal geography where the very laws of the physical world—and thus of the terms capable of defining or differentiating geographical space—are gone. Rivers in Cooper's novels narrow and widen arbitrarily from one chapter to the next, bullets miraculously speed to their targets across impossible distances, architectural structures magically shrink and expand.[55] Citing *The Deerslayer* as the source of these Cooper extravagances (a point to whose irony I will return), Twain concludes that the whole Cooper wilderness has "a sort of air of fictitiousness and general improbability over it."[56] Twain says Cooper had no "real knowledge of Nature's way of doing things"; "even the eternal laws of Nature have to vacate"[57] when he gets to work.

Evacuated of nature and extended across an unreal, limitless sea of fictitiousness, the vital, regenerative "frontier" of expansionist promise is here presented as utterly incapable of delivering on the racial and national distinctions it promises. Like Harte's parody, which depicts the confusion of scalps/skins and hairpieces as coextensive with a larger disintegration of biological and geographical differentiation, so that even animal species (the wildcat, the Spanish bull) wander aimlessly in a world evacuated of environmental and organic compasses, Lowell and Twain emphasize that on the Cooper frontier, all populations are interchangeable. Distinctions based on race, class, region, nation, and even gender vanish in a blur of costume and surface inscription. Thus in Lowell's formulation, the Cooper frontier is ultimately only productive of a multitude of samenesses:

> His Indians, with proper respect be it said,
> Are just Natty Bumpo daubed over with red,
> And his very Long Toms are the same useful Nat,
> Rigged up in duck pants and a sou'-wester hat,
> (Though, once in a Coffin, a good chance was found
> To have slipt the old fellow away underground.)
> All his other men-figures are clothes upon sticks,
> The dernier chemise of a man in a fix,
> (As a captain besieged, when his garrison's small,
> Sets up caps upon poles to be seen o'er the wall;)
> And the women he draws from one model don't vary,
> All sappy as maples and flat as a prairie.[58]

Twain elaborates Lowell's metaphor of interchangeable dummies. "In the matter of intellect," says Twain, "the difference between a Cooper Indian and the Indian that stands in front of the cigar shop is not spacious."[59] Etherealized into a surface of costumes and texts, racial and class verities, far from actualizing themselves on this frontier, dissolve into a confusion of unfixed discourses and unreal personages. Among Cooper's eighteen "literary offenses" out of a possible nineteen, is his breaking of rule number 7, which requires "that when a personage talks like an illustrated, gilt-edged, tree-calf, hand-tooled, seven-dollar Friendship's Offering in the beginning of a paragraph, he shall not talk like a negro minstrel at the end of it."[60] A like dissolution of the divisions between the classes is at work in Natty. "In

The Deerslayer story he lets Deerslayer talk the showiest kind of book-talk sometimes, and at other times the basest of base dialects."[61] Invoking again a disintegration of differences and bounded individualities, Twain not only depicts the Cooper frontier as destructive of all "laws" and "rules," but he also signals the surface interchangeability of all the figures in this lawless realm by dubbing the simulacra that wander in the Leatherstocking landscapes "Cooper people."[62]

It is worth noting that *A Fable For Critics*, which is mostly a sendup of the late 1840s' literary scene and its authors, is also punctuated by often violent abolitionist and anti-imperialist sentiments whose rhetorical markers match up with Lowell's attack on Cooper. Cooper is the only writer that Lowell attacks for his production of "empty," replicable "casks" and "clothes." By contrast, writers sympathetic to Lowell's politics, including John Greenleaf Whittier and Lydia Maria Childe, while they do not go unsatirized, are ultimately redeemed for their individuated depth, their "naturalness" and "heart." The full significance of these metaphors of empty replication is revealed at the end of *A Fable For Critics*, which pictures a nightmarish global "graveyard" filled with meaningless, unnatural replications in which national particularity and individual human worth are dissolved. Strewn with the empty detritus of transnational literary, cotton, and political economies, this endless graveyard (and Lowell's inventory takes up five pages of text) contains "masses" of "American Bulwers, Disraelis, and Scotts," American "Miltons and Dantes," "as much of a staple as corn is, or cotton"; "Irish heroes," "Saxons," Teutonic republicans"; "Forty fathers of Freedom, of whom twenty bred / Their sons for the rice-swamps, at so much a head"; "sixty two second Washingtons: two or three Jacksons"—"And so forth and so forth and so forth and so on. / With this kind of stuff one might endlessly go on."[63]

Like the "frontier" in *The Deerslayer*, then, whose powers to adjudicate racial, national, and proprietary boundaries are vanquished in its evisceration of the "eternal laws of Nature" and its endless scenes of paint and costume, the Cooper frontier in the satires is invalidated through its sheer constructedness as a site for the plausible realization of racial and national destiny. And yet precisely to the extent that this "artificial" Cooper—a creation, it should be stressed, largely of his critics—had the power to flatten barriers and dissolve embodied populations into a hazy realm of fiction, he was rehabilitated by the end of the nineteenth century to signify the sweep and potentiality of an empire freed of its debt to "natural" limits. Whereas the satires of Cooper stop at a decimation of the romantic frontier, in other words, Cooper's admirers, starting in the 1860s, began to invoke the additional logic that Cooper himself had invoked: that the evacuation of the "laws of Nature" does not just destroy the romantic, regenerative frontier but also creates conditions for a new imperial order that can extend itself over a surface whose mediated, cultural composition means that it has ceased to contain organic limits. It is important to stress here, accordingly, that whereas Kaplan understands the essentialist "self-contained white male body," as well as its correlative, the cozy bourgeois family, as crucial delimiting structures within discourses of later nineteenth-century U.S. empire, and thus as entities whose integrity had to be protected, Cooper's celebrants by the end of the century hypothesized a "frontier" similar to *The Deerslayer*'s (and to the satires') in which conventional racial and region-based verities, especially those involving the white body, are openly advertised as hollow constructions and tricks of culture.

"Theater by Day-Light"

Initially, the tradition of attack on Cooper's naturalness, which was inaugurated by Lowell in 1848 during violent debates around pro-imperialist plans to annex all of Mexico, was experienced by celebrants of Manifest Destiny and the regenerative frontier as an attack upon the principles of "America" and its future of "national grandeur." Thus admirers of Cooper fired back not only by accusing Lowell and his compatriots of "hypercritical" and "dilettantish" introversion, by implication the opposite of the manly, daring frontier spirit, but also by defending Cooper—and presumably the imperial frontiers his novels had come iconically to represent—as the purveyor of a fulsome, exemplary naturalness, crucial to what *The Democratic Review* called "the necessities of the American race."[64] In distinction to Lowell and in accord with visions of the frontier as a vital space of renewal in nature, *The Democratic Review* told readers in 1849 that contrary to what they might have heard, Cooper's characters "are living and breathing men, whose future we divine as clearly as that of our relatives and acquaintances of long standing."[65] So "true to nature" is Cooper, said Francis Parkman in 1852, that his wilderness vistas "exhale[] the odors of the pine woods and the freshness of the mountain wind," and Cooper's characters are no "mere abstract ideas, or unsubstantial images," but "solid embodiments in living flesh and blood," full of "vitality and truth" and rooted in a "deep, rich soil."[66] In the 1860s, however, the idea, so prevalent among Cooper's detractors both at the time and for decades to come, that Cooper was empty and unnatural began to acquire a sunnier aspect among his celebrants.[67]

In his extended contemplation of Cooper in *The Atlantic Monthly* in 1862, for example, G. S. Hillard grants—indeed, aggressively insists—that Cooper's frontier is indeed a trumped-up sham. Not only is Cooper's frontier like "the theatre by gas-light," but even more glaringly, it is "like the theatre by day-light."[68] On the one hand, this is a source of great disappointment and cynical clarity for Hillard. Looking back on Cooper's 1820s' novels from the perspective of wise old age as opposed to delirious youth (and the temporal distance here is precisely that between the wonderful visions of an endlessly growing nation in the 1820s and their result in the Civil War in 1862), Hillard sees that all the glamour and promises of the Cooper frontier were, after all, part of a cheap, worthless machinery. "[T]he gold was pinchback, the gems were glass, the flowers were cambric and coloured paper, the goblets were gilded pasteboard" (54). Invested with this perspective of age, Hillard sees that so many of Cooper's characters are "a formal piece of mechanism, as destitute of vital character as Maelzel's automaton trumpeter" (60). Indeed, not only are Cooper's male characters all interchangeable, but his young ladies are as "deficient in individuality as the figures and faces of a fashion print" (58). Invoking the language of disintegration and borderless chaos typical of Cooper's detractors, Hillard wonders whether Cooper has any respect at all for the rules of narrative. "Are his stories, simply as stories, well told? Are his plots symmetrically constructed and harmoniously evolved? Are his incidents probable . . . ? Or are they merely a series of sketches strung together without any relation of cause and effect?" (56). The answer to these questions, Hillard decides, is no. Cooper's whole expansionist vision, says Hillard, in almost an exact anticipation of the words Twain would use, is a "violation of the laws of Nature" (56).

But then Hillard wonders: Do we really need Nature? In Hillard's view, some of Cooper's grossest violations of the "laws of Nature" are to be found in his depictions of Indigenous peoples. By investing Indigenous peoples with "delicacy and refinement," Cooper's novels are "wholly inconsistent with the inexorable facts of the case," as if "a painter should represent an oak-tree bearing roses." The real state of nature (and by implication the real frontier) is not the home of these poeticized fabrications, says Hillard, but of hordes "who stand upon the base-line of civilization." In contrast to Cooper's silly images of the noble savage, "the 'noble savage' . . . is really a very ignoble creature when seen in the 'open daylight' of truth. He is selfish, sensual, cruel, indolent, and impassive." A character like Uncas is for Hillard "a graceful and beautiful image; but he is no Indian" (61). And yet apparently to the extent that Cooper's unnatural nature is able to remake these biological realities into so many "mechanisms," Hillard discovers in it paradoxical terms of redemption in which unnatural nature ("gilded pasteboard," "automatons," "fashion plates," "images") can simply replace biological nature as a new order of reality. In this conceptual twist, as Hillard sees it, "the so-called state of Nature . . . is an essentially unnatural state" (61).

Freed of the logic of "essential" nature, Hillard is on the one hand free to redeem Cooper, and indeed to celebrate him, purely on the basis of his capacities as an exemplary "painter." If Cooper has no representational accountability to conventional foundational bodies and subjects—that is, if the "real" world he transcribes in his novels is conceived as itself a theater or wash of paint—Cooper can be reconfigured as a writer who excels at the organization of certain overall "designs" and surface forms. In Hillard's view, "We can pardon in a portrait-gallery of such extent here and there an ill-drawn figure or a face wanting in expression" (62). Liberated of the burden of "expression," Cooper's novels can be exalted on the basis of their breathtaking descriptions, or "paintings," of landscapes and scenic backdrops alone. But more importantly, once Hillard announces that nature is unnatural—that Cooper's attackers are actually correct and his frontier is a surface contrivance of culture—he is also at liberty to perform a startling about-face and to reread Cooper's novels as, in fact, faithfully transcribing (or more accurately retroactively inscribing) "the aspects of Nature and the movements of natural man" (64). Whereas at first in Hillard's review, actual, living persons—not just the "ignoble" Indigenous people but also such figures as General Webb and George Washington—had stood at the back of Cooper's "mechanical" and "faulty" efforts, their organic livingness and solid factualness a glaring contrast to the silly thinness of Cooper's art, these fleshly figures fade in the realm of unnatural nature. In their very artificiality—their endless replication of "caricature" (64), their "faulty" "drawings" whose "colors" are "more brilliant than those of life" (52)—Cooper's novels have "the power to present the broad characteristics of universal humanity" and the "healthy taste of the natural man" (65). With "essential" nature and its innatist subjects vaporized into an extended portrait gallery, a series of interchangeable dummies and poetic phrases, and a blur of featureless fashion-plates, the Cooper frontier, no longer clogged with a failed naturism and its bulky subjects, is reimagined as a space of a wonderful possibility. Violating "the laws of Nature," merely "dressed in the natural garb in which a vigorous mind clothes its conceptions" (63), Cooper "is the swan on the lake, the eagle in the air, the deer in the woods" (63). "[P]aint[ing] with a pencil dipped in the glow of our sunset skies and the crimson of our autumn maples" (60), Cooper's art "sweeps and soars with victorious and irresistible wing" over a "wide horizon" (63).

Virtually the same language of clumsy unnaturalness and redeeming greatness defines the celebrations and biographies of Cooper published later in the century. Evidenced in Thomas R. Lounsbury's biography, *James Fenimore Cooper*, published in 1886 as part of Houghton, Mifflin's American Men of Letters series, for example, is precisely the dynamic we see in Hillard. Here again we hear how Cooper's stories are "cheap and commonplace," "unintelligible and absurd," and "grossly improbable."[69] Indeed, like Cooper's satirists and Hillard, who stress the bizarre, "lawless" formations of Cooper's narratives of national destiny, Lounsbury stresses that "Many of the incidents [in Cooper's novels] are more than improbable, they are impossible" (51); "Plot, in any genuine sense of the word 'plot,' is to be found in very few of his stories" (275), which are marked by "bungling and incompetent development" (275). Even more shoddy are Cooper's characters, which are "unnatural if not ridiculous" (276). Most of Cooper's characters do not "bear any near kinship to humanity" (155); their "talk is of a kind not known to human society"; his books are full of "imbeciles" and "actors . . . acting like idiots" (51). Yet the end of all this, remarkably, is not to trounce Cooper. Precisely to the extent that Cooper's frontier, wholly ridiculous and artificial, is dismissed as a repository of providential truth and biological actualization, Lounsbury is able to refigure it for a new order of greatness unhindered by foundational frameworks. It is not necessarily true, says Lounsbury, that we live in a world of "facts." "Modern research," on the contrary, stresses that so much of what "we . . . look upon as fact is nothing more than fable." And so why not, Lounsbury wonders, "instead of going to history for our fiction we . . . turn about and go to fiction for our history"? (50). With "facts" the same as "fable" and "fiction," Cooper's novels, released from mimetic accountability, acquire a whole new "vividness and power." Not simply mimicking but constituting reality and nature, "The pictures [Cooper] draws are as real to the mind as if they were actually seen by the eye" (282). Indeed, so irrelevant are boundaries between fact and fiction and nature and artifice in Lounsbury's account that Cooper himself, who "looked at nature with the eye of a painter" (283), is transformed into the sole repository of the natural order he "pictures"; in his "portrayal of these scenes," says Lounsbury, "Cooper is like nature" (282).

It is not insignificant that, like Hillard, Lounsbury is hardest on Cooper when it comes to his portrayal of Indigenous people and genteel white women, for these were the two groups whose changeless essentialness conventionally fixed the romantic settler frontier as an arena of danger and promise. The Indigenous people (or, more broadly, any nonwhite population) threatened Anglo-Saxon victory and undermined ideals of white racial destiny, and genteel white women constituted objects of vulnerability and protection, their bodies the literal promise of a regenerative, procreative future for the white race. But precisely to the extent that in Lounsbury's account Cooper's Indigenous people and genteel ladies are the cheapest, most shabbily textual of all of Cooper's imaginings, their presence in Cooper's fiction a mere hasty scrawl of citation and "book talk," they cease to function as bounded biological entities whose genetic fixity might constitute a frontier or border at all. Cooper's frontier instead comprises a vast "moving panorama, in which the mind is no sooner sated with one picture than its place is taken by another" (282). Nowhere is Lounsbury's implicit renunciation of the regenerative, bordered frontier represented by these figures of biological depth more amply manifested than in his opinion that Cooper's finest achievement is *The Deerslayer*, with *The Pathfinder*, the other novel that overtly proposes and rejects a domestic future for the white frontiersman, a close second. These two works "stand at the head of Cooper's novels as artistic creations" (239); they are "pure works of art" (240). Substituting aesthetic design for racial purity, Lounsbury theorizes a frontier that is remarkably like *The Deerslayer*'s: an expanse of painted "landscape" with human agents a transient inscription on its surface. "The . . . uniform excellence of Cooper . . . lies in the pictures he gives of the life of nature. Forest, ocean, and stream are the things for which he really cares; and men and women are the accessories, inconvenient and often uncomfortable, that must be endured" (283). Implicitly presented here is the inconsequence not just of colonized peoples but also of the white colonizers themselves, who disintegrate in the general "nonhumanness" of the Cooper frontier, their conventionally providential, genetic purity and righteousness no longer called upon to authorize imperial grandeur and thus presumably no longer placing any "inconvenient" limits on it either. In the end, the only real occupant of the Cooper frontier is Cooper, not because he appears as a personage in his own tales, but because he figures as a retroactively inscribed power, the charismatic maker of a superficial, surface design who appears in his texts as "nature."[70]

It is a final irony in this remaking of the Cooper frontier in the second half of the nineteenth century, in which an anti-imperialist attack on the naturist frontier was transformed into a pro-imperialist logic, that Twain's satire of Cooper begins by quoting Lounsbury. Twain's project is to laugh down the idea that *The Deerslayer* and *The Pathfinder* might be "pure works of art" and to this end, as we have seen, he sets about ruthlessly exposing the Cooper's romantic frontier as a piece of incoherent, unnatural trumpery. But, of course, both Lounsbury and *The Deerslayer* itself had already done the wrecking job on the romantic frontier that Twain proposes. It is no coincidence, therefore, that Twain, perversely put into the position of affirming a pro-imperialist logic in his attack on an imperial writer, is obsessed throughout his satire not with *The Pathfinder* or with Cooper's other Leatherstocking Tales, but with *The Deerslayer*, the novel whose marriage of empty scenery and possessive desire threatens to transform Twain's very exposure of the romantic frontier's bogusness into a validation of imperialist appetite.

A New Wild West

Written as an attack on the frameworks of white racial destiny, *The Deerslayer* contains mechanisms that elsewhere in antebellum culture were being utilized to undermine the opinions of metropolitan groups—the English and other Europeans—in whose derisive sights the antebellum United States found itself caught. In these fantasy scenarios, the American body, instead of having positive qualities subject to derision and abjection, presents a front of confusing and distracting surfaces that deflect the ethnicizing and racializing gaze. Instead of positing the "American" subject as the apotheosis of "Anglo-Saxon" providential design, as antebellum white nationalists did, these unorthodox cultural nationalist texts posited the American subject as a hallucinatory wash of surface forms, often hinting at a kind of invisible impresario behind this cheap show, a canny manipulator of visual scenery. For Cooper, who was attacking white settler ideology, the same hollow constructions offered themselves as instruments of vengeful fantasy; the white settler dream itself, Cooper decided, was a rickety, hollow mechanism and he himself was the impresario behind the scenes.

While Cooper's strategies in *The Deerslayer* were unusual for the time and were ultimately aimed at addressing a fundamentally local and idiosyncratic problem, his idea of a highly "artificial" frontier eviscerated of its debt to providential and biological frameworks would come alive in U.S. nationalist and expansionist thinking in the last decades of the nineteenth century. Indeed, in the 1870s and 1880s, this idea of a surface "America," contained solely in its trumpery, entered into the U.S. cultural mainstream and finally came to dominate nationalist ideas of "America" as both settler colonial and imperial power. The reasons for this gradual normalization of a gimmicky, artificial America as a conceptual and figural touchstone for nationalist representation are not difficult to divine.

In his study of the often odd match between scientific racial theory and U.S. settler colonial and imperial ambitions, Eric Love makes the point that from the middle of the 1840s onward U.S. formal imperialism was hobbled rather than enabled by powerful racist belief.[71] Most obviously, in the 1840s and 1850s, U.S. expansion was closely linked to the interests of the slaveholding states and their seemingly bottomless thirst for fresh lands and fresh sources of enslaved labor. It was proslavery factions, eager to shore up their lands and their supporters in Congress, who agitated for the expansion of U.S. interests in the Caribbean, Mexico, and Central America. Many U.S. politicians, however, were reluctant to follow this course. How would the newly annexed populations, many of whom would be people of color, be incorporated into the nation? Would they enter as free citizens or as slaves? Would they be represented in Congress? Love shows that at several points before the 1880s, including 1848, when the United States won its war with Mexico, the U.S. government might easily have pressed for more land. Why stop the Texas border at the Rio Grande, for example? These were the years of Manifest Destiny, after all. Continental expansion was presumed to be part of the United States's mission as a modern, divinely sanctioned settler nation. Why not take all of Mexico? Love argues that the complexities of incorporating large non-Anglo-Saxon populations, including the Spanish, Black, creole, and Indigenous people inhabiting Mexico, together with deep anxiety over sectional conflict between slave and free states, made the idea of U.S. expansion into new territories peculiarly fraught.

North American Indigenous people were, as we have seen, interior to settler colonial mythology. They were figured as an ancient race destined to die out and to clear the way for the vigorous white race, leaving the land "virginal" and waiting. Their extermination, according to this way of thinking, could be justified. It was less easy for U.S. white, northern, upper- and middle-class people to imagine the United States as an entity gloriously destined to be a slaveholding nation, especially as abolitionist sentiment and free soil white nativism became widespread in the North in the 1840s and 1850s. Nor was it easy for most white northern U.S. people to imagine themselves in a nation that had deliberately decided to include large numbers of people of color. In the words of the *Cincinnati Herald*, the United States, if it took Mexico, would have to incorporate into itself eight million Mexicans "with their idol worship, heathen superstition, and degraded mongrel races?"[72] Indeed, precisely because race and land were so closely allied in early nineteenth-century racial and ethnic ideology, the appropriation and settlement of land opened up disturbing contemplations of how white settlers might bond with lands that were densely populated not just by Indigenous people but by those of mixed-race, African, and southern European descent who were, it was now increasingly believed, slated to thrive.

These problems around the racist and political dimensions of expanded colonization did not subside with the end of the Civil War. In the years after the Civil War, the Republican-led government, which feared the imminent resurgence of the Confederacy, sought to foreclose the possibility of plantation and slave-powered agriculture in new territories by populating the West with homesteaders on small farms. In theory, the Homestead Acts were supposed to open the West to settlement by farmers both white and Black, giving ex-slaves and Civil War veterans a chance to leave the South and start anew. These acts opened the settler dream to Black Americans as well as white. In practice, the Homestead Acts not only spelled disaster for Plains Indigenous people but also opened up the West to land grabs and fevered resource speculation, as capitalists quickly realized that the new value of these lands lay not in agricultural yields but in resource extraction, including mining and water rights. At the same time, as the post–Civil War U.S. economy turned into an industrial powerhouse, U.S. business interests and imperialist ideologues agitated for overseas imperialism, hoping to imitate the newly militaristic, and now often overtly racist, imperial direction of many European nation-states.

Nineteenth-century racial and ethnic ideology did not always fit well with these agendas, especially given the changes that these ideologies underwent in the second half of the nineteenth century. Polygenetic-based biological racial theory, far from retreating after the abolition of slavery, surged in its power and sway, becoming hegemonic in both the United States and Europe and often melding itself with new Darwinian models of evolution. Racial theory by the 1880s was a "science" that took special authority from its examination, measurement, and dissection of the unadorned body. Once essential to the elaboration of racial characteristics, clothes and other cultural appurtenances declined in importance, giving way to the morphological body and phenotypical characteristics—blonde or black hair, blue or dark eyes, height, body shape, skin shade—as the ultimate signs of a character that was now assumed to be indelible, baked into genetic material and unrelated to regional origin. This branch of racial thinking reached its apotheosis in Madison Grant's 1916 *The Passing of the Great Race*.[73] One of the features of this new brand of racial ideology was its fear of pollution and contamination, the fear that "Nordics" would mix themselves with "inferior strains" and thus commit "race suicide." Vaunting the purity of the Anglo-Saxon race, now conceived as a hard, genetic category, late nineteenth-century racial ideology feared the imminent decline of the globe's white populations and warned against too much racial mingling and contact. It is not insignificant to these issues that the abolitionists of the 1840s and 1850s, fearing a resurgence of the Confederacy, turned into anti-imperialist crusaders in the decades that followed the Civil War. Anti-imperialist agitation culminated with the creation of a formal league, the American Anti-Imperialism League, in 1898 to fight pro-imperialist agitation in the wake of the U.S. war with Spain. For many in the immediate post–Civil War era, the new extremes of scientific racial theory, combined with fears of a Confederate resurgence, made the idea of formal empire and new frontiers both politically and morally frightening and undesirable.

It is not surprising under these circumstances that U.S. nationalist symbol systems underwent significant revision in the later part of the nineteenth century, incorporating the shallow, surface formations hypothesized in antebellum entertainment culture, precisely, we might suppose, for their ability to deflect and confuse questions of racial difference and land appropriation and disposal. Written as an attack on white racial destiny, *The Deerslayer* utilizes loopholes in prevailing ethnoracial symbol systems to scramble the coordinates of both race and destiny when it comes to continental settlement. These were the same loopholes that were being utilized by U.S. writers and entertainment professionals seeking to undermine the visual and semiotic frameworks of British and European metropolitan supremacy. In these scenarios, the American body is imagined not as impeccably "white" or impeccably "Anglo-Saxon," but rather as something confusing and distracting, a composite of shifting surfaces potentially animated by an unseen "operator."

In the 1870s and 1880s, this idea of a surface "America" entered into the U.S. cultural mainstream and finally came to dominate nationalist ideas of "America" as both settler colonial and imperial power. One of the things this domination suggests is the extent to which these surface formations did not automatically challenge racist beliefs in the human body as a system of codes and signs. Indeed, racial science and racist belief reached a kind of terrifying crescendo in the late nineteenth century in both the United States and Europe. Rather, the idea of a "surface American," these materials suggest, readily worked within ethno-racial symbol systems by confusing and short-circuiting code and signs, turning what should have been sites of transparency into noise and incoherent visuality for its own sake. To be sure, this noisy visuality proposed to interrupt traditional ways of understanding the body as a system of signals. But this very quality of excess visuality, in all its meaninglessness, could itself register as "*American*"; it could circulate as a peculiar property of the people of the United States, in a way that left larger ethno-racial frameworks unharmed.

Nowhere is this notion of U.S. settler colonial and imperial power as showiness for its own sake more powerfully illustrated than in the figure who replaced Natty Bumppo as the signature frontier hero of the West, actor and showman William F. Cody, or Buffalo Bill. A kind of proto "reality" celebrity, Cody originally worked as a scout in the Plains Wars that raged across the 1860s and 1870s between the United States and Lakota (Sioux), Navajo, Cheyenne, and Arapaho people. One of Cody's jobs was to hunt buffalo for meat to feed U.S. troops. He also hired himself out as a guide for European aristocrats who came to the plains to hunt big game. In 1872, Ned Buntline, a writer of cheap fiction who had been toiling in the New York entertainment world since the 1840s, wrote a novel loosely based on Cody's adventures and featuring Cody as the hero. It was published serially in the *Chicago Tribune*. That same year, Buntline developed his novel into a stage play and convinced Cody to come to Chicago to star in it as himself. Cody's career as a performer was launched.

Over the next few years, Cody would establish an elaborate Barnum-like touring show, called Buffalo Bill's Wild West, that purported to recreate for eastern and European audiences the thrilling dramas taking place on the western frontier. Staged for tens of thousands around a central arena and featuring sharpshooters, stunt riders, and vivid sets that conjured up the scenery of the plains, the Wild West introduced U.S. and European audiences to such characters as Annie Oakley, Sitting Bull, Geronimo, the Rough Riders, and Buffalo Bill himself. The shows were gargantuan, involving at their peak more than six hundred performers, hundreds of animals, musicians, costumes, guns, and elaborate sets. Richard Slotkin underlines the extent to which the Wild West, which began as an effort to mythologize frontier warfare as a necessary step in the providential fulfillment of U.S. destiny, turned at the end of the century to representing scenes of heroic U.S. empire building in Cuba and the Philippines. In both cases, Slotkin argues, the Wild West turned reality into "myth."[74] What is less often noted is the extent to which the scenes of empire in the Wild West also confusingly offered American empire itself as something staged and unreal. In other words, it wasn't just that audiences were encouraged to mystify real violence through the compensatory consumption of romanticized scenes on a stage, but rather that real-life violence—and it was always racialized violence against colonized groups—was sewn into the show in a way that made it difficult to distinguish from the dazzlement of the show itself.

In one of the signature episodes of his career, for example, Cody quit the stage for a while to return to his job as a scout. It was 1876 and Cody and his company were the ones to discover the defeat of Lieutenant Colonel George Custer's troops at the Little Bighorn. Ordered to head off a possible attack by the Cheyenne people, Cody and his battalion were surprised at Hat Creek by a Cheyenne scouting party. Cody, according to a report, was at the head of his men. He and the leader of the Cheyenne party, a young man named Heova'ehe, in English Yellow Hair, exchanged gunfire and the Cheyenne man died. Accounts of this episode report that Cody scalped him. To be sure, while Heova'ehe did die and somebody, apparently Cody, sliced off his scalp and hair, the precise sequence and even the truth of some of these events is unclear because they were immediately densely mythologized. The key point to note for my purposes is the extent to which, as it circulated in U.S. popular culture, this storied incident combined horrific, racialized violence and often incongruous images of the stage, complete with extravagant costumes.

In his autobiography, Cody described the incident with Yellow Hair thus: "My usual luck did not desert me on this occasion, for his bullet missed me, while mine struck him in the breast. He reeled and fell, but before he had fairly touched the ground I was upon him, knife in hand, and had driven the keen-edged weapon to its hilt in his heart. Jerking his war-bonnet off, I scientifically scalped him in about five seconds. . . . As the soldiers came up, I swung the Indian chieftain's top-knot and bonnet in the air, and shouted: '*The first scalp for Custer.*'"[75] Accounts of this incident that circulated in its aftermath highlighted this gruesome violence, while also putting Cody in his stage costume. "Cody went into that fray all dressed up in one of his stage costumes, a handsome Mexican suit of black velvet, slashed with scarlet and trimmed with silver buttons and lace. Why he should be wearing such regalia, far in the hills, at dawn, after an eighty-mile ride, when the regiment was in its working clothes, is impossible to explain, except as studied showmanship."[76] It is unclear whether Cody was actually dressed in his costume at the time. Whether or not he was, however, the artifacts involved in this "duel," including the scalp, were certainly sent east specifically for display, and they were put in a clothing store; Cody wrote his wife to expect "the war bonnet, shield, bridle, whip, arms and his scalp to Kerngood [owner of a clothing store in Rochester] to put up in his window."[77] The deadly fight with Heova'ehe was subsequently incorporated into Cody's theatrical extravaganzas, in which Cody, dressed in one of his gaudy stage costumes, played himself.

The strange mix of theater and life purveyed in this incident was endlessly repeated in Cody's shows. The Wild West, for example, employed as actors the very people responsible for the death of Custer and his men. The star among these actors was Tȟatȟáŋka Íyotake, in English Sitting Bull, a Hunkpapa Lakota leader who organized years of resistance to United States government colonial policies and played a central role in the massacre of Custer's troops. In the aftermath of Custer's defeat, Cody paid Sitting Bull to ride around the Wild West ring as himself before the crowds. A famous set of photographs of Cody and Sitting Bull taken in 1885 by Montreal photographer William Notman show them in mutually striking costumes covered with ornament (see fig. 33). These costumes, which were stage costumes worn by Cody and Sitting Bull for performances,[78] exploit the tropes of the ethnographic and anthropological artifact. Like the folk and regional costumes depicted in nineteenth-century costume geographies, they are heavily layered, nuanced, dense with decoration, embroidery, and pattern. Sitting Bull wears a flowing war bonnet and ceremonial dress; Buffalo Bill wears a satiny shirt thickly embroidered with a floral pattern and unusual tall boots.

In the early nineteenth century, ethnic dress of this kind had adjudicated racial and ethnic differences among the various peoples of the world. Indeed, these photographs count on the viewer's knowledge of these ethnic costume tropes. Viewers are invited to marvel at the detail and beauty of the clothes, which transmit the authenticity, the peculiarity, and nonmetropolitan character of these "frontier" people. At

Fig. 33. William Notman, *Sitting Bull and Buffalo Bill*. 1897. Black and white photograph. Library of Congress Prints and Photograph Division LC-DIG-ds-07833.

Fig. 34. R. H. Furman, *William F. Cody, John B. Omohundro, Elisha Green, Eugene Overton, and James B. Butler*. 1872. Black and white photograph. Buffalo Bill Center of the West, Cody, Wyoming, USA; Buffalo Bill Museum; MS 006 William F. Cody Collection; P.6.0908.

the same time, Cody's costume is garbled. Is it Mexican? Is it English? Is it its own frontier genre? The presence of Cody's costume, which seems to contain ornament for its own sake, undermines the potential authenticity of Sitting Bull's. In other words, the uniformity and lavishness of ornament tends to flatten the scene as a site of transmission, nullifying what viewers might potentially see as ethnic, racial, and regional differences among the actors. In this sense, these photographs—and the Wild West and Cody's career in general—perform the operations of artificialization and dazzlement intimated in James Fenimore Cooper's project, deflecting the audience's eye from the reality of the Plains Wars, pursued through policies of land expropriation and genocidal effacement, to a scene of staged amity that cannot, at the same time, precisely be separated from the real thing, a real thing that, purely by association, seems more hollow and unreal than it usually would.

Fig. 35. *E. Z. C. Judson, William F. Cody, Mlle. Giuseppina Morlacchi, and John B. Omohundro.* Amos Photo Service, c. 1873. Black and white photograph. Buffalo Bill Center of the West, Cody, Wyoming, USA; Buffalo Bill Museum; MS 006 William F. Cody Collection; P.69.0028.

Moreover, Buffalo Bill's costume in this photograph is not as elaborate as was often the case. Earlier photographs of Cody among other "frontier" performers highlight the extent to which elaborate, overwrought costumes, fringed, embroidered, and beaded on virtually every surface, were part of their characters as celebrity figures (see figs. 34 and 35).

This flattening of scenes of transmission, and thus the confusion of reality and stage, worked across the Wild West show as a whole, something that becomes clear if we look for a moment at accounts of Indigenous people's experience working in the Wild West. The most comprehensive account of the Wild West from the perspective of its Indigenous performers comes from the biographies and memoirs written by Óta Kté, in English, Luther Standing Bear, in the late 1920s and early 1930s (see fig. 36). Standing Bear, an Oglala Lakota man who traveled to England with the Wild West show in 1902, refers constantly to clothing in his writing. Standing Bear's accounts make clear that clothing in the Wild West did not occupy the

Fig. 36. Gerhard Sisters, *Luther Standing Bear*. c. 1905. Black and white photograph. Library of Congress Prints and Photographs Division LC-USZ62–119406, LOT 3796 [item] [P&P].

place we would expect of ethnic or "tribal" clothes in this period. Instead, Standing Bear's clothes while he is in contact with the Wild West come to occupy the same shifting, unreal territory that Buffalo Bill's clothes occupy.

On the one hand, clothing exists in Standing Bear's autobiographies as an object of lament. Writing in *Land of the Spotted Eagle* (1933), Standing Bear is aware of the extent to which by the early twentieth century, traditional Lakota culture is being lost to modernization. In particular, he protests the ossification of traditional Lakota dress that was happening through the settler fetishization of "primitive" arts. He informs readers, "Many books have been written telling of the significance" behind the "beautiful designs and colors" on "Bags, purses, trunks, warbonnet and awl cases, garments and robes."[79] For Eurocentric culture these cultural objects and designs have all become "meaningful" and indelibly indicative of timeless "Sioux" character. But Standing Bear insists that these objects and designs have no mysterious spiritual meaning or "significance." The designs now worshipped by anthropologists were absent-mindedly scrawled by his grandmother with a stick in the dirt, just for something to do while she laughed with her friends. The meaning of Lakota objects and designs lies not in some transcendent ability to transmit racial and ethnic character but in their everyday use inside the living Lakota community. Accordingly, Standing Bear's memoir tries to recover this lost experience of intimacy and community. He details with loving precision the clothes he knew as a child: the "soft warm clothing made from buffalo calf skin" in which he was wrapped as a baby; the "gayly colored hood with tassels of eagle feathers dyed in bright colors" that decorated his cradle; the cumbersome hair ornament consisting of "six or eight silver discs" adorning his hair, and "the breastplate made of imitation bone beads . . . and put together with small brass beads" that he was forced to wear for a coming-of-age ceremony when he was ten.[80] Remembering his childhood, Standing Bear is all too aware that his people have been dispossessed of these objects, for they are regarded by white academia not as the materials of everyday life but as symptoms and manifestations of a racial personality, the "Sioux" character. To counteract this perspective, Standing Bear emphasizes that these objects are intimately tied to the real everyday livingness of his family and their immediate social group.

Yet Standing Bear also implicitly tells the story of how these objects—clothes in particular—entered the powerful symbol systems of the Wild West not as anthropological or personal objects, as we might expect, but as odd surface formations that both did and did not refer to Indigenous peoples and cultures.[81] We can see this process, through which Indigenous clothes are "operationalized" and co-opted into tricky meanings, played out repeatedly in Standing Bear's account of the Wild West in *My People, The Sioux*. Initially recruited for the Wild West as a translator, Standing Bear tells of how he first traveled to Rushville, Nebraska, to meet with the show managers, William McCune and Jim Esay. His first contact with McCune and Esay involves the show's "costumes." "Indians," Standing Bear learns, are required to have a costume when they audition; if they don't have one already, Esay "ha[s] a store and provide[s] costumes for those of the Indians who had none themselves."[82] Now it is never clear in Standing Bear's account whether he is talking about clothes the Indigenous performers wear specifically as costumes in the Wild West show or clothes they already own or clothes they make or purchase for wear on an everyday basis. But the fact that Standing Bear himself never makes a distinction indicates, I am suggesting, the slippery role that clothes and other objects of everyday life, including habitat, played in relation to the Wild West's theatrical project. Here again, as in the butchering of Heova'ehe (Yellow Hair), the collapsing together of veridical life and performance has the quality of a modern "reality" television show in which the conflation of the real and the performance is the point.

In many cases, for example, we are given to believe that the Indigenous performers wear their own clothes both on stage and off. At the beginning of *My People, the Sioux*, Standing Bear makes a point of telling readers that, contrary to popular belief, Indigenous people do not wear feathers all the time. "Some white people have the idea that Indians wear feathers all the time—in fact, I imagine they have an idea that we go to bed with them on." Standing Bear makes clear, "We wore feathers only when we were going to dress up—just as the white people put on their evening clothes for a party or dance" (78). Apparently, for their journey by train to London in 1902, the Indigenous men dress up. "Every time the train stopped, the Indians stuck their heads out the windows to see where we were. As many of the boys had their faces painted and wore feathers in their hair, this sight must have appeared funny to onlookers" (251). But these scenes of personal dressing up, in which the Indigenous people put on their good clothes, are never fully distinguished from the costumes worn for performances in the Wild West. When Standing Bear and McCune audition new performers for the show in Standing Bear's second season, they give a "feast." He says, "[A]ll the Indians who wanted to go out with the show were invited to come in full costume, so we could 'size them up' and select those who had good outfits." They end up selecting "those having the finest outfits and who were the best dancers" (270). But are these clothes dress-up wear, like evening clothes? Are they theatrical costumes meant for the stage? The narrative does not specify. In this same paragraph describing the auditions, Standing Bear relates how his baby girl died just before the show was to go on tour. To honor Standing Bear and his family, McCune and Esay "had all the Indians who were to accompany me with the show dress in full Indian costume and march to the cemetery. . . . It was a solemn and impressive sight" (270).

During the time the Indigenous performers are actually working in London, their clothes figure in Standing Bear's narrative as obvious costumes. Thus, Standing Bear reports that during the winter, when the shows suffer from the damp London weather, Standing Bear is asked by the show managers to save his "Indian" dress—"a very fine outfit" (254)—for days when the Wild West has a large audience. To protect his costume, Standing Bear dresses in a cowboy costume and plays the part of one of the cowboys instead. Similarly, Standing Bear recounts how his little son, also named Luther and also in the show, is an object of adoration for the other performers who dress him up and paint his face each day. "He had a full costume of buckskin, very much like the one I wore, and every day his face must be painted and his hair combed and braided for the two performances. The Indian boys seemed to think it was a pleasure to get the little chap ready for exhibition" (266). At the same time, the nonstage lives of the Indigenous people traveling with the Wild West are part of a sideshow attraction. First arriving at the site of the Wild West camp when he initially joins the show, Standing Bear is surprised to see, like magic, a whole Lakota village with its forest of tipis spread out around the Cody headquarters (248). Erected by the Indigenous performers according to the standards of the villages they were living in before they joined the show, this village is, in fact, at once the living quarters of the Indigenous performers and their families (the performers transported the tipis, which were easily dismantled, from show site to show site) and a sideshow attraction that tourists can pay to enter. When Standing Bear and his wife have a baby during their tour in London (the little girl who would later die), the birth is announced with great fanfare in the British papers. Cody asks if they would mind letting Londoners see the baby. Standing Bear consents and a little stage is set up, featuring a traditional cradle or "hoksicala postan," where mother and child can be displayed. Londoners line up in the road to see the first Indigenous child born in England. In these scenes, everyday clothes and stage clothes are the same clothes.

Now it is clear from his account that Standing Bear is not critical of Cody or the Wild West. He feels that he and the other Indigenous performers were treated fairly and generously and he is grateful for the opportunity to see London. He does not see Cody and the Wild West as part of the violent colonizing project that was destroying the lives of Indigenous people across the Plains, including his own. Nevertheless, we might think of the references to clothes and costumes in Standing Bear's narrative of the Wild West as a kind of traumatic haunting of his thoughts by the operational aesthetic that was clearly at work in Cody's shows. Here material culture objects do not play the part of museum or art pieces; instead, they morph into the slippery, ethereal, quasi-real sartorial objects that played such a large part in Cody's career itself. In effect, Standing Bear's clothes and habitats, which occupy a strange land between real and unreal, are like Buffalo Bill's; they etherealize and make hallucinatory the violence of colonization, rendering its precise nature and parameters unclear. Unlike appropriated Indigenous museum and art objects—which, under the aegis of Western anthropology, suffer from an excess of essentialist meaning, endowed with an import they were never meant to have—the clothes in the Wild West are like the clothes in *The Deerslayer*: they are unburdened of their historical, situated properties, set free into a world of uncanny performances and staged gimmicky "realities," where they confuse and distract the viewing eye from discerning or properly assessing the colonizing events their wearers enact. Like the audacious scarlet letter in Hawthorne's novel or the flicker of revolving costumes in the *Confidence Man*, the clothes of the Wild West performers send out a confusing signal that inveigles and distracts the perceiving eye.

In the early nineteenth century, the sartorial tricks used by Willis, Hawthorne, and Melville to fantasize the foiling of the Anglo-European eye when it came to perceptions of "Americans" were a marginal response to transatlantic anti-Americanism. Most antebellum cultural nationalist constituencies, as we have seen, replied to British and European criticism by admonishing U.S. citizens to dress more plainly. Continuing to insist on foundationalist notions of Anglo-Saxon purity, these constituencies believed that such purity transmitted itself without flaw in monochrome, unornamented clothing that did not draw attention to itself. By the end of the century, however, the tricky, overdressed sartorial figures of midcentury fantasy, which were in the first place developed inside local and transatlantic entertainment industries, had clearly become central to evolving concepts of the nation. No longer limited to the expressions of an urban entertainment intelligentsia, they were being deployed on a mass scale for the mounting of celebratory spectacles of "America" as both empire and settler colonial power.

The career and posthumous reputation of James Fenimore Cooper, I have shown here, provide a kind of conceptual road map to the twists and turns these ideas about "America" took. Cooper had been the principal architect of romantic settler frontier mythology in the 1820s. Fed up with this ideology when it came to asserting his imagined privileges over the land owned by his own family in Cooperstown, Cooper set out to destroy its underlying ontological structures by unraveling the continuities between racial destiny and continental land that had long underwritten the settler project. Instead of being deeply enmeshed within the millennial machinery of Anglo-Saxon Manifest Destiny, the "frontier" figures in *The Deerslayer* are bits of nothing, so much flotsam and jetsam in the wide, anonymizing eddies of modern global capital. But while unusual in the 1840s, this picture of U.S. settler colonial scenes would find favor among later nineteenth-century entertainers and ideologues whose purpose was not the accentuation of white imperial conquest, necessarily, but the artificialization of imperial violence and the garbling of the racialized bodies upon which the U.S. imperial project depended.

It is important to stress that at the end of the century the ideal of the United States as a white Anglo-Saxon nation equal to other white nations in the world was in no way diminished. In fact, Anglo-Saxon supremacy ideologies, which had died down in the aftermath of the Civil War, experienced a powerful resurgence at the end of the century as the United States, seeking to join the triumphalist imperialist projects being launched by Germany, England, and France, embarked on plans of formal overseas imperialism for itself. In the 1890s, Cody's Wild West was not populated by the denizens of western North America alone. Rather, seeking to cash in on the newly globalized focus of U.S. ambition and also conscious of its own

Fig. 37. *Buffalo Bill's Wild West and Congress of Rough Riders of the World [The Real Sons of Soudan]*. 1899. Chromolithograph poster. Library of Congress Prints and Photographs Division LC-DIG-ppmsca-54874.

Fig. 38. William Herman Rau, *Eight Cossacks.* 1901. Black and white photograph. Buffalo Bill Center of the West, Cody, Wyoming, USA; Buffalo Bill Museum; MS 006 William F. Cody Collection; P.69.0052.

emerging status as a touring show in Europe, the Wild West incorporated a striking ethnic nationalist element in its show in 1893. Calling itself "Buffalo Bill's Congress of Rough Riders of the World," the Wild West included stunt riders not just from among Indigenous Plains people but from all over the world (and indeed Cody did recruit stunt riders from all parts of the globe). Recalling the nationalistic fervor that had preoccupied Europe, Britain, and the United States in the 1820s, these riders performed in Cody's show wearing their national costumes, with horses caparisoned to match.[83] Promotional materials made much of these regional types in their ethnic costumes. Audiences were invited to see "The Real Sons of the Soudan, whose brawn and muscle have amazed the world, vividly illustrating their feats of strength, marvelous horsemanship, athletic achievements, gun spinning and pyramid building" (see fig. 37). They were invited to see "The Brave Cossacks of the Caucasus in wild strange feats and fearless equitation" (see fig. 38).

What did the "American" person in this cheap global scenery look like? He was the showman, Cody, dressed in a gaudy outfit of uncertain provenance. In these shows, Fenimore Cooper's vision of the settler frontier as a play staged on an insubstantial reflective surface in which stick-figure characters perform in transient costumes was essentially mounted, the ring of the circus and its performers imagined as the very materialization of "America" as world-scale empire. This trope of America as a gaudy show, a set of tricks performed before a dazzled viewer, was something that would be repeated at international events as the century closed. In the next chapter, I turn to the materializations of this visually tricky "America" that flourished not only in theatrical spectacles and circuses but at world's fairs at the end of the century. I argue that while these visions of "America" as an elaborate show on the one hand challenged essentializing racial and ethnic ascriptions, they also themselves became curiously "ethnic" features. They became deeply linked to what was now seen as an enduring, timeless national personality, a personality that manifested itself in cheap visual dazzle.

FOUR

SOME INSCRUTABLE FLATTERY OF THE ATMOSPHERE

THE ETHNIC NATION IN THE WHITE CITY

The hologram is akin to the world of phantasy. It is a three-dimensional dream and you can enter it as you would a dream. Everything depends on the existence of the ray of light bearing the objects. If it is interrupted, all the effects are dispersed and the reality along with it. You do indeed get the impression that America is made up of a fantastic switching between similar elements, and that everything is only held together by a thread of light, a laser beam, scanning out American reality before our eyes.

—JEAN BAUDRILLARD, *AMERICA*

American woman, get away from me
American woman, mama, let me be
Don't come a-knockin' around my door
Don't wanna see your shadow no more
Colored lights can hypnotize
Sparkle someone else's eyes
Now woman, I said get away
American woman, listen what I say, hey

—THE GUESS WHO, "AMERICAN WOMAN"

I began this book by quoting Russian novelist Maxim Gorky's 1906 account of his trip to Coney Island. I want to begin this chapter by returning to that episode to look more closely at what exactly Gorky was seeing. As we will recall, Gorky is stupefied by the glittery, fiery light he sees. "From the very first moment of arrival at this city of fire, the eye is blinded. It is assailed by thousands of cold, white sparks, and for a long time can distinguish nothing in the scintillating dust round about. Everything whirls and dazzles and blends into a tempestuous ferment of fiery foam." These bewildering assaults on the "eye" have a deadening effect on the subject. "[T]he visitor is stunned; his consciousness is withered by the intense gleam."

Millions of electric lights "prick the eye with the sharp needles of their dead, indifferent sparkle." Gorky observes how "people wander about in the flashing, blinding fire intoxicated and devoid of will."[1]

Gorky's description of Coney Island as a glittering, surreal visual extravaganza with no spiritual or political content was typical of descriptions of the United States. Late nineteenth- and early twentieth-century chroniclers of what was called U.S. "civilization" agreed that "America" was distinguished by empty sparkle, flashiness, and vistas of highly colored facades, lights, and signs. The quotes with which I opened this book are worth repeating. Describing various American "broadways" and boardwalks in 1922, Lewis Mumford noted, "The dazzle of white lights, the colour of electric signs, the alabaster architecture of the moving-picture palaces, the aesthetic appeals of the shop windows." He concluded, "Broadway . . . is the façade of the American city: a false front."[2] This idea of America achieved a kind of climax in the writing of Jean Baudrillard, for whom "America" is to be found in all its technologized, hyperactively visual soullessness, "in the speed of the screenplay, in the indifferent reflex of television, in the film of days and nights projected across an empty space, in the marvellously affectless succession of signs, images, faces."[3]

In twentieth-century critical traditions, such descriptions were typically thought to chronicle the devious materializations of capital. For William Leach in *Land of Desire* (1993), America's "facades of colour, glass, and light" are the apparatus of consumer modernity; the superficial, tricky quality of these visual displays mimics the trickiness of the commodity itself, an object that seems magnificent and magical but is in reality trivial.[4] Recent scholars reject the political terms of traditional consumer theory. Instead of trying to define the political aims of late nineteenth-century visual extravaganzas, recent material culture scholars, including Robert Rydell and Rob Kroes in *Buffalo Bill in Bologna* (2005) and Lauren Rabinovitz in *Electric Dreamland* (2012), see them as part of the interactive relationships between subjects and modern embodied entertainment experience. Rydell argues that as it was exported around the world, U.S. mass entertainment, though understood as "American" and "capitalist," performed a variety of functions that cannot reliably be mapped onto to racial, national, imperial, or economic ideologies.[5] According to Rabinovitz, the amusement park's assault on the senses helped Americans weave new industrial and manufacturing technologies into both their sensible lives and into "a sense of national belonging." "Uniquely *modern mechanized* responses" to a changing nation, amusement parks "taught Americans to revel in a modern sensibility that was about adapting to new technologies, to hyperstimulation analogous to the nervous energies of industrial cities, to mechanical rhythms and uniformity, and to this perceptual condition as itself American."[6]

It is not insignificant, however, as I've already pointed out, that while Rydell and Rabinovitz renounce the idea of coherent political meaning in the experiences of material culture, they continue to understand the forms of the new entertainments as "American" and "national."[7] The question I have asked in the course of this study is why visual overload of the kind described by Gorky would be understood as American in the first place. Can a display of light—the glare of sunlight, the glow of electric bulbs—be "American" without first being part of a regime of meaning that articulates connections between certain visual effects and the imputed characteristics of a nationality or ethnicity?

In fact, a closer look at the origin of the kind of scenery that strikes Gorky and others as typically "American" reveals the extent to which these scenes were in the first place generated not around consumer pleasure or technology or urban entertainment, as scholars suggest, but around literal performances of national and ethnic characteristics. Touring Coney Island in 1906, Gorky was viewing a set of architectural and scenographic elements that had first been developed for competitive national displays at the World's Columbian Exposition in Chicago in 1893. The three Coney Island amusement parks, Steeplechase, Luna Park, and Dreamland, were all constructed between 1897 and 1904 in frank imitation of the Midway Plaisance and White City that had been the most distinctive and profitable features of the Columbian Exposition. What is revealed in descriptions of these features at the Columbian Exposition is the extent to which both the language used to describe them and the material and visual components of the features themselves drew on an existing repertoire of national and ethnic stereotypes, in which "America" already appeared as a site of emptiness and visual overload. In other words, what Gorky encountered at Coney Island was neither the metaphysical emptiness of commodity capitalism nor precisely some actual embodied experience produced by electric bulbs and giant machines but a conventional way of imagining the material instantiation of "America" in the international community of the late nineteenth and early twentieth century. Indeed, it is only possible to understand how indebted these descriptions of America were to the larger complexes of Western ethnic nationalist thinking by examining American scenes as part of a network of culturally differentiated ethnic and national scenes that crystallized at the end of the nineteenth century.

In previous chapters of this book, I looked at how, from the early nineteenth century onward, clothes worked as technologies of ethnicity and nationality, purporting to materialize in their details the true character of their wearers, which was then beamed to viewers wholesale. In addition, I looked at how U.S. nationalist iconography tinkered with these ethnic nationalist sign and symbol systems, refiguring "America" not as a nation of transparent subjects whose bodily surfaces spoke unproblematically of their essential character as a people, but as sites of blockage and distraction. Encountering the surface of the "American" body, the eye of Europe was blocked and distracted by a confusing wash of meaningless visual noise. By the late nineteenth century, as my last chapter showed, these aggressive, meaningless visual surfaces were not just symbols in certain urban literary and entertainment venues; they had become a central part of spectacles that identified themselves as "American."

In this chapter I continue this line of thought by considering the transference in the late nineteenth century of the properties of "American" appearance away from the body to the surfaces of built environments. To be sure, as earlier chapters have shown, habitats had always been central to the ethnic nationalist vision. Early racial theorists and Germanic supremacists had identified the land of a given people as a powerful force in shaping their essential character and destiny. But such theories were brought to new life in the late nineteenth century in the international system of world's fairs, which mandated that nationalities materialize themselves in buildings and landscape features. As I will show, ethnic and national dress, with their implications of embodied character, continued to be central to exhibition culture. Often, indeed, landscapes and built environments were only given regional specificity through their containment of personages wearing ethnic or national dress. At the same time, the world's fair system turned topography into the new ethnic dress, reimagining the regions of the globe not just as distinctively clothed but also as distinctively shaped by or productive of a given people.

In the following pages, then, I begin by tracing the interweaving of nation and ethnicity with architecture and landscape in the composition of the Chicago Exposition's community of international edifices. I spend considerable time on my description and analysis here, partly because there is little scholarship on the architectural tropes of national difference and ethnic personality at world's fairs and partly because it is only by understanding the principles at work in the construction of nationality and race in the non-U.S. buildings that we can understand the comparable constructions of "America" within the fair's scenographic idioms. I then turn to an examination of the Chicago Exposition's instantiations of "Americanness," focusing in particular on the fair's famous White City, which I consider in both its visual and discursive formations.

Scholars have almost unanimously understood the White City, which was in fact painted all white, as a sincere and direct tribute to white racial supremacy. But if we compare the White City to the way race and ethnicity were materialized in other national buildings and exhibits at the fair, this reading becomes more complicated. Instead, I argue, the White City, which fairgoers described not as an enclave of authentic white racial substance but as a blaze of lights and reflections, functioned in the way that antebellum clothes functioned, as a site of visual overload that foiled the transmission of national, racial, and ethnic personality from object to the eye of the viewer. Including in its landscape and architectural elements the recognizable features of "Old World" cities, most prominently the city of Venice in Italy, the White City offered "America" as a set of technological surfaces that both parodied and hollowed out the ethnic body in order to re-present it as a meaningless blaze of light, an assault on the eyes that blocks and distracts from proper perception.

Throughout the chapter, I argue that the performance of national, racial, and ethnic identity in the fair's scenographic media closely mimicked the performance of embodied identity established earlier in the century through costumes; architecture and costumes were understood as cognate sites of transmission when it came to the apprehension of the alleged spirit of nation, race, folk, or ethnic group. This later nineteenth-century insistence on America as a place of dazzling lights devoid of content was thus a kind of architectural fruition of earlier typifications of Americans as dressed in dazzling clothes that also had no discernible content or personality behind them, something made clear if we look at the use of ethnic and national costumes at the fair. In the final section of the chapter, I discuss the afterlife of the White City, whose brilliant white forms were almost immediately duplicated and re-erected to become the staple features of a new kind of popular entertainment: the amusement park. Although the amusement park was a global phenomenon not linked to any one nation, its visual grammar was henceforth "American." Its whirling lights, machines, and scenographic elements seemed to capture an enduring American personality.[8] I suggest in these final sections that although these glittering, technological surfaces were part of a symbolic complex originally devised to challenge ethnic nationalism's presuppositions, they emerged as themselves ethnic structures, seeming in their very emptiness and reflectivity to beam out "Americanness" to eye of the world.

The Scenes of the Foreign

To understand the extent to which the World's Columbian Exposition reconstituted an existing repertoire of nationalist visual idioms in its creation of "American" spaces, it is useful to begin by looking at the extent to which the fair as a whole called upon nations to actualize themselves in exhibitionary landscape and architecture. Nineteenth-century nationalism had thrived on the romanticization of landscapes and architectural formations, forging powerful links, as Lloyd Kramer says, between "territorial homeland and distinctive national cultures."[9] Naturally occurring geographical formations, such as mountains, seas, prairies, deserts, and lakes, were incorporated into nationalist imaginaries as signs and embodiments of national spirit and unity. These were complemented by architectural remains and monuments. In the nineteenth century, Anthony Smith notes, "Castles, tells, temples, and dolmans" were "naturalized" as part of a nation's character, "integrated into the landscape and treated as part of [the nation's] special nature," as Stonehenge was for England.[10] Architecture too, often accompanied by regional topographic and landscape features such as gardens or canals, came to play an increasingly central role in ideas of national and ethnic materialization. In particular those architectural elements associated with a romantic past or folk culture were believed to transmit in particularly pure form the national character and "peculiar genius" of the nation's people.[11]

Nowhere were these conventions of national and ethnic materialization more peculiarly realized than at late nineteenth-century world's fairs. In one sense, world's fairs, the modern form of which was launched by the Crystal Palace Exhibition in London in 1851, were not rooted in parochial, regional, or national interests.[12] "Established to exhibit mercantile capitalism's internationalist and expansionist ambitions," according to Roger Luckhurst, world's fairs hypothesized an amorphous, "borderless" globe; they "aimed to condense the world into a single, easily traversable site encompassed by the harmonious utopian vision of free-trade capital triumphant."[13] Sometimes funded by sovereign nation-states but more often bankrolled by venture capitalist and commercial interests, world's fairs oriented themselves around the display and circulation of technology, raw commodities, manufactured goods, knowledge, the arts, and entertainment attractions. In their commercial features, world's fairs purported to encapsulate not the world's sovereign powers but modernity itself. In Alexander Geppert's words, "the exhibition's significance far exceeded any local context. Not only was the exposition modern but modernity itself was on display; the continuous attempts to create an illusionary unity, a fictitious, transitory and largely self-contained realm in which the audience could immerse itself on each such occasion, was reflexively considered modern."[14]

Nevertheless, world's fairs achieved this "illusionary unity" through the ethnic and national branding of their separate parts. Conceived as elaborate trade and technology fairs, world's fairs were also sites of nationalist celebration and "global encounter."[15] That is, the corporations and entertainment entrepreneurs that financed world's fairs offered themselves as representatives of nations, sometimes with the sanction and direct support of the governments involved, and sometimes not. In the often fictional performance of sovereign nationality that went on at fairs, host countries vied to outdo each other in the splendor, cost, and size of their buildings, the ingenuity of their exhibits, and the innovation and monumentality of their designs. Visiting countries (or their representative commercial interests) displayed themselves in what were now conceived as characteristic scenic and architectural vernaculars. Often the displays offered fairgoers an immersive virtual experience; fairgoers seemed to enter into or behold a synechdochal fragment of a distant place, a foreign country, a city. In Geppert's words, world's fair sites were conceived as a lively patchwork of "fleeting microcosms of national self-representation" inside the grand conceptual space of the "metropolis."[16] In the late 1880s, when world's fairs began advertising themselves as a kind of miniature grand tour in which attendees could visit all the regions of the earth in a day or two, there was a positive demand that the various countries, nations, colonies, and population groups represented in the exhibition not merely display goods or technologies but appear to perform and personify themselves in some characteristic, often caricatured, form. In these circumstances fair designers drew not just on well-known regional landscape and architectural elements (the Tower of London, Versailles) but also on a variety of objects, colors, costumes, and insignia that only became associated with specific countries in the turn-of-the-century world's fair system. Indeed, Paul Greenhalgh underlines that it was the world's fair system that helped popularize the crude national signs that proliferated in tourist hubs all over the turn-of-the-century West and are still found in souvenir shops today; half-timbered houses with wattle and daub infill, for example, which were found all over northern Europe, suddenly became signs of "Englishness," the very soul of "Olde Englande."[17] Porcelain steins were "German."

Held to honor the quadricentenary of Columbus's voyage to the Americas, the World's Columbian Exposition in Chicago in 1893 was organized and financed by Chicago millionaires. The largest, costliest, and most widely attended of the late nineteenth-century international expositions, the Columbian Exposition represented the United States's bid to compete among the newly self-conscious, militaristic theaters of empire being consolidated among nations in Europe. As *Harper's* proclaimed, "It is America putting its best foot forward."[18] Costing twenty-eight million dollars and covering almost seven hundred acres of Jackson Park on Lake Michigan, the fair was home to 65,000 exhibits from forty-six countries.[19] In addition to introducing Europe to U.S. power and grandeur, the fair was also organized, most historians agree, to have a palliative effect on affairs inside the United States. The brainchild of financial elites striving to quell fears around economic volatility and waves of violent dissent sweeping through U.S. working-class and immigrant communities, the Chicago Exposition sought to shift attention away from domestic strife and turn it instead toward visions of utopian amity among the peoples of the world. Like other world's fairs, it sought to bolster and narrativize the supremacy of the West while also offering pictures of all the nations and populations of the world coming together in a benign, productive collage of cultures.

The "display" of national character at the fair took three major forms: designated "foreign buildings," built by countries or their commercial representatives; displays set up by nations and colonies inside the various "great buildings"; and elaborate immersive environments or "attractions" that recreated distant places in virtual form. Before tracing more closely how these sites worked as signs and purveyors of nationality, it is worth describing what fairgoers would have encountered as they moved among these seemingly virtualized regions of the earth.

Most prominent among the national sites were the "foreign buildings," state-sponsored edifices and exhibits that were typically designed by renowned vernacular architects and rendered in picturesque architecture associated with the country's history. In some cases, the foreign buildings served as offices for fair bureaucrats; in others they served as exhibitionary structures. They featured interiors of a characteristic national style and were filled with local products, food, arts and crafts, and curiosities. Some of the more famous of these national buildings included the Japan and Spain pavilions. The Japan pavilion, called the Ho-o-den, consisted of three annexes built on Wooded Island, each of which was inspired by architectural styles dominant in Japan's long history. The annexes were filled with examples of Japanese décor and material culture: screens, porcelains, silks, and rare artifacts from Japan's Imperial Museum. The exterior of the Spanish Building was inspired by fifteenth-century Spanish gothic architecture. The interior, according to visitors, was one of the most ingenious and breathtaking at the fair; it recreated the magnificent hall of columns in Valencia's Llotja de la Seda.

The second form that displays of nationality took involved the exhibits inside the various exhibition or "Great Buildings." In these cases, nationalistic or regional decorative features often served as little more than ethnic and national branding; they gave otherwise anonymous products an air of cultural heritage. Inside the Agricultural Building stood a booth sponsored by a cigarette manufacturer located in Cairo, which displayed its tobacco products inside a structure made to look like an Egyptian temple. In the Mines and Mining Building, great piles of silver-bearing rocks from New South Wales, indistinguishable from rocks from anywhere else, were given regional flavor with surrounding tropical plants and signs printed with the names of Australian towns. In the Manufactures Building, English and Irish manufacturers mounted extensive exhibits of porcelain, silver, woolens, and linens; these were given heritage status by being displayed behind quaint storefronts evocative of late eighteenth-century London. Although Russia did not have a building at the fair, its representatives contrived a spectacular exhibit in the Manufactures Building, constructing a pavilion within a pavilion inspired by the colorful turrets and domes of St. Basil's Cathedral in Red Square. Upon entering, fairgoers seemed to enter an "ancient cathedral" and were treated to displays of lavish garments made of rare Russian furs and artworks in silver, bronze, and glass.[20]

The third way that nations and regions were performed and materialized at the fair was in the form of elaborate virtual or recreated environments. Instead of being sponsored by countries and open to all fair visitors, these environments were typically financed by entertainment entrepreneurs who charged admission. Conceived as sideshow attractions rather than ambassadorial or edificatory structures, these re-creations often traveled from fair to fair. Their status at fairs—did they belong inside or outside the formally curated grounds?—was often contentious. Partly to deal with their ambiguous position, the Chicago fair organizers decided to design a street dedicated purely to rides and sideshows. They called it the Midway Plaisance. It not only became the model for the "midways" that would henceforth emerge as standard features of exposition space, but it also originated the modern amusement park, which almost as soon as the fair closed was developed in the United States and Britain. Even more than other parts of the fair, the Midway was designed as a tour of the world. Indeed, its various parts offered fairgoers virtual, immersive journeys into exotic lands that were supposed to be indistinguishable from what an actual journey to these locations would be like.

One of the most famous of the attractions, for example, was the Street in Cairo, where visitors seemed to enter an actual section of the city of Cairo, complete with noisy bazaars, ancient domiciles, a temple, donkeys, snakes, dogs, and seemingly native Egyptians in their customary clothes going about their daily lives. Another popular attraction was Old Vienna, a recreation of an eighteenth-century Viennese square of shops and "antique houses" with a bandstand and beer garden at its center (see fig. 39). The German Village featured a life-size village scene with Bavarian houses, a saloon, a library, and a marketplace. The most infamous attractions were the "native villages" where groups of people from distant locales worked on contract (which frequently shaded into indentured servitude), essentially performing caricatures of themselves for fairgoers.[21] First making their appearance at the Paris Exposition Universelle in 1889, these villages were central attractions on the Midway at Chicago and included an Algerian and Tunisian Village, a Samoan Village, an American Indian Village, an Eskimo Village, a Chinese Village, a Dahomey

PLATE 108

OLD VIENNA, ON THE MIDWAY.

Fig. 39. Charles Dudley Arnold, "Old Vienna on the Midway," *Official Views of the World's Columbian Exposition, Issued by the Department of Photography*. Ed. C. D. Arnold and H. D. Higinbotham. Chicago: Press Chicago Photo-Gravure, 1893. Plate 108. Author's collection.

Village, and a Javanese Village, among others (see, for example, fig. 40).[22] Like other recreations, the "native villages" were elaborately contrived to give fairgoers a sense of having traveled to a distant locale. The Javanese village, in the words of one journalist, encompassed more than eighty huts "composed of wickerwork, the huts being thatched with palm leaves." In addition, visitors could attend a Javanese "theatre and watch a contingent of royal dancers."[23]

It is important to stress that in their effort to particularize regions and populations and to find their equivalents in architecture, these sites developed elaborate taxonomies and interpretive systems intended to school fair attendees in fine and often arbitrary discriminations. The Chicago Exposition as a whole came with an enormous textual apparatus—an army of gigantic guidebooks, catalogues, publicity packages, and narrativizations—that told attendees how to read, interpret, historicize, order, and particularize everything they saw. This textual apparatus forms

PLATE 96

THE SAMOAN VILLAGE, ON THE MIDWAY.

Fig. 40. Charles Dudley Arnold, "The Samoan Village on the Midway," *Official Views of the World's Columbian Exposition, Issued by the Department of Photography*. Ed. C. D. Arnold and H. D. Higinbotham. Chicago: Press Chicago Photo-Gravure, 1893. Plate 96. Author's collection.

an often jarring contrast to the photographic record of the fair; sites that seem crude and shabby in photographs are given texture and vivacity through narrative description. But precisely to the extent that these discursive aids seemingly differed from the scenes caught in photographs, they illustrate the fair's reliance on pregiven interpretive and visual rubrics; fairgoers were intended to project points of view onto what they saw. What becomes apparent from a reading of the textual materials related to "foreign" structures and environments is their reliance on a set of semiotic codes that matches almost exactly the codes used to elaborate the workings of ethnic, national, and racialized bodies and costumes. The guiding principle of these codes was communicative transparency; architectural edifices, landscape arrangements, and decorative objects were all assumed to divulge information to attendees and to effortlessly communicate their origins and interior logics. Like the national, ethnic, and racialized bodies developed over the course of the nineteenth century and studied at length in chapter 1, world's fair scenographic entities were assumed to be transmitting authentic and verifiable information about the character of the people to whom these entities belonged.

In many cases, sites that offered to transport visitors to distant lands rested their claims to the conveyance of truth on simple re-creation; a well-known architectural icon, such as Valencia's Llotja de la Seda, was replicated in all its detail using modern construction materials. In other cases, buildings relied for their conveyance of national and ethnic authenticity on sign and symbol systems. Frequently at work in these were "signs," in the sense meant by Roland Barthes in his famous essay in *Mythologies*, "The Romans in Films." Writing in the 1950s, Barthes notes that characters in contemporary Hollywood films about ancient Rome convey Roman-ness to audiences by sporting a short fringe of hair on their foreheads. All the Roman characters have this fringe. According to Barthes,

> We . . . see here the mainspring of the Spectacle—the *sign*—operating in the open. The frontal lock overwhelms one with evidence, no one can doubt that he is in Ancient Rome. And this certainty is permanent: the actors speak, act, torment themselves, debate "questions of universal import," without losing, thanks to this little flag displayed on their foreheads, any of their historical plausibility. Their general representativeness can even expand in complete safety, cross the ocean and the centuries, and merge into the Yankee mugs of Hollywood extras: no matter, everyone is reassured, installed in the quiet certainty of a universe without duplicity, where Romans are Romans thanks to the most legible of signs: hair on the forehead.[24]

In the world's fair system, signs of nationality frequently worked like the fringe in Hollywood films about Rome. A certain window style announced "Vienna"; the curve of a stone wall was "Ireland."

At the same time, this simple system of signs worked in tandem with the idioms of embodied character. In an ad for the Woolson Spice Company, for example, the conveyance of national character at foreign sites exploits the verbal and visual tropes of embodied nationality, ethnicity, and race. Fairgoers in the ad are invited to see not China, but the "Chinaman with wooden shoes and pigtail"; they are promised a glimpse not of Scotland but of "the Scottish Chief and his highland Bride" (see fig. 41).

Writing in *Toward a Global Idea of Race*, Denise Ferreira Da Silva underlines the extent to which the creation of nineteenth-century globality hinged upon a conceptual confusion of "global regions" and "bodily and social configurations." Transforming "race (a term previously employed to describe collectivities in terms

Fig. 41. Woolson Spice Co., "Going to the World's Fair." *World's Columbian Exposition.* 1893. Library of Congress via Internet Archive.

of blood relationship) into the racial (a scientific concept)," post-Enlightenment Europe produced "the human body as an exteriorization of productive *nomos*," rewriting the "manifoldness of human bodies into signifiers (exteriorizations) of the mind (intellectual and moral attributes)." Nineteenth-century nationalist and ethnic symbol systems extended themselves outward from these primary propositions; regalia, manners, personal decoration, national and ethnic dress, were all theorized as coextensive with the body in their supposed exteriorization of national, ethnic, and racial spirit. By extension, the "various social configurations found across the globe"—regional populations, customs, architecture, landscape—were now understood as "actualizations of different minds."[25] In other words, the creation at world's fairs of visual and tactile panoplies that seemed to belong to specific regions of the globe drew on the figurations that already described regional and racialized bodies, for it was the body, by seeming to be an exteriorization of invisible inclinations and moral and intellectual abilities, that most clearly registered regional difference and particularity. Thus one of the first things we notice about the typification of nationality through architecture and topography at world's fairs is its resemblance to the typification of nationality through dress.

Invented in the nationalist movements of the nineteenth century, cults of ethnic dress centered on the fantasy of a timeless past in which a people or folk existed in a state of unselfconsciousness, their cultural artifacts, unadulterated by modernity, constituting pure expressions of their peculiarity as a tribe. Closely related to the racialized body, which promised to convey the true inner character of a person or population group through biovisual features (hair, stature, skin, etc.), national and ethnic costume hypothesized a spontaneous, unmediated, expressive relationship between clothes and their wearers. Instead of being conceived as cultural additions to the body, national, ethnic, and tribal dress was conceived as spillover, the bubbling up to the surface of a body's pregiven internal spirit and genius.

These features of national and ethnic costume—their refusal of modern Western temporality and embrace of the ancient past, their claim to transmit a people's authentic, unadulterated spirit through the disposition of visible material forms—were precisely the principles that governed the architecture and landscape of the foreign sites at the Chicago Exposition. To convey their "nationality," the foreign sites and attractions engaged in two fundamental maneuvers. They rejected the modern West and created visual and discursive links to a fantasized, romantic past, often a past associated with an ethnic or racialized population group. They also insisted on the notion that architecture and scenic designs opened a window into the true spirit of the people, something that was achieved through the literal incorporation of seemingly authentic artifacts in the design and interior decoration of buildings. The goal here was to indicate a continuity between the surface of the buildings and their insides that would echo the similar relationship between the inner spirit and outer surface of the ethno-racialized body.

It was understood, for example, that national, ethnic, and "tribal" spirit expressed itself most profoundly in the architecture understood as "rustic," "picturesque," and "romantic" rather than modern. The division here was similar to the one between timeless heritage clothing and ever-changing modern fashion. In his report on the architecture of the Chicago Exposition, Henry Van Brunt, one of the fair's judges, explained the logic behind architectural edifices in general. "In each case [the structure's] general form and the character of its detail, especially its decorative detail, are developed from the spirit and essential characteristics of its contemporary phase of civilization or semibarbarism."[26] Brunt does not, however, place modern architecture in this category. It belongs, on the contrary, to the same category as "fashion." It is constantly changing, bodying forth design for its own sake. "[M]odern architecture has become so conscious of itself that it is in a measure sophisticated, affected, insincere and therefore apparently not so accurately representative of its era."[27] Like the curators of ethnic costumes, the architects of the national buildings purported to reach into the past, to a time before modernity, to find appropriate expressive idioms through which to convey national character in its ostensibly purest form.

In their descriptions of national structures, guidebooks to the Chicago fair's exhibits emphasized the special authenticity suffusing those architectural designs that called upon some ancient, long-lost moment in a country's past. The fair's promotional materials, which were handed out to journalists and writers of guidebooks, extolled the ancient past of a nationality as a privileged site of inspiration in the design and making of the foreign buildings. By extension, it was a prerequisite of the legitimacy of these buildings that they seem to reach into the past as a changeless site of national, ethnic, and racial authenticity. In Trumbull White and William Igleheart's gigantic guidebook, the words "ancient" and "old" are included in virtually every description. The elaborate Japan annex is "copied from one of the finest specimens of ancient Japanese architecture."[28] The Ceylon building's "architecture partakes of the Dravidian style as it appears in the ruins of ancient temples throughout the islands" (548). The Norway building "is built after the model of the old 'Stavkirk,' a peculiarly Norwegian style of architecture which dates back to the twelfth century" (549). Describing the German building, "The handsomest and most expensive of all the foreign edifices," White and Igleheart note, "The centre is in the form of a chapel, rich in decoration. Bay windows, projecting balconies and turrets lend it a most picturesque appearance, closely resembling an old German city-hall, such as may be seen even now in some of the ancient towns of the empire" (549).

Like national and ethnic clothing, which purported to ferry the inner spirit of the ancient people to the visible surfaces of their living representatives in unmediated form, these architectural edifices offered themselves as sites of authenticity and plenitude in which there was an utter continuity between the national or ethnic spirit and its material manifestation. Guidebooks and journalistic commentary frequently mention that certain national buildings are not just made in imitation or re-creation of certain architectural styles but are in their very materials extensions of the organic substance of their home countries; they are constructed of raw materials from their region and even built by local residents of the nation or colony. Of the Japan pavilion, White and Igleheart say, "The lumber of which this edifice was constructed was all prepared at Japan and was brought here and put together by Japanese workmen" (543). They say of the Ceylon building, "The beautiful Singhalese woods used in this building were cut and fitted in Ceylon and shipped here to be put together" (548) (see fig. 42). Similarly, "The steep roof" of the German building "is covered with shining glazed tiles imported from Germany" (549). The contents of these buildings amplify this conceit of organic extension between exhibit

Fig. 42. Charles Dudley Arnold, "The Ceylon Building," *Official Views of the World's Columbian Exposition, Issued by the Department of Photography*. Ed. C. D. Arnold and H. D. Higinbotham. Chicago: Press Chicago Photo-Gravure, 1893. Plate 79. Author's collection.

site and parent country by being full of indigenous products and artifacts: spices, silk, teas, sculptures, preserves, missals, prayer books, illuminated manuscripts, bells, etc. Indeed, the indigenized innards of these buildings emphasize their interchangeability with the clothed ethnic nationalist body whose internal and external composition are the same.

These same principles—architecture channels the spirit of the people and materializes this spirit much as the body and clothes do—governed the national and ethnic immersive environments offered as entertainment on the Midway. Here again, advertisements and guidebooks stressed organic connections to the home country or region. *Conkey's Guidebook* informed visitors that the Midway included a German Village, "which came from Germany in a shipment of over 6,000 pieces, representing farm buildings, markets, shops, meeting hall and church, all in the style of the twelfth century. It contains many interesting antiquities from the German museum at Mayence."[29] The Irish villages that appeared on the Midway like-

PLATE 95

DONEGAL CASTLE, ON THE MIDWAY.

Fig. 43. Charles Dudley Arnold, "Donegal Castle," *Official Views of the World's Columbian Exposition, Issued by the Department of Photography*. Ed. C. D. Arnold and H. D. Higinbotham. Chicago: Press Chicago Photo-Gravure, 1893. Plate 95. Author's collection.

wise claimed to be connected to an ancient and organic Irishness. Sponsored by the Countess of Aberdeen, these villages consisted of two "picturesque" hamlets, including "a street of typical cottages, market people, and the ruins of Drogheda Castle."[30] "At the end of the courtyard," according to White and Igleheart, "stands a portion of the 'Wishing Chair' of the Giant's Causeway. It stands on real Irish soil."[31] Channeling the spirit and organic specificity of their distant home places, the Midway's immersive recreations offered themselves as the equivalent of a voyage to the place itself (see fig. 43). According to British journalist Frederick Villiers, the Midway's famous "street in Cairo" was thronged with "Egyptians, Arabs, Soudanese and other Africans," as well as "shopkeepers, camels, donkeys, dancing girls." "I know my Cairo well, but I must say, after what I saw at Chicago, that I think that Cairo must be entirely stripped of its old lattice work, for it seemed to be all there by the shore of Lake Michigan, in fact, only the walls were artificial; the doors and woodwork were veritable relics of the past" (see fig. 44).[32]

Fig. 44. Photo by Weber [Street of Cairo Section of the Midway at the World's Columbian Exposition, Chicago, Illinois]. 1893. Photographic print, albumen. Library of Congress Prints and Photographs Division LC-DIG-ds-05104.

This description of the Street in Cairo, as well as descriptions of the fair's other immersive national and ethnic environments, draw attention to their reliance not just on a particular architectural idiom but on the interplay of architecture and bodies as companion signifiers and dual transmitters of authenticity. It is by encountering not just the Cairo-esque latticework but also the "Egyptians, Arabs, Sudanese and other Africans" in the Cairo Street that Villiers experiences Cairo virtually. Indeed, as the popularity of the many populous native villages suggests, sites were brought to life by the presence of seemingly real inhabitants who appeared in what fairgoers could read as ethnic or indigenous dress.[33] This was true not only of the native villages and colonial exhibits that featured Indigenous people, but also of the European ones. The Hungarian Orpheum, which consisted of a café and concert pavilion, featured "Hungarian artists, brought direct from Budapest." "The native costumes and modes of life of the different nationalities which compose this empire are shown."[34] The French Cider-Press consisted of "an open pavilion where cider is made from apples, in a typical French press, by French peasants, and served to visitors by French country maidens in Normandy caps and short skirts."[35] The Turkish Bazaar exhibit not only offered customers exotic trinkets but also salespersons dressed in lavish regional clothing (see fig. 45). One of the most popular sites on the Midway was the exhibit of the International Dress and Costume Company, in which "forty-five or more beauties" "display their charms of form and face, and their striking national costumes."[36] At these sites, costumes and architecture worked as mutually reinforcing, interacting structures of transmission in ways that equated the outside and inside of the body and outside and inside of the building with the characterological demands of Western ethnic nationalist ideology. Fairgoers were offered the chance to taxonomize, decode, and experience the world's regional populations in their seemingly real, viscerally present, microcosmic forms.

In this chapter so far, I have detailed the visual rubrics according to which fair buildings and sites constructed nationality, ethnicity, and race. As we have seen, these sites drew not just on the imitation of regional landscape and architecture but also on the regimes of intelligibility that had been established earlier in the century for national and racial bodies. Assumed to be instruments of transmission or communication, the surfaces, including the costumes, of these bodies conveyed the character of a people or person in transparent and unambiguous ways. It was precisely this same regime, I will now argue, that reigned over the flamboyantly "American" parts of the fair. As in the case of the foreign sites, the American sites were organized around the visual schematics of racialized and ethnic bodies, but instead of acting as media of transmission, the surface of the "American" site was distinguished by its visual noise. As in the case of the foreign buildings, moreover,

Fig. 45. Charles Dudley Arnold, "In the Turkish Bazaar," *Official Views of the World's Columbian Exposition, Issued by the Department of Photography*. Ed. C. D. Arnold and H. D. Higinbotham. Chicago: Press Chicago Photo-Gravure, 1893. Plate 102. Author's collection.

the American sites were anchored by a body, not the transparent body of Western racialist and nationalist fantasy, but the overclothed, radiant, and garish body of the "American," a figure associated with visual overload and lack of meaning.

The American Scene

Understanding the principles through which the "foreign" was actualized in the architecture and landscape of the fair allows us to see these principles at work in the "American" portions of the fair as well. The U.S. presence at the World's Columbian Exposition was, of course, immense. As host country, the United States provided an envelope for all of the fair's exhibits. In addition, acres of space in the great buildings were devoted to the display of everything from American technological wizardry, the highlights of which were Edison's Kinetoscope and Tower of Light, to American-made agricultural products and works of art. But Americanness, as a peculiar national quality, was materialized at the fair in highly specific ways.

On the one hand, the United States offered itself on the model of the various ethnic and incipiently nationalist regions contained within the old empires of Britain, Europe, South America, the Middle East, and Asia. Just as Scotland and England appeared at the fair as discrete units inside the United Kingdom, the United States displayed itself as a composite of regions and ethnicities that were discreet in their character and history. Each state of the United States constructed its own building at the fair (though in some cases where states could not raise capital for their own state building they shared buildings or went unrepresented). These were all designed on the same pattern as the foreign buildings at the fair: they were regional in their design referents; they offered themselves in romantic, rustic, and picturesque styles; they summoned some past moment in the state's history; they purported to be constructed of materials indigenous to the region; and they were often full of material goods and products indicative of the state's economy, geography, populations, resources, and biome. The Texas State Building was constructed, according to White and Igleheart, "after the style of the old Spanish Mission, and is a good example of Spanish renaissance architecture." The Florida State Building is "an exact reproduction of old Ft. Marion, St. Augustine's remarkable Spanish Fort. . . . The fortress was erected in 1565. The reproduction is faithful; bridge and moat, watch-tower, sentry box and parapet, curtain and bastion are exactly as in the original."[37] Also prominent were British Colonial and early national styles. The Virginia Building was "an exact representation of Mount Vernon, the building in which George Washington lived and died." The Massachusetts State Building was "a reproduction of the residence of John Hancock, which stood on Beacon Hill."[38]

But the most spectacular, memorable "American scene" at the Chicago Exposition was the vast, magnificent "White City" that formed the heart of the exhibition grounds. The late nineteenth-century expositions held in European cities tended to exploit existing urban infrastructure, gardens, and topographical features. The Paris Exposition in 1889 was particularly memorable for taking advantage of Paris's legendary gardens and palaces, its shady riverbanks, bridges, and islands, to create luxurious exhibition and leisure spaces. Having nothing similar to work with, the Chicago Exposition designers, Daniel H. Burnham and Frederick Law Olmstead, decided to make their own city and waterways from scratch. They designed a set of massive pavilions and gardens, all of which they arranged around engineered waterways and canals cut out of the Lake Michigan coastline.

The buildings were unusual. Massive in scale, majestically neoclassical, they were all painted a brilliant white.

Entering the fair by boat from the Lake Michigan side, fairgoers passed under a vast white-columned peristyle to emerge at one end of a large blue lake, called the Grand Basin. On either side of the lake, their terraces running down to the water, were two majestic, white-columned, glass-roofed exhibition buildings. On the right was the Manufactures Building, its forty acres of floor space making it at that time the largest building in the world; on the left was the almost as large Agriculture Building. Straight ahead, across the length of the Grand Basin, stood the domed, Renaissance-revival—and again all white—Administration Building. On all sides of the Grand Basin were fountains and pure white statues of personifications and creatures caught in mid-motion. These statues were gigantic; some were four and five stories tall. On the waterways beyond the Grand Basin were islands and little bridges and black gondolas gliding in the water. The total effect—the dazzling white palaces, the white columns unfolding themselves into seeming infinity, the blue water, sparkling fountains, and pearly domes—was, by all reports, breathtaking. As we have seen, it would be the White City structures that became the signature architectural feature at amusement parks in the United States, Britain, and Europe (see figs. 46 and 47).

In an important sense, the White City did not abide by the standards of other buildings at the fair. Though clearly meant to signal "America," it was unrelated to U.S. history or traditions; it did not refer to any recognizable feature of U.S. geography or landscape. In the words of one journalist, the White City "looks least like America of any place this side of the world of the obelisks."[39] Fantastical in its conception, the White City was not done in the rustic or picturesque style. Indeed, Beaux Arts neoclassical and renaissance architectural motifs, of which the White City made liberal use, were considered the opposite of the picturesque; they were considered generic and characteristic of metropolitan space. Writing about the White City at the time of its construction, architect Henry Van Brunt, whose equation of ethnic architecture with the picturesque is cited above, described the aims of the White City's architects. Wanting "a uniform and ceremonious style" expressive of the "highest civilizations in history," they rejected "any form of romantic, archaeological, or picturesque art."[40] In addition, the White City exhibition buildings or Great Buildings, as they were called, were not made out of definably local or even durable materials. What looked like white stone and marble from a distance was actually a material called "staff," a mixture of hemp, plaster, and cement that could be molded and painted to look like stone but would last only through the six months of the fair. The insides of the buildings had nothing to do with the outsides.

Fig. 46. Charles Dudley Arnold, "Looking West from the Peristyle," *Official Views Of The World's Columbian Exposition, Issued by the Department of Photography.* Ed. C.D. Arnold and H.D. Higinbotham. Chicago: Press Chicago Photo-Gravure, 1893. Plate 102. Author's collection.

Built to house a large variety of exhibits from places all over the world, the Great Buildings were the equivalent of a series of malls or covered markets.

Given its abstract, generic function, the White City seems to belong to a different framework of intelligibility than, for example, the German Building. It was characteristic for host cities to erect some kind of marvelous, largely technical or abstract structure through which to figure the inclusiveness, the purely structural rather than hereditary relations of civic nationalism. Summoned in these structures was not a folk or ethnic past but the exposition's ties to metropolitan life and its reach forward into an as-yet unrealized future. The Eiffel Tower in Paris, then the tallest structure ever built, had served this purpose at the Exposition Universelle in 1889. Before that, it was the glass and iron Crystal Palace, built in 1851 for London's Great Exhibition. With its unconventional color and design, its gargantuan spaces, and engineered water and landscape features, the White City as a whole followed in the footsteps of these previous demonstrations of the technological mastery of space and form. William Dean Howells called it the "greatest marvel of the competitive world." It struck him as a premonition. "I feel as if I had caught a glimpse

Fig. 47. Frances Benjamin Johnson, *Palace of Mechanic Arts and Lagoon at the World's Columbian Exposition, Chicago, Illinois.* 1893. Library of Congress Prints and Photographs Division LC-USZC4-2097.

of the glorious capitals which will whiten the hills and shores of the east and the borderless plains of the west."[41] This prophetic role was not purely speculative. The White City went on to inspire the "City Beautiful" movement in the United States, in which architects were hired to imagine cities not as parcels of land for commercial developers but as areas intended for public edification, entertainment, and aesthetic pleasure.

And yet the White City did not strike observers as strictly abstract either. Several important U.S. architects condemned the White City as an imitation of obviously European designs and flourishes; for Louis H. Sullivan it was "a naked exhibition of charlatanry in the higher feudal and domineering culture" of Europe.[42] Celebrated at the time and copied in U.S. pavilions at subsequent fairs, the White City quickly became an object of ridicule. Modern scholars feel that it gives material form to late nineteenth-century U.S. capitalist and racialist imperialism. Many, for example, see the White City as a symptom of capitalist ideology, brewed in the effort of U.S.

capitalists to build what Alan Trachtenberg memorably calls the "incorporated" state. In this analysis, the White City, with its implications of luxury and references to Old World grandeur, exists to mystify the cynical workings of capitalist consumerism, providing a "landscape of fantasy in which goods might be displayed as progress, as emblems of a beneficent future."[43]

Other scholars argue for the White City's racialist itineraries. Writing in the 1980s, Robert Rydell offered an innovative and compelling reading of the designers' use of the color white. Built to display U.S. imperial power during the era of Jim Crow, the Great Buildings with their pearly exteriors and imposing white statues, according to Rydell, literalized beliefs in white racial supremacy. Rydell argues that the Midway Plaisance was arranged as an illustration of human progress and evolutionary hierarchy, with the various Indigenous villages representing the least developed forms of humanity, the Chinese and Japanese the next most developed, and western Europe and the United States the most advanced, with the White City at the apex. Visitors to the fair drew this conclusion as well. In the words of one journalist, "the best way of looking at these races is to behold them in the ascending scale, in the progressive movement; thus we can march forward with them starting with the lowest specimens of humanity and reaching continually upward to the highest stage."[44] These topographies mimicked the scientific racism of the fair's ethnological exhibits curated by the Smithsonian, which, according to ethnologist Harlan Ingersoll Smith, were "arranged and grouped to teach a lesson; to show the advancement and evolution of man."[45]

In other words, while the White City did not offer itself as an ethnic or racialized structure precisely—at least within the rubrics set out in the other national sites and buildings—it also did not offer itself as purely abstract, as free of the symbol systems that determined racialized and nationalized entities. That is, for all its seeming rejection of conventional signifiers of ethnic nationality, the White City clearly made itself available as a structure that could be read on the same terms as the foreign and ethnic sites at the fair. The bridge between these two modes of reading, I would suggest, was what I have called in this study the "American" body. Instead of participating in the production of embodied ethnicity as this was articulated in the foreign edifices at the fair, the White City represented the extension of the principles behind the stereotypical flashy, empty American body into the realm of scenographic and architectural design.

As it was devised in the U.S. nationalist imaginary over the course of the nineteenth century, the American body was conceived not as a positive entity in and of itself but as a kind of broken or perverse version of the conventional ethnic and racial body. Nineteenth-century science and epistemology privileged the surface of the typical ethnic body as the site of definitive information about character, intelligence, evolutionary stage, predilections, and so on. The same was true of the American body. But instead of existing as a transparent set of surfaces whose visual features ferried forth a stable moral, intellectual, and genetic character, the American body, covered in its garish clothes, was understood as a set of surfaces that impeded the transmission of information. Instead of announcing its own transparency and organic coherence as a national or ethnic entity, the American body presented itself as a site of visual noise, distraction, and reflexivity that deflected precise racial and ethnic attribution; it was thus characterized as empty and meaningless, little more than a set of dazzling tricks and reflections. The surface of the American body was the site where interpretive systems that depended on the decoding of visual clues got lost in a scene of visual clutter, glare, and reflections.

Accounts of the White City figure it in precisely these terms. It features in contemporary accounts not as white, precisely, but as an array of lights, reflections, and dizzying colors that confuses attempts to discern character. Moreover, in the same way that the American body appeared as a kind of parody of the Western racialized body (its surfaces should have transmitted debased character and origins but did not), the White City functioned as a kind of parody of the interpretive frameworks of fair architecture. The White City's architects were vocal in their rejection of the picturesque, but they nevertheless included in the design of the White City substantial references to picturesque architecture, in particular the architecture of Venice, Italy. Exploiting European façades and design elements while at the same time repudiating their powers of referentiality, the White City was able to suggest that the inner areas of the edifice where spirit might dwell were missing and vacant. It replaced the signature sites of European transparency and authenticity with forms that announced themselves as hollow and stagey, reinforcing the impression of meaninglessness as a central feature of Americanness.

I want to stress here again that I do not mean necessarily to suggest that the White City actually looked the way it was described. As we have seen, verbal description of the sites at the fair potentially overstates the glamour and allusiveness of the material structures. Nevertheless, these rhetorical flourishes articulate the conventions of viewing, the expectations, fantasies, and projections, that fairgoers and commentators brought to the material forms. Just as certain seemingly arbitrary signs could indicate "Norway" or "Java," a certain arrangement of surfaces and effects indicated "America." In addition, while I do not want to suggest that fair designers consciously devised buildings that would possess the same qualities as the fabled loud, overdressed American types that peopled the scenery of late nineteenth-century globality, I do want to argue that contemporary investments in national, ethnic, and racial stereotypes and their unique visual vocabularies led designers to work within certain frameworks of intelligibility, which were then revived in accounts by fairgoers, journalists, and others recording their impressions of the fair.

In the reading ventured here, the signal features of the White City, its white paint, its European-inspired façades, and its Venetian flourishes, are not intended as transmissions of a European or racially white moral and intellectual character, but as sites at which the European emphasis on visual markers as fail-safe clues to character is parodied and reflexively turned back on itself. Thus, the very markers that should point to the genetic history and living spirit of the folk turn out to be mechanical and inert. The whiteness of the white city, instead of transmitting racial character, turns out to be a mere technology of reflecting light and color. The Venetian exteriors, which should be connected to the spirit of Europe, advertise themselves as hollow constructions. The White City contains the same elements as the foreign buildings and sites at the fair, but it does so in order to show visitors that, in fact, there is no meaningful information being transmitted through its visual spectacle. The spectacle is all there is. As I will propose at the end of this chapter, however, this quality of spectacle for its own sake was also what made the White City seem quintessentially "American"; the love of spectacle was elaborated as a kind of ethnic characteristic of the American people.

The Light of the White City

In her discussion of contemporary paintings of the Columbian Exposition, Margaretta M. Lovell underlines, as Rydell does, the insertion of the White City into racialized Western imperial history. "As though haunted by the memory of Thomas Cole's *Consummation of Empire* painted a half century earlier and the popular phylogenic concept of civilization that it embodies," artists who painted the fair, according to Lovell, "were careful to fix this moment in what they understood to be American historical progress. As in Cole's work, the buildings are metaphors for a cultural state, the acme of political evolution, artistic sophistication, and economic dominance." Lovell adds, "The Midway . . . was not simply the White City's foil (popular, commercial, visually heterogeneous, multinational); it related to its blond neighbor as a cluster of architectural and cultural predecessors, an outgrowth of Charles Garnier's History of Human Habitation in forty-four dwellings (from Stone Age to contemporary) at the Paris Exposition of 1889."[46]

In one sense, of course, Lovell and Rydell are correct. The fin de siècle world's fairs were all Western imperialist phenomena; many of them were overtly called "colonial fairs" and sought to sell empire as an instrument of Western wealth and prosperity. However, it is also the case that the White City, for all its seeming references to the peoples of northern Europe, did not call upon the architectural tropes of northern Europeanness set out in the more clearly northern European buildings at the fair. These buildings, as I outline above, operated according to the conceits of ethnic nationalist historicity, locality, and heritage; the quality of being Norwegian was conveyed not in the coloring of the Norway Building but in its allegedly archaic design, its regional contents, its use of building materials peculiar to the forests of northern Europe, and its seeming ability to transmit to present viewers the changeless past of the Norwegian folk. In this sense, the White City was not racially "white" in the same way that the Norway or German buildings were racially "white." References to its color almost invariably stress radiance and light over pigment. The whiteness of the buildings, instead of serving as a signifier of an Anglo-Saxon or Teutonic heritage and character, is understood in contemporary accounts as a technology through which light is refracted and bounced back to the eye of viewers.

Even before the White City had been built, when the fair was still in the early planning stage, Lyman Gage, the first president of the Chicago fair's board of directors, imagined it purely as an array of colors and reflections. He pictured fairgoers climbing to the top of an Eiffel Tower–like structure to "see beautiful buildings radiate with color and flashing the sunlight from their gilded pinnacles and domes."[47] Descriptions of the completed White City are not unlike Gage's in their emphasis on it as a spectacular visual display, a bold, disorienting panoply of color, radiance, and reflections. Indeed, descriptions of the White City tend to emphasize no other sensible features of it outside of the overwhelming impression it makes on the sight. Although the color white features in these descriptions, the white is often important chiefly for its reflective qualities, its ability to redouble and refract the effects of light and color.

In a children's novel, *Two Little Pilgrims' Progress*, that tells the story of two orphans' lone journey to the Chicago fair, Frances Eliza Hodgson, author of *The Secret Garden*, describes their first sight of the fair as they "passed beneath the snow-white stateliness of the great arch" of the peristyle. Before them "The water of blue lagoons lapped the bases of white palaces." The children see nothing but these white colonnaded "marvels," whose surfaces reflect "the green of sward and broad-leaved plants, the sapphire of water, the flood of color and human life passing by." The narrator goes on, "It was so white—it was so full of the marvel of color—it was so strange—it was so radiant and unearthly in its beauty."[48] The same emphasis on disorienting color and radiance is found in Candace Wheeler's account, "A Dream City," published in *Harper's New Monthly Magazine* for their special series on the Columbian Exposition. The fair is filled with "shining architectural wonders."[49] Fairgoers see "aerial domes of gold or crystal, flashing facets of color against the sky" and "waving flags and gonfalons, softened in outline, varied in color and crimped by ripples from moving launches and gondolas." All of this, "seen under the sunset sky, filled with bits of winged and floating cloud, is enough to overfill the heart of the most prosaic of mortals, or to delight stray spirits of the air."[50]

In many accounts, all that fairgoers see is a blinding array of lights. "The white walls of the Court of Honor, with their heroic statues, and allegories in plaster, shone in the sun in blinding glory. . . . At the end of the lagoon rose . . . the Peristyle, white as glistening marble."[51] Owen Wister reported that "a bewilderment at the gloriousness seized me . . . until my mind was dazzled to a stand-still."[52] The whiteness of the buildings both dazzles the eyes with its glare but also intensifies, by reflecting and refracting, the play of colors. "Multiform and many-colored flags bloomed like flowers over and against all these colossal walls of white."[53] One journalist, reporting how "the sun shone brightly on the dazzling white buildings" during the day, goes on to describe how at night white and colored lights lit up the Court of Honor and Grand Basin. "The fountains start and are brilliantly illuminated in colours, as the vast floods of water splash and the spray is blown away." Lit by flood lamps at the top of the buildings, the basin flashes and "ripples with a sheen of silver."[54]

Motifs of reflection and reflexivity, of surface visuality for its own sake, as well as motifs of theatricality, run through discussions of the White City. Candace Wheeler notes how the White City, surrounding as it does the pool of the Grand Basin, "owes its last and crowning charm to color and reflection. The doubling of beauty gained by water reflection could hardly have been taken into adjunct, and its effect upon the general glamour is beyond calculation." She adds that this doubling of beauty is again doubled through "The constant repetition of beautiful forms of architecture, starting in immaculate and ivory whiteness from the green strip of lawn."[55]

Unlike the foreign buildings, which locate meaning in a fantasized transparent relationship between the visible parts of the edifices and their heritage spirit, the White City fixes interpretation on the surface of the structure, a surface that, instead of transmitting positive information about the culture of the American people, bounces back and distorts light and color. Something similar was at work, I would suggest, in the White City's references to Venice. Scholars who discuss the White City as a racialist construct assume that the fair designers were meditating on problems internal to the United States, on conflicts over segregation, immigration, working-class disaffection and anxiety around the United States's future as an imperial power. In this analysis, the fair was designed to assuage internal discontent. In the words of Jackson Lears, "Class and race conflict dissolved in the neoclassical vision of regeneration through art and culture—a dream of universal unity that reinforced the developing discourse of empire."[56]

But evidence suggests that fair designers were worried less about assuaging internal problems than about what kind of figure the United States would cut on the global stage among what one guidebook called "skeptical European minds," that is, minds unconvinced that the United States would be able to match the high standard of expositions recently held in France in particular. Located in Chicago, far away from the Atlantic circuit, the World's Columbian Exposition began, according to this report, with a "great handicap" and "did not receive the impetus that was given to previous expositions held in London, Paris, or Vienna."[57] Informed of the Exposition, Britain and France were "lukewarm" and "perfunctory" in their support.[58] The designers' focus on Europe rather than the domestic United States as a problematic scene of competition is nowhere more cogently revealed than in the "European" themes of the White City.

As I mention above, picturesque architecture was rejected as a basis for the White City. Nevertheless, the White City contained powerful references to one of the world's most picturesque spots: the city of Venice in Italy. Scholarship on the fair, while it acknowledges the influence of Venetian architecture on the fair's design, does not examine the oddity and full implications of this choice nor the lengths to which designers went to achieve the Venice effect. Designing the White City's navigable waterways, with their bridges, towers, and islands, Burnham and Olmstead had been directly inspired by Venice's signature canals, islands, lagoons, docks, bridges, and towers. The construction of the canals was the same. In the words of one historian, "By making the edges of the channels vertical and then filling in behind the walls they could create an effect similar to the canals of Venice."[59] The Exposition's Administration Building, which stood at one end of the Court of Honor, was inspired by Venice's luminously white Santa Maria della Salute basilica, which guards the entrance of the Grand Canal (see fig. 48). To emphasize the connection, the canals of the White City were filled with imported black gondolas and gondoliers in Venetian costume, which ferried fairgoers around the grounds. These connections were not lost on fairgoers. Visitors to the fair routinely talked about feeling as if they had been transported to Venice. Candace Wheeler felt she had entered "the floating hours of Venice."[60] Wandering about the fair in *Two Little Pilgrims' Progress*, the children find "a gondola with a rich-hued, gay-scarfed gondolier." Meg exclaims, "Now we are in Venice!"[61]

But why refer to Venice at all? The neoclassical elements of the White City, the rows of white columns, for example, clearly refer to the culture of Athens and

Fig. 48. Frances Benjamin, [Exposition grounds, World's Columbian Exposition, Chicago] 1893. Library of Congress Prints and Photographs Division LC-USZC4-2097.

Rome. This was not an unconventional connection. Links between the United States, commonly considered a modern democracy and republic, and ancient Athens and Rome, the supposed origins of democracy and republicanism, were not unusual. Neoclassical architecture, in addition, was considered more abstract and metropolitan, less attached to a specific locale than other styles and therefore less likely to seem out of place in Chicago. In addition, the buildings of the White City could vaguely evoke the White House and Capitol Building in Washington, DC. In this context, the choice of Venice is puzzling. Venice was not metropolitan. Its signature canals and architectural landmarks were not, at this period, commonly reproduced in architectural motifs. And they were very much associated with Italy and its vernaculars, much as St. Basil's in Red Square was associated with Russia. But the very fact that Venice was not considered reproducible suggests that this was in fact the quality of it that attracted fair designers. Indeed, if we look more closely at the position of Venice in European and U.S. discourse of this period, we can see that fair designers were interested in architectural forms that would both read as quintessentially European and parochial and yet lend themselves to parody and anonymization. Valued as a richly ethnic space that was often racialized and orientalized, Venice, I argue, could perform in tandem with the white paint to suggest the White City's strategic deployment of ethnicized and racialized forms that had been emptied of their ethnic and racial content.

In the Vapor of the Lagoons: Venice in the White City

In the early twentieth century, Venice would be transformed into the "tourist maze" it is today,[62] but in the late nineteenth century Venice was still associated with the stereotypically exotic, orientalized world of the "East." According to Margaret Doody, following its surrender to Napoleon in 1797, Venice emerged as an object lesson for western Europe, illustrating the cyclical nature of empire. A once great Mediterranean power, Venice, in this formulation, had succumbed to the inevitable forward march of civilization by disintegrating and falling victim to such newer, fresher empires as France and Austria-Hungary. Venice was thus famous among nineteenth-century intellectuals as an object of colonization and a place of backwardness and decay.[63]

To a degree not usually remarked by historians, U.S. authors and intellectuals were centrally involved in the orientalist construction of Venice. Writing his Venice novel, *The Bravo*, in 1831, James Fenimore Cooper described Venice in much the same terms as he described Indigenous populations in North America. Venice was an ancient, exhausted world, doomed to succumb to the Western empires. He said of Venice, "Men lived among her islands in the state of incipient lethargy which marks the progress of a downward course, whether the decline be that of a moral or a physical decay."[64] Describing the child beggars who swarmed tourists on the island of Torcello in the Venetian Lagoon, Henry James, writing in the early 1880s, wrote, "They were very nearly as naked as savages, and their little bellies protruded like those of infant cannibals in the illustrations of books of travel." "Savage" and "cannibalistic," these children are to James like Venice itself, stranded "on the lonely margin of a decaying world, in prelude to how blank or to how dark a destiny?" The cathedral at Torcello, instead of reminding James of a mutual Christian past, reminds him of some "primitive orthodoxy":

> [T]he terribly distinct Apostles are ranged against their dead gold backgrounds as stiffly as grenadiers presenting arms—intensely personal sentinels of a personal Deity. Their stony stare seems to wait for ever vainly for some visible revival of primitive orthodoxy, and one may well wonder whether it finds much beguilement in idly-gazing troops of Western heretics—passionless even in their heresy.[65]

At the end of the century, the Harvard scholar Charles Eliot Norton was one of the world's great experts on "the rise and fall of Venice."[66] Indeed, Venice's fame in the United States had just reached its apex in the 1890s as Venice replaced Rome as a hub for U.S. imperial tourists, its dilapidated palazzi playing host to such U.S. luminaries as Anders Zorn, John Singer Sargent, Henry James, Francis Marion Crawford, Julia Ward Howe, and Isabella Stewart Gardner.

Like other racialized sites in the Western global imaginary, Venice was understood as a transparent precinct, suffused with its own peculiar spirit. Its allegedly decadent, exhausted character was for contemporaries embodied in its architecture, with its peculiar colors and the condition of its masonry. Henry James' pictures of Venice in "The Aspern Papers" conjure "a mausoleum" of "repaired breaches, crumblings of plaster, extrusions of brick that had turned pink with time."[67] In *Italian Hours*, James imagines Venice possessing a deep, hidden energy that lives behind its visible surface. In tropes linking architecture and flesh, James says this hidden Venice is like a "creature" and "varies like a nervous woman. . . . She has high spirits or low, she is pale or red, grey or pink, cold or warm, fresh or wan, according to the weather or the hour."[68] In a fantasy of mutual affection, James goes on, "The place seems to personify itself, to become human and sentient and conscious of your affection. You desire to embrace it, to caress it, to possess it; and finally a soft sense of possession grows up and your visit becomes a perpetual love-affair."[69]

But it was precisely James's Venice, with its flesh-colored surfaces and moody interiors, that was missing from the White City. Although clearly citing Venice, the White City eschewed the colors and trompe l'oeil effects that might have recreated Venice on the same terms as, for example, the recreated Lonja de la Seda or the recreated Monticello. Indeed, this architectural refusal of virtuality and the poetics of re-creation is highlighted if we consider the probable origins of the White City.

In 1891, at about the same time that designers began planning the Columbian Exposition, the Hungarian-born spectacle producer Imre Kiralfy, who had trained in Paris and worked for two and a half decades in the United States, mounted an extravaganza in London called "Venice in London" (sometimes called "Venice: The Bride of the Sea"). Utilizing the five-acre space of London's Olympia Exhibition Centre, Kiralfy built gargantuan "Modern" and "Ancient" life-size replicas of Venice that included a Grand Canal and exact duplicates of Venetian buildings. One half of the exhibition building was devoted to "Modern Venice" and was an immersive, virtualized site, the city "as it exists today." In this section were re-creations of Venice streets along which visitors could wander as if walking the actual streets of the city. The other side, "Ancient Venice," was a stage with seating for many thousands of spectators. This stage section was built for spectacle, again on a vast scale. Between the audience and the stage was a huge indoor lake, the Grand Canal, on which the performances took place. Audiences watched "the most imposing spectacle of its kind ever witnessed in London," a "ballet on an immense scale" and a "grand aquatic carnival." According to the *Times*, "A hundred gondolas [were] imported from Venice," along with "Venetian gondoliers." Ballet dancers numbering in the hundreds performed on "the uncertain footing" of "ornamental gondolas and flat-bottomed *zatarre*." Afterwards there were "exciting gondola races," as well as enactments of "several dramatic and historical episodes connected with medieval Venice." The stage scenery resembled "a gigantic and splendid panorama."[70]

As a producer of spectacles, Kiralfy worked closely with world's fairs in the United States and Europe from the 1880s to the 1910s. It is probable that his Venice extravaganza in London influenced the White City architects, who likewise mounted a large-scale theatrical set piece built around Venice's signature architectural features. There were, however, important differences in the way these two Venices were conceived and described, differences that suggest the extent to which the Chicago Venice, built only a year later, was keyed to a set of expectations, characteristics, and visual effects already typified as something other than "Venetian."

Kiralfy's "Venice in London" was discussed in much the same way as the foreign buildings and exotic immersive sites at the Chicago fair. It was offered as a piece of the real Venice, in all its sensuous detail and particularity. After visiting "Venice in London," the reviewer for the *Times* of London wrote, "Every house has been copied from some Venetian original, and various styles of architecture, from the severity of the early Gothic to the voluptuous delicacy of the renaissance are represented with fidelity and skill." In contrast to the White City in Chicago, which was described as a set of lights and shining surfaces, "Venice in London" took pains to invoke temporal layering and interiority, the mystery of things hidden. Visitors glimpsed little peculiarities. "Here, in a niche in a wall, from which the plaster has fallen in flakes, leaving visible the bricks beneath in picturesque red patches, is the miniature figure of a Madonna with the *bambino* in her arms." Like Chicago's foreign buildings and immersive ethnic sites, Kiralfy's "Venice in London" called upon the visual and tactile rubrics of late nineteenth-century regionalism, ethnicity, raciality, and their architectural and design equivalents, like the picturesque. Like James's Venice in *Italian Hours*, "Venice in London" is conceptualized by the reviewer as a flowing, living, organic thing. "Close at hand the tendrils of a climbing plant twine round a small wooden balcony of singular simplicity and gracefulness, while below a canal flows noiselessly along its narrow channel and winds in and out between the houses and beneath the little bridges which lead from *calle* to *calle*."[71]

By contrast, the Chicago Venice, although built only a year later, called upon an entirely different set of scenographic tropes. Even as it included the formal shapes of Venetian architecture—a canal, a bridge, a cathedral dome—these were anonymized; they were literally whitewashed and blended into the scenery of the White City as a whole, made part of its disorienting and undifferentiated play with reflections of light and color. Not a single account of the White City mentions its faithfulness to the details or essential nature of Venice. Instead, like the glare of the white paint on the exhibition buildings, Venice themes, I would venture, were included at the fair so that they could emphasize that the essence of Venice is, in fact, *not there*. Gesturing at a famous, ethnically saturated heritage site that it makes no effort to virtualize or recreate, the White City can produce impressions of vacancy, of things missing. Venice is present but only as a façade, a spurious shell or outline of itself. In this way, the architects and designers included Europe in the conceptual frame of the American fair, but Europe appears as a kind of parody or emptying of itself. The march of the buildings from lowest to highest, from the most barbaric to the most civilized—and then finally to the most American—can be understood as a purification of contents until the contents disappear completely in a wash of light.

It is important to stress that contemporary descriptions of the White City corroborate this reading. Whereas commentators describing the foreign and state buildings go to some lengths to draw connections between their appearance and the essential spirit, history, and heritage of the peoples they purport to represent, which are understood to be organically coextensive and mutually reinforcing, descriptions of the White City tend to dwell on its ephemerality and its hollowness. The White City is frequently described as transitory and meaningless.

The White City buildings were built in much the same way that stage sets would have been built. A steel or wood frame was covered with pieces of "staff," a mix of gypsum, glycerine, dextrin, and hemp that had been cast in molds and shaped to look like stone or marble. Staff had first been used four years before in the Paris Exposition.[72] Extremely lightweight and easy to shape, staff covered the wood and steel armatures of the buildings. In the case of the White City, the staff coverings were painted to look like white marble. It is important to note that many of the foreign and state buildings were also made of staff, as were most sites on the Midway, but the flimsy impermanence and the mere trumpery of the outsides of these structures were not understood as fundamental to their identity. On the contrary, those sites infused with conventional ethnicity, raciality, historicity, and regional character—the reproductions of Monticello or Drogheda Castle, for example—were assumed, despite the transience of the materials with which they were built, to be sincere; they transmitted the spiritual character, the truth, of the spaces they represented. The staff in this instance was ignored. In discussions of the White City, the opposite was true. Commentators drew attention to flimsiness, transience, and superficiality as central to its identity.

Describing the White City, Van Brunt emphasized its tricky, superficial qualities. The great buildings will be "an unsubstantial pageant of which the concrete elements will be a series of vast covered inclosures . . . faced with a decorative mask of plaster composition on frames of timber and iron, as the romans of the Empire clothed their rough structures of cement and brick with magnificent architectural veneers." The emphasis on bodily coverings here is not coincidental. In the case of ethnic clothing, the coverings of the body are assumed to convey information about the moral and intellectual character of the clothed subject; here, on the other hand, the "masks," "faces," "clothes," and "veneers" are themselves the chief points of interest. Van Brunt goes on to specify that the buildings are ethereal, without density. "Mr. Burnham, the Chief of Construction, rubs his wonderful lamp of Aladdin . . . and the sudden result is an exhalation, a vast phantasm of architecture, glittering with domes, towers, and banners, like the vision of Norumbega, which presently will fade and leave no trace behind."[73] Another architect, Montgomery Schuyler, wondered at the end of the fair "Whether the cloud-capped towers and the gorgeous palaces of the World's Fair are to dissolve, now that the insubstantial pageant of the fair itself has faded." Schuyler hypothesized that in the White City buildings, classic masonic shapes had lost "touch with their origins," leaving only the outline of a "form"; these formal outlines can now be used without a "suggestion of any real structure or any particular material."[74]

Moreover, contemporary descriptions of the White City fortify the idea that it was organized around the idea of evacuation; they emphasize its emptiness, its lack of proper heft, with respect to its pointedly European signs. The painter Edwin H. Blashfield remembered arriving at the workshop where the pieces of the White City were being constructed. He had just come from studying "classical columns in the Roman Forum where drum upon drum had been piled by antique enginery and years of labor." At the White City workshop, by contrast, he sees

> groups of a half dozen men debonairly picking up a colossal fluted thing that looked like a monolith, standing it on end and with light tackle fitting a Corinthian cap to it; white walls were rising as you watched and domes seemed big iridescent bubbles in the vapor of the lagoons. . . . What was it all? This was staff, they told me—and what was staff? Something light to juggle with and stop out wind and weather long enough for exhibition purposes.[75]

Unlike the monumental marbles of Rome or the famous "stones of Venice" contemplated by John Ruskin, the White City is a "bubble" in a "vapor." Montgomery Schuyler called the White City "a success of illusion." It is an example "not of work-a-day building, but of holiday building" and "display." Barely three-dimensional in Schuyler's account, the White City is a "painter's dream of Roman architecture."[76] More critical than his peers, Louis H. Sullivan, architect of the Chicago fair's Transportation Building, which stood out from the rest of the exhibition buildings by eschewing white paint and opting instead for a huge gilded doorway, disdained the rest of the White City for its superficial imitation of European forms. It was "an imposition of the spurious upon [the] eyesight; the White City was comprised of the 'bogus antique.'"[77]

In its hollow performance of ethnicity, then, the White City duplicated the overly clothed and hollow "American" figures that had peopled the world of antebellum entertainment and that were coming alive again in late nineteenth-century traveling shows. Like the figures in Melville's *The Confidence Man*, the White City presented a distracting surface of formal flourishes that dazzled the eye, preventing coalescence of the positive ethnic and racial properties organizing other national sites at the fair. These were properties whose absence the White City also emphatically recorded in its tributes to and evacuation of a colonized Venice. At the same time, the hollow emptiness of the White City's features, their tricky, purely technical mastery of visual space, were not qualities devoid of ethnic and national meaning. Like other national sites and virtualized habitats at the fair, the White City had a populace, a brace of seeming "occupants," both real and pictured. These included employees like the gondoliers who rowed guests around the canals, as well as updated national personifications like Columbia and Uncle Sam, who featured in contemporary cartoons and promotional materials. Like the White City, which was imagined as a hollow formal contrivance, a kind of shining mask of paint, these denizens and personifications of

"America" were understood as a hollow, gaudily clothed population associated with cheap theatricality. What is made plain by an examination of these costumed personages is the extent to which qualities of tricky hollowness and theatricality, even as they defied Western standards of ethnic and racial transparency, had themselves come to represent a kind of "American" ethnicity.

We can see this notion of American ethnicity coalesce in journalist Amy Leslie's account of the fair. Unlike most fairgoers, Leslie found fault with the White City. She took a special dislike to the contrivance of the gondolas and gondoliers, which she found inaccurate and inauthentic. Focusing on the costumes of the gondoliers, she disabused her readers of the "supposition that actual gondoliers of Venice array themselves in such noisily comic-opera regalia" as the fair commission had consigned to the gondoliers of the White City. "[H]itherto no conversational satin stripes nor tawdry fringes have found room around the Venetian gondolier's sinuous hips outside of a summer burlesque." No one in Venice, she says, is wearing "azure jackets with lawn-tennis trowsers made of awning canvas, *a la* Turk, tinsel fringe." She goes on, "[S]ong-and-dance sleeves and melodramatic collars never thrust their bellowing glares against the blues of Italy."[78] Emphasizing images of reflectiveness (tinsel, glare) and theater (comic-opera, burlesque, song-and-dance, melodrama), Leslie condemns the contrivance of the gondoliers. But, as Leslie specifies elsewhere in her chronicle, it is also this quality of vacant theatricality, of the shiny "tinsel" and "song-and-dance sleeves," that makes these overdone uniforms characteristically *American*. In other words, in Leslie's account, these tinseled, theatrical outfits without content figure as the equivalent of ethnic clothing; they are the sincere expression of the American personality.

According to Leslie, each region in the world has its own expressive forms. In this explicitly racist formulation, there are "Turkish odah gyrations, Egyptian sorcery, African nudity and French rhodomontades [vainglorious boasting or bragging]." What is the form of expressiveness most typical of the United States? Leslie claims that U.S. national identity is contained in this quality of fake showiness. "Addled variety shows and theatrical pugilism are indigenous to the reputed civilization of America."[79] For Leslie, the cheap tinsel and glitter are for Americans what "nakedness" is for "Africans": both convey the essential personality and traits of their respective nationalities, both are "indigenous." It is important to note that even as Leslie disdains the garb of the American gondoliers, her emphasis on them as not Venetian also obscures and displaces their potential ethnic and national content, making them, in effect, unreadable within accepted nationalist rubrics. Like the White City whose waters they ply, these gondoliers are American to the extent that they are recognizable as gaudy shells, theatrical displays.

Themes of brilliant reflexivity and theatrical display were at work not just in Leslie's account but also in contemporary cartoons and illustrations of American fair-going culture. That is, when Americans and personifications of America were pictured in fair-related materials they tended to be pictured in the terms set out by Leslie. In some cases, the dazzling, distracting features of American personages were made cheekily overt. In a full-color, centerfold political cartoon in *Puck*, titled "The Cue for the Transformation Scene," the Columbian fair is depicted as a theatrical event that takes place on a stage. Female personifications of the Republican and Democratic parties stand downstage dressed in spangled medieval costumes, smiling and shaking hands in delighted amity. Upstage is the glimmering set of the White City. Meanwhile, the stage trap door is open below, busily swallowing up the monstrous domestic political problems from which the dazzling, faux medieval damsels distract. With its female allegories vaguely reminiscent of Columbia but outfitted in sparkles and colorful drapery, this cartoon literalizes the idea of "America" as a set of glittery surfaces and dazzling scenographic elements that distract the eye and thus prevent it from seeing a "real" America (see fig. 49).[80]

This hollow showiness as a feature of the "American" character on the world stage was also present in the fair's iconic "American" figures. Americanness was most frequently represented in fair materials through images of Uncle Sam. In the 1870s, Uncle Sam had replaced Columbia and Brother Jonathan as the preferred personification of the United States among cartoonists on both sides of the Atlantic. Uncle Sam (whose initials spelled "U.S.") had in fact existed since the late eighteenth century as a close cousin of Brother Jonathan and was often conflated with him. Like Jonathan, he was a "Yankee" and the artifact of an early nineteenth-century transatlantic comedy and cartoon circuit that gloried in ethnic caricature. Early stage and cartoon Yankees, we will recall, purported to represent unsophisticated backcountry New Englanders and appeared to audiences in the overbright, loudly patterned coat, vest, and pants that signaled ethnicity. In these early incarnations, as we have seen, Jonathan's costume was the equivalent of a European ethnic costume, offering to relay the peculiar folk spirit and personality of a regional population through that population's unique form of dress. But as the figure of Brother Jonathan faded away and Uncle Sam took its place in the 1870s, largely through the work of political cartoonists, his earlier links to ethnic stereotyping and to specific New England populations, class structures, and customs vanished. Only the bright costume, now covered in the abstract pattern of the U.S. flag, remained. Whereas the old Brother Jonathan had come equipped with what audiences assumed was his peculiar regional or folk heritage, the more modern Uncle Sam was developed in Civil War–era political cartoons as a vaguely northern, republican but ultimately

Fig. 49. W. A. Rogers, "Puck: World's Fair Chicago" ["The cue for the transformation scene"]. 1893. Chromolithograph centerfold in *Puck Magazine* [unknown issue]. Author's collection.

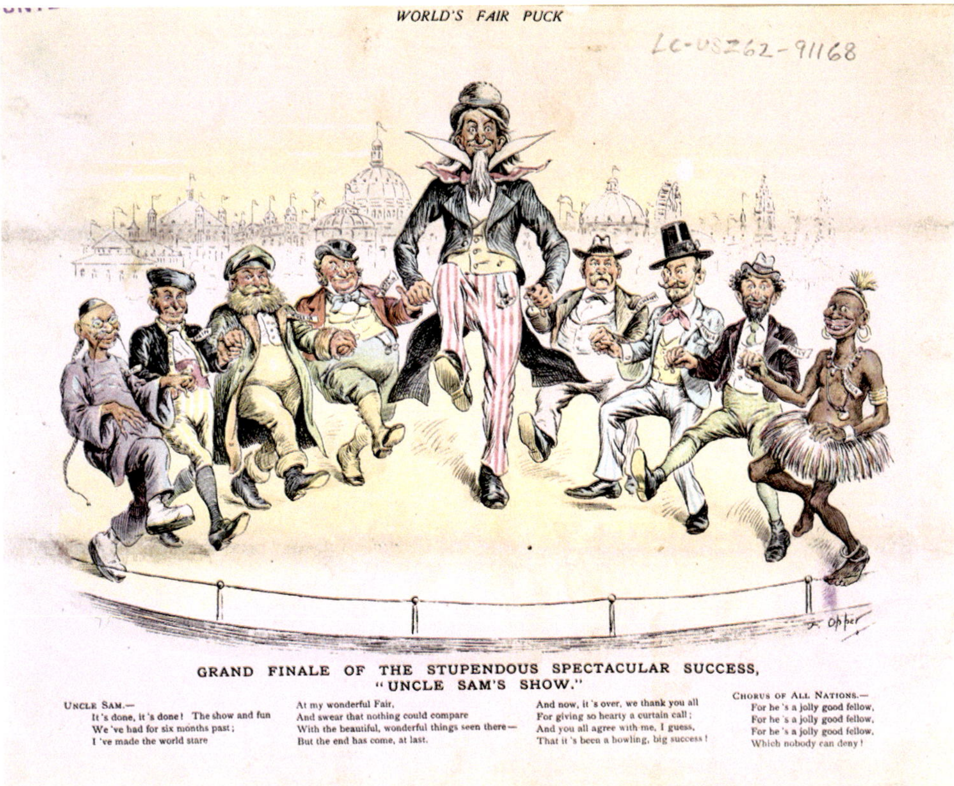

Fig. 50. Frederick Burr Opper, "Grand Finale of the Stupendous Success Uncle Sam Show." 1893. *Puck Magazine* (unknown issue), 1893. Chromolithograph print. Alamy Stock Photo.

nonpartisan, personification who did not embody any local virtues or characteristics but who was instantly recognizable as "American." In an important sense, in other words, Uncle Sam worked in much the same way that the White City worked. He was a hollow shell, a remnant of an ethnic structure whose putative spirit had been expunged and whose meaningless bright surface was all that remained. He was also associated, like Yankee characters generally, with the theater.

In keeping with Leslie's sense that "Americanness" conveys itself in "bogus" and self-consciously stagy forms, the dress of Uncle Sam, although no longer referring to familiar heritage and ethnicity, features in Chicago Fair promotional materials as the equivalent of ethnic dress. In a cartoon titled "Grand Finale of the Stupendous Spectacular Success Uncle Sam Show," Uncle Sam is depicted celebrating the end of the fair surrounded by representatives of the world's nations in caricatured national and ethnic costume (see fig. 50).The implication here is that Uncle Sam is in his national/ethnic costume as well.

This equivalency, however, is not exact. The clothes of other racial and ethnic caricatures in these illustrations purport to open a window onto the population group's history, intellect, and culture. Uncle Sam's costume, by contrast, is intended, in the words of the "Grand Finale" song, to "make the world stare." In the "Grand Finale" cartoon, what distinguishes Uncle Sam from the crowd of other ethnic and racialized peoples is not some quality that can be linked to embodied character but merely the noisy extravagance and brightness of his dress. The points of his collar are exaggeratedly long, as are the matching points of his bright red neckerchief, and his red-striped pants, yellow vest, and blue coat are the most vivid on the page. The other ethnic costumes are muted by comparison. Instead of communicating information about the American past or culture, Uncle Sam is the equivalent of the faux gondoliers, a figure in a cheap stage costume whose only purpose is to stand out, to draw the eye. In other words, what other ethnic costumes achieve through a network of signs and referential markers, in which clothes offer to transmit the intrinsic ethnic national character of their wearer, Uncle Sam's costume achieves through bright visual display for its own sake. Uncle Sam's bold and meaningless visuality *is* his ethnic character.

Pictorial images of Americans at the fair amplify this visual assertiveness in ways that chime with the reflective visual effects of the White City. An illustration of Leslie herself, which again hints at ethnic status, features Leslie standing proud among cringing, unflattering caricatures of the representatives of the world's nations (see fig. 51). Leslie disappears behind an assault of light caused by her giant journalist's star, which sends out violent, dazzling rays before which the rest of the world bows and cowers. The stripes on Leslie's dress link the journalist's star to the stars and stripes of the U.S. flag and the Uncle Sam suit, inserting Leslie into the narrative of Americanness not as a positive identity but as a bold panoply of light, a piercing effect on the eyes. Leslie's distinctiveness as an American lies in the fact that whereas those surrounding her are instantly legible as racial and ethnic subjects, our perception of Leslie's features is unavailable, lost behind the rays of her star. Leslie is a kind of nobody, an empty if dazzling form.

In this chapter, I have tried to show the extent to which, as a self-conscious site of Western nationalist competition, the World's Columbian Exposition incorporated long-established stereotypes of Americanness in its design. By the end of the century, certain visual arrangements—scintillating light, reflection, glaring whiteness, signs that seemed to fail in their summoning of a designated presence—had come to mean "Americanness" as surely as plaid meant Scottishness or the prow of a Viking ship meant Danishness. While the White City architects did not perhaps consciously summon these stereotypes, they devised buildings and landscapes that could readily be included in an existing nationalist visual repertoire that plaited

Fig. 51. Amy Leslie, Frontispiece, *Amy Leslie At the Fair.* Chicago: Conkey, 1893. Buffalo Bill Center of the West.

together American character and forms of aggressive visual display that defied standards of transparency. These rubrics would go on to define the amusement parks and other entertainment sites that blossomed directly out of the Chicago fair. Like the White City, these new sites emphasized an American look: the shine of lights, the reflection of white façades, and the incorporation of identifiably ethnic, often European or orientalist architectural and topographic motifs that could signify the absence of the thing at which they gestured. As we will see, it is precisely this arrangement of glittery surfaces that Gorky confronts on Coney Island and assumes, correctly, that this—the fiery light, the blazing sparkle, the dead and meaningless forms—is the epitome of all that is "American."

Reflections of the White City

As soon as the World's Columbian Exhibition was dismantled in the fall of 1893, entertainment entrepreneurs took its signature architectural motifs and used them as the basis for a newly invented entertainment phenomenon: the amusement park. Inspired by the success of the Columbian Exposition attractions, the first amusement parks, which sprang up in the United States and Britain in the 1890s and early 1900s, were basically permanent "Midways," versions of the Chicago Exposition's Midway Plaisance without any of the edificatory paraphernalia. Amusement parks were made up of the rides, sideshows, concessions, and virtual entertainments that had proved so popular at Chicago. Partly because they seem to extend from the World's Columbian Exposition, amusement parks are often understood as a peculiarly "American" mass cultural form. In their opening up of lavish entertainment to millions of ordinary people, amusement parks are often considered the first true instances of modern mass culture, shortly to be followed by cinema. They are often understood to be forces of "Americanization." Rydell argues that in Britain and Europe amusement parks were considered "American" partly because they extended the Chicago Exposition's mixing together of high-culture exhibits and popular sideshow attractions. "At precisely the moment some Americans were starting to force culture into categories of 'high' and 'low,' the World's Columbian Exposition, by encouraging millions of fairgoers to travel freely between the Midway Plaisance and White City as part of their exposition experience, had the effect of loosening those categories and making mass culture seem quintessentially American."[81]

It is also true, however, that in the 1890s and 1900s, amusement parks, whatever their origination within cultural hierarchies, were made to *look* American. A central portion of all new entertainment complexes in both the United States and Britain contained "White Cities," architectural façades and landscape designs that imitated the famed Venetian topography and white paint used in Chicago. In fact, these were sometimes called "White Cities."[82] The moniker "White City" emerged as an informal but potent entertainment brand, indicating to customers of new amusement venues that those parks incorporating a "White City" were on the cutting edge of the entertainment business. It is important to stress that these entertainment ventures were not attached to the United States in any literal sense. The development of modern mass entertainments like amusement parks was a Western phenomenon that grew out of world's fair activities. But the framing of these new amusement ventures as "American" illustrates the extent to which Americanness emerged at the fin de siècle as a kind of national and ethnic look divorced from actual origination in or even connection to the United States, something that is made apparent if we look more closely at the evolution of the White City phenomenon.

To be sure, the first amusement parks to copy the White City architecture and typography were in the United States. Visiting the World's Columbian Exposition in 1893, entertainment entrepreneur George Tilyou returned to Coney Island determined to imitate its signal features. When Tilyou opened the first of the modern Coney Island amusement parks, Steeplechase, in 1897, he included not only a version of the Ferris Wheel, which had made its debut on the Midway Plaisance of the Columbian Exposition, but also "a boat ride along the Grand Canals of Venice."[83] Versions of Venetian architecture, often painted brilliant white or covered in light bulbs, were henceforth a signature of the new amusement parks and themed cities that flourished across the global West. Featured at Steeplechase, Venice played an even more important role in the two subsequent Coney Island amusement ventures, Luna Park and Dreamland. Built by architect Frederic Thompson, who had started as a janitor at the Chicago Exposition, and Nebraska showman Elmer Dundy, Luna Park was an agglomeration of faux Venetian domes, canals, bridges, and Campanile towers, painted white with bright candy-red accents. At night these features were lit up, bathing Coney Island in, to use Thompson's phrase, "the glare of thousands of electric light bulbs" (see fig. 52).[84] Equally indebted to the White City's design tropes was Luna Park's more upscale neighbor, Dreamland, which opened in 1904 and was the brainchild of state senator William H. Reynolds. Whereas Luna Park adulterated the purity of its white city with bright red accents, Dreamland returned to form with an emphasis on sparkling white surfaces and more pronounced Venetian architectural features, which included lagoons, Campanile tower, and a façade reproducing Venice's Doge's Palace (see fig. 53). All three amusement parks featured waterways and gondolas, effectively offering the White City in virtualized form (see fig. 54).

Venice themes proliferated in new themed cities as well. Inspired by the White City, which he had visited in 1893, tobacco millionaire Abbot Kinney founded "Venice of America" (today Venice, California) in 1905 as a theme park and beach resort town fourteen miles west of Los Angeles. Like the White City, Venice, California was built around a series of canals dug out of the Pacific coastline. There were gondolas to ferry tourists from site to site, as well as storefronts and arcades, the architecture of which imitated the Doge's Palace and Loggia (see figs. 55 and 56).[85]

While these U.S. ventures were unfolding, Kiralfy, whose "Venice in London" had inspired the Chicago White City designers, opened a permanent exhibition site called the "White City" near Shepherd's Bush in London in 1908. Still the site of the BBC today, the White City in London, sometimes called the "Great White City," would serve as the site of the Franco-British Exhibition in the year it opened. Included in it were canals, boat rides, and a "Court of Honour" that mimicked almost exactly the Chicago White City (see fig. 57).

The exhibition site hosted the Imperial International Exhibition in 1909 and the

Fig. 52. *Electric Tower at Night, Luna Park.* 1893. Black and white photograph. Detroit Publishing Company. Library of Congress Prints and Photographs Division LC-DIG-det-4a11114.

Japan-British Exhibition in 1910. The final two exhibitions to be held there were the Latin-British Exhibition (1912) and the Anglo-American Exhibition (1914), which was brought to a premature end by the outbreak of the First World War. The White City Stadium in the north of the area, known as the Great Stadium and seating 66,000, was officially opened by King Edward VII on April 27, 1908, for the Olympics.

It is worth noting that at first, as the White City structures became part of amusement park architecture in the early 1900s, they were still directly associated with "America." When the United States was invited to design a building for itself at the 1900 Paris Exposition Universelle, it chose a version of the White City's domed Horticulture Building, the building that resembled Venice's Santa Maria della Salute. As in the case of the White City, some U.S. journalists were dismayed. A journalist for the *New York Times* called the American building "slavishly imitative":

Fig. 53. *Dreamland Park, Coney Island New York.* c. 1905–10. Black and white photograph. Detroit Publishing Company. Library of Congress Prints and Photographs Division LC-DIG-det-4a11114.

> The "American building" at the Paris Fair cannot be an object of patriotic pride to any "good American." While the national building of almost every other country carries its nationality unmistakably impressed upon its architecture, we have contented ourselves with a bad imitation of European work in a building which seems to have been modeled after that Venetian church which is known to flippant tourists as "Santa Maria Della Volute."[86]

Of course, as we have seen, the White City structures were by this time already "American." Not only did they conform to visual stereotypes of Americanness, but they were also now central to U.S. national self-presentation in Paris; they were white and they used Venetian forms without endowing these forms with the conventions associated with Venetian content (interiority, agedness, temporal layering).

What Gorky sees at Coney Island, then—the thing that dazzles and pierces his

Fig. 54. *Canals of Venice, Dreamland, Coney Island.* 1906. Postcard. Author's collection.

Fig. 55. *One of the Saltwater Canals, Venice of America, California.* 1911. Postcard. Author's collection.

Fig. 56. *The Miniature Railway, Venice, Cal.* 1916. Postcard. Western Pub. and Novelty Co., Los Angeles, CA. Author's collection.

Fig. 57. *Grandstand and Canal, Franco-British Exhibition, London 1908*. 1908. Postcard. Official Franco-British Exhibition. Author's collection.

eyes—are copies of the scenographic elements of the White City, reconstituted for the demands of the amusement park venue. Coney Island from a distance, says Gorky, is a string of "beautiful white buildings"; "the fiery magic castles are tall white buildings;" the island's "flimsy white structures are enveloped in a translucent sheet"; the "transparent buildings" stand out against the yellow sand "like thin white silk embroidery."[87] For Gorky, this whole panoply is a vacant fiery nothingness, a "dead magnificence and spiritual penury."[88] But as I have shown, it was precisely this seeming dead nothingness produced by brilliant reflections and façades emptied of their seemingly original ethnic meaning that signaled "America" at the end of the century. Gorky closes his essay with an image of light and fire: Coney Island at night. Like Hester's glowing scarlet letter, which leaves her gray and spectral, Gorky's Coney Island deflects the ascription of particularity, turning all those who follow in its wake shadowy and difficult to assess. "[W]hen night comes, a fantastic magic city, all of fire, suddenly blazes up from the ocean. Without consuming, it burns long against the dark background of the sky, its beauty mirrored in the broad, gleaming bosom of the sea. In the glittering gossamer of its fantastic buildings, tens of thousands of gray people, like patches on the ragged clothes of a beggar, creep along with weary faces and colourless eyes."[89] Unlike Hawthorne's description of Hester and her scarlet badge, Gorky's analysis of this phenomenon is violently negative. He loathes the United States and its capitalist apparatus. Still, his imagery—the glittery light, the technological surface, the spectral physicality, the "people" with their "colourless" eyes and their vague undifferentiated bodies—is the same.

At Coney Island, then, which was quite literally built to look like "America," Gorky found what audiences the world over by this time expected to find when they saw "America": a sea of "glittering gossamer," a distracting reflection that prevented the nation and its people from properly cohering or coming into view. And by this point, this glare *was* "America." America's essence, its exceptional and irreducible quality as a nation, was coalesced in the glitch it produced within otherwise limpid lines of sight.

CONCLUSION

Attending the cinema during his trip to the United States in the 1920s, French author Georges Duhamel recalled how difficult it was to tell the real from the fake as he traveled. Casting his eyes up from the screen to the painted ceiling of the movie theater, he seemed to see "a sky where stars are twinkling and light clouds are drifting past. Of course, it is a false sky, with false stars, and false clouds. . . . For indeed, everything here is false. False is the life of the shadows on the screen. The world is false. Perhaps I myself am no longer more than a simulacrum of a man, imitation of Duhamel."[1] Duhamel was not alone. Throughout the early twentieth century, visions of "America" as a place of aggressive visuality, of glittering façades and false fronts, continued to dominate tourist literature and cultural history. Dutch historian Johan Huizinga's description of the United States condemns it as a place of "superficiality" where all pleasures are delivered "mechanically."[2] America, he says, is a civilization of "pictures" and "screens." "Picturizing" is an American ideal."[3]

But in addition to remaining touchstones among travelers and cultural commentators, these visions of "America" as a land of false screens and superficial "pictures" came to form a powerful site of political disaffection for an emerging generation of U.S. authors. In the *Scarlet Letter* or in Buffalo Bill's Wild West, the surface of the body is incontrovertibly understood as a site of "nationality," where the history of a people is crystallized and made apparent to the perceiver. To be sure, in these cases, the "history" itself is obscured. Hester's scarlet badge and Buffalo Bill's sequined shirts are there to distract from underlying sins and depredations, but by the end of the century this distracting mechanism, as I have shown, was itself a feature of American nationality. Americans were considered a people who worshiped distracting surfaces and flickering pictures.

But in the early twentieth century, this equation of American nationality and glitter acquired another dimension that was not necessarily part of its system of meanings in the early nineteenth century; the glittery, false scenes of "America" became associated not with embodied or essentialized nationality and ethnicity but with class inequality, consumerism, and capitalism writ large. The dazzling surfaces of "America" now emerged among the U.S. intelligentsia as sites of seductiveness, as alluring consumerist dreamscapes produced by modern capital itself. The goal of these dreamscapes, this branch of political discourse believed, was not to trick the eye of a judgmental Europe but to trick U.S. workers and consumers into believing in capitalism's promises of wealth and self-betterment. I opened this study with a summary of traditional scholarship on the meaning of glittering surfaces and lights in twentieth-century descriptions of American landscapes. For traditional scholars, these glittering surfaces and lights were features of capitalist modernity. It is worth closing now by noting the extent to which these equations of glitter and capitalist modernity, rather than inhering in descriptions of America all along, appear to have been consolidated in early twentieth-century political discourse itself.

Nowhere are these new capitalistic qualities of the glittering surface more amply apparent than in F. Scott Fitzgerald's famous 1925 novel *The Great Gatsby*. The tale of a social climbing "roughneck," Jay Gatsby, who makes millions in order to win the love of wealthy socialite Daisy Buchanan, *The Great Gatsby* offers up a kind of apotheosis of "America" as surreal vista of lights and glittery clothes.[4] In the early nineteenth century, the United States was associated with "gaudy" colors, shining brass, "tinsel," garish cosmetics, and overly fine suits. These are precisely the qualities that typify the titular protagonist in Fitzgerald's tale. Gatsby's vast, wild parties, held in his "palace" on Long Island Sound, are "gaudy with primary colors" and filled with "hair bobbed in strange new ways, and shawls beyond the dreams of Castile." There are "enough colored lights to make a Christmas tree of Gatsby's enormous garden," banquet tables of "glistening hors d'oeuvres . . . salads of harlequin designs" (51). In describing Gatsby's palace, Fitzgerald several times refers directly to amusement parks and world's fairs. At one point, the novel's narrator, Nick Carraway, comes upon Gatsby's mansion in the middle of the night, "blazing with light, which fell unreal on the shrubbery and made thin elongating glints upon the roadside wires." Nick tells Gatsby, "Your place looks like the World's Fair." Gatsby himself is like Nathaniel Parker Willis or a figure out of the *Confidence Man*. He has endless beautiful shirts of "sheer linen and thick silk," with "stripes and scrolls and plaids in coral and apple-green and lavender" (117). At one point he appears in a pink suit; at another he appears in "a white flannel suit, silver shirt, and gold-colored tie" (106). He reminds Nick of a cheap stage dummy, his speech tinny and unreal. "The very phrases were worn so threadbare that they evoked no image except that of a turbaned 'character' leaking sawdust at every pore as he pursued a tiger through the Bois de Boulogne" (83).

In the *Confidence Man* or the work of Willis, these artificial, glittering contrivances are a plus. They distract the viewing eye, preventing it from detecting the embodied dimensions of American character. In the *Great Gatsby*, these surfaces are represented as treacherous. They are meant to symbolize the delusive contrivances of modern American capitalism and what Fitzgerald's generation began to call the "American Dream." Writing in his *Epic of America* in 1931, James Truslow Adams, who coined the term "American Dream," consolidated a long-standing celebration of the possibilities of U.S. social mobility. He sang the praises of "that dream of a land in which life should be better and richer and fuller for every man," "regardless of the fortuitous circumstances of birth or position."[5] Luring "tens of millions of all nations to our shores in the past century," the "American dream," said Adams, is not "a dream of merely material plenty." It is "a dream of being able to grow to fullest development as man and woman, unhampered by the barriers which had slowly been erected in the older civilizations, unrepressed by social orders which had developed for the benefit of classes rather than for the simple human being of any and every class."[6]

Gatsby's pursuit of Daisy allegorizes the pursuit of the American Dream. Climbing out of poverty to great wealth, Gatsby personifies all the self-makers of the U.S. past, from Benjamin Franklin and John Jacob Astor to the robber barons of the Civil War. He both represents and longs for the possibility of a "richer and fuller" life "unrepressed by social orders." But Fitzgerald's point is that this "dream" of a richer and fuller life free of entitlements is illusory. In the United States there is no social mobility. The United States is a society full of rigid class hierarchies policed by old money and recalcitrant power systems. Gatsby believes that his lack of money is all that stands between him and Daisy. He not only determines to get rich but he also pursues the wealthy lifestyle made available to the rich through America's vast consumer marketplace, buying hundreds of shirts and shimmery suits and hosting Hollywood-style parties. What he does not understand is that wealth alone does not buy a membership in the American aristocratic class. Gatsby's wealth cannot bridge the distances erected by class systems that remain as powerful in the United States as they are in Britain or France.

In this novel, the shimmering surfaces, the glamorous parties, the twinkling swimming pool and pink suit, are meant to symbolize this illusory apparatus of the American Dream. Instead of representing and actualizing Gatsby's wealth, these consumer objects collectively act as a kind of trap, their dazzling, beguiling surfaces tricking Gatsby into believing that mere money can buy him fulfillment and happiness. They represent, in the novel's words, "A new world, material without being real, where poor ghosts breathing dreams like air, drifted fortuitously about" (203). In this context, the images of world's fairs and amusement parks in this novel promote the notion that such mass entertainments are not manifestations of national personality. They are a kind of vehicle of dream ideology, offering a spectacular, shimmery scenery that seems to actualize the promises of American capitalist empire. Fittingly, Gatsby ends as a scapegoat of the American rich, of the aristocracy represented by Daisy and her husband Tom. Taking the rap for Daisy's criminal hit-and-run car accident, he becomes the target of the grief-stricken husband of the victim, Wilson, who shoots him in revenge. Gatsby dies in his luxury swimming pool, the pool a symbol of both the American dream in all its materialistic dimensions and its treacherous worthlessness.

Nevertheless, even as *The Great Gatsby* divorces America's shimmering surfaces from the frameworks of ethnic nationalist personality in which they were originally concocted, ethnic nationalities survive in it as a kind of deep structure of American personality, one not strictly covered by the American Dream and its capitalistic ideology. In other words, even as this novel elaborates consumer material culture as the site of a treacherous belief in American promises of wealth, success, and social mobility, it also elaborates them as a kind of dazzling visual scenery through which ethnicity and race are voided or made illegible. For Gatsby is not just a working-class character. The implication is that Gatsby is descended from an ethnic minority, German, Slav, or Jew. His real name is not Jay Gatsby, but James or "Jimmy" Gatz. He makes his money bootlegging and by partnering with the Jewish gangster, Meyer Wolfsheim. Thus, even as the shimmer of the American dream apparatus acts as a kind of seductive miasma that entices naïve, striving souls like Gatsby, gaudiness and glitter also act here in the same way that they did in earlier manifestations of American national personality, as instruments of effacement and distraction. The glitter and gaudiness distract from Gatsby's origins in or affiliations with an ethnic group. When Fitzgerald has to invent a quintessential American personality, in other words, he invents not just a bootstrapping, working-class character determined to climb into high society but also someone who is trying to hide his ethnic and racial provenance from a curious viewing world. In an important sense, Gatsby's overclothed body, with its silver and gold coverings, evokes earlier figures of American nationality. It is meant to block and distract perception of Gatsby's ethnic origins. For all its implication in the discourses of early twentieth-century modernity, for all its emphasis on the deceptive scenes of capitalist promise and celebration, *The Great Gatsby*, I am suggesting, is tethered to an earlier framework of nationalistic definition, in which Americanness is equated not with materialistic aspiration and consumer avidity but with the legacy of early nineteenth-century transatlantic nationalism, with its insistence on immemorial ethnic and racialist essences. We can assume that scholars studying early twentieth-century consumer culture imbibed some of this conflation of empty glitter and consumerism while forgetting the extent to which such images had long been linked to the architecture of British and European ethnic nationalism.

In the early nineteenth century, this book has argued, as ethnic nationalism rose to prominence in Britain and Europe, the United States joined a roster of nationalities that were being defined not according to their political alliances or traditional imperial or religious affiliations but according to the appearance of their clothes and habitats. These new sartorial and material culture taxonomies sewed the various populations of the globe into a hierarchy of nations and peoples marching up through the stages of modernization, with the most plainly and modestly dressed of the ethnicities and races at the top of the hierarchy and the most peculiarly or audaciously clothed standing near the bottom. Like other precincts on the peripheries of British and European empire, the United States was characterized as a backward place. It was typified as a place full of curious personalities wearing odd, colorful clothes, clothes that by common consent stood in for backwardness and degeneracy.

But in the 1830s and 1840s, as we have seen, significant figures in U.S. literature and performance culture began tinkering with the visual arrays presupposed in ethnic nationalist ideology. They experimented not with gaudy American clothes precisely but with the audacious surface itself as a site where the critical eye of Europe could be short-circuited and turned back on itself in a flare of light and visual noise. From Nathaniel Parker Willis, Nathaniel Hawthorne, and Herman Melville to P. T. Barnum, James Fenimore Cooper, and the entertainers in minstrel shows, U.S. intellectuals and performers experimented with as they theorized the possibility of changing the terms under which the American body was perceived. Already associated with garishness and glitter, the surface of the American body was now hypothesized as a site not just of gaudiness but of noise, of masking and blockage. When the eye of the Old World hit the surface of the gaudy American body, it did not see the indelible signs of degeneracy. Instead, the perceiving eye was blocked and distracted by an incoherent wash of color or a flare of light that foiled perception. In this fantasy, the organic, allegedly essential nature of the American body was impossible to detect. The American body thus seemed to be empty, a dead technological shell.

Originally conceived as a challenge to Eurocentric models of race and ethnicity, over the second half of the nineteenth century these glittering, impenetrable surfaces were themselves normalized as a sign of Americanness, intimately associated not just with American bodies, which now entered transatlantic ethnic nationalist lore as mysterious veiled figures devoid of meaning, but also with American habitats and landscapes. In settler colonial nationalism, they became part of a complex ideological response to racial scientific doctrines. At the World's Columbian Exposition in Chicago in 1893, fair designers concocted a scenographic equivalent of the flashy but empty American figure devised in popular culture, constructing a set of ersatz European façades and a blaze of white light and reflections that assaulted the eye. By the end of the century, the glittery masked American earlier hypothesized as a challenge to the ethnic body came itself to be regarded as an ethnic property, the fail-safe sign of a quintessential American national personality. Appearing in everything from Buffalo Bill's Wild West to national sites as world's fairs, the visual rhetoric of flashiness and assaulted vision, of fake scenes and tinseled clothes, became as indelibly "American" as the Wild West itself.

For Baudrillard, America unfolds itself in a series of gleaming frictionless images, "a new experience of space."[7] "American reality," says Baudrillard, "was there before the screen was invented, but everything about the way it is today suggests it was invented with the screen in mind, that it is the refraction of a giant screen." For this reason, says Baudrillard, Americans are different from Europeans. "A fusion of the kinetic and the cinematic produces a different mental configuration and overall perception *from our own*" (emphasis mine). Comparing this "reality" to Europe's, Baudrillard remarks, "You do not find mobility or the screen taking precedence over reality in the same way in Europe, where things most often remain with the static form of territory, the palpable form of substances." America for Baudrillard is like the automobile ride he takes across the desert. The quintessence of modernity, America unfurls noiselessly along a smooth endless road "as if you were on a cushion of air." "Europe" and its "old obsessions" are in the rearview mirror.[8] But in fact, the sense of leaving Europe behind in the rearview mirror was itself an illusion, for the "America" Baudrillard thinks he sees, I have argued here, was never not a creation of the community of British and European nations, its mirrored surfaces deflecting and defying the Old World eye.

NOTES

Introduction

1. Maxim Gorky, "Boredom," *The Independent*, August 8, 1907, 310.

2. Edwin Lawrence Godkin, *Reflections and Comments, 1865–1895* (New York: C. Scribner's Sons, 1895), 192.

3. Lewis Mumford, "The City," in *Civilization in the United States: An Inquiry By Thirty Americans*, ed. Harold E. Stearns (New York: Harcourt, Brace), 1922), 9.

4. Jean Baudrillard, *America* (London: Verso, 2010), 5.

5. William Leach, *Land of Desire: Merchants, Power, and the Rise of a New American Culture* (New York: Pantheon, 1993), 111.

6. See Robert W. Rydell and Rob Kroes, *Buffalo Bill in Bologna: The Americanization of the World, 1869–1922* (Chicago: University of Chicago Press, 2005), 8–10, 49, and chap. 4.

7. Lauren Rabinovitz, *Electric Dreamland: Amusement Parks, Movies, and American Modernity* (New York: Columbia University Press, 2012), 2.

8. See, for example, Rabinovitz, *Electric*, where she argues that amusement parks offered to "'Americanize' Americans," 10.

9. Charles Dickens, *American Notes for General Circulation*, vol. 1 of 2, 2nd ed. (London: Chapman and Hall, 1842), 194.

10. George G. Foster, *New York by Gas-Light and Other Urban Sketches*, ed. Stuart Blumin (Berkeley: University of California Press, 1990), 70.

11. Foster, *New York*, 70.

12. James Fenimore Cooper, *Gleanings in Europe: England*, 2 vols. (Philadelphia: Carey, Lea, and Blanchard, 1837), 2:187.

13. Benedict Anderson, *Imagined Communities: Reflections on the Origin and Spread of Nationalism*, rev. ed. (London: Verso, 1991 [1983]), 62.

14. Lloyd S. Kramer, *Nationalism in Europe and America: Politics, Cultures, and Identities Since 1775* (Chapel Hill: University of North Carolina Press, 2011), 126.

15. See Michael Warner's *Letters of the Republic: Publication and the Public Sphere in Nineteenth-Century America* (Cambridge, MA: Harvard University Press, 1990) for a now-classic analysis of the critical role played by the abstract spaces of the eighteenth-century print sphere in the creation of the United States as a nation-state.

16. Étienne Balibar and Immanuel Wallerstein, *Race, Nation, Class: Ambiguous Identities* (London: Verso, 1991), 86.

17. For extended studies of ethnic nationalism see John Breuilly, "Nationalism and National Unification in Nineteenth-Century Europe," in *The Oxford Handbook of the History of Nationalism*, ed.

John Breuilly (Oxford: Oxford University Press, 2013). See also, in this volume, "Introduction: Concepts, Approaches, Theories," for Breuilly's account of the complexity of talking about the history of nationalism and for a useful overview of the problems of definition. In addition, see John Breuilly, *Nationalism and the State*, 2nd ed. (Chicago: University of Chicago Press, 1994); and *Austria, Prussia, and the Making of Germany, 1806–1871*, 2nd ed. (London and New York: Routledge, 2011). Important studies of Irish and Scottish nationalism include David Lloyd, *Nationalism and Minor Literature: James Clarence Mangan and the Emergence of Irish Cultural Nationalism* (Berkeley: University of California Press, 1987) and Katie Trumpener, *Bardic Nationalism: The Romantic Novel in the British Empire* (Princeton: Princeton University Press, 1997). For an account of how race and sexuality interact with nationalism, see the essays in Andrew Parker, Mary Russo, Doris Sommer, and Patricia Yaeger, *Nationalisms and Sexualities* (New York and London: Routledge, 1992).

18. Balibar and Wallerstein, *Race*, 71.

19. I discuss white nationalism and Germanic supremacy theory at length in chapter 1. The standard study of the birth of white nationalism in the United States is Reginald Horsman, *Race and Manifest Destiny: The Origins of American Racial Anglo-Saxonism* (Cambridge, MA: Harvard University Press, 1981).

20. James Fenimore Cooper, *Gleanings in Europe*, 2 vols. (Philadelphia: Carey, Lea & Blanchard, 1837), 2:60.

21. Ralph Waldo Emerson, *English Traits* (Boston: Phillips, Samson, 1856), 60.

22. J. Hector St. John [de Crèvecoeur], *Letters from an American Farmer* (London: T. Davis, 1783), 48.

23. Henry David Thoreau, "Our Country," in F. B. Sanborn, *The Personality of Thoreau* (Boston: Charles E. Goodspeed, 1901), 65.

24. See Caroline M. Kisiel, "Utopian Ideals in Transatlantic Context: Frances Wright's American Vision," in *Nineteenth-Century British Travellers in the New World*, ed. Christine Devine (Farnum, UK: Ashgate, 2013), 52.

25. Rob Kroes, *If You've Seen One, You've Seen the Mall: Europeans and American Mass Culture* (Urbana: University of Illinois Press, 1996), 40.

26. Michael Zakim, *Ready-Made Democracy: A History of Men's Dress in the American Republic, 1760–1860* (Chicago: University of Chicago Press, 2003), 43.

27. See Karen Halttunen, *Confidence Men and Painted Women: A Study of Middle Class Culture in America, 1830–1870* (New Haven: Yale University Press, 1982); John F. Kasson, *Rudeness and Civility: Manners in Nineteenth-Century Urban America* (New York: Hill and Wang, 1990); and Richard L. Bushman, *The Refinement of America: Persons, Houses, Cities* (New York: Random House–Vintage, 1993 [1992]).

28. See Monica Miller, *Slaves to Fashion: Black Dandyism and the Styling of Black Diasporic Identity* (Durham: Duke University Press, 2009).

29. Lori Merish, *Sentimental Materialism: Gender, Commodity Culture, and Nineteenth-Century American Literature* (Durham: Duke University Press, 2000), 64.

30. See Jesper Gulddal, *Anti-Americanism in European Literature* (London: Palgrave Macmillan, 2011).

31. See Jared Gardner, *Master Plots: Race and the Founding of an American Literature, 1787–1845* (Baltimore: Johns Hopkins University Press, 1998); Elisa Tamarkin, *Anglophilia: Deference, Devotion, and Antebellum America* (Chicago: University of Chicago Press, 2008); Lara Langer Cohen, *The Fabrication of American Literature: Fraudulence and Antebellum Print Culture* (Philadelphia: University of Pennsylvania Press, 2012); J. Gerald Kennedy, *Strange Nation: Literary Nationalism and Cultural Conflict in the Age of Poe* (New York: Oxford University Press, 2016); and Jason Richards, *Imitation*

Nation: Red, White, and Blackface in Early and Antebellum US Literature (Charlottesville: University of Virginia Press, 2017).

32. Kennedy, *Strange Nation*, 33.

33. Baudrillard, *America*, 10.

34. Studies of such objects are available in the Bloomsbury Object Lessons book series. See, for example, Alison Kinney, *Hood* (London: Bloomsbury, 2016) and Rafia Zakaria, *Veil* (London: Bloomsbury, 2017). These objects conform in some ways to the "sign" described in Roland Barthes' *Mythologies*, which I discuss in chapter 4. I discuss masks and veils at length in chapter 2.

35. Michelle Ann Stephens, *Skin Acts: Race, Psychoanalysis, and the Black Male Performer* (Durham: Duke University Press, 2014), 4.

36. Stephens, *Skin Acts*, 7.

37. Anne Anlin Cheng, *Second Skin: Josephine Baker and the Modern Surface* (New York: Oxford University Press, 2011), 13.

38. Anne Anlin Cheng, *Ornamentalism* (New York: Oxford University Press, 2019), 4.

Chapter 1

1. Charles Dickens, *American Notes for General Circulation*, vol. 1 of 2, 2nd ed. (London: Chapman and Hall, 1842), 194.

2. Cornelius Mathews, *A Pen-and-Ink Panorama of New York City* (New York: J. S. Taylor, 1853), 131–32.

3. Michael Zakim. *Ready-Made Democracy: A History of Men's Dress in the American Republic, 1760–1860* (Chicago: University of Chicago Press, 2003), 43.

4. See Richard L. Bushman, *The Refinement of America: Persons, Houses, Cities* (1992; New York: Random House-Vintage, 1993) and Karen Halttunen, *Confidence Men and Painted Women: A Study of Middle Class Culture in America, 1830–1870* (New Haven: Yale University Press, 1982). Lori Merish, *Sentimental Materialism: Gender, Commodity Culture, and Nineteenth-Century American Literature* (Durham: Duke University Press, 2000).

5. See Monica Miller, *Slaves to Fashion: Black Dandyism and the Styling of Black Diasporic Identity* (Durham: Duke University Press, 2009).

6. Dickens, *American Notes*, 59–60.

7. Ethnic clothes might be considered an instance of what Alexander G. Weheliye calls "racializing assemblages"; see *Habeas Viscus: Racializing Assemblages, Biopolitics, and Black Feminist Theories of the Human* (Durham: Duke University Press, 2014); they multiplied opportunities for scopic differentiation.

8. Quoted in T. H. Breen, *The Marketplace of Revolution: How Consumer Politics Shaped American Independence* (New York: Oxford University Press, 2005), 125. For an account of colonial clothing, particularly homespun, see Linda Baumgarten, *What Clothes Reveal: The Language of Clothing in Colonial and Federal America* (New Haven: Yale University Press and Colonial Williamsburg Foundation, 2002), 96–97, figs. 141–43.

9. "Advertisement 1," *The North-Carolina Magazine; or, Universal Intelligencer* [Newbern, NC], vol. 2, no. 33 (Jan. 11, 1765): 11.

10. "Advertisement 1," *The Censor* [Boston], vol. 2, no. 5 (April 18, 1772): 86.

11. Breen, *Marketplace*, 265.

12. Quoted in Breen, *Marketplace*, 211.

13. "American Patriotism," Number CIII, *Public Ledger*, Thursday, January 25, 1770, rpt. in *The Repository or Treasury of Politics and Literature, 1770*, 2 vols. (London: J. Murray, 1771), 1:229.

14. Quoted in Breen, *Marketplace*, 266.

15. *New-London Gazette*, November 27, 1767.

16. Claude Rawson, *Satire and Sentiment, 1660–1830: Stress Points in the English Augustan Tradition* (New Haven: Yale University Press, 2000), 158.

17. Thomas Paine, *Common Sense* (Girard, KS: Appeal to Reason, 1920), 15.

18. See Thorstein Veblen, *Theory of the Leisure Class: An Economic Study of Institutions*, ed. Martha Banta (1899; New York: Oxford University Press, 2007).

19. See Roland Barthes, *The Fashion System*, trans. Matthew Ward and Richard Howard (London: Cape, 1985), and Umberto Eco, "Social Life as a Sign System," in *Structuralism: An Introduction*, ed. David Robey (Oxford: Clarendon Press, 1973).

20. Fred Davis, *Fashion, Culture, and Identity* (Chicago: University of Chicago Press, 1992) 5, 11.

21. Ann Rosalind Jones and Peter Stallybrass, *Renaissance Clothing and the Materials of Memory* (London: Cambridge University Press, 2000), 3.

22. Jones and Stallybrass, *Renaissance Clothing*, 2, 4.

23. Webb Keane, "Signs Are Not the Garb of Meaning: On the Social Analysis of Material Things," in *Materiality*, ed. Daniel Miller (Durham: Duke University Press, 2005).

24. *Virginia Gazette*, December 14, 1769: 2; Colonial Williamsburg Digital Library, https://www.encyclopediavirginia.org/Excerpt_from_the_Virginia_Gazette_December_14_1769

25. Quoted in Jones and Stallybrass, *Renaissance Clothing*, 6.

26. Keane, "Signs," 184.

27. Susan Manning, *Poetics of Character: Transatlantic Encounters, 1700–1900* (Cambridge: Cambridge University Press, 2013), 15.

28. Joan Copjec, *Read My Desire: Lacan Against the Historicists* (Cambridge, MA: MIT Press, 1995).

29. Anthony D. Smith, *National Identity* (1991; Reno: University of Nevada Press, 1993), 11. For discussions of nineteenth-century ethnic nationalism see Lloyd Kramer, *Nationalism in Europe and America* (Chapel Hill: University of North Carolina Press, 2011); John Breuilly, *Nationalism and the State*, 2nd ed. (Chicago: University of Chicago Press, 1994); and John Breuilly, *Austria, Prussia, and the Making of Germany, 1806–1871*, 2nd ed. (London and New York: Routledge, 2011). Important studies of Irish and Scottish nationalism include David Lloyd, *Nationalism and Minor Literature: James Clarence Mangan and the Emergence of Irish Cultural Nationalism* (Berkeley: University of California Press, 1987) and Katie Trumpener, *Bardic Nationalism: The Romantic Novel in the British Empire* (Princeton, NJ: Princeton University Press, 1997). Critical definitions of ethnicity are offered in Étienne Balibar and Immanuel Wallerstein, *Race, Nation, Class: Ambiguous Identities* (London: Verso, 1991), especially chaps. 4, 5, and 6.

30. Johann Gottlieb Fichte, *Addresses to the German Nation*, trans. and ed. Gregory Moore (Cambridge: Cambridge University Press, 2008), 186.

31. J. G. Herder, *Outlines of a Philosophy of the History of Man*, trans. T. Churchill (1800; New York, 1966), 249.

32. Edmund Burke, *Reflections on the Revolution in France* (London: John Sharpe, 1820), 48.

33. Quoted in Reginald Horsman, *Race and Manifest Destiny: The Origins of American Racial Anglo-Saxonism* (Cambridge: Harvard University Press, 1981) 12.

34. Fichte, *Addresses*, 54.

35. Quoted in Rohan Butler, *Roots of National Socialism, 1783–1933* (London: Faber and Faber, 1941), 103.

36. Quoted in Horsman, *Race and Manifest Destiny*, 18–23. For a discussion of Jefferson's Anglo-Saxonism and his relationship to enslavement, see Amanda Louise Johnson, "Thomas Jefferson's Anglo-Saxon Genesis: A Romance," *Modern Philology* 114, no. 3 (2017): 680–701.

37. Ralph Waldo Emerson, *English Traits* (Boston: Phillips, Samson, 1856), 60.

38. John O'Sullivan, "Annexation," *The United States Magazine and Democratic Review* 17 (July and August 1845): 9.

39. The most famous costume albums were lavishly illustrated early modern productions by painters and illustrators. For information on these early costume albums see Christoph Weiditz, *Authentic Everyday Dress of the Renaissance* (Berlin: Nachdruck der Ausgabe, 1927; rpt. New York: Dover, 1994); *The First Book of Fashion: The Book of Clothes of Matthäus and Veit Konrad Schwarz of Augsburg*, ed. Ulinka Rublack and Maria Hayward (London: Bloomsbury Academic, 2015); *The Clothing of the Renaissance World: Europe, Asia, Africa, the America: Cesare Vecellio's Habiti Antichi et Moderni*, essay and trans. Margaret F. Rosenthal and Ann Rosalind Jones (New York: Thames and Hudson, 2008). For general information on clothes in early modern global cosmopolitan culture, see Ulinka Rublack, *Dressing Up; Cultural Identity in Renaissance Europe* (New York: Oxford University Press, 2010).

40. See, for example, Joanne B. Eicher and Barbara Sumberg, "World Fashion, Ethnic, and National Dress," in *Dress and Ethnicity: Change Across Space and Time*, ed. Joanne B. Eicher (Oxford: Berg, 1995), 299, and Malcolm Chapman, "Freezing the Frame: Dress and Ethnicity in Brittany and Gaelic Scotland," in *The Visible Self: Global Perspectives on Dress, Culture, and Society*, ed. Joanne B. Eicher, Sandra Lee Evenson, and Hazel A. Lutz (New York: Fairchild, 2008), 8.

41. See the essays in Joanne B. Eicher, ed., *Dress and Ethnicity*. These essays attack the idea that ethnic dress is "traditional" and without change (2). See especially Chapman, "Freezing the Frame" (7–28); see also Suzanne Baizermane, Joanna B. Eicher, and Catherine Cerny, "Eurocentrism in the Study of Ethnic Dress," in *The Visible Self: Global Perspectives on Dress, Culture, and Society*, ed. Joanne B. Eicher, Sandra Lee Evenson, and Hazel A. Lutz (New York: Fairchild, 2008). Useful studies of the history and semiotics of fashion include Elizabeth Wilson, *Adorned in Dreams: Fashion and Modernity* (London: Virago, 1985); Joanne Entwhistle, *The Fashioned Body: Fashion, Dress, and Modern Social Theory* (Cambridge: Polity Press, 2000). Useful, if Eurocentric, histories of world fashion include François Boucher, *20,000 Years of Fashion: The History of Costume and Personal Adornment* (New York: Harry N. Abrams, 1967); and DK, *Fashion: The Definitive History of Costume and Style* (London: DK, 2012).

42. Edmund Burke, *Reflections on the Revolution in France*, in *Revolutionary Writings: Reflections on the Revolution in France and the First Letter on a Regicide Peace*, ed. Iain Hampsher-Monk (Cambridge: Cambridge University Press, 2014), 89. https://doi.org/10.1017/CBO9781139046268.009

43. [Walter Scott] *Ivanhoe: A Romance*, 3 vols. (Edinburgh: Archibald Constable, 1820), 3:303.

44. Jones and Stallybrass, *Renaissance Clothing*, 7.

45. I discuss the idea of monogenesis and other race science theories at length in chapter 3.

46. Denise Ferreira da Silva, *Towards a Global Idea of Race* (Minneapolis: University of Minnesota Press, 2007), 105.

47. See Johann Caspar Lavater, *Essays on Physiognomy*, trans. Thomas Holcroft (London: Tegg, 1853).

48. Edward Harding, *Costume of the Russian Empire: Illustrated By Upwards of Seventy Richly Coloured Engravings* (London: R. H. Evans, 1811), n.p.

49. Harding, *Costume of the Russian Empire*, 105. In Silva's framework race does not reside in the body of the raced person. Race is rather a way of *seeing*. Likewise, Paul Gilroy writes, "The textbooks of classical, eighteenth-century raciology were studded with images. . . . "[C]ognition of 'race' was

never an exclusively linguistic process and involved from its inception a distinctive visual and optical imaginary." See Gilroy, *Against Race: Imagining Political Culture Beyond the Color Line* (Cambridge, MA: Belknap Press of Harvard University, 2000), 35.

50. Keane, "Signs."

51. David Batchelor, *Chromophobia* (London: Reaktion, 2001), 22–23.

52. Charles Blanc, *The Grammar of Painting and Engraving*, trans. Kate Newell Doggett (Chicago: S.C. Griggs, 1891), 4–5; quoted in Batchelor, *Chromophobia*, 25.

53. See Andrew Benjamin Bricker, "After the Golden Age: Libel, Caricature and the Deverbalization of Satire" *Eighteenth-Century Studies* 51, no. 3 (2018), which shows that in the late eighteenth-century, censorship drove satire from textual to visual media (both performance and illustration), which were difficult to prosecute.

54. Benjamin Disraeli, *Vivian Grey*, vol. 3 of 3 (London: Henry Colburn, 1827), 87.

55. See, for example, the series "Costumes of All Nations" which ran in *Godey's Lady's Book* 44 (1852): 45, 138, 189, 259, 331, 469.

56. For accounts of transatlantic theater in this period, see Jeffrey H. Richards, *Drama, Theatre, and Identity in the American New Republic* (Cambridge: Cambridge University Press, 2005); S. E. Wilmer, *Theatre, Society and the Nation: Staging American Identities* (Cambridge: Cambridge University Press, 2007); and Elizabeth Maddock Dillon, *New World Drama: The Performative Commons in the Atlantic World, 1649–1849* (Durham: Duke University Press, 2014).

57. J. Aspin, *Cosmorama: A View of the Costumes and Peculiarities of All Nations* (London: J. Harris, 1825), 3, 128. For information on early nineteenth-century children's geographies, see Megan A. Norcia, *X Marks the Spot: Women Writers Map the Empire for British Children, 1790–1895* (Athens: Ohio University Press, 2010).

58. [John Dadley], "A Female Inhabitant of Lapland," in *Costume of the Russian Empire, Illustrated by a Series of Seventy-Three Engravings* (London: William Miller, 1803), plate 2.

59. Harding, *Costume of the Russian Empire*, plate 2. There were two versions of this book put out, one by Harding, and one, the original, by John Dadley. Both were important influences on contemporary costume drawing and I quote from them both here.

60. "A Mordvin Woman," in Harding, *Costume of the Russian Empire*, plate 12. See also, in the same volume, "A Female Mestscheraik," plate 28.

61. Harding, *Costume of the Russian Empire*, plate 5.

62. William Alexander, *The Costume of China: Illustrated in Forty-Eight Colour Engravings* (London: William Miller, 1805), n.p.

63. Joseph Reinhard, "Costumes du Canton de Zoug," in *Collection de Costumes Suisses en 44 feuilles* (J. Whatman, 1808), Swiss National Library, Prints and Drawings Department, on Wikimedia Commons; and Johan Fredrik Eckersberg, "Costumes from Hitterdal in Tellemarken," in *Udvalgte Norske Nationaldragter* (*A Selection of Norwegian National Costumes*) (Christiania: Chr. Tønsberg, 1861), plate 2, National Library of Norway.

64. [George Scharf], "Unterwalden," in *Swiss Costume* (London: Rodwell and Martin, 1824), Swiss National Library, Bern.

65. The populations of Western and Southern Africa and of South America were not, as far as I can tell, a major focus of interest in English language ethnic costume books, but numerous studies of the varied and intricate regional costumes of these continents were published in French, Dutch, and German. Virtually all the books I consulted treat the world's populations according to monogenesis models of late eighteenth-century race pseudoscience, according to which all humans were descended from Adam and Eve, after which climate became the major determinant of both morpho-

logical and cultural difference in human groups. In one English-language children's book, *Costumes of All Nations*, the entry for "Africans" features a family with a mother, a child, and a father who carries arrows and bow. They are minimally clothed and painted pale gray. The description reads, "The poor Africans inhabit the quarter of the globe called Africa, which is very hot, and a great part of it a desert. The burning sun is supposed to be the cause of their being black. They are generally very ignorant and uncivilized. Some wicked and foolish people despise and ill-treat them on account of their colour, forgetting that the same good God made us and them, and that he will punish all pride and cruelty." See *Costumes of All Nations* (London: William Darnton and Son, 1836?) n.p. I discuss monogenesis theory at more length in chapter 3.

66. "Otaheitans," [Tahitians] in *Costume, Manners, and Peculiarities*, 12.

67. *Finden's Tableaux. A Series of Picturesque Scenes of National Character, Beauty, and Costume* [ed. Mary Russell Mitford] (London: Charles Tilt, 1838).

68. See [Edward] Finden, "England," in *Finden's Tableaux*, n.p.

69. See W. Hall, "Venice," E. Scriven, "Scotland," and H. Egleton, "India," in *Finden's Tableaux*, n.p.

70. For a study of how the racially charged color white determined the desirability of material culture objects, see Bridget T. Heneghan, *Whitewashing America: Material Culture and Race in the Antebellum Imagination* (Jackson: University Press of Mississippi, 2007).

71. Richards, *Drama, Theatre, and Identity*, 6.

72. Francis Hodge, *Yankee Theatre: The Image of America on the Stage, 1825–1850* (Austin: University of Texas Press, 1964), 61. Other important discussions of the Yankee on the transatlantic stage are Maura L. Jortner, "Throwing Insults Across the Ocean: Charles Mathews and the Staging of "the American" in 1824," in *Portrayals of Americans on the World Stage*, ed. Kevin J. Wetmore Jr. (Jefferson NC: McFarlane, 2009), 26–49; Matthew Pethers, "That Eternal Ghost of Trade: Anglo American Market Culture and the Antebellum Stage Yankee," in *The Materials of Exchange Between Britain and North East America, 1750–1900*, ed. Daniel Maudlin and Robin Peel (London: Routledge, 2013), 83–115.

73. See "Mathew-o-rama, Or Pretty Considerable D—d Particular, Tit Bits" [1824], in Charles Mathews, Theatrical Portrait Prints (visual works), ca. 1700–1900, Harvard Theatre Collection, Holis ID 01293422, Barcode: 4694853.

74. *The London Mathews: Containing an Account of this Celebrated Comedian's Trip to America* (Philadelphia: Morgan and Yeager, 1824), 8.

75. *The London Mathews*, 48.

76. Brother Jonathan Administering a Salutary Cordial to John Bull, 1813 Print, hand-colored engraving, Author/Creator: Amos Doolittle; Publisher: Yankee-Doodle Scratch't; New Haven, Connecticut; Courtesy of the American Antiquarian Society, Polit. Cart. B872.

77. [James Kirke Paulding], *The Diverting History of John Bull and Brother Jonathan* (Philadelphia: Robert Desilver, 1827), 7.

78. Hodge, *Yankee Theatre*, 96.

79. "Costumes," *Jonathan in England: A Comedy in Three Acts* (New York: Samuel French, n.d.), n.p. Technologies of color printing in the United States were well behind those of Paris and London, where artists and lithographers had long been experimenting with color processes before they finally perfected chromolithography in 1837. For a general history of this technology, see Michael Twyman, *A History of Chromolithography: Printed Colour For All* (London: British Library, 2013).

80. [George Hill], *Scenes from the Life of an Actor* (New York: Garret, 1853), 91.

81. Hugo Playfair and Robert Cruikshank, *The Playfair Papers, or, Brother Jonathan, the Smartest Nation in All Creation*, vol. 1 of 3 (London: Saunders and Otley, 1841), 116. Future references are to this edition; page numbers are inserted in brackets in the text.

82. Thomas Chandler Haliburton, *The Clockmaker, Or, the Sayings and Doings of Samuel Slick, of Slicksville*, 4th ed. (London: Richard Bentley, 1838), 3, 13.

83. William Oliver, *Eight Months in Illinois* (1843; rpt. Chicago: Walter M. Hill, 1924), 68.

84. Lady Emmeline Stuart Wortley, *Travels in the United States, Etc. During 1849 and 1850*, vol. 1 of 3 (London: Richard Bentley, 1851), 265, 267–68.

85. [Michel] Chevalier, *Society, Manners and Politics in the United States: Being a Series of Letters on North America* (Boston: Weeks, Jordan, 1839), 431, 342.

86. Aspin, *Cosmorama*, 39.

87. Aspin, *Cosmorama*, 50–51.

88. Aspin, *Cosmorama*, 165–67.

89. For general information on travelogues dealing with the antebellum United States see Max Berger, *The British Traveller in America, 1836–1860* (Gloucester, MA: Peter Smith, 1964); Jesper Gulddal, *Anti-Americanism in European Literature* (London: Palgrave, 2011); Christine Devine ed., *Nineteenth-Century British Travelers in the New World* (Farnham: Ashgate, 2013).

90. See J. Gerald Kennedy, *Strange Nation: Literary Nationalism and Cultural Conflict in the Age of Poe* (New York: Oxford, 2016), 11–35.

91. Charles Dickens, *The Life and Adventures of Martin Chuzzlewit* (London: Chapman and Hall, 1859), 217. Future references are to this edition and included in parentheses in the body of the text.

92. Aspin, *Cosmorama*, 371.

93. See Hodge, *Yankee Theatre*, 74–76.

94. Harriet Beecher Stowe, *Uncle Tom's Cabin*, ed. Ann Douglas (New York: Penguin, 1981), 2.

95. Aspin, *Cosmorama*, 215.

96. [Frances] Trollope, *Domestic Manners of the Americans*, 4th ed. (London: Whittaker, Treacher; New York: Reprinted For the Booksellers, 1832), 34. Future references are to this edition and are included in parentheses in the body of the text.

97. Amy S. Greenberg, *Manifest Manhood and the Antebellum American Empire* (Cambridge and New York: Cambridge University Press, 2005), 21. For Anglo working-class culture see also David Roediger, *The Wages of Whiteness: Race and the Making of the American Working Class* (London: Verso, 1991) and Shelley Streeby, *American Sensations: Class, Empire, and the Production of Popular Culture* (Berkeley: University of California Press, 2002).

98. See Peter Adams, *The Bowery Boys: Street Corner Radicals and the Politics of Rebellion* (Westport, CT: Praeger, 2005).

99. George G. Foster, *New York By Gas-Light, and Other Urban Sketches*, ed. and intro. Stuart M. Blumin (Berkeley: University of California Press, 1990), 177.

100. Foster, *New York By Gas-Light*, 175, 176.

101. [William M. Bobo], *Glimpses of New-York City, by a South Carolinian* (Charleston: J. J. McCarter 1852), 164.

102. Foster, *New York*, 170.

103. Trollope, *Domestic Manners*, 154.

104. "Mrs Trollope," *Traveller and Spirit of the Times*, January 26, 1833, 1, 48, American Periodicals, 2.

105. "Yankeeisms," *New England Magazine*, November 1832, American Periodicals, 377.

106. Horace Bushnell, "The Age of Homespun," in *Work and Play; or Literary Varieties* (New York: Charles Scribner, 1864), 374, 375.

107. Anna Cora Mowatt, *Fashion* in *Early American Drama*, ed. Jeffrey Richards (New York: Penguin, 1997), 312.

Chapter 2

1. Jacques Lacan, *Four Fundamental Concepts of Psychoanalysis*, ed. Jacques-Alain Miller, trans. Alan Sheridan (New York and London: W.W. Norton, 1981), 100.

2. Henry D. Thoreau, *Walden; or, Life in the Woods* (Boston: Ticknor and Fields, 1854), 18. All future references are to this edition and are inserted in parentheses in the body of the text.

3. See Laura Dassow Walls, "'Are You the Brothers of Mine': Thoreau and the Irish," *New England Quarterly* 88, no. 1 (March 2015): 5–36.

4. See "La Comptess Walewski" and "The Princess Wagram," in *Godey's Lady's Book and Magazine* 49 (August 1854): 100, 101.

5. Emma C. Embury, "The Count and the Cousin," *Godey's Lady's Book* 37 (1848): 90.

6. Richard L. Bushman, *The Refinement of America: Persons, Houses, Cities* (1992; New York: Random House-Vintage, 1993), 414.

7. Eric Lott, *Love and Theft: Blackface Minstrelsy and the American Working Class* (New York: Oxford, 1995), 89.

8. Elisa Tamarkin, *Anglophilia: Deference, Devotion, and Antebellum America* (Chicago: University of Chicago Press, 2008), xxvii. See also Leonard Tennenhouse, *The Importance of Feeling English: American Literature and the British Diaspora, 1750–1850* (Princeton: Princeton University Press, 2009).

9. See Lewis Leary, introduction to *Home As Found*, by James Fenimore Cooper (New York: Capricorn Books, 1961), xvii–xviii, who suggests that Cooper's Steadfast Dodge in *Homeward Bound*, described by Cooper as "an American in a European mask," was a satire of Willis.

10. See Homi K. Bhabha, "Of Mimicry and Man," in *The Location of Culture* (London: Routledge, 1994), 91.

11. Fred Lewis Pattee, *The Development of the American Short Story: An Historical Survey* (New York: Harper, 1923), 78. General information on Willis is from Henry E. Beers, *Nathaniel Parker Willis* (Boston: Houghton, Mifflin, 1885), and Thomas Nelson Baker, *Sentiment and Celebrity: Nathaniel Parker Willis and the Trials of Literary Fame* (New York: Oxford University Press, 1998).

12. Willis's relationship to the culture of aspiration is treated at length in Sandra Tomc, *Industry and the Creative Mind: The Eccentric Author in American Literature and Entertainment, 1790–1860* (Ann Arbor: University of Michigan Press, 2012), chap. 4. For general discussions of the mythology of self-making, see Irvin G. Wyllie, *The Self-Made Man in America* (New York: Free Press, 1954), and John G. Cawelti, *Apostles of the Self-Made Man: Changing Concepts of Success in America* (Chicago: University of Chicago Press, 1965).

13. For class structure and dynamics in the antebellum northeast, see Stuart M. Blumin, *The Emergence of the Middle Class: Social Experience in the American City, 1760–1900* (1989; New York: Cambridge University Press, 1994); Frederic Cople Jaher, *The Urban Establishment: Upper Strata in Boston, New York, Charleston, Chicago, and Los Angeles* (Urbana: University of Illinois Press, 1982); and Martin J. Burke, *The Conundrum of Class: Public Discourse on the Social Order in America* (Chicago: University of Chicago Press, 1995).

14. Quoted in Baker, *Sentiment and Celebrity*, 39.

15. "Nathaniel Parker Willis to J. B. Van Schaick," 18 Feb. [1829]. Simon Gratz Collection, Historical Society of Pennsylvania, Philadelphia; and Fanny Fern, *Ruth Hall and Other Writings*, ed. Joyce W. Warren (New Brunswick, NJ: Rutgers University Press, 1986), 16.

16. Quoted in M. A. DeWolfe Howe, *American Bookmen: Sketches, Chiefly Biographical, of Certain Writers of the Nineteenth Century* (New York: Dodd, Mead, 1898), 104–5.

17. "Editor's Table," *American Monthly Magazine* 1 (1829): 285; and quoted in Beers, *Willis*, 122–23.

18. Jaher, *Urban Establishment*, 83.
19. "Editor's Table," *American Monthly Magazine* 1 (1829): 285, and passim.
20. "The Editor's Table," *American Monthly Magazine* 2, no. 2 (May 1830): 132.
21. Quoted in Beers, *Willis*, 90.
22. "Eight Pages," *Harvardiana* 1 (1835): 315.
23. Michael Zakim, *Ready-Made Democracy: A History of Men's Dress in the American Republic, 1760–1860* (Chicago: University of Chicago Press, 2003), 105.
24. Michael Paul Rogin, *Subversive Genealogy: The Politics and Art of Herman Melville* (New York: Alfred A. Knopf, 1979), 243.
25. *New-York Herald*, July 8, 1849.
26. Timothy S. Arthur, *Advice to Young Men on Their Duties and Conduct in Life* (Philadelphia: G. G. Evans, 1860), 12.
27. Joel Hawes, *Lectures to Young Men on the Formation of Character*, 3rd ed. (Hartford, CT: Cooke and Co., 1829) 76.
28. Henry Ward Beecher, *Seven Lectures to Young Men* (Indianapolis: Cutler, Davis, 1844), 6, 84.
29. Beecher, *Seven Lectures*, 7.
30. Rufus W. Clark, *Lectures on the Formation of Character, Temptations and Mission of Young Men* (Boston: Albert Colby, 1861), 232.
31. Rogin, *Subversive Genealogy*, 243. Karen Halttunen's *Confidence Men and Painted Women: A Study of Middle Class Culture in America, 1830–1870* (New Haven: Yale University Press, 1982) describes the broader phenomenon of the confidence man as urban fable.
32. Zakim, *Ready-Made*, 187–88.
33. N. P. Willis, *New Mirror* 2, no. 3 (October 21, 1843): 47.
34. Oliver Wendell Holmes, *A Mortal Antipathy*, Riverside Edition (Boston: Houghton, Mifflin, 1891), 4; [John Moncure Daniel], rev. of Edgar Allan Poe in the *Southern Literary Messenger* 16 (1850): 172–87, rpt. in *Edgar Allan Poe: The Critical Heritage*, ed. I. M. Walker (London: Routledge & Kegan Paul, 1986), 360; Child's comments are quoted in Carolyn L. Karcher, *The First Woman in the Republic: A Cultural Biography of Lydia Maria Child* (Durham: Duke University Press, 1994), 50; and James Parton, *Triumphs of Enterprise, Ingenuity and Public Spirit* (New York: Virtue & Yorston, 1874), 16.
35. James Russell Lowell, *A Fable For Critics* (New York: G. P. Putnam, 1891), 51.
36. Fern, *Ruth Hall*, 70.
37. "Editor's Table," *American Monthly Magazine* 1, no. 6 (Sept. 1829): 437.
38. Beecher, *Seven Lectures*, 94.
39. Edgar Allan Poe, "The Duc de L'Omelette," in *Tales*, vol. 2 of *The Complete Works of Edgar Allan Poe*, ed. James A. Harrison, 15 vols. (1902; New York: AMS, 1965), 198. Kenneth L. Daughrity, in "Poe's Quiz on Willis," *American Literature* 5 (1933–34): 55–62, identifies "The Duc de L'Omelette" (1836) as a satire of Willis.
40. "Editor's Table," *American Monthly Magazine* 1, no. 5 (August 1829): 357.
41. Quoted in Beers, *Willis*, 198.
42. Quoted in Joyce W. Warren, *Fanny Fern: An Independent Woman* (New Brunswick, NJ: Rutgers University Press, 1992), 52.
43. [Untitled Notice], *Morning Courier and New York Enquirer* Feb. 7, 1845, 2.
44. "Editor's Table," *American Monthly Magazine* 2 (1830): 141.
45. Homi K. Bhabha, *The Location of Culture* (London and New York: Routledge, 1984), 86. See also Judith Butler, *Bodies that Matter* (New York and London: Routledge, 1995), 124–37; and Michelle

Ann Stephens, *Skin Acts: Race, Psychoanalysis, and the Black Male Performer* (Durham: Duke University Press, 2014), chap 1. Miller is discussed below.

46. Bhabha, *Location*, 89.

47. Monica L. Miller, *Slaves to Fashion: Black Dandyism and the Styling of the Black Diasporic Identity* (Durham: Duke University Press, 2009), 14.

48. Beecher, *Lectures*, 82.

49. Jirí Veltruský, "Man and Object in the Theatre," in *A Prague School Reader on Esthetics, Literary Structure, and Style*, trans. Paul L. Garvin (Washington, DC: Georgetown University Press, 1964), 85.

50. Nathaniel Hawthorne, "The Minister's Black Veil," in *Twice-Told Tales*, ed. William Charvat et. al., vol. 9 of the Centenary Edition of the Works of Nathaniel Hawthorne (Columbus: Ohio State University Press, 1974), 38. All future references are to this edition. Page numbers are in parentheses in the body of the text.

51. Nathaniel Hawthorne, *The Scarlett Letter*, ed. William Charvat et. al., vol. 1 of the Centenary Edition of the Works of Nathaniel Hawthorne (Columbus: Ohio State University Press, 1962), 47. All future references are to this edition. Page numbers are in parentheses in the body of the text.

52. Bhabha, *Location*, 88.

53. Bhabha, *Location*, 91.

54. Jacques Lacan, *The Four Fundamental Concepts of Psychoanalysis*, ed. Jacques-Alain Miller and trans. Alan Sheridan (New York and London: W.W. Norton, 1981), 95.

55. Lacan, *Four Fundamental Concepts*, 95.

56. Nathaniel Hawthorne, *The Blithedale Romance* (Boston: Ticknor, Reed, and Fields, 1852), 234.

57. Hawthorne, *Blithedale*, 229–30.

58. Hawthorne, *Blithedale*, 235, 236. It is worth noting the extent to which these models of distracted or occluded sight were able to function partly, we might surmise, because nineteenth-century Western societies associated power, self-expression, truthfulness, and sincerity with degrees of visibility. Writing in *Veil* (London: Bloomsbury Academic, 2017) on the controversies around veiling that plague Muslim and Western societies in the twenty-first century, Rafia Zakaria hypothesizes that the veil is an object of contention not because of its religious overtones but because we live in a world where "visibility signifies power and control" (6). The function of the niqaab or burqa, which conceal the wearer's face and body, Zakaria believes, is to "eliminate physicality from the identity equation, enabl[ing] the creation of a third state of being, a limbo between existence and non-existence where either can be actualized but neither really is" (9).

59. Hawthorne, *Blithedale*, 234.

60. P. T. Barnum, *The Art of Money Getting; Or, Golden Rules for Making Money* (Project Gutenberg EBook, July 30, 2009 [EBook #8581]), loc. 82 of 696.

61. Jonathan Elmer, *Reading at the Social Limit: Affect, Mass Culture, and Edgar Allan Poe* (Stanford: Stanford University Press, 1995), 184.

62. Elmer, *Reading*, 185.

63. Elmer, *Reading*, 187.

64. P. T. Barnum, *The Humbugs of the World: An Account of Humbugs, Delusions, Impositions, Quackeries, Deceits and Deceivers Generally, in All Ages* (New York: Carleton, 1866), 20.

65. Ralph Waldo Emerson, *English Traits* (Boston: Phillips, Samson, 1856), 110. Future citations are from this edition and appear in parentheses in the body of the text.

66. See Michael Pickering, *Blackface Minstrelsy in Britain* (London: Ashgate, 2008), 6–7.

67. Philip Deloria, *Playing Indian* (New Haven: Yale University Press, 1998), 6. For studies of blackface minstrelsy, see Dale Cockrell, *Demons of Disorder, Early Blackface Minstrels and their World*

(New York: Cambridge University Press, 1997); Louis Chude-Sokei, *The Last "Darky": Bert Williams, Black-on-Black Minstrelsy, and the African Diaspora* (Durham: Duke University Press, 2006); Brian Roberts, *Blackface Nation: Race, Reform, and Identity in American Popular Music, 1812–1925* (Chicago: University of Chicago Press, 2017); and Robert Hornback, *Racism and Early Blackface Comic Traditions: From the Old World to the New* (Basingstoke: Palgrave Macmillan, 2018).

68. Robert P. Nevin, "Stephen C. Foster and Negro Minstrelsy," *Atlantic Monthly* 20 (1867): 609, 610.

69. James Fenimore Cooper, *The Last of the Mohicans; A Narrative of 1757*, vol. 1 of *The Leather-stocking Tales*, 5 vols. (New York: State University of New York Press, 1985), 499, 500–501, 499, 500.

70. "Editor's Table," *American Monthly Magazine* 1 (1829): 580.

71. Washington Irving, "England and America," *Godey's Magazine and Lady's Book* 36 (1848): 55.

72. Washington Irving, *The Sketchbook of Geoffrey Crayon, Gent.*, ed. Haskell Springer, vol. 8 of *The Complete Works of Washington Irving*, 30 vols. (Boston: Twayne, 1978), 63.

73. James Fenimore Cooper, *Gleanings in Europe: England*, ed. Donald Ringe, James P. Eliot, et al., in *The Writings of James Fenimore Cooper* (Albany: State University of New York Press, 1982), 65.

74. Ralph Waldo Emerson, "The American Scholar," in *Nature, Addresses, and Lectures*, ed. Robert Spiller et al., vol. 1 of *The Collected Works of Ralph Waldo Emerson*, 12 vols. (Cambridge, MA: Harvard University Press, 1960–1976), 52.

75. Quoted in Beers, *Willis*, 123.

76. Quoted in Beers, *Willis*, 140.

77. N. P. Willis, *Pencillings By the Way*, vol. 3 of 3 (London: John Macrone, 1835), 60. Willis's 139 letters to the *New York Mirror* appeared under various titles and at various intervals between February 13, 1832, and January 14, 1836. Most were published in expurgated form as *Pencillings By the Way* in 1835. To save confusion around the titles, the original *Mirror* letters are hereafter referred to as "Pencillings." Where possible, however, I cite from the expurgated 1835 edition of *Pencillings By the Way*, partly because of its subsequent influence, and partly in order to give a sense of what Willis felt he could legitimately present to British audiences.

78. Willis, *Pencillings*, 3:82.

79. Quoted in Joy S. Kasson, *Artistic Voyages: Europe and the American Imagination in the Works of Irving, Allston, Cole, Cooper, and Hawthorne* (Westport, CT: Greenwood, 1982), 10.

80. Willis, *Pencillings*, 3:83.

81. The Blessington circle is detailed in Michael Sadleir, *The Strange Life of Lady Blessington* (Boston: Little, Brown, 1933). Willis is discussed on 197–208. For a reading of Willis's travels as landmarks in a history of publicized intimacy, see Glenn Hendler, *Public Sentiments: Structures of Feeling in Nineteenth-Century American Literature* (Chapel Hill: University of North Carolina Press, 2001), chap. 5.

82. Willis, *Pencillings*, 3:151.

83. R. R. Madden, *The Literary Life and Correspondence of the Countess of Blessington*, 2 vols. (New York: Harper, 1855), 2:329.

84. Quoted in Beers, *Willis*, 97.

85. Ellen Moers, *The Dandy: Brummell to Beerbohm* (New York: Viking, 1960), 17–18.

86. N. P. Willis, *Lecture on Fashion*, Mirror Library (New York: Morris & Willis, 1844), 6, 7.

87. Domna C. Stanton, *The Aristocrat as Art: A Study of the* Honnête Homme *and the Dandy in Seventeenth- and Nineteenth-Century French Literature* (New York: Columbia University Press, 1980), 115.

88. Quoted in Stanton, *Aristocrat as Art*, 159.

89. Frances Trollope, *Paris and the Parisians in 1835*, 2nd ed. 2 vols. (London: Richard Bentley, 1836), 1:105–6.

90. James Eli Adams, "The Hero as Spectacle: Carlyle and the Persistence of Dandyism," in *Victorian Literature and the Victorian Visual Imagination*, ed. Carol T. Christ and John. O. Jordan (Berkeley: University of California Press, 1995), 217.

91. N. P. Willis, "Pencillings," *New York Mirror* Apr. 25, 1835: 340; and Willis, *Pencillings*, 167.

92. For an account of the legacy of the Carlyle dandy in antebellum U.S. culture, see Nicola Nixon, "Men and Coats; or, The Politics of the Dandiacal Body in Melville's 'Benito Cereno,'" *PMLA* 114 (1999): 359–72, which argues that Carlyle's figure of the dandy as decadent aristocrat offered Melville a way of critiquing the myth of a classless, egalitarian northern United States.

93. Willis, *Pencillings*, 197, 198, 200.

94. Willis, "Pencillings," *New York Mirror*, Mar. 14, 1835, 292.

95. Willis, "Pencillings," *New York Mirror*, June 6, 1835, 388.

96. Willis, "Pencillings," *New York Mirror*, Mar. 21, 1835, 297; and *New York Mirror*, Apr. 14, 1835, 317.

97. Willis, "Pencillings," *New York Mirror*, Mar. 14, 1835, 292.

98. Willis, "Pencillings," *New York Mirror*, Apr. 18, 1835, 332.

99. It is important to stress that while Willis revealed himself as a fraud, he did not, as a consequence, produce a positive or fixed knowledge of his actual contents but only presented audiences, once again, with a surface front that demanded guesswork and conjecture.

100. [Frances] Trollope, *Domestic Manners of the Americans*, 4th ed. (London: Whittaker, Treacher; New York: Reprinted For the Booksellers, 1832), 241.

101. Travelers like Irving and Cooper were cast by the British as familiar commodities, the one with all "his flattering pictures of Christmas life in old ancestral halls" ("American Poetry," *Edinburgh Review* 61 [1835]: 23), the other with his fear of the "general subjection of America" ("Cooper's *England*," *Fraser's Magazine* 16 [1837]: 234).

102. Review of *Melanie and Other Poems, Pencillings By the Way* and *Inklings of Adventure*, by N. P. Willis, *North American Review* 43 (1836): 412.

103. "Cooper's *England*," *The Spectator* 10 (1837): 493; and "Willis's Pencillings," *Fraser's Magazine* 13 (1836): 195.

104. "Willis's *Pencillings By the Way*," *Quarterly Review* 54 (1835): 457.

105. "Willis's *Pencillings*," *Fraser's* 13 (1836): 195.

106. See Beers, *Willis*, 196. It is worth emphasizing the consonance of conservative American and prevailing English opinion, doubtless a result of the fact that both constituencies were invested in transparency and in the legibility of the emissaries of each nation to the other.

107. "Willis's *Pencillings By The Way*," *Quarterly Review* 54 (1835): 469.

108. "Willis's *Pencillings*," *Fraser's* 13 (1836): 195.

109. "Willis's *Dashes At Life With a Free Pencil*," *Edinburgh Review* 82 (1845): 472; and "On an American Traveller," *Punch* 19 (1850): 7. For details of the Willis-Thackeray relationship see Harold H. Scudder, "Thackeray and N.P. Willis," *PMLA* 57 (1942): 589–92.

110. See Beers, *Willis*, 119.

111. See Beers, *Willis*, 119. Henry James patterned his "international novel" on Willis's fictional retelling of his European adventures in his one novel, *Paul Fane* (1857); see Van Wyck Brooks, *The World of Washington Irving* (New York: E. P. Dutton, 1944), 442.

112. "Literary Gossipings," *Spirit of the Times: A Chronicle of the Turf, Agriculture, Field Sports, Literature and the Stage* 12, no. 22 (July 30 1842): 264.

113. See Lara Langer Cohen, *The Fabrication of American Literature: Fraudulence and Antebellum Print Culture* (Philadelphia: University of Pennsylvania Press, 2012).

114. "American Travelers," *Putnam's Monthly* 5 (1855): 563, 564, 570, 576.

115. Herman Melville, *The Confidence Man: His Masquerade* (New York: Dix, Edwards, 1857), 10.

116. Melville, *Confidence Man*, 204–5.
117. James Salazar, *Bodies of Reform* (New York: New York University Press, 2010), 47.
118. N. P. Willis, *The Ragbag, a Collection of Ephemera* (New York: Charles Scribner, 1855), 56.
119. [George Foster], *New York in Slices: By An Experienced Carver*, revised by the author (New York: William H. Graham, 1849), 76.
120. Willis, *Ragbag*, 45–46, 48.
121. N. P. Willis, *Loiterings of Travel*, vol. 1 of 3 (London: Longman, Orme, Brown, Green, & Longmans, 1840), 68–69.
122. Bhabha, "Of Mimicry and Man," 92.
123. Reginald Horsman, *Race and Manifest Destiny* (Cambridge, MA: Harvard University Press, 1991), 164.
124. Henry James, *The American* (London: Macmillan, 1879), 7.
125. James, *The American*, 47–48, 44.
126. James, *The American*, 7.

Chapter 3

1. See James D. Wallace, *Early Cooper and His Audience* (New York: Columbia University Press, 1986).
2. Jared Gardner, *Race and the Founding of American Literature, 1787–1845* (Baltimore: Johns Hopkins University Press, 1998), 110–12. For significant discussions of Cooper and race, see also Barbara Alice Mann, "Race Traitor: Cooper, His Critics, and Nineteenth-Century Literary Politics," in *A Historical Guide to James Fenimore Cooper*, ed. Leland Person (New York: Oxford University Press, 2007), 155–85, which makes a case for the complexity of Cooper's representation of Indigenous people; Ezra Tawil, *The Making of Racial Sentiment: Slavery and the Birth of the Frontier Romance* (Cambridge: Cambridge University Press, 2009), chap. 2; Robert S. Levine argues that Cooper became increasingly critical of racist and anti-Indigenous doctrine in the second half of his career and uses *The Deerslayer* as evidence. See *Race, Transnationalism, and Nineteenth-Century American Literary Studies* (Cambridge: Cambridge University Press, 2017), chap. 2.
3. Biographical information on Cooper is from Wayne Franklin, *James Fenimore Cooper: The Early Years* (New Haven: Yale University Press, 2007) and *James Fenimore Cooper: The Later Years* (New Haven: Yale University Press, 2017).
4. The books that address the Three-Mile Point problem are *Homeward Bound* (1838), *Home As Found* (1838), *The American Democrat* (1838), *Chronicles of Cooperstown* (1838), and *The Deerslayer* (1841).
5. D. H. Lawrence, *Studies in Classic American Literature*, ed. Ezra Greenspan, Lindeth Vasey, and John Worthen (Cambridge and New York: Cambridge University Press, 2003), 65.
6. In *The Prairie* (1827) the prospective settlers are convinced to move back east, but the land is not by any means left vacant; it still belongs to its Indigenous inhabitants and to Natty himself, who is buried in the prairie's sublime expanse. *The Deerslayer* is notable for its complete depopulation of the Otsego Lake "frontier."
7. Franklin, *Cooper: Later Years*, 261.
8. James Fenimore Cooper, *The Deerslayer or, The First War-Path*, intro. and notes by James Franklin Beard (Albany: State University of New York Press, 1987), 547. All future references are to this edition and are included in parentheses in the main body of the text.
9. For a study of graves and Indigenous land claims in Cooper see Sarah Klotz, "The Red Man

Has Left No Mark Here: Graves and Land Claim in the Cooperian Tradition," *ESQ: A Journal of the American Renaissance* 60, no. 3 (2014): 331–69.

10. John P. McWilliams Jr., *Political Justice in a Republic: James Fenimore Cooper's America* (Berkeley: University of California Press, 1972), 288.

11. Stephen Germic, "Land Claims, Natives, and Nativism: Susan Fenimore Cooper's Fealty to Place," *American Literature* 79, no. 3 (2007): 476.

12. Johann Gottfried Herder, *Outlines of a Philosophy of the History of Man*, trans. T. Churchill (1800; rpt. in facsimile, New York: Bergman, 1966), 169.

13. Herder, *Outlines*, 169.

14. Herder, *Outlines*, 167.

15. Samuel Stanhope Smith, *An Essay on the Causes of the Variety of Complexion and Figure in the Human Species* (New Brunswick, NJ: J. Simpson and Williams and Whiting, 1810), 80. For relevant studies of the history of race ideology in the United States see Thomas F. Gossett, *Race: The History of an Idea in America* (1963; New York: Oxford University Press, 1997); Dana D. Nelson, *National Manhood: Capitalist Citizenship and the Imagined Fraternity of White Men* (Durham: Duke University Press, 1998); Betsy Erkkila, *Mixed Bloods and Other Crosses: Rethinking American Literature from the Revolution to the Culture Wars* (Philadelphia: University of Pennsylvania Press, 2005); Ibram X. Kendi, *Stamped from the Beginning: The Definitive History of Racist Ideas in America* (New York: Nation Books, 2016). For a general history of the ongoing structure of racist thought in Europe and its empires see Miriam Eliav-Feldon, Benjamin H. Isaac, and Joseph Ziegler, eds., *The Origins of Racism in the West* (Cambridge: Cambridge University Press, 2009), and Francisco Bethencourt, *Racisms: From the Crusades to the Twentieth Century* (Princeton: Princeton University Press, 2013).

16. Smith, *Essay*, 45.

17. Smith, *Essay*, 75.

18. Lorenzo Veracini, *Settler Colonialism: A Theoretical Overview* (London: Palgrave Macmillan, 2010), 21. For the settler colonial contexts of U.S. continental expansion and settler-based democracy, see Walter L. Hixson, *American Settler Colonialism: A History* (London: Palgrave Macmillan, 2013); Adam Dahl, *Empire of the People: Settler Colonialism and the Foundations of Modern Democratic Thought* (Lawrence: University Press of Kansas, 2018); Gerald Horne, *The Apocalypse of Settler Colonialism: The Roots of Slavery, White Supremacy, and Capitalism in Seventeenth-Century North America and the Caribbean* (New York: Monthly Review, 2018). For a study of settler colonialism and mid-nineteenth-century settler literature, see Mark Rifkin, *Settler Common Sense* (Minneapolis: University of Minnesota Press, 2014). Tony Hughes-d'Aeth places Cooper in the settler colonial tradition; see "Cooper, Cather, Prichard, 'Pioneer': The Chronotope of Settler Colonialism," *Australian Literary Studies* 31, no. 3 (2016): 1–26. For a general discussion of the merits of settler colonialism as a lens through which to see U.S. history, see the special issue of *William and Mary Quarterly* 76, no. 3 (July 2019) on "Settler Colonialism in Early American History," ed. Jeffrey Ostler and Nancy Shoemaker. The settler colonial model fits particularly well with beliefs in white racial destiny and the mythical western direction of white settlement consolidated in early nineteenth-century ethnic nationalism.

19. Veracini, *Settler Colonialism*, 100, 99.

20. Alexis de Tocqueville, *Democracy in America* (Chicago: University of Chicago Press, 2000), 393–94.

21. James Fenimore Cooper, *The Last of the Mohicans: A Narrative of 1757*, intro. by James Franklin Beard, ed. James A. Sappenfield and E. N. Feltskog (Albany: State University of New York Press, 1983), 30.

22. James Fenimore Cooper, *Notions of the Americans: Picked Up by a Travelling Bachelor*, ed. Gary Williams (Albany: State University of New York Press, 1991), 483, 242, 486.

23. James Fenimore Cooper, *Home as Found* (New York: Capricorn Books, 1961), 166.

24. Cooper, *Home as Found*, 164–65.

25. See, for example, George Dekker, *James Fenimore Cooper: The American Scott* (New York: Barnes and Noble, 1967), 185; William P. Kelly, *Plotting America's Past: Fenimore Cooper and the Leatherstocking Tales* (Carbondale: Southern Illinois University Press, 1983), 185; Louise K. Barnett, "Speech in the Wilderness: The Ideal Discourse of the *The Deerslayer*," in *Desert, Garden, Margin, Range: Literature on the American Frontier*, ed. Eric Heyne (New York: Twayne, 1992), 20.

26. James Fenimore Cooper, *The Pioneers*, ed. Lance Schachterle and Kenneth M. Andersen, Jr., intro. by Donald A. Ringe (New York: Penguin, 1988), 18.

27. Samuel George Morton and George Combe, *Crania Americana; or, A Comparative View of the Skulls of Various Aboriginal Nations of North and South America* (Philadelphia: J. Dobson; London: Simpkin, Marshall, 1839), 3.

28. See, for example, Charles Hansford Adams, *The Guardian of the Law: Authority and Identity in James Fenimore Cooper* (University Park: Pennsylvania State University Press, 1990), 112.

29. James Fenimore Cooper, *The Pathfinder, or The Inland Sea*, intro. and notes by William P. Kelly (Oxford: Oxford University Press, 1992), 27.

30. James Fenimore Cooper, *Home as Found* (New York: Capricorn Books, 1961), 200–201, 202, 205.

31. See Donald Pease, "Introduction," in *The Deerslayer* by James Fenimore Cooper (New York: Penguin 1987).

32. Franklin suspects that *The Deerslayer* is a meditation on Cooper's troubles with the press. The character who most closely resembles Cooper, for Franklin, is Judith, with her fine imported clothes, her homelessness, and her decimated reputation. See *Cooper: Later Years*, 262.

33. For Cooper's debt to picturesque landscape painting and his affiliation with the Hudson River School, see Blake Nevius, *Cooper's Landscapes: An Essay on the Picturesque Vision* (Berkeley: University of California Press, 1976); and Daniel H. Peck, *A World by Itself: The Pastoral Moment in Cooper's Fiction* (New Haven: Yale University Press, 1977). Peck argues that whereas Cooper's other novels punctuate dialectical history with brief pastoral moments of picturesque stillness and "aesthetic rapture," the whole of the *The Deerslayer* is itself a "prolonged" "pastoral moment" (181–82). All picturesque, in other words, the natural world of *The Deerslayer* is developed as all aesthetic or all cultural.

34. See, for example, Gordon Brotherston, "The Prairie and Cooper's Invention of the West," in *James Fenimore Cooper: New Critical Essays*, ed. Robert Clark (London and New York: Vision and Barnes & Noble, 1985), 162–86.

35. Accounts of midcentury filibustering and proexpansion politics and culture can be found in Alexander Saxton, *The Rise and Fall of the White Republic: Class, Politics, and Mass Culture in Nineteenth-Century America* (London: Verso, 1990); Shelley Streeby, *American Sensations: Class Empire, and the Production of Popular Culture* (Berkeley: University of California Press, 2002). Especially useful for this study is Amy S. Greenberg, *Manifest Manhood and the Antebellum American Empire* (Cambridge: Cambridge University Press, 2005), which deals with the racial and proslavery elements of pre–Civil War expansionist agitation. See also Michel Gobal, *Empire by Invitation: William Walker and Manifest Destiny in Central America* (Cambridge, MA: Harvard University Press, 2018), which discusses the antislavery, egalitarian spirit in which some filibustering campaigns were waged.

36. See Amy Kaplan, *The Anarchy of Empire in the Making of U.S. Culture* (Cambridge MA and London: Harvard University Press, 2002). For studies of late nineteenth-century U.S. formal imperialism, see Amy Kaplan and Donald Pease, eds., *Cultures of United States Imperialism* (Durham: Duke University Press, 1993); Matthew Frye Jacobson, *Barbarian Virtues: The United States Encounters For-*

eign Peoples at Home and Abroad, 1876–1917 (New York: Hill and Wang, 2000); and Daniel E. Bender and Jana K. Lipman, eds., *Making the Empire Work: Labor and United States Imperialism* (New York: New York University Press, 2015).

37. James Fenimore Cooper, *The American Democrat*, ed. and intro. George Dekker and Larry Johnston (London and New York: Penguin, 1989), 187. All future references are to this edition and are inserted in parentheses in the body of the text.

38. Saxton, *Rise and Fall*, 137.

39. Quoted in James Grossman, *James Fenimore Cooper*, The American Men of Letters Series (n.p.: William Sloane Associates, 1949), 132.

40. Quoted in Grossman, 133.

41. James Fenimore Cooper, *The American Democrat; or, Hints on the Social and Civic Relations of the United States of America* (Cooperstown, NY: H. & E. Phinney, 1838), 130, 133. All future references are to this edition and are placed in parentheses in the body of the text.

42. For an account of Benjamin's career in New York and Boston see, Sandra Tomc, *Industry and the Creative Mind: The Eccentric Writer in American Literature and Entertainment, 1790–1860* (Ann Arbor: University of Michigan Press, 2012), chap. 3.

43. Frederic Hudson, *Journalism in the United States from 1690 to 1872* (New York: Harper, 1873), 459.

44. "Gallery of Literary Characters, No. XVI: James Fenimore Cooper," *The Athenaeum* (November 15, 1832): 106.

45. "Cooper's Works: The Leatherstocking Tales," *The United States Democratic Review* 28 (March 1851): 2.

46. The racial bases of anti-imperialism are detailed by Horsman, *Race and Manifest Destiny*, chap. 5, and Streeby, *American Sensations*, passim, in their accounts of the Mexico crisis; it should be noted that Streeby sees racism as a "contradiction" within anti-imperialist argument (chap. 6). Eric T. L. Love, however, demonstrates the continuity of these positions. Pro-imperialists in the era of Manifest Destiny fantasized a "United States of the World," but Love shows that virtually every overseas colonization or annexation project launched by these groups between 1840 and 1890 stumbled—and failed—over the issue of racial and republican purity. See Love, *Race Over Empire: Racism and U.S. Imperialism, 1865–1900* (Chapel Hill: University of North Carolina Press, 2004), passim; see also Ronald Takaki, *Iron Cages: Race and Culture in Nineteenth-Century America* (1979; New York: Oxford, 2000).

47. Francis Bret Harte, "Muck-a-Muck: A Modern Indian Novel After Cooper," *Condensed Novels* (New York, 1867); rpt. in George Dekker and John P. McWilliams, eds., *Fenimore Cooper: The Critical Heritage* (London: Routledge & Kegan Paul, 1973), 270.

48. Harte, "Muck-a-Muck," 273.

49. Harte, "Muck-a-Muck," 274.

50. Harte, "Muck-a-Muck," 275.

51. [James Russell Lowell], *A Fable for Critics, by James Russell Lowell With Vignette Portraits of the Authors De Quibis Fabula Narratur* (London: Gay and Bird, [n.d.]), 66.

52. Lowell, *A Fable*, 66.

53. Mark Twain, "Fenimore Cooper's Literary Offenses," *North American Review* clxi (July 1895): 1–12; rpt. in George Dekker and John P. McWilliams, eds., *Fenimore Cooper: The Critical Heritage* (London: Routledge & Kegan Paul, 1973), 280.

54. Twain, "Fenimore Cooper," 278.

55. Critics have pointed up that Twain, pretending to a minute reading of Cooper's "facts," actually fabricated some of these details, but the point to be made here is that Twain is intent upon elaborat-

ing a "frontier" in which distinctions between fact and fiction have ceased to operate, and Twain's "source" here is *The Deerslayer*, where there *is*, I am suggesting, something off and artificial about the landscape.

56. Twain, "Fenimore Cooper," 282.

57. Twain, "Fenimore Cooper," 279–80.

58. Lowell, *A Fable*, 66.

59. Twain, Fenimore Cooper, 282.

60. Twain, Fenimore Cooper, 277.

61. Twain, Fenimore Cooper, 285.

62. Twain, Fenimore Cooper, 280.

63. Lowell, *A Fable*, 93, 96, 95.

64. "Cooper's Works," *The United States Democratic Review* 25 (July 1849): 55.

65. "Cooper's Works," *The United States Democratic Review*, 54.

66. Francis Parkman, "The Works of James Fenimore Cooper," *North American Review* lxxiv (January 1852): 147–61. Rpt. in George Dekker and John P. McWilliams, eds., *Fenimore Cooper: The Critical Heritage* (London: Routledge & Kegan Paul, 1973), 258, 256, 250, 257, 260.

67. The idea that Cooper was a shoddy craftsman had been part of his reputation since the early 1820s. This, however, had always been understood as a demerit. The critics I look at in the following pages regard Cooper's bad craftsmanship as a positive, saving feature of Cooper's art.

68. [G. S. Hillard], "James Fenimore Cooper," *The Atlantic Monthly* 9 (January 1862): 54. All future references are to this edition; page numbers are inserted in parentheses in the body of the text.

69. Thomas R. Lounsbury, *James Fenimore Cooper* (Boston: Houghton, Mifflin, 1886), 276, 51, 277. All future references are to this edition; page numbers are inserted in parentheses in the body of the text.

70. The identical patterns present themselves in Brander Matthews' short tribute for the Cooper centenary in 1889. See Brander Matthews, "The Centenary of Fenimore Cooper," *The Century* 38 (Sept. 1889): 796–98.

71. See Love, *Race Over Empire*, 11–26.

72. *Cincinnati Herald and Philanthropist*, June 17 1846; quoted in Horsman, *Race and Manifest Destiny*, 238.

73. Madison Grant, *The Passing of the Great Race* (New York: Charles Scribner's Sons, 1916), 43.

74. See Richard Slotkin, "Buffalo Bill's 'Wild West' and the Mythologization of the American Empire," in Kaplan and Pease, *Cultures*, 164–81. For a study of the role played by the imitation and performance of Indigeneity in the United States see Philip Deloria, *Playing Indian* (New Haven: Yale University Press, 1999).

75. Henry Inman and William F. Cody, *The Great Salt Lake Trail* (New York: MacMillan, 1898), 444–45. For an extended study of the mixing of reality and entertainment in Cody's shows see Joy Kasson, *Buffalo Bill's Wild West: Celebrity, Memory, and Popular History* (New York: Hill and Wang, 2000). For the show's European context see Robert Rydell and Rob Kroes, *Buffalo Bill in Bologna: The Americanization of the World, 1869–1922* (Chicago: University of Chicago Press, 2005).

76. Richard J. Walsh, *The Making of Buffalo Bill* (Indianapolis, IN: Bobbs Merrill, 1928), 190–91.

77. Quoted in Robert A. Carter, *Buffalo Bill Cody: The Man Behind the Legend* (New York: John Wiley, 2000), 200.

78. See Kasson, *Buffalo Bill*, 178.

79. Luther Standing Bear, *Land of the Spotted Eagle* (Lincoln: University of Nebraska Press, 1978), 91.

80. Standing Bear, *Land*, 1, 3, 23, 24.

81. For significant accounts of Standing Bear and the Wild West see, Ryan E. Burt, "'Sioux Yells'

in the Dawes Era: Lakota 'Indian Play,' the Wild West, and the Literatures of Luther Standing Bear," *American Quarterly* 62, no. 3 (2010): 617–37; and Coll Thrush, *Indigenous London: Native Travelers at the Heart of Empire* (New Haven: Yale University Press, 2016), chap. 6.

82. Luther Standing Bear, *My People, the Sioux* (Lincoln: University of Nebraska Press, 1975), 246. All future references are to this edition. Page numbers are inserted in parentheses in the body of the text.

83. Carter, *Buffalo Bill*, 361.

Chapter 4

1. Maxim Gorky, "Boredom," *The Independent*, August 8, 1907, 310.

2. Lewis Mumford, "The City," in *Civilization in the United States: An Inquiry By Thirty Americans*, ed. Harold E. Stearns (New York: Harcourt, Brace), 1922), 9.

3. Jean Baudrillard, *America* (London: Verso, 2010), 5.

4. William Leach, *Land of Desire: Merchants, Power, and the Rise of a New American Culture* (New York: Pantheon, 1993), 111.

5. See Robert W. Rydell and Rob Kroes, *Buffalo Bill in Bologna: The Americanization of the World, 1869–1922* (Chicago: University of Chicago Press, 2005), 8–10, 49, and chap. 4.

6. Lauren Rabinovitz, *Electric Dreamland: Amusement Parks, Movies, and American Modernity* (New York: Columbia University Press, 2012), 2.

7. See, for example, Rabinovitz, *Electric*, where she argues that amusement parks offered to "'Americanize' Americans," 10.

8. In contrast to most scholarship on world's fairs, this chapter does not take up the issues of imperial display, racialist exclusivity, and exploitation of Indigenous or indentured people that stood at the heart of the world's fair system. That said, my reading does not in any way exclude these histories and may contribute to a clearer understanding of the stakes of models of national self-performance in which nations were encapsulated in their ability to stage and sell allegedly unique characteristics.

9. Lloyd Kramer, *Nationalism in Europe and America: Politics, Cultures, and Identities Since 1775* (Chapel Hill: University of North Carolina Press, 2011), 59.

10. Anthony D. Smith, *National Identity* (Reno: University of Nevada Press, 1991), 66.

11. Smith, *National Identity*, 90.

12. General information on nineteenth-century world's fairs is from Robert Rydell, *All the World's a Fair: Visions of Empire at American International Expositions, 1876–1916* (Chicago: University of Chicago Press, 1984); Alexander Geppert, *Fleeting Cities: Imperial Expositions in Fin-de-Siècle Europe* (London: Palgrave MacMillan, 2010); Paul Greenhalgh, *Ephemeral Vistas: The Expositions Universelles, Great Exhibitions and World's Fairs, 1851–1939* (Manchester: Manchester University Press, 1988); Peter Henry Hoffenberg, *An Empire on Display: English, Indian, and Australian Exhibitions from the Crystal Palace to the Great War* (Berkeley: University of California Press, 2001); David Raizman and Ethan Robey, eds. *Expanding Nationalisms at World's Fairs: Identity, Diversity, and Exchange, 1851–1915* (New York: Routledge, 2017); Zeynep Çelik, *Displaying the Orient: Architecture of Islam at Nineteenth-Century World's Fairs* (Berkeley: University of California Press, 1992). For a material culture analysis of U.S. spectacle culture, see Susan Tenneriello, *Spectacle Culture and American Identity: 1815–1940* (New York: Palgrave Macmillan, 2013).

13. Roger Luckhurst, "Global Space-Time: Science-Fictionality and the World's Fairs, 1851–1939," *Science Fiction Studies* 39, no. 3 (November 2012): 385.

14. Geppert, *Fleeting Cities*, 2.

15. Luckhurst, "Global Space-Time," 385.

16. Geppert, *Fleeting Cities*, 223.

17. Greenhalgh, *Ephemeral Vistas*, 122.

18. "Editor's Study," *Harper's* 86, no. 513 (Feb. 1893): 477.

19. Norman Bolotin and Christine Laing, *The World's Columbian Exposition: The Chicago World's Fair of 1893* (Urbana: University of Illinois Press, 2002), 4.

20. Bolotin and Laing, *World's Columbian*, 124.

21. The native villages were typically run by an entertainment corporation that contracted with individuals and families to secure their services on the fairgrounds for a specified amount of time. For a study of the complexities of these exhibits and the often-punishing rules to which performers had to conform, see Melissa Rinehart, "To Hell with the Wigs: Native American Representation and Resistance at the World's Columbian Exposition," *American Indian Quarterly* 36, no. 4 (Fall 2012): 403–42. See also Sadiah Qureshi, *Peoples on Parade: Exhibitions, Empire, and Anthropology in Nineteenth-Century Britain* (Chicago: University of Chicago Press, 2011).

22. Bolotin and Laing, *World's Columbian*, 107.

23. Frederick Villiers, "An Artist's View of Chicago and the World's Fair," *Journal of the Society of the Arts* 42 (November 17, 1893–November 16, 1894): 52.

24. Roland Barthes, *Mythologies*, trans. Annette Lavers (1957; New York: Hill and Wang, 1972), 26.

25. Denise Ferreira da Silva, *Toward a Global Idea of Race* (Minneapolis: University of Minnesota Press, 2007), 116.

26. Henry Van Brunt, "Architecture of the World's Columbian Exposition," *Report of the Committee of Awards of the World's Columbian Commission*, 2 vols. (Washington, DC: Government Printing Office, 1901), 1:7.

27. Brunt, "Architecture," 1:7.

28. Trumbull White and William Igleheart, *The World's Columbian Exposition, Chicago, 1893* (Philadelphia: P. W. Ziegler, 1893), 542. Page numbers hereafter cited in parentheses in text.

29. *Conkey's Complete Guide to the World's Columbian Exposition* (Chicago: W. B. Conkey, 1893), 169.

30. Villiers, "An Artist's View," 52.

31. White and Igleheart, *World's Columbian Exposition*, 569.

32. Villiers, "An Artist's View," 52.

33. It should be noted that the necessity of always appearing in costume was a burden for those performers required to stage their daily lives. The Inuit people who had traveled from Labrador to work at the "Esquimaux Village" were required to always wear furs, even when the weather was warm, a circumstance that eventually led to revolt and scandal for the corporation that hired them. See Rinehart, "To Hell," 415.

34. *Rand, McNally and Co.'s Advance Guide to The World's Columbian Exposition* (Chicago: Rand, McNally, 1893), 212.

35. *Rand, McNally*, 315

36. *Rand, McNally*, 219.

37. White and Igleheart, *World's Columbian Exposition*, 506–7.

38. White and Igleheart, *World's Columbian Exposition*, 528.

39. Amy Leslie, *Amy Leslie at the Fair* (Chicago: W. B. Conkey, 1893), 19.

40. William A. Coles and Henry Hope Reed Jr., *Architecture in America; A Battle of Styles* (New York: Appleton-Century-Crofts, 1961), 155.

41. W. D. Howells, "Letters of an Altrurian Traveller," *The Cosmopolitan* 15, no. 5 (Sept. 1893): 218.

42. Louis H. Sullivan, *The Autobiography of an Idea* (New York: Dover, 1956), 322.

43. Alan Trachtenberg, *The Incorporation of America: Culture and Society in the Gilded Age* (New York: Hill and Wang, 1982), 217.

44. Denton J. Snider, *World's Fair Studies* (Chicago: Sigma Publishing Company, 1895), 237; quoted in Rydell, *All the World's a Fair*, 65.

45. Harlan Ingersoll Smith, "Man and His Works," *American Antiquarian* 15 (1893): 117; quoted in Rydell, *All the World's a Fair*, 57.

46. Margaretta M. Lovell, "Picturing 'A City for a Single Summer': Paintings of the World's Columbian Exposition," *The Art Bulletin* 78, no. 1 (March 1996): 43.

47. Lyman Gage, *The World's Columbian Exposition: First Annual Report of the President* (Chicago: Knight and Leonard Company, 1891), 22.

48. Frances Hodgson Burnett, *Two Little Pilgrims' Progress: A Story of the City Beautiful* (New York: Charles Scribner's Son, 1895), 95.

49. Candace Wheeler, "A Dream City," *Harper's New Monthly Magazine* 86, no. 516 (May 1893): 835.

50. Wheeler, "Dream City," 835.

51. Hezekiah Butterworth, *Zigzag Journeys in the White City: With Visits to the Neighbouring Metropolis* (Boston: Estes and Laurier, 1894), 132.

52. Quoted in Trachtenberg, *Incorporation of America*, 218.

53. Butterworth, *Zigzag Journeys*, 135.

54. "The World's Columbian Fair. From Our Philadelphia Correspondent," *The Times* (London), Saturday, October 7, 1893, 4.

55. Wheeler, "Dream City," 835.

56. Jackson Lears, *Rebirth of a Nation: The Making of Modern America, 1877–1920* (New York: Harper Perennial, 2009), 167.

57. *The Artistic Guide to Chicago and the World's Columbian Exposition* (Chicago: Columbian Art Company, 1892), 270.

58. *Artistic Guide*, 271.

59. Bolotin and Laing, *World's Columbian*, 9.

60. Wheeler, "Dream City," 831.

61. Burnett, *Two Little*, 100.

62. See Robert C. Davis and Garry R. Marvin, *Venice, The Tourist Maze: A Cultural Critique of the World's Most Touristed City* (Berkeley: University of California Press, 2004).

63. See Margaret Doody, *Tropic of Venice* (Philadelphia: University of Pennsylvania Press, 2007).

64. Davis and Marvin, *Venice*, 19, 6.

65. Henry James, *Italian Hours*, #45 in the Henry James Series, Project Gutenberg (August 2004), accessed October 5, 2010, http://www.gutenberg.org/ebooks/6354

66. Charles Eliot Norton, *Notes of Travel and Study in Italy* (Boston: Houghton, Mifflin, 1859), 196.

67. Henry James, *The Aspern Papers, Louisa Pallant, The Modern Warning* (London: Macmillan, 1888), 8.

68. James, *Italian Hours*.

69. James, *Italian Hours*.

70. "Venice in London," *The Times*, Dec. 28, 1891, issue 33519, 8. For Kiralfy and his career see Bolossy Kiralfy, *Creator of Great Musical Spectacles: An Autobiography*, ed. Barbara M. Barker (Ann Arbor, MI: UMI Research Press, 1988). See also Geppert, *Fleeting Cities*, chap. 3.

71. "Venice in London," *The Times*, Dec. 28, 1891, issue 33519, 8.

72. *The Artistic Guide to Chicago and the World's Columbian Exposition* (Chicago: Columbian Art Company, 1892), 268.

73. Henry Van Brunt, "Architecture at the World's Columbian Exposition," *The Century Magazine* xliv (1892); rpt. in William A. Coles and Henry Hope Reed Jr., *Architecture in America: A Battle of Styles* (New York: Appleton-Century-Crofts, 1961), 154.

74. Montgomery Schuyler, "Last Words about the Fair," *The Architectural Record* 3 (1893); rpt. in Coles and Reed, *Architecture*, 197, 200.

75. Edwin H. Blashfield, "A Painters Reminiscences of a World's Fair," *New York Times Magazine* (March 18, 1923); rpt. in Coles and Reed, *Architecture*, 150.

76. Montgomery Schuyler, "Last Words about the Fair," *The Architectural Record* 3 (1893); rpt. in Coles and Reed, *Architecture*, 204.

77. Sullivan, *Autobiography of an Idea*, 324.

78. Leslie, *Amy Leslie at the Fair*, 29.

79. Leslie, *Amy Leslie at the Fair*, 105.

80. W. A. Rogers, "The Cue for the Transformation Scene," from an unknown issue of *Puck* magazine (New York: Puck Pub. Co., 1893?, and New York: J. Ottmann Lith. Co.), centerfold.

81. Rydell and Kroes, *Buffalo Bill*, 69.

82. See Josephine Kane, *The Architecture of Pleasure: British Amusement Parks, 1900–1939* (London: Routledge, 2013), 17, 48, and chap. 1 in general. For the early history of amusement parks see John F. Kasson, *Amusing the Million: Coney Island at the Turn of the Century* (New York: Hill and Wang, 1978); and Gary S. Cross and John K. Walton, *The Playful Crowd: Pleasure Places in the Twentieth Century* (New York: Columbia University Press, 2005).

83. Louise J. Parscandola and John Parascandola, eds. *Coney Island Reader: Through the Dizzy Gates of Illusion* (New York: Columbia University Press, 2015), loc. 507.

84. Woody Register, *The Kid of Coney Island: Fred Thompson and the Rise of American Amusements* (New York: Oxford University Press, 2001), 132.

85. For a history of Venice, California, see Carolyn Elayne Alexander, *Venice*, Images of America, Presented by Venice Historical Society (Charleston SC: Arcadia, 2004).

86. "Nationality in Art," *New York Times*, 17 June 1900: 20; in *Historical Newspapers*, Proquest, 6 April 2015.

87. Gorky, "Boredom," *The Independent*, 310.

88. Gorky, "Boredom," *The Independent*, 311.

89. Gorky, "Boredom," *The Independent*, 317.

Conclusion

1. G. Duhamel, *Scènes de la vie future* [Scenes from future life] (Paris: Mercure de France, 1931). This passage is translated in Rob Kroes, *If You've Seen One, You're Seen the Mall: Europeans and American Mass Culture* (Urbana: University of Illinois Press, 1996), 47.

2. Johan Huizinga, *America: A Dutch Historian's Vision, from Afar and Near*, trans. and intro. Herbert Rowen (New York: Harper and Row, 1972), 110.

3. Huizinga, *America*, 312, 251, 312.

4. F. Scott Fitzgerald, *The Great Gatsby* (New York: Charles Scribner's Sons, 1968), 62. Future references are to this edition and are inserted in parentheses into the body of the text.

5. James Truslow Adams, *The Epic of America* (Boston: Little, Brown, 1931), 308, 404.

6. Adams, *Epic*, 405.

7. Jean Baudrillard, *America* (1986; London and New York: Verso, 2010), 57.

8. Baudrillard, *America*, 57.

INDEX